KASHMIR AT THE CROSSROADS

Kashmir at the Crossroads

Inside a 21st-Century Conflict

Sumantra Bose

YALE UNIVERSITY PRESS
NEW HAVEN AND LONDON

For information about this and other Yale University Press publications, please contact:
U.S. Office: sales.press@yale.edu   yalebooks.com
Europe Office: sales@yaleup.co.uk   yalebooks.co.uk

Set in Adobe Caslon Pro regular by IDSUK (DataConnection) Ltd
Printed in Great Britain by TJ Books, Padstow, Cornwall

Library of Congress Control Number: 2021944148

ISBN 978-0-300-25687-1

A catalogue record for this book is available from the British Library.

10 9 8 7 6 5 4 3 2 1

In loving memory of my luminous mother

Krishna Bose

(26 December 1930–22 February 2020)

writer, academic, institution-builder, parliamentarian

and

the personification of dignity, integrity, courage and compassion.

Forever my inspiration.

Proshno (A Query)

Rabindranath Tagore (1861–1941)

Translated from the Bengali by Sumantra Bose

India's greatest poet of modern times composed this poem in December 1931, during a peak of British repression of Indians agitating through mass civil disobedience, as well as armed struggle by youth groups.

Dear God, You have, down the ages, sent your messengers
To this benighted Earth.
They have preached 'Forgive them all'.
They have preached 'Learn to love, banish the poison of hate from
    your heart'.
They are worthy of respect, worthy of remembrance.
But still, in this evil time
I have turned them away from the outer door with the briefest of
    salutations.

For I have seen the defenceless subjected to cruel violence under
    cover of night.
For I have seen justice weep in silence from the unredressed crimes
    of the powerful.
For I see tender youths, driven to madness
strike their heads against stone in vexation and meet agonizing
    deaths.

My voice is stifled today, my flute has lost its music.
This pitch-dark prison has turned my world into a nightmare.
That is why I ask You in tears, dear God
Those who have poisoned your air, snuffed out your light
Have You truly forgiven them? Have You really given them your
    love?

Contents

Illustrations

8. Insha Mushtaq at her home in a Kashmir Valley village (May 2017). TAUSEEF MUSTAFA / Stringer / Getty Images.
9. Riyaz Naikoo addresses the crowd at the funeral of a slain comrade in the Kashmir Valley (July 2017). ZUMA Press, Inc. / Alamy Stock Photo / Getty Images.
10. Thousands attend the funeral of a slain insurgent in the Kashmir Valley (August 2018). SOPA Images / Contributor / Getty Images.
11. Srinagar under lockdown (August 2019). SAJJAD HUSSAIN / Contributor / Getty Images.
12. Indian soldiers in Ladakh (February 2021). TAUSEEF MUSTAFA / Contributor / Getty Images.

MAPS

Preface

THIS IS NOT a book I had particularly wished to write.

I first visited Kashmir in autumn 1976, as a little boy, on a family holiday with my parents. I still remember being terribly excited. At the time, it was the farthest I had travelled anywhere. Instead of flying, we took the train from my hometown Calcutta (now Kolkata) in eastern India. The journey took two nights and was thrilling in itself, as the train rolled through the vast farming plains of northern India and I tried to memorise the names of the dozens of stations we passed through. As we neared the final halt – the city of Jammu – I woke up in the morning to the verdant fields of the Punjab on either side, and shortly afterwards we crossed into the state of Jammu and Kashmir.

Jammu railway station was crowded, raucous and dirty – as large Indian terminuses typically were then – and the weather was hot. I was tiring from the long ride yet still full of excitement when we boarded a bus to Srinagar, the capital of the Kashmir Valley, 200 miles north. We were seated in front and the bus's engine was mind-numbingly noisy. From the town of Udhampur, about 40 miles north of Jammu, the road began to climb steeply in sharp twists and turns into the mountains. The engine's noise increased as our vehicle laboured on the upward gradients, and it belched acrid fumes which spread through the bus. I felt sick and threw up. My mother splashed cold water on my face and told me that we would be in a very beautiful place in a few hours. To raise my flagging spirits, she also reminded me that our destination had another element of excitement – there had been no fewer than three wars over the place in the preceding three decades. I was almost passed out and don't recall much of the rest of the journey until we arrived in salubriously cool Srinagar in the early evening, except that we passed through a tunnel – bored into the Banihal Pass, which connects the Jammu region and the Valley.

The next fortnight was an idyll. We stayed in a wooden houseboat moored on Srinagar's Dal Lake, a far superior experience to any hotel, fussed over by the family who owned the houseboat and their staff. I woke up in the mornings to the gentle swaying of the houseboat on the lake's waters and to steaming *kahwa* – Kashmiri tea flavoured with saffron, almonds, cinnamon and cardamom – served with delicious, warm Kashmiri bread. The home-cooked meals were all local cuisine, to which I would develop something of an addiction later in life. I sat on the houseboat's deck and contemplated the ethereal mountains framing our location; I think my love of mountains has its origins in that trip to Kashmir. To reach the shore and go sightseeing in the city of Srinagar, we took a *shikara*, the distinctive canopied boat of the waterways of Kashmir. My efforts to help a local boy a little older than me to row his family *shikara* were not successful – I was too small and unpractised and almost fell into the water.

We made, as I recall, three out-of-town trips. One was to Gulmarg (Flower Meadow), a resort 30 miles west of Srinagar. It literally was blooming with flowers in the autumn, and I remember being stunned by the beauty of the scenery as I rode a pony there. The highlight was a funicular ride to a hilltop. The only downside was that the place was jam-packed with tourists, mostly Indian, and we had to queue for a long time for our turn on the funicular. The next time I passed through Gulmarg was twenty years later, in August 1996. Its verdant meadows were absolutely deserted. No local visitors, let alone tourists, had been there after 1989 because insurgency engulfed the Kashmir Valley from 1990. I and my Kashmiri companion rented horses from a local family and galloped through the empty landscape, feeling a bit like cowboys in a Wild West movie.

In 1976, we also drove to Sonamarg (Golden Meadow), a picture-perfect alpine valley 55 miles north-east of Srinagar, close to the Zojila Pass which connects the Valley to the Ladakh region, a vast high-altitude desert. Standing in Sonamarg, I looked up at the towering peaks all around and marvelled at the snow trickling down their slopes from glaciers ('like *doi*', the Bengali word for yoghurt, I informed my amused parents). We also spent a couple of nights in Pahalgam, another resort south-east of Srinagar. There we stayed in a log cabin, and I mostly remember feeling cold – it was October and the harsh Kashmiri winter was imminent. But I also remember playing by the local rivulet, a boulder-strewn stream called the Lidder, and riding on horseback on treacherous tracks in the surrounding mountains.

I did not know then that I was to make some twenty more trips to Kashmir as an adult – from 1994 to 2020 – during which I would come to know almost every nook and corner of not just the Kashmir Valley but also the Jammu and Ladakh regions. It is that conflict-riven Kashmir – a grim contrast to the childhood idyll I experienced – which is recounted in this book. But there is one aspect that has held constant from the time of my childhood vacation: the gentle and gracious nature of the highly cultured people whom I first met in 1976.

During one of my first research visits in the mid-1990s, I needed to extend my stay for a few days to complete some fieldwork. At the time, being a nearly penniless graduate student at Columbia University, I had naturally bought the cheapest possible air ticket, which did not allow for changes or refunds. Nonetheless, I went to the airline office in Srinagar's city centre. The two young men there were somewhat bemused to see me, as a visiting outsider was very rare during that period, and they were curious about my purpose. They checked to confirm that there were plenty of seats available, and got on the telephone to their head office in Delhi. Then they said, all smiles, that they would do as I asked, 'but you must write the truth about what you see here'.

The Kashmir conflict is most commonly known as a stubborn territorial dispute between India and Pakistan which originated with the partition of the subcontinent in 1947. Since January 1949, when the first India–Pakistan war over Kashmir ended, the territory has been divided into a larger and much more populous part under Indian authority and a smaller, less populous part under Pakistani authority. The dividing line was known as the Ceasefire Line (CFL) from 1949 until 1972, and relabelled as the Line of Control (LoC) by an intergovernmental agreement in July 1972. The Kashmir conflict has been the bane of the subcontinent ever since the emergence of India and Pakistan as sovereign countries. There was another India–Pakistan war in 1965 over Kashmir, and Kashmir also saw fighting during the third India–Pakistan war in December 1971, which was sparked by the crisis in East Pakistan (Bangladesh). In 1999, India and Pakistan fought a limited war on a stretch of the LoC, just a year after both countries successfully tested nuclear weapons. And since 1990, at least 60,000 people – guerrillas, civilians and Indian military and police personnel – have been killed in insurgency, counter-insurgency and civil unrest in Indian Kashmir.

This book is a comprehensive account of the Kashmir conflict's trajectory over the past seventy-five years. It is written in a lucid, accessible style and draws liberally on my three decades of field experience in Indian Kashmir. The view from the grassroots, which brings the human story of Kashmir into central focus, is essential to understanding how the conflict has evolved, over the past three decades in particular. But *Kashmir at the Crossroads* also illuminates the other crucial elements of the conflict as it stands today: the troubled politics of India in the age of Hindu nationalist ascendancy as well as that of its chronically unstable neighbour Pakistan, and the complexity of the regional and global geopolitics in which the contemporary conflict is situated.

The organisation of this book is straightforward. Chapter 1 narrates the India–Pakistan territorial dispute over Kashmir as it unfolded from its inception in 1947 until 1989, and fills in historical information from centuries past essential to understand the twentieth-century conflict. Chapter 2 is about the bloodiest phase of the conflict, from 1990 to the mid-2000s, when tens of thousands met brutal deaths in the course of protracted insurgency and counter-insurgency. Chapter 3 covers the next, more nebulous, period from the mid-2000s until 2019, punctuated by stone-pelting uprisings in the Kashmir Valley. Chapter 4 discusses the present conjuncture since August 2019, when India's Hindu nationalist government decided to implement its vision of a solution to the Kashmir problem and ushered in a new and dangerous phase of the conflict. Finally, Chapter 5 provides an analytical perspective on all aspects of the twenty-first-century conflict's current and emerging context, and especially its regional and global geopolitics – which now increasingly involves China in the foreground in addition to the United States in the background.

Around and shortly after the time I published my previous book on the Kashmir conflict, *Kashmir: Roots of Conflict, Paths to Peace*, in autumn 2003, a flicker of hope emerged that fifteen years of unrelenting violence might yield to a peace process to resolve the conflict. Although far from confident about such a process, I was sure about its necessity and urgency. So, using my training as a comparative political scientist specialising in conflicts of this type, that book formulated a framework for settling the Kashmir conflict which, somewhat to my surprise, quickly gained currency. *Kashmir at the Crossroads* appears at a dark time when it is difficult to visualise a better future for the region, at least in the near term. But I remain convinced of the necessity and urgency of settling the conflict, now in its seventy-fifth year, through diplomacy and statecraft, and believe that the framework I formulated two decades ago will be useful if it happens.

This book is dedicated to the memory of my mother, Krishna Bose, who passed away suddenly on 22 February 2020. She was 89 but full of life, energy and curiosity. A multi-faceted personality, she was at once an author, professor, institutional leader and a politician-parliamentarian. My mother visited Kashmir three times – in 1954, 1976 and 2003. On the first two occasions, she was largely unaware of the depths and the complicated dimensions of the conflict. But on the third visit in the summer of 2003 – when she led a delegation of Indian parliamentarians on a tour of the Jammu, Kashmir Valley and Ladakh regions – she was well equipped to understand the conflict in all its depth and complexity. A democrat and a humanist to her core, she was delighted that a prominent ex-leader (presently again incarcerated, since February 2019) of the Kashmiri armed struggle that erupted in 1989–90 had taken to addressing her as 'Mummy' ever since they first met in Calcutta in January 1995. She was distressed by the turn of events in August 2019 and told me: 'My heart bleeds for them [the people of

Kashmir]'. This book is written in the hope that a time will come when no Kashmiri mother's heart will have to bleed for her children. It is also written in the hope that the ideals my late father – the renowned paediatrician Dr Sisir Kumar Bose (1920–2000) – imbibed in his youth as a fearless fighter for India's freedom will define India's future in the twenty-first century.

At Yale University Press (London), I would like to especially thank Joanna Godfrey, my commissioning editor. Joanna has been of immense support throughout, from the time we first discussed the book in late 2019. I am also grateful to Rachel Bridgewater, Lucy Buchan, Percie Edgeler, Rachael Lonsdale and Katie Urquhart for their work on this book. It has truly been a pleasure collaborating with them. Martin Brown drew the maps. Having worked as an author with many publishers, including several other leading university presses, I found the professionalism and courtesy of the staff at Yale to be really exemplary.

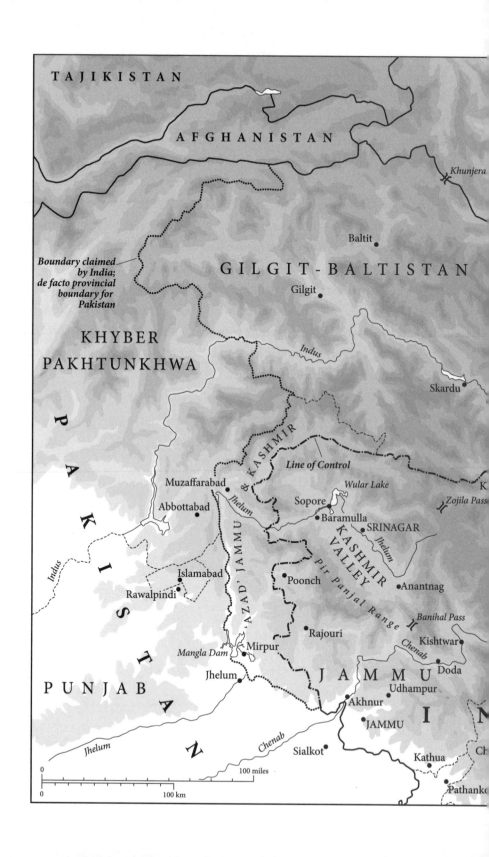

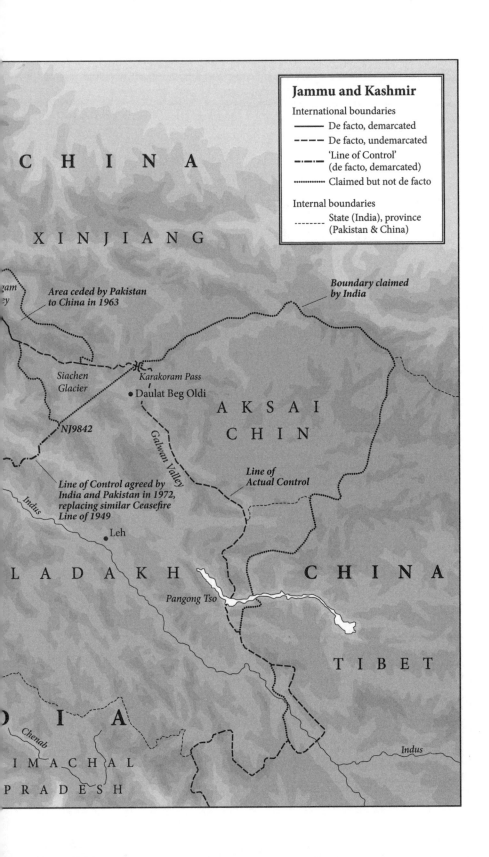

Jammu and Kashmir

International boundaries

——— De facto, demarcated

– – – De facto, undemarcated

–·–·– 'Line of Control' (de facto, demarcated)

··········· Claimed but not de facto

Internal boundaries

- - - - - - State (India), province (Pakistan & China)

C H I N A

X I N J I A N G

gam
ey

Area ceded by Pakistan to China in 1963

Boundary claimed by India

Siachen Glacier

Karakoram Pass

• Daulat Beg Oldi

NJ9842

A K S A I

C H I N

Galwan Valley

Line of Actual Control

Line of Control agreed by India and Pakistan in 1972, replacing similar Ceasefire Line of 1949

Indus

• Leh

L A D A K H

C H I N A

Pangong Tso

T I B E T

Chenab

Indus

D I A

I M A C H A L

P R A D E S H

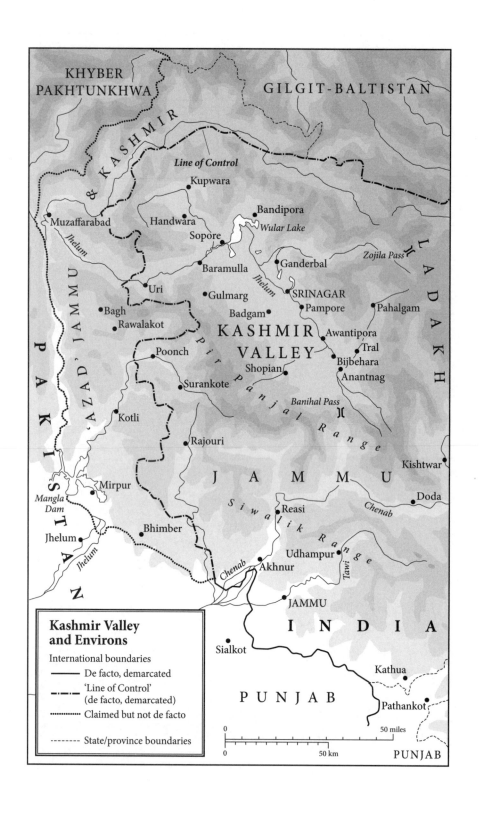

KHYBER
PAKHTUNKHWA

GILGIT-BALTISTAN

& KASHMIR

Line of Control

Kupwara

Bandipora

Muzaffarabad
Handwara
Sopore
Wular Lake

Zojila Pass

Baramulla
Ganderbal

Jhelum

Uri
Gulmarg
SRINAGAR
Pampore
Pahalgam

Bagh
Badgam
Awantipora

Rawalakot
KASHMIR
VALLEY
Tral

Poonch
Shopian
Bijbehara

Surankote
Anantnag

Banihal Pass

Kotli

Rajouri

Kishtwar

J A M M U
Doda

Siwalik
Chenab

Mirpur

Mangla
Dam
Reasi

Bhimber
Udhampur

Jhelum

Chenab
Akhnur

JAMMU

I N D I A

Kashmir Valley
and Environs

Sialkot

Kathua

International boundaries

De facto, demarcated

'Line of Control'
(de facto, demarcated)

Claimed but not de facto

State/province boundaries

P U N J A B

Pathankot

0   50 miles

0   50 km

PUNJAB

CHAPTER ONE

The Dispute

1947–89

J AWAHARLAL NEHRU, INDIA'S first prime minister (1947–64), wrote in a private letter in July 1948, a year after the partition of India: 'Partition came and we accepted it because we thought that perhaps that way, however painful it was, we might have some peace to work along our own lines. Perhaps we acted wrongly. It is difficult to judge now. And yet, the consequences of that partition have been so terrible that one is inclined to think that anything else would have been preferable'.[1]

Sheikh Mohammad Abdullah, the first prime minister of the Indian state of Jammu and Kashmir (1948–53), said in a message to the people of India on 26 January 1968, India's eighteenth Republic Day:

Respect for the rule of law, the independence of the judiciary, the integrity of the electoral process – are all sought to be guaranteed by the Indian constitution [proclaimed on 26 January 1950]. It is not surprising that many other countries have drawn upon this constitution, particularly the chapter on fundamental rights. Yet it must at all times be remembered that the constitution provides the framework, and it is for the men who work it to provide it life and meaning. In many ways the provisions of the constitution have been flagrantly violated in recent years [in Indian

1

Kashmir] and the ideals it enshrines completely forgotten. Forces have arisen which threaten to carry this saddening and destructive process further still ... What we have in Kashmir bears some of the worst characteristics of colonial rule.[2]

The Kashmir conflict is a by-product of the partition of India in August 1947. The partition's violence caused the brutal deaths of hundreds of thousands – Hindus, Muslims and Sikhs – and made several tens of millions of survivors into refugees. It also gave birth to the Kashmir conflict. The conflict over ownership of Kashmir caused two India–Pakistan wars in less than twenty years: in 1947–48 and again in 1965. At the end of the 1980s, the conflict entered a new phase as, for the first time, an armed rebellion against Indian authority developed within Indian Jammu and Kashmir, which has contained the bulk of the area and nearly three-fourths of the population of the territory disputed between the two countries since the end of the first Kashmir war in the late 1940s (the rest have been under Pakistani control and authority). The armed rebellion which began at the end of the 1980s rapidly evolved into a protracted insurgency that raged from 1990 until the mid-2000s and claimed tens of thousands of lives. The brutal legacy of that period casts a long, dark shadow over the contemporary conflict. The root cause of the descent into insurgency against Indian authority is captured by what the Kashmiri leader Sheikh Abdullah said in 1968. This introductory chapter surveys the Kashmir conflict from 1947 to the beginnings of insurgency in late 1989.

THE PRINCELY STATE OF JAMMU AND KASHMIR

Through the long nineteenth century, India's British masters created an edifice of 'Indirect Rule' in the subjugated subcontinent as the second pillar of their colonial state. This pillar was a vast network of so-called princely states, vassal principalities with native Indian rulers who accepted the 'paramountcy' of British power. When decolonisation finally arrived in 1947, 45 per cent of the subcontinent's land area consisted of a patchwork of about 562 such princely states. The rest of India was under direct British

2

authority. The princely states represented probably the most extensive collaborator network ever devised by a modern colonial power. Their rulers were a motley collection of maharajas and nawabs – Hindu, Muslim and Sikh – who in return for their allegiance were permitted by the British to run their fiefdoms more or less as they chose. Many princely states were tiny, but some had sizeable territories and populations. The princely state of Jammu and Kashmir (J&K), located in the far north of the subcontinent, belonged in the latter category. It sprawled across nearly 86,000 square miles of sub-Himalayan, Himalayan and high Himalayan land and had a population of 4 million in 1947.

The subcontinent's partition into two new 'Dominions', India and Pakistan, became final in early June of 1947 as the leadership of the Indian National Congress, the standard-bearer of the anti-colonial movement, conceded the All-India Muslim League's demand for a sovereign Muslim state in Muslim-majority regions of north-western and eastern India. At that point, the question arose of what would happen to the hundreds of princely states, which had been run by the British-sponsored native 'royal' families – tinpot despots who had operated as sub-contractors of colonial power for a century or longer. Until 1857, the English East India Company represented Britain's colonial rule in the subcontinent. In 1857, a large-scale Indian insurrection across the plains of northern and central India initiated by Indians serving in the Company's army of occupation – known as the 'Sepoy [ordinary soldiers] Mutiny' or the 'Indian Mutiny' in the British lexicon and retrospectively as the 'First War of Independence' in the Indian nationalist narrative – came close to driving the British out of the subcontinent. But the 1857–58 revolt eventually failed due to its fragmented and uncoordinated character. Hindus and Muslims alike led and participated in the uprising and suffered brutal retribution after its suppression. Following this, the Company's authority over India was replaced by direct Crown rule: the 'Raj', which ended abruptly and in chaos ninety years later in 1947. After the traumatic watershed of 1857, which put an end to any notions of a benign, civilising British colonial presence in India, the loyalty of the rulers of the princely states became even more important to the reformatted edifice of colonial control. In 1911, at a time of Indian nationalist awakening against colonial subjugation, these native 'princes' featured prominently in the osten-tatious transfer of the capital of the Raj from Calcutta – the capital of Bengal and the springboard of the East India Company's colonisation of India – to Delhi in the north.[3]

On decolonisation, the princely states technically had three options: to join India or Pakistan, or to become independent states. Lord Louis Mountbatten, the last viceroy and overseer of Great Britain's shambolic exit from the subcontinent, was, however, clear that the third option was purely notional. In late July of 1947, he told a gathering of princes and their ministers convened in Delhi that they should make up their minds forth-with – and preferably before mid-August, when India and Pakistan would emerge as independent countries – to join either of those two Dominions. Mountbatten advised that they should consider two criteria in making the decision: geographic embeddedness or contiguity to India or Pakistan, and the wishes of their subjects.

Under this common-sense formula, the accession of the large majority of princely states to India was a fait accompli on grounds of geographic loca-tion, and the rest to Pakistan. Problems arose with only three princely states: Junagadh, Hyderabad and Jammu and Kashmir. Junagadh, a small princely state located in western India (in the present-day Indian state of Gujarat) had a Muslim ruler presiding over a largely Hindu population. On the advice of his *diwan* (equivalent of prime minister), who was the father of Zulfiqar Ali Bhutto, a future prime minister of Pakistan, the ruler declared his domain as part of Pakistan and then fled to Pakistan to escape the wrath of his subjects. Junagadh became part of India.

Hyderabad was one of the major princely states. Centred on the epony-mous city, its territory was a huge sprawl across the Deccan plateau and parts of southern India and its population was over 16 million. Like Junagadh, Hyderabad had a hereditary Muslim ruler, known as the *nizam*, and a subject population that was about 80 per cent Hindu. The last *nizam* prevaricated under mounting pressure from pro-Pakistan hardliners in his administra-tion and armed forces. A pro-Pakistan militia called the *razakars* (volun-teers) emerged and launched an escalating campaign of terror against the Hindu population in autumn 1947, leading to widespread unrest and flight.

Some who fled beyond the borders of the princely state into Indian territory then started waging cross-border guerrilla warfare, with Indian support. Finally, in September 1948 the Indian government sent its army into Hyderabad. The Indian army's 'Operation Polo', which had limited air force support, defeated the *nizam*'s army and the *razakar* militia within a week, and this settled the Hyderabad question. It was a bloody end to the crisis that had festered for a year. Tens of thousands of Muslim civilians were killed in reprisals by the Indian Army and local Hindus during and in the immediate aftermath of Operation Polo.

The outcomes in Junagadh and Hyderabad could not have been other-wise. Both princely states were geographically embedded in India and had large Hindu majorities.

Jammu and Kashmir was a mirror image of Hyderabad and Junagadh, in that a hereditary Hindu ruler presided over a population – of 4 million – of whom the large majority (76–77 per cent) were Muslims and 20–21 per cent Hindus (the rest were mainly Sikhs and Buddhists). However, the application of Mountbatten's two common-sense criteria, very simple and decisive in the Hyderabad and Junagadh cases, did not yield an obvious answer to Jammu and Kashmir's future.

First, J&K was contiguous to both Pakistan and India. Its contiguity to Pakistan – with western Punjab and the North-West Frontier Province (NWFP) – was markedly more extensive than to India (eastern Punjab). The princely state's external links in trade, transport and commerce were also predominantly with areas to the west that became part of Pakistan. For example, the otherwise remote Kashmir Valley's lifeline was the 'Jhelum Road' (so known after the Jhelum, a major regional river) that ran from Srinagar, the capital of the Kashmir Valley, to Rawalpindi, an old city which is adjacent to Islamabad, Pakistan's custom-built capital. There were also ties of culture and kinship because a sizeable population of Kashmiri origin, descendants of nineteenth-century migrants from the princely state, lived in western Punjab. Nonetheless, the fact remained that the princely state had borders with both Pakistan and India.

Second, the political preferences of the J&K population were divided and the overall picture indeterminate, notwithstanding the demographic fact of a three-fourths Muslim majority. It could be assumed that the one in five subjects who were Hindus, as well as the small Sikh and Buddhist communities, would prefer India over Pakistan, an avowedly Muslim state. But the Muslim population was split – between those inclined towards Pakistan and those not so. Why is explained below. Of the princely state's two populous regions, the first group was strong in the Jammu region and the second in the Kashmir Valley. The variation, and divide, which was hugely consequential to the outcome of the first India–Pakistan war over Kashmir in 1947–48, is elaborated later in this chapter.

The princely state of Jammu and Kashmir came into being in 1846. Its founder was Gulab Singh (1792–1857), a warrior chieftain from the Jammu region. Singh belonged to a traditionally martial Rajput sub-caste of the Dogras, an ethnolinguistic group found in significant numbers in the Jammu region. Hence the princely state is often recalled, especially in the Kashmir Valley which lies to the north of the Jammu region, as 'Dogra rule' or the 'Dogra monarchy'. Gulab was a courtier and commander of Ranjit Singh, the great Sikh ruler who established a mini-empire across vast tracts of northern and north-western India in the early nineteenth century with its capital in the Punjab city of Lahore (in Pakistan post-August 1947). But after the Sikh monarch's death in 1839, Gulab Singh colluded with British schemes to undermine and eliminate Sikh power, which proved successful within a decade.

During the 1820s and 1830s, Gulab Singh's forces – led by his most intrepid commander, Zorawar Singh – had gradually expanded his territories northward from the plains and sub-Himalayan foothills of the southern parts of the Jammu region to mountainous areas in the Jammu interiors, and then to the sparsely populated high Himalayan regions of Ladakh and Baltistan (Zorawar was killed in 1841 when he forayed further east from Ladakh into Tibet). In 1846, as Sikh power unravelled, the Kashmir Valley – under Sikh rule since 1819 – was up for grabs and the British rewarded Gulab Singh for his collaboration by selling him the Kashmir Valley, along with the remote region of Gilgit to the north of Baltistan. The British were not interested in garrisoning and governing far-flung Himalayan territories and it suited them to sub-contract their authority to Gulab Singh.

First, under the Treaty of Lahore (9 March 1846), the British got a compliant son of Ranjit Singh to cede to them 'perpetual sovereignty' over 'the hill countries' of the disintegrating Sikh kingdom, 'including the provinces of Cashmere and Hazarah'. Then, on 16 March 1846, a second agreement, the Treaty of Amritsar, followed (Amritsar, a city in India's Punjab state, is home to Sikhism's holiest shrine, the Golden Temple). The Treaty of Amritsar stated: 'The British Government transfers and makes over, for ever, in independent possession, to Maharaja Gulab Singh and the heirs male of his body, all the hilly or mountainous country ... being part of the territories ceded to the British Government by the Lahore state'. Gulab Singh had gained the fertile, scenic and populous Vale of Kashmir, or the Kashmir Valley, in a bloodless commercial transaction. In return, he paid the East India Company 75 lakh (7.5 million) rupees and agreed to lend his military forces to the British whenever required. He also recognised 'the supremacy of the British Government' and undertook, 'in token of such supremacy, to present annually to the British Government [a tribute of] one horse, twelve perfect shawl goats of approved breed (six male and six female), and three pairs of Kashmir shawls'.[4] People in the Kashmir Valley like to recall how their land and ancestors were sold in sordid circumstances to a petty raja from Jammu by the predatory colonisers of the subcontinent.

The princely state born in the mid-nineteenth century cobbled together vast and disparate territories: the Jammu region, the Kashmir Valley and the high Himalayan expanses of Gilgit, Baltistan and Ladakh. Since 1947, almost the whole of the Kashmir Valley and Ladakh and most of the Jammu region have been under Indian authority. The western fringes of the erstwhile Jammu region, along with Gilgit and Baltistan, have been under Pakistani authority.

The immense social, cultural and political heterogeneity of the princely state which existed from 1846 to 1947 – the territory of the India–Pakistan dispute since 1947 – merits special emphasis. The territory of the former princely state consists of several distinct regions and a potpourri of religions, ethnicities, languages and castes. Since 1947, this diversity is especially pronounced on the larger and much more populous Indian side, but it very much exists on the Pakistani side as well. C.E. Tyndale Biscoe, a British missionary and educator who worked in the Kashmir Valley a hundred years ago – one of Srinagar's best schools carries his name – noted in a book published in 1922: 'To write about the character of the Kashmiris is not easy, as the country of Kashmir, including the province of Jammu, is large and contains many races of people. Then again, these various countries included under the name of Kashmir are separated the one from the other by high mountain passes, so that the people of these various states differ considerably the one from the other in features, manner, customs, language, character and religion.'[5]

The eternal jurisdiction promised to the newfound royal family of the princely state of Jammu and Kashmir by the Treaty of Amritsar lasted just over one hundred years, from March 1846 to October 1947. The century-long reign of Gulab Singh and his successors was an ordeal not much short of calamity for the Muslim subjects, especially in the Kashmir Valley.

In a book titled *Cashmere Misgovernment*, published in 1868, a British army officer called Robert Thorp wrote that 'in no portion of the treaty made with Gulab Singh was the slightest provision made for the just or humane government of the people of Cashmere, upon whom we forced a government they detested'. A review of the book in the London weekly *Saturday Review* in 1870 conceded that 'Mr. Thorp has succeeded in showing that Cashmere is under an extremely bad Government', with the vast majority living 'virtually in a state of slavery'.[6]

Walter Lawrence, a British official deputed to try and reform the princely state's punitive land revenue system in 1889 in the wake of recurrent famines, spent six years in the Kashmir Valley and published a major book on that region in 1895. Lawrence noted the geographic remoteness of 'Kashir', as the Valley is known to locals, which appears on maps as 'a white footprint set in a mass of black mountains . . . about 6000 feet above the sea, 84 miles in length and 20 to 25 miles in breadth . . . north, east and west, range after range guard the valley from the outer world, while in the south it is cut off from the Panjab by rocky barriers'. The Valley's population was then 814,241: '52,576 are Hindus, 4,092 are Sikhs and the rest are Musalmans [Muslims], who thus form 93 percent'.

Lawrence was struck by the wretched condition of the 93 per cent: 'When I came to Kashmir in 1889, I found the people sullen, desperate and suspicious. They had been taught for many years that they were serfs without any rights ... It will suffice to say that the system of administration had degraded the people and taken all heart out of them.' Lawrence was especially horrified by the practice of *begar*, forced labour without compensation which was the daily lot of the mass of landless serfs:

> It is to be regretted that the interests of the State and its people should have been entrusted to one class of men and that these men, the Pandits [the small community of Kashmiri Brahmins indigenous to the Valley] should have systematically combined to defraud the State and rob its people ... In a country where education has not made much progress it is only natural that the State should employ the Pandits, who can read and write and have depended on office as a means of existence for many generations ... [But] though this generosity in the matter of official establishments was an enormous boon to the Pandit class, it was a curse and misfortune to the Musalmans of Kashmir.

In 1890 Colonel R. Parry Nisbet, the British 'Resident' (supervisor) posted in the princely state, echoed Lawrence in a letter to his superiors: 'Kashmir should no longer be governed solely to benefit the ruling family and the rapacious horde of Hindu officials and Pandits, but also for its people, the long-suffering indigenous Muhammadans'.[7]

Nothing changed in the new century. In 1922 Tyndale Biscoe, the educator, observed: 'If we Britishers had to undergo what the Kashmiris have suffered, we might also have lost our manhood ... Gradually are the Kashmiris rising from slavery to manhood. I trust they will become once more a brave people, as they were in the days of old when their own kings led them into battle.'[8] In 1925 George Roerich, a young Russian scholar, spent several months in the Valley. He wrote: 'Comparing the beauties of nature, and the unique gardens of Nishat and Shalimar laid out by the Great Moguls Akbar and Jehangir with the sad realities of the native city of Srinagar, one is struck by the deep contrast. We were glad to leave the "Indian Venice" [Srinagar is built on the banks of the Jhelum river and has two large lakes, Dal and Nageen].' Roerich described the locals as simply 'a sad sight'.[9]

Indeed, in a book titled *Kashmir Then and Now* published in 1924, Gwasha Nath Kaul, a Kashmiri Pandit, described Srinagar as a 'frightful' city infested with beggars, thieves and prostitutes and overflowing with disease and filth.[10] According to Kaul, 90 per cent of the squalid Muslim dwellings in the city were mortgaged to Hindu moneylenders. Until 1924, the Kashmiri historian Mohammad Ishaq Khan writes, 'there was not a single newspaper printed or published in the State of Jammu and Kashmir'.[11]

In 1929 Sir Albion Bannerji, a Bengali Christian civil servant, dramatically resigned as the princely state's 'foreign and political minister' after two years in the post. He explained why to the *Associated Press*: 'Jammu and Kashmir State is labouring under many disadvantages with a large Muhammedan population absolutely illiterate, labouring under poverty in the villages and practically governed like dumb-driven cattle. There is no touch between the Government and the people, no suitable opportunity for representing griev-ances, and the administrative machinery requires overhauling from top to bottom. It has at present little or no sympathy with the people's wants and grievances.'[12] The phrase 'dumb-driven cattle' caught on and is still used by Valley Muslims to describe their sub-human treatment by those wielding power over their lives.

Still nothing changed. In 1941 Prem Nath Bazaz, a Kashmiri Pandit who joined a growing movement for change that emerged during the 1930s and gained mass support in the Valley in the 1940s, wrote: 'The poverty of the Muslim masses is appalling. Dressed in rags and barefoot, a Muslim peasant presents the appearance of a starving beggar. Most are landless labourers, working as serfs for absentee landlords. Rural indebtedness is staggering.'[13]

A unique characteristic of the princely state of Jammu and Kashmir that warrants emphasis is its overtly Hindu character. Thorp's late 1860s account describes floggings of subjects accused of killing cows, an animal sacred in Hindu orthodoxy. Until 1920 a death sentence was mandatory in J&K for killing a cow; under British pressure this was reduced to ten years in prison in 1920 and later to seven years. But more important, Muslim subjects – more than three-fourths of the population – were barred from becoming officers in the princely state's military and were almost non-existent in the civil administration.

Although seven decades have passed since the end of the princely state in October 1947, that oppressive era casts a long shadow even today, especially in the Kashmir Valley. Once popular protest and resistance developed in the Valley from the 1930s, the context – a dehumanised Muslim population at the mercy of a tinpot Hindu monarchy – meant that protest and resistance would be articulated through the Muslim identity of the oppressed masses. This continued over subsequent decades post-1947, as Kashmiri Muslims endured uniquely oppressive conditions in the independent and nominally secular Indian republic. The wave of repression unleashed by India's overtly anti-secular Hindu nationalist government since August 2019 is in some ways a twenty-first-century throwback to the princely state, the historical experience that shaped political consciousness in the Valley.

THE EVOLUTION OF THE KASHMIR VALLEY'S IDENTITY

The mass conversion of the Kashmir Valley to Islam occurred in the fourteenth century. This was catalysed by Mir Sayyid Ali Hamadani, a Persian Sufi mystic from Hamedan in western Iran, who visited Kashmir thrice in the 1370s and 1380s accompanied by hundreds of disciples, many of whom settled in Kashmir. Hamadani is known as 'Shah Hamdan' in Kashmir. After his death, a mosque – the Khanqah-e-Maula – was erected in his honour in the 1390s on the Jhelum river in Srinagar, where it currently stands in a rebuilt eighteenth-century version.

The Kashmiri transition to Islam is, however, identified above all others with a locally born Sufi saint, Sheikh Nooruddin Noorani. He was born around 1377 in a village south of Srinagar and lived until about 1440. Noorani is referred to in the Valley as Alamdar-e-Kashmir (patron saint) and is also known among Muslims and non-Muslims alike by the Sanskrit name Nund Rishi (Nund the Sage). Noorani was greatly influenced by Lalleshwari, a woman mystic of Shaivite Hinduism (which worships the deity Shiva), who lived from about 1320 to 1392. Lalleshwari is known as Lal Ded (Mother) in Kashmir, and Srinagar's main maternity hospital is named after her. Lalleshwari is also the founder of the Kashmiri literary tradition. She expressed her spirituality in couplets in Kashmiri, which belongs to the Dardic group of Indo-Aryan languages. Sheikh Noorani, Lal Ded's follower, was a 'Muslim Shaivite' who 'translated Islam into Kashmir's [pre-existing] spiritual and cultural idiom'.[14] Noorani's mausoleum-shrine is located in Charar-e-Sharief, a town about 20 miles south-west of Srinagar. In 1995 the mausoleum-shrine was razed by a fire that broke out during a gun-battle between Indian Army troops and insurgents who had occupied the holy site. It has since been rebuilt and continues as a place of pilgrimage not just for Kashmiri Muslims but also for Hindus and Sikhs who live in the Valley.

The specifically Kashmiri version of Islam pioneered by Sheikh Nooruddin Noorani was taken forward in the fifteenth century by Kashmir's greatest indigenous ruler (sultan) Zain-ul-Abidin, who reigned from about 1423 to 1474. He is known in the Valley as Badshah (Emperor), and Badshah Chowk, a large square in the centre of Srinagar, is named in his honour. Zain-ul-Abidin foreshadowed the syncretistic policies of India's greatest Mughal monarch, Akbar, who ruled from 1556 to 1605 and tried to implement an innovative official religion, Din-i-Ilahi, a hybrid of Hinduism and Islam. Among other initiatives, Zain-ul-Abidin sponsored a Persian translation from the original Sanskrit of an epic chronicle of Kashmir from antiquity to the eleventh century composed around 1149 by a poet called Kalhana. Kalhana's legendary chronicle *Rajatarangini* (The Flow of Kings) consists of 7,826 verses in 8 books. Centuries later, *Rajatarangini* was translated into English in 1900 by Marc Aurel Stein, a British explorer and scholar.[15]

The version of Islamic faith implanted in Kashmir by Shah Hamdan, Sheikh Noorani/Nund Rishi and Zain-ul-Abidin proved enduring and resilient, and defines the everyday practice of Islam in the Valley 600 years later. The Kashmir Valley's towns and villages abound with *ziarat*s, shrines dedicated to Sufi saints down the centuries, some of whom are women. Relic worship, which has its roots in Kashmir's pre-Hindu Buddhist past, also persists. Its most famous example lies in the gleaming-white Hazratbal shrine on Srinagar's outskirts where a hair believed to be from the beard of the Prophet Mohammad is preserved. The Kashmiri literary tradition that began with Lalleshwari/Lal Ded also continues. In the late sixteenth century Habba Khatun, a woman poet and singer, composed verses suffused with loss and longing. The outstanding heir to this tradition is the twentieth-century poet Ghulam Ahmad Mahjoor.[16] The result is a very distinctive ethnolinguistic identity, infused with religious faith, that is peculiar to the Kashmir Valley.

This dominant tradition of faith and culture in the Kashmir Valley was not really challenged until the second half of the twentieth century. The main challenge came from the local wing of Jama'at-i-Islami (Islamic Rally, JI), a Sunni fundamentalist movement in the subcontinent inspired by the teachings of Maulana Abul Ala Maududi (1903–79). It made inroads into Kashmiri society in the 1970s and 1980s, and from the early 1990s, when insurgency erupted in the Kashmir Valley, JI's version of Sunni orthodoxy was actively promoted by the Pakistani state and its agencies in the Valley. It remains a minority tendency, at odds with the deeply rooted historical traditions of the Kashmir Valley.

THE RISE OF POPULAR PROTEST IN THE PRINCELY STATE

The absence of significant unrest in the princely state until the early 1930s was attributed by a British scholar writing in the 1960s to 'the exceptionally docile nature of the peasantry' who comprised the vast bulk of the subjects.[17] But on 13 July 1931, violence erupted in the city centre of Srinagar. The spark was the trial of a man accused of making hostile remarks about the government to a mosque congregation. The police fired on a crowd protesting the trial, killing twenty-two persons. Rioters then ransacked shops owned by Kashmiri Pandits and Hindu traders from the Punjab in a commercial quarter of the city. In Maisuma, a warren of old wooden homes on narrow, winding streets next to the city centre, women came out and confronted cavalry charges by the police (seven decades later, in 1989–90, Maisuma would emerge as a hub of insurgents seeking independence from Indian rule).

After the demise of the princely state in late 1947, 13 July was declared 'Martyrs' Day' and made a holiday in the Indian state of Jammu and Kashmir, which had the greater part of the territory and over 70 per cent of the population of the erstwhile princely state since the late 1940s. After India's Hindu nationalist government dismembered the state into two centrally administered 'union territories' (Jammu and Kashmir, and Ladakh) in August 2019, the date was struck off the holiday calendar.

Who would provide leadership and build an organised opposition? The initiative came from a handful of young men with higher education who had established a 'Reading Room Association' in Srinagar in 1930. Their leader was Sheikh Mohammad Abdullah, a schoolteacher in his mid-twenties who was from Soura, then a village outside Srinagar and now a neighbourhood of the city. Abdullah had benefited from scholarships for higher studies outside the princely state given by an association of Kashmiri émigrés in Lahore. He graduated from Lahore's Islamia College and then gained a master's degree in chemistry from the Aligarh Muslim University located in post-independence India's Uttar Pradesh (Northern Province), known in British India as the United Provinces. His family were late converts; his ancestors were Hindu Brahmins until the late eighteenth century, when they were influenced by a Sufi mystic. Abdullah, a very tall man with a gentle face, was a rousing orator who could mesmerise audiences. According to a police report on a 'seditious speech' he made in a village in 1933, he urged the crowd to 'take revenge' and 'turn out the Hindus'.[18]

Abdullah was among the founders of the princely state's first organised opposition – the All Jammu and Kashmir Muslim Conference (MC), launched in October 1932. By the late 1930s, however, he toned down the fiery Muslim rhetoric and started to speak of a national movement inclusive of all faiths. In 1938, primarily at the initiative of Valley activists grouped around him, the MC resolved to 'end communalism by ceasing to think in terms of Muslims and non-Muslims' and invited 'all Hindus and Sikhs who believe in the freedom of their country [J&K] from the shackles of an irresponsible rule' to join the organisation.[19] The following year, 1939, the MC was formally renamed the All Jammu and Kashmir National Conference (NC).

Kashmir's syncretistic heritage may have been a factor underlying Abdullah's shift from 'communal' to 'national'. The example of the Indian National Congress, which sought to represent all Indians opposed to British rule, may also have been a model. From 1939 the NC's doors were open to non-Muslims, though only a handful of Pandits, and other Hindus and Sikhs, actually joined.

Although 173 of the 176 delegates present at the MC convention in 1939 had approved the renaming, there was much internal debate, and many leaders had misgivings. In 1941, a large faction broke away from the NC and revived the Muslim Conference. Their leader was Chaudhary Ghulam Abbas, from the Jammu region, who had been secretary-general of the original MC formed in 1932 (Abdullah was president). Those who revived the MC were by and large religious and social conservatives, and most were from the Jammu region, though there was also an anti-Abdullah group from the Valley led by the head priest (*Mirwaiz*) of Srinagar's Jama Masjid (Grand Mosque). As the 1940s progressed, Abdullah and the NC became more and more dominant in the Valley, but the rival MC remained the stronger force in the Jammu region. This Kashmir/Jammu split, and the divide in Muslim politics more generally, played out in the second half of 1947 as the princely state collapsed.

That was presaged by the MC drawing closer to the All-India Muslim League, the party of the Pakistan movement, and the NC to the Indian National Congress. In 1944 Mohammad Ali Jinnah, the supreme leader of the campaign for Pakistan, visited the Valley and certified the MC as representative of '99 percent' of the princely state's Muslims.[20] In 1945, the NC's annual convention was attended by a galaxy of Congress leaders released from prison upon the end of World War II in Europe. They included Jawaharlal Nehru, soon to be India's first and as yet longest-serving prime minister (1947–64), whose Kashmiri Pandit forebears had migrated from the Valley to the plains of northern India. Maulana Abul Kalam Azad, Congress's most prominent Muslim figure, also attended, as did Khan Abdul Ghaffar Khan, a famous Congress-aligned anti-colonial and pacifist leader from the North-West Frontier Province known as the 'Frontier Gandhi'.

In 1946, the NC decided to mark the princely state's centenary with a 'Quit Kashmir' campaign of mass protests and civil disobedience against the ruler and his government. 'The time has come to tear up the Treaty of Amritsar,' Sheikh Abdullah declared. The agitation was modelled on the Congress's 'Quit India' movement against the British Raj launched in August 1942. Launched in April 1946, the Quit Kashmir campaign wilted by June under brutal repression and large-scale arrests of leaders (including

Abdullah) and grassroots organisers. Its main impact was in the Kashmir Valley, the NC's bastion, where the atrocities of the princely state's police and military 'caused tremendous commotion, leaving bitter memories of cruelties in the minds of the normally peaceful Kashmiris'. Speaking from Lahore, the MC leader Ghulam Abbas condemned Quit Kashmir as 'an agitation started at the behest of Hindu leaders'. This echoed the Muslim League's denunciation of the Quit India uprising in 1942.[21] Nehru entered the princely state in a symbolic show of solidarity with the NC and was promptly arrested and deported.

The National Conference's 1938–39 shift to a supra-religious stance had been followed a few years later by a marked leftward turn. At its annual convention in September 1944 held in Sopore, a town in the northern part of the Valley, the party adopted a manifesto called 'Naya Kashmir' (New Kashmir), which embodied a detailed vision of the future of Jammu and Kashmir. The hereditary monarchy would be purely ceremonial, and sovereignty would be vested in a National Assembly elected through universal adult franchise. Governance would be decentralised to districts, *tehsils* (subdivisions of districts), towns and villages. Due to the multilingual character of J&K – the largest spoken language, Kashmiri, being restricted to the Valley and some contiguous parts of the Jammu region and Dogri, the second largest, mostly to the southern Jammu plains and low uplands to its north – the manifesto said that Urdu, the hybrid of Sanskrit and Persian written in the Arabic script which emerged under the Mughal Empire, would be the state's official language. Kashmiri, Dogri, Punjabi, Hindi, Balti and Dardi would all be recognised as national languages. The most significant promise made was the transformation of rural J&K and its agrarian society. The Naya Kashmir charter called for the abolition of parasitic landlordism without any compensation, transfer of land to the masses of landless tillers, and cooperative farming associations. This was something the Indian National Congress could never commit to in India proper, because the party was a 'broad church' that included various shades, from arch-conservatives to centrists to socialists. The charter also visualised rapid social progress through education for downtrodden groups and, remarkably for the time, included a separate section on the rights of women.

The extraordinarily progressive charter reflected the influence of socialist and even communist (pro-Soviet) thinking within some elements of the NC leadership. The party's chief ideologue at the time, G.M. Sadiq, was known for pro-Soviet leanings. On taking control of Srinagar in the autumn of 1947, the NC named the main downtown square with its distinctive clocktower Lal Chowk, or Red Square, after the Moscow original.

For all of this, the NC's appeal to its core base in the Kashmir Valley remained rooted in the pious, God-fearing Sufi Islam of six centuries which constituted the spiritual refuge of a desperately impoverished, oppressed population. Sheikh Abdullah drew crowds mainly because he enthralled illiterate audiences by reciting beautifully from the Holy Koran. His rise to political dominance in the Valley during the 1940s was above all because his followers were able to take control of most of the Valley's mosques, and therefore their congregations, at the expense of traditional religious preachers. When he was asked in the twilight of his life, in 1978, how he had managed to marginalise the clergy, he chuckled and replied: 'By becoming a *mullah* [cleric] myself'.[22] When he launched the Quit Kashmir movement in April 1946, Abdullah's headquarters was the Hazratbal shrine on the shores of Srinagar's Nageen Lake, venerated because it has a hair believed to be from the beard of the Prophet Mohammad. The general secretary of the National Conference was a cleric, Maulana Mohammad Sayyid Masoodi, who was also the editor of *Khidmat*, the National Conference party's paper. Maulana Masoodi was 'highly respected by the people for the depth of his views and the sobriety of his judgment'.[23]

KASHMIR AND THE ENDGAME OF THE BRITISH RAJ

After the violent suppression of the Quit Kashmir movement in mid-1946, a deceptive lull ensued in the princely state even as the subcontinent as a whole moved towards partition into India and Pakistan.

The lull was broken in spring 1947. The scene was not the temporarily cowed Valley but the Jammu region's Poonch district. The Poonch district lies just south and west of the Valley but is separated from it by the majestic Pir Panjal mountain range. Overwhelmingly Muslim then as now, the historic district has been divided between Indian and Pakistani jurisdictions since 1949 by the Ceasefire Line (CFL, which was renamed the Line of Control, or LoC, in 1972). As in the Jammu region as a whole – on both sides of the dividing line – most Poonch Muslims are not Kashmiris in the ethnolinguistic sense but belong to other ethnolinguistic groups, which makes them distinct from the Valley's largely Kashmiri-speaking population.

Poonch had been an autonomous principality within the princely state until World War II, when the local raja (ruler) was deposed by the Dogra dynasty. The princely state's government then started levying punitive taxes on the Poonch peasantry, which sparked a rebellion in spring 1947. The princely state's Sikh and Dogra troops reacted with brutal reprisals against the population. This was a grave error. Along with nearby districts in west Punjab and the NWFP, Poonch had been a prime recruiting ground for the British-Indian army during World War II. Of the 71,667 men from J&K who had served in the British forces during the war, 60,402 were from Poonch.[24] The district was thus full of recently demobilised soldiers and, unlike in the Kashmir Valley, the princely state's forces ran into fierce armed resistance. By August 1947, the Poonch revolt took on a strongly pro-Pakistan character, and by September the rebels controlled the entire district barring the town of Poonch, where they besieged the remnants of the princely state's forces. Flush with success in the fighting, a bunch of pro-Pakistan *sardars* (feudal clan-chieftains) of the western Jammu districts – Poonch, Mirpur to its south as well as Muzaffarabad to the north – declared a provisional 'Azad' (Free) Jammu and Kashmir government in Rawalpindi, Pakistan on 3 October 1947.

Meanwhile on 15 August – the day after Pakistan's birth – the princely state's government had signed a 'standstill agreement' with the government of Pakistan. Standstill agreements between a princely state and a Dominion (India or Pakistan) were normally indicative of the state's formal accession to that Dominion. Under the 15 August agreement, the Pakistan government was supposed to take charge of J&K's post and telegraph system and to supply the state with foodstuffs and other essentials.

This was a strange dalliance between the subcontinent's new Muslim state and a despotic Hindu monarchy that had not only oppressed its Muslim subjects for a century, but whose forces had very recently perpetrated grave abuses against Muslims both in the Kashmir Valley and in Poonch. But it was not as counter-intuitive as it appeared. The last maharaja, Hari Singh, and his coterie of advisers were concerned only about his throne, the ruling family's palatial properties, and their privileges. They knew that many Indian National Congress leaders held the princely rulers in contempt as British stooges. Moreover, the Congress had friendly ties with Abdullah and his National Conference party and had been openly supportive of the Quit Kashmir agitation in 1946. The princely state's oligarchy could not be faulted for thinking – or at least hoping – that Pakistan's leaders would be more receptive to their interests and demands than India's. Pakistan's leaders, for their part, were aware that while geographic contiguity and religious demographics were favourable to Jammu and Kashmir becoming part of Pakistan, only Maharaja Hari Singh could sign a legally binding accession of the state to either Dominion.

The dalliance unravelled in the first half of October. On 3 October, the day the 'Azad' Kashmir government was proclaimed in Rawalpindi, the princely state's government cabled Pakistan's foreign ministry in Karachi, accusing the Pakistan government of violating the terms of the standstill agreement, and of complicity in cross-border raids by armed bands into J&K along a lengthy stretch of the border with Pakistani Punjab, from Rawalpindi in the north to Sialkot in the south. On 18 October a second cable sent to Liaquat Ali Khan, Pakistan's prime minister, and M.A. Jinnah, its governor-general, accused the Pakistan government of an economic blockade against Jammu and Kashmir. Pakistani officials responded by calling for talks to discuss cross-border problems and noted with disapproval the J&K government's release of Sheikh Abdullah from sixteen months in detention on 29 September, while the incarceration of leading pro-Pakistan figures continued.

The stage was set for the final act of Kashmir's post-partition drama.

THE FIRST KASHMIR WAR

That endgame unfolded from 21 October 1947. On that day a motorised force of several thousand armed Pashtuns swept into the north-west of J&K

from the adjoining Hazara district of the NWFP (today Pakistan's Khyber-Pakhtunkhwa province). Although the ingress has been referred to ever since as the 'tribal invasion' of Kashmir, the operation showed clear signs of careful organisation and strategic planning. While many of the raiders were, as it turned out, primarily motivated by the prospect of loot and rape, they were 'led by experienced military men familiar with the terrain and equipped with modern arms, and poured down in numbers estimated at 5000-strong initially, with a fleet of transport vehicles of about 300 trucks'. The trucks and some of the weaponry had been provided by the government of the NWFP. This government of Pakistan loyalists had been installed in Peshawar just two months earlier after the province's pro-Congress government, elected in 1946, was dismissed by Pakistan's governor-general, M.A. Jinnah. A Jinnah acolyte, Abdul Qayyum Khan, whose father was from the Kashmir Valley, was made the new NWFP chief minister and was closely involved in planning the Kashmir operation. Liaquat Ali Khan, the Pakistani prime minister who had been Jinnah's deputy in the Pakistan movement, railed unconvincingly on 4 November that portraying 'the rebellion of an enslaved people' against the Maharaja's 'illegal and immoral' rule as 'an invasion from outside, just because some outsiders have shown active sympathy with it', amounted to 'a dishonest rewriting of history'.[25]

The raiders first captured Muzaffarabad, a town close to the princely state's border with Pakistan, where they terrorised and massacred Sikh and Hindu residents (Muzaffarabad was to become the capital of Pakistan's 'Azad' Kashmir). Then, using the Jhelum Road, they advanced rapidly into the Kashmir Valley and seized Baramulla, the major town in the northern part of the Valley. Srinagar was just another 20 miles by road, and there was no sign of any resistance from the princely state's forces. On 24 October the Maharaja's government sent an SOS to Delhi, urgently seeking military assistance to repel the raiders. Nehru and his home (interior) minister, Vallabhbhai Patel, were advised by Mountbatten, the governor-general of the Indian Dominion, that sending in troops without first securing the accession of J&K to India would be an Indian invasion of a neutral territory. On 26 October Hari Singh signed the Instrument of Accession to India and handed it over to an emissary of the Indian government in the city of

Jammu, who immediately flew back to Delhi. On 27 October Mountbatten accepted the accession but noted that once the raiders had been expelled, the accession should be ratified by 'a reference to the people [of Jammu and Kashmir]'. On 2 November Nehru clarified the nature of this reference when he announced a 'pledge ... not only to the people of Kashmir but to the world ... to hold a referendum under international auspices such as the United Nations' to determine whether a majority of J&K's people wished to join India or Pakistan. He regularly repeated this commitment until 1952.

Meanwhile, Sheikh Abdullah had arrived in Delhi from Srinagar on the evening of 25 October and was staying at Nehru's residence on 26–27 October. In his first public speech after release from prison, to a huge gathering at Srinagar's Hazratbal shrine on 5 October, Abdullah had declared the issue of accession to be secondary to the establishment of a people's government in Jammu and Kashmir. But on 27 October, he told the *Times of India* newspaper in Delhi that the raiders had to be resisted to prevent the forcible absorption of J&K into Pakistan. He certainly knew that his home region and stronghold, the Kashmir Valley, was in dire peril and that he and his movement had no place in Jinnah's scheme of things.[26]

The first Indian Army units arrived by airlift in Srinagar on the morning of 27 October, where they were warmly welcomed by National Conference leaders. The Indians almost immediately encountered groups of raiders on the outskirts of Srinagar. Over the next few days, they also 'discovered that they were dealing with an organized body of men armed with light and medium machine-guns and mortars' led by 'commanders thoroughly conversant with modern tactics and use of ground', and supported by 'considerable engineering skill'.[27]

The military tables turned swiftly in the Kashmir Valley. The Indian Army units first pushed the raiders out of the vicinity of Srinagar, eliminating the threat to the city's airfield. Then, reinforced by armoured cars that arrived by road through the Banihal Pass, which connects the Kashmir Valley to the Jammu region to its south through the Pir Panjal range, they went on the offensive. Baramulla was retaken on 8 November and Uri, a smaller town on the Valley's edge which has straddled the border between the Indian and Pakistani Kashmirs ever since, on 14 November. By the time fighting subsided as the snowy winter set in, the raiders had been driven back to the Valley's peripheries.

The Indian success was enabled by two factors. First and most important, local help and support from the well-oiled National Conference organisation was crucial. Thousands of volunteers enrolled in a Kashmiri 'National Militia' quickly put together by senior NC leaders Bakshi Ghulam Mohammed and G.M. Sadiq, which included a women's unit. In late November Liaquat Ali Khan, the Pakistani prime minister, vented his frustration at the turn of events: 'Sheikh Abdullah has been a paid agent of Congress for two decades and with the exception of some gangsters he has purchased with Congress money, he has no following among the Muslim masses [of Kashmir]'.[28] Second, some of the raiders committed looting, murder and rape against the overwhelmingly Muslim population of the Valley as they advanced, spoiling any possibility of cooperation. Baramulla was pillaged, and killings and rapes occurred there and in other northern Valley towns taken by the raiders, such as Handwara. Memories of this brutality would linger in the Kashmir Valley for several decades.

During the winter lull in the fighting, the Kashmir dispute was internationalised when Nehru's government complained to the UN about Pakistani aggression against a territory that had acceded to and become part of India. In January 1948, the UN Security Council established a United Nations Commission for India and Pakistan (UNCIP). As spring arrived and fighting resumed in April 1948, the Security Council passed a resolution 'instruct[ing] the Commission to proceed at once to the Indian subcontinent and there place its good offices and mediation at the disposal of the Governments of India and Pakistan ... both with respect to the restoration of peace and order and the holding of a plebiscite'. The resolution urged the government of Pakistan 'to use its best endeavours ... to secure the withdrawal from the State of Jammu and Kashmir of tribesmen and Pakistani nationals not normally resident therein who have entered the State for the purpose of fighting'. Once UNCIP was satisfied of such a withdrawal, the government of India was urged to 'put into operation in consultation with the Commission a plan for withdrawing their own forces from Jammu and Kashmir and reducing them progressively to the minimum strength required for the support of civil power in the maintenance of law and order'. The resolution further said that 'the Government of India should undertake that there will be established in Jammu and Kashmir a Plebiscite Administration to hold a plebiscite as soon as possible on the question of the accession of the State to India or Pakistan'.[29] In August 1948 UNCIP called on India and Pakistan to reach a ceasefire agreement in Kashmir. Once such a ceasefire came into effect on 1 January 1949, UNCIP announced, on 5 January, the imminent formation of a Plebiscite Administration.

That the plebiscite was never held is regarded by Pakistanis, as well as pro-Pakistan and pro-independence people in the contested territory, as evidence of Indian perfidy. The Indian rejoinder is that Pakistan never vacated the parts of J&K under its control, the first requirement specified by the UN for holding the plebiscite.

It was the Jammu region, rather than the Valley, that bore the brunt of the first India–Pakistan conflict over Kashmir. In the autumn of 1947 the sizeable Hindu and Sikh populations of towns in the western Jammu districts – Mirpur, Bhimber, Kotli, Rawalakot, Bagh and Muzaffarabad – were expelled amid large-scale killings and rapes. In October and November 1947, the Hindu-dominated areas in the south-eastern part of the Jammu region – the city of Jammu, Kathua, Samba, Udhampur – saw mass murder and forced expulsion of the local Muslims. This violence involved Sikh and Hindu refugees who had arrived from the western Jammu districts as well as from western (Pakistani) Punjab. But it was directed by officials of the princely state and local activists of the Rashtriya Swayamsevak Sangh (National Volunteer Organisation, RSS), a militant Hindu group which forms the core of post-independence India's Hindu nationalist movement and is the ideological parent of India's present ruling party, the Bharatiya Janata Party (Indian People's Party, BJP). The Jammu RSS chief, Prem Nath Dogra, who was a key instigator, went on to become the all-India president of the Bharatiya Jana Sangh (BJS), the Hindu nationalist political party launched in 1951 and renamed BJP in 1980.

The renewed military hostilities of 1948, which pitted the Indian and Pakistani armies in direct combat, went in India's favour. The Indians were able to secure the Kashmir Valley and in April–May made gains on the

Jammu front, retaking the strategic town of Rajouri, south of Poonch. The final phase of fighting came in late autumn of 1948 when an Indian force with light tanks evicted the Pakistanis from the strategically vital Zojila Pass, which at 11,300 feet connects the Kashmir Valley to Ladakh, a high-altitude desert, and provides a gateway to the Valley from the north. Following the Zojila victory, the Indians recaptured the small western Ladakh towns of Drass and Kargil and fully secured the road running from the Valley through these towns to Leh, the major town in eastern Ladakh. The Pakistanis withdrew northward to the mountainous Skardu area.

The territorial division of Jammu and Kashmir at the end of the 1947–48 war has endured unaltered, barring very minor changes from fighting during the third India–Pakistan war in December 1971. This means that India has been in possession of the bulk of the territory, and the population, of the erstwhile princely state: practically the whole of the Kashmir Valley, most of the Jammu region, and almost all of Ladakh except Skardu. Pakistan was left with a long finger-like sliver of territory mostly running along the western edge of the Jammu region (the area of 'Azad' Kashmir) and the mountainous, sparsely populated zones of Gilgit and Baltistan in the high Himalayas. Today, the Indian regions of the princely state that existed until 1947 have about 14 million people – approximately 8 million in the Kashmir Valley, 6 million in the Jammu region, and 300,000 in Ladakh. The Pakistani regions have 5 to 6 million in all – 4–4.5 million in 'Azad' Kashmir and 1–1.5 million in Gilgit-Baltistan.

Consequently, India has been an essentially status-quo power in the territorial dispute. As early as 1955, Prime Minister Nehru suggested to his Pakistani counterpart that Pakistan should agree to the Ceasefire Line between the Indian and Pakistani jurisdictions becoming a permanent international border, which would formalise the division to India's advantage. Pakistan has consistently held the opposite view and been the perennially revisionist party in the territorial dispute. Pakistan sought to change the territorial status quo by war in 1965, and repeatedly tried to challenge the status quo through sub-conventional conflict with India thereafter.

The Pakistanis' restless revisionism is rooted in the historic centrality of Kashmir to Pakistan as a political concept and subsequently a movement ideology. Kashmir had been an integral part of the *idea* of Pakistan ever since the term Pakistan (Land of the Pure) was coined by an Indian Muslim student at Cambridge University in 1933. The 'P' denoted Punjab, the 'K' Kashmir, the 'S' Sind and 'tan' Baluchistan. So Kashmir, as part of a swathe of Muslim-majority regions in the north-west of the subcontinent, was a constitutive element of the imagined Pakistan long before the formation of the sovereign Muslim state in August 1947. In this ideological framework that charged the Pakistan movement, particularly during the 1940s, Pakistan as a state is incomplete without Kashmir. This became a permanent part of Pakistan's political discourse. As prime minister nearly five decades later, Benazir Bhutto declared in 1994: 'Kashmir is the *shah rug* [jugular vein] of Pakistan and the day is not far when it will be a part of this country'.[30]

India initially did not have such an ideologically driven claim to posses-sion of Kashmir. But once the war of 1947–48 concluded – with the new Indian state of Jammu and Kashmir containing the bulk of the territories and the large majority of the population of the dissolved princely state – such an ideological justification developed rapidly. It was at first articulated by Sheikh Abdullah, who declared in November 1951:

> The real character of a state is revealed in its Constitution. The Indian Constitution [which came into effect on 26 January 1950] has set before the country the goal of secular democracy based on justice, freedom and equality for all without distinction ... The national movement in our State [J&K] naturally gravitates towards these principles of secular democracy ... This affinity in political principles, as well as past associa-tions and our common path of suffering in the cause of freedom, must be weighed properly while deciding the future of the State [this was a time when the UN-administered plebiscite was still considered possible].[31]

In August 1952 Abdullah reiterated this ideological argument: 'The supreme guarantee of our relationship with India is the identity of demo-cratic and secular aspirations, which have guided the people of India as well as those of Jammu and Kashmir in their struggle for emancipation, and before which all constitutional safeguards [a reference to Article 370 of the Indian Constitution, which guaranteed autonomy to J&K in all matters except defence, foreign affairs, and currency and communications] will take a secondary position.'[32]

The argument that Muslim-majority Kashmir and Hindu-majority India had a natural affinity due to a shared commitment to democracy and, especially, 'secularism' – the equality and coexistence of all religious faiths and communities – became the basis of the Indian ideological claim to Kashmir from the early 1950s onward. In this quasi-official narrative, India as a 'secular' state – i.e., the antithesis of Pakistan – would be incomplete without its only Muslim-majority constituent, J&K. Equally, so the argument ran, the Muslims of J&K – and especially those of the Kashmir Valley with their syncretistic cultural heritage – naturally belonged with India. The narrative romanticised that heritage (*Kashmiriyat*, or Kashmiriness) and represented the Kashmir Valley as the ultimate repository of India's 'secular' ethos, and therefore the jewel in the crown of the Indian secular state. The narrative of harmonious Kashmir–India symbiosis derived from shared democratic and secular values was fatally damaged after four decades of hegemonic circulation in India, when in 1990 a furious uprising for *azaadi* (freedom) from Indian rule erupted in the Valley and a new generation of young Kashmiri Muslim men took to armed struggle.

THE RISE AND FALL OF SHEIKH ABDULLAH

Sheikh Mohammad Abdullah ruled the Indian state of Jammu and Kashmir in the style of an uncrowned monarch for almost six years, from October 1947 to August 1953. He officially became its almost all-powerful prime minister in March 1948 (Hari Singh remained the titular head of state until 1952, when he was succeeded by his son, Karan Singh). Abdullah was the first indigenous Muslim ruler to emerge in Kashmir in over 350 years, since the time the last Kashmiri dynasty, the Chaks, were deposed by the forces of the Mughal emperor Akbar in 1586.

After the proclamation of the Republic of India in January 1950, India embarked on the path of parliamentary democracy, holding its first general election in late 1951 and early 1952. It was a genuinely democratic election. The Congress party won three-fourths of the seats in parliament, but it won only 45 per cent of the votes polled. The mismatch between votes and seats was due to the 'first-past-the-post' electoral system, which disproportionately favours the party with the single largest vote share. In other words, 55 per cent of Indians who turned out in the founding election of India's democracy voted freely for a wide range of opposition parties.

The autonomous Indian state of Jammu and Kashmir, the subject of an international dispute, did not participate in this election (Indian parliamentary elections were not held there until 1967). But quite separately, a J&K Constituent Assembly was elected around the same time, in autumn 1951, at the initiative of Abdullah's National Conference party. The UN Security Council disapproved of the initiative and had passed a resolution in March 1951 which reiterated that 'the final disposition of the State of Jammu and Kashmir will be made in accordance with the will of the people, expressed through the democratic method of a free and impartial plebiscite conducted under the auspices of the United Nations'. The resolution noted that previous UNSC resolutions in April 1948, June 1948 and March 1950, as well as UNCIP resolutions in August 1948 and January 1949, had all affirmed 'the above principle'.[33]

The manner in which the J&K Constituent Assembly was formed presented a stark contrast to the democratic exercise simultaneously underway in India. There was no voting and all 75 seats in the J&K Constituent Assembly – 43 from the Kashmir Valley, 30 from Jammu and 2 from Ladakh – were filled by NC candidates without any contest (25 further seats were kept vacant for the Pakistani-controlled areas, making a nominal total of 100 members). Abdullah's Muslim opposition – represented by his old rivals in the Muslim Conference – had been decimated by the events of late 1947. The MC's leaders from both the Jammu region and the Valley had fled into exile in Pakistan's 'Azad' Kashmir territory, which from January 1949 lay beyond the Ceasefire Line. Two non-NC candidates who tried to stand for election in the Valley were forced to withdraw, according to Josef Korbel, an UNCIP official.[34] The situation was somewhat different in the Hindu-populated southern parts of the Jammu region where the

Praja Parishad (Subjects' Forum), an organisation launched in late 1947 by ex-officials of the princely state and backed by the local RSS, was active. The Praja Parishad tried to field candidates from twenty-eight of the thirty Jammu seats – thirteen were arbitrarily disqualified and the others withdrew in protest.

The National Conference's slogan during the Abdullah premiership was 'One Leader, One Party, One Programme'. Balraj Puri, a Jammu-based activist and writer, was disturbed by the strong-arm authoritarianism of the Abdullah regime and met Nehru in Delhi to voice his concern. Puri specifically requested that a small dissident NC group led by Ghulam Mohiuddin Karra – the former Srinagar NC chief and a leader of the 1946 Quit Kashmir movement who had fallen out with Abdullah – be allowed to operate as a political opposition in the Valley. Nehru, Puri wrote four decades later, conceded 'the theoretical soundness of my argument but maintained that India's Kashmir policy revolved around Abdullah and therefore nothing should be done to weaken him'.[35]

The authoritarianism of the Abdullah regime was, however, offset for the majority of ordinary people by its fulfilment of a key promise of the National Conference's 1944 'Naya [New] Kashmir' charter – the 'One Programme' alluded to in the NC's post-1947 slogan. On 13 July 1950, the anniversary of the 1931 events in Srinagar which marked the beginning of popular resistance to the princely state, Abdullah's government 'introduced the most sweeping land reform [ever seen, then and since] in the entire subcontinent'.[36] Until then, almost all of (Indian) J&K's privately owned farmland of 2.2 million acres was the property of 396 big landlords and 2,347 medium-sized landlords, 'who rented to [landless] peasants under medieval conditions of exploitation'. Between 1950 and 1952 about 700,000 serfs became peasants working their own land as over 1 million acres expropriated without compensation from the feudal lords were transferred to them, and another sizeable chunk passed to government-run collective farms. The majority of the beneficiaries were Muslims in the Kashmir Valley but about a third were in the Jammu region, including tens of thousands of poor, low-caste Hindus. In the Valley the Pandit community, less than 5 per cent of the population, owned one-third of the arable land, and

Abdullah softened the blow for them. They were allowed to retain their fruit orchards and 10 per cent of jobs in the J&K state government were reserved for them.[37]

By the early 1960s, 2.8 million acres of farmland and fruit orchards (the latter in the Valley), including previously state-owned land, had become the property of smallholding peasant-proprietors. Visiting the Kashmir Valley in the mid-1950s, Daniel Thorner observed that despite 'defects in implementation, many [tenant] tillers have become landowners and some land has even gone to the landless. The peasantry of the Valley were not long ago fearful and submissive. No one who has spent time with Kashmiri villagers will say the same today.'[38] Another scholar, Wolf Ladjensky, noted that 'whereas virtually all land reforms in India lay stress on the elimination of the *zamindari* [large estates] system with compensation, or rent reduction and security of tenure [for tillers], the Kashmir reforms call for distribution of land among tenants without compensation for the erstwhile proprietors ... [and] whereas land reform enforcement in most of India is not so effective, in Kashmir enforcement is unmistakably rigorous'.[39]

This transformation of the overwhelmingly rural and agrarian society of Indian Jammu and Kashmir had profound political consequences. It elevated Sheikh Abdullah to nearly divine stature in the eyes of the Muslim peasantry of the Kashmir Valley. The NC party flag, which depicts a plough, the peasant's essential implement, in white against a red background, now aptly reflected the party's support among the masses of emancipated serfs. Abdullah, already worshipped by his supporters as Sher-e-Kashmir (Lion of Kashmir), now became the Baba-e-Qaum (Father of the Nation), a twentieth-century addition to the Valley's pantheon of Sufi saints.

In August 1953, Sheikh Abdullah was deposed as Indian J&K's prime minister and spent almost all of the next twenty-two years – until 1975 – as a political prisoner. Abdullah's undoing was his insistence on 'maximum autonomy for the local organs of [J&K] state power, while discharging obligations as a unit of the [Indian] Union', as he put it in August 1952.[40] The Instrument of Accession to India signed by Maharaja Hari Singh on 26 October 1947 had limited New Delhi's jurisdiction to three subjects: defence, foreign affairs, and currency and communications. This was standard practice with accession agreements and did not normally preclude further integration of princely states into India or Pakistan. Jammu and Kashmir, however, was a unique case because of multiple UNSC resolutions calling for a plebiscite, and the existence of UNCIP. There was also Mountbatten's call for 'a reference to the will of the people' (27 October 1947) and Nehru's 'pledge' about a UN-sponsored referendum, first made on 2 November 1947 and repeated by him several times until 1952.

So in October 1949, India's Constituent Assembly inserted a provisional clause, Article 306A, into the Indian constitution, which specified that New Delhi's jurisdiction would remain limited to the three subjects specified in the Instrument of Accession. Once the constitution was enacted and India became a republic on 26 January 1950, the same guarantee was incorporated into the Indian constitution as its Article 370. Under Article 370, which formally remained in India's constitution until 5 August 2019, India's parliament could legislate even on the three subjects assigned to it only 'in consultation with the Government of Jammu and Kashmir state', and on any other subjects on the Union List with 'the final concurrence of the Jammu and Kashmir Assembly'.

Jammu and Kashmir's asymmetric autonomy within the Indian Union became the lightning rod for a reactionary agitation that developed from 1949 onward in the southern part of the Jammu region, centred on the city of Jammu, which is Indian J&K's second largest after Srinagar and its winter capital. Indian J&K's Hindu population is mostly concentrated in this southern swathe of the Jammu region. The agitation was led by the Praja Parishad (Subjects' Forum), an organisation formed in Jammu city just after the shambolic demise of the princely state by ex-officials in the last maharaja's administration and leaders of the local wing of the RSS, the militant Hindu nationalist group.[41] These elements would not quietly accept the ascendancy, and supremacy, of a new Valley-based Muslim political elite. The agitation was joined from 1950 by Jammu's Hindu landlords dispossessed by the National Conference government's land reforms (unlike Pandit landlords in the Valley, there were no concessions to them). The Praja Parishad's campaign of protest meetings, marches and civil disobedience steadily intensified through 1952 and the first half of 1953, after the strong-armed formation of the one-party J&K Constituent Assembly in late 1951. Its rallying cry was *Ek Vidhaan, Ek Nishaan, Ek Pradhaan* (One Constitution, One Flag, One Premier, for all of India). This targeted the making of a separate J&K state constitution, the J&K state flag (a slight variant of the NC party flag, with the addition of three vertical white lines to represent the three regions of the Indian state), and Sheikh Abdullah's 'prime minister' title. Balraj Madhok, a fiery Praja Parishad leader who went on to become the all-India president of the Bharatiya Jana Sangh (the BJP's name before 1980), called for 'full integration of Jammu & Kashmir State with the rest of India like other acceding [princely] States and the safeguarding of the legitimate democratic rights of the people of Jammu from the communist-dominated and anti-Dogra government of Sheikh Abdullah'.[42] The agitation received support from the leader of eastern Ladakh's Buddhist clergy, who feared that the NC government would turn its attention next to the clergy's immense landholdings in that remote part of the state.

The agitation escalated, and climaxed, in mid-1953. In May 1953 Syama Prasad Mookerjee, a Hindu nationalist politician from the eastern Indian state of West Bengal who had become the first all-India president of the Bharatiya Jana Sangh, entered the agitation zone in southern Jammu in solidarity with the protesters and was promptly arrested. Transferred to the Kashmir Valley, he died in detention near Srinagar the following month, apparently of natural causes.

Abdullah was rattled by the agitation. In April 1952, he described that demand for 'full integration' as 'unrealistic, childish and savouring of lunacy' in a combative speech in Ranbirsinghpora – a town on the border of Indian J&K with Pakistani Punjab and part of the Jammu Hindu heartland (the town is named after Ranbir Singh, the second ruler of the princely state).[43] He asserted that the agitation was backed not just by the RSS and the Hindu nationalist BJS party but by elements in the Congress party and the Union government. The speech was widely reported in the Indian press and the controversy deepened. Talks were then held in Delhi in June and July of 1952 between a J&K government delegation headed by Abdullah and Indian officials led by Nehru. The latter pressed the J&K delegation for concessions that might dampen the raucous clamour for 'full integration' without compromising the asymmetric autonomy framework. Abdullah held out, and turned down proposals to extend the fundamental rights provisions of the Indian constitution to J&K and make India's supreme court the final court of appeal for J&K civil and criminal cases. He did make a few lesser concessions, such as agreeing to fly India's national tricolour in a 'supremely distinctive' position alongside the J&K state flag.

The result of the talks was an unwritten modus vivendi, the 'Delhi Agreement' of August 1952. Nehru reported on the talks to India's parliament in a weary tone. He said he wanted 'no forced unions' and if J&K wished 'to part company with us, they can go their way and we shall go our way'.[44] Abdullah reported on the talks to his hand-picked J&K Constituent Assembly in the state's summer capital, Srinagar, in a very different tone. He emphasised the 'maximum autonomy' theme, and while he lauded 'the identity of democratic and secular aspirations' between Kashmir and India, he warned: 'I would like to make it clear that any suggestion of arbitrarily altering the basis of our relationship with India would not only constitute a breach of the spirit and letter of the [Indian] Constitution, but might invite serious consequences for the harmonious association of our State with India'.[45]

In April 1953, Abdullah appeared to back-track a bit and held out an apparent olive branch to his internal enemies. The basic principles committee of the J&K Constituent Assembly proposed devolution of power to the Jammu and Ladakh regions. Under the scheme, in addition to the J&K state legislature, the Kashmir Valley and Jammu regions would have directly elected assemblies to legislate on specified subjects, as well as ministerial councils for regional affairs. Ladakh would also have a directly elected regional council. It was even proposed to change the name of the Indian state of J&K to 'Autonomous Federated Unit of the Republic of India'. In response, the Jammu Hindu agitators simply reiterated their full-integration stance and Muslim-dominated areas in the northern half of the Jammu region protested against the prospect of becoming part of an autonomous Hindu-majority Jammu.

The entry of S.P. Mookerjee, the Hindu nationalist leader, into the fray in May 1953 aggravated the situation, and Abdullah decided to switch back to a confrontational line. In May the NC's working committee, the party's highest body, tasked a sub-committee with suggesting options for the future of the entire princely state. On 9 June 1953 the sub-committee reported back. It recommended a plebiscite but with a third option, independence, in addition to India and Pakistan. In private correspondence during July with Nehru and Abul Kalam Azad, India's education minister, Abdullah refused to back down. He then announced that he would convene the NC's working committee and its much larger general council in late August to discuss the sub-committee's report. This was to be preceded by a mass rally in Srinagar on 21 August, the day of the Muslim religious festival Bakr-Id.

There had been earlier signs that Abdullah did not regard his alliance with India as set in stone. In an interview with London's *Observer* newspaper in April 1949, he mused that rather than be permanently trapped in a bitter India–Pakistan dispute, it might be better for the people of the former princely state to live in an independent state which would have friendly relations with both countries – if India, Pakistan, world powers and the UN would support such a solution. These remarks aroused great alarm in India, and Abdullah recanted a month later in another interview given to *The Hindu*, a major Indian daily.[46]

Just before dawn on 9 August 1953, Sheikh Abdullah was arrested by state police from Gulmarg, a famous resort 30 miles from Srinagar. He was detained under the J&K Public Security Act, used until then against his opponents, and taken away to a prison in the Jammu region. The same day, Abdullah was dismissed as Indian Jammu and Kashmir's prime minister – 'in the interest of the people of the state' – by Karan Singh, the last maharaja's 22-year-old son, who held the ceremonial title of *sadr-e-riyasat* (head of state).

Bakshi Ghulam Mohammed, Abdullah's deputy prime minister and the state's home (interior) minister, took over immediately as prime minister. On 10 August, he denounced his leader as the agent of an unspecified imperialist power. The events bore all the hallmarks of a carefully engineered coup d'état. In September, Nehru justified Abdullah's deposition to India's parliament on the grounds that he had lost the confidence of the majority of his cabinet. This was correct – of the five-man cabinet, Shyamlal

Saraf (a Kashmiri Pandit) and Giridharilal Dogra (a Jammu Hindu) sided with Bakshi, leaving Mirza Afzal Beg as the Sheikh's only supporter. But Nehru was unable to offer any explanation for why it had been necessary to arrest and imprison Abdullah, beyond a claim that his conduct had caused 'distress to the people'.[47]

The reason for Abdullah's incarceration was revealed by the public reaction in the Kashmir Valley. Syed Mir Qasim, a NC leader from the southern Valley town of Anantnag/Islamabad, who sided with the coup, became a minister in Bakshi's cabinet and would go on to serve as Indian J&K's chief minister from 1971 to 1975. He recalled in his memoir, published in 1992, that Abdullah's removal 'gave rise to a grim situation and a bitter sense of betrayal. The news spread like wildfire, giving rise to widespread agitations and protest marches. In Anantnag, where the news reached a day late, I sat in my [law] chamber for three days, watching wave after wave of protest marches surge past. Some people were killed in police firing.' On 12 August, Qasim and the top NC leader G.M. Sadiq, also a coup supporter, travelled from Anantnag to Srinagar with a police escort. 'On our way,' Qasim wrote, 'we passed through Kulgam, Shopian and Pulwama [towns] and saw the people's angry, rebellious mood.' In Kulgam, crowds at a graveyard were burying people who had been killed in police firing. When they saw Qasim with a police escort, they asked him: 'So you are also with them?' 'In Shopian we faced a graver situation,' Qasim wrote, as 'a 20,000-strong crowd menacingly surged towards where we were staying, to attack us.' When they arrived in the capital, 'Srinagar was in chaos. Bakshi Saheb's own house, despite the police guard, was under attack. He was nervous and wanted to step down as prime minister in favour of Mr Sadiq.'[48] Indian Army troops were deployed alongside state police to control the insurrection-like situation. This was achieved at the cost of hundreds of deaths and thousands of arrests. The latter included 33 senior National Conference leaders, including Afzal Beg, the former cabinet minister, who were taken into custody on 9–10 August. In special sessions held in October, 60 of the 75 J&K Constituent Assembly members and 90 of 110 members of the NC's general council ratified the new leadership; most of the rest were in jail.

The watershed of August 1953 heralded a permanent police state in the Kashmir Valley. Abdullah's six-year reign was authoritarian, but it had a significant degree of popular legitimacy, especially in the Valley. The governments that followed his for the next two decades, until the mid-1970s, were run by stooges of New Delhi – Bakshi Ghulam Mohammed (1953–63), Khwaja Shamsuddin (1963–64), G.M. Sadiq (1964–70) and Mir Qasim (1971–75). They were installed through farcically rigged elections and dispensed with by their masters once they outlived their usefulness. Their sole qualification was that they were prepared to do the bidding of Indian governments without any question or dissent, and because they did not owe their office to the people, they had no accountability to the people. The result was a dysfunctional polity bordering on dystopia, ruled by a host of draconian laws: the J&K Public Security Act, the Defence of India Rules (a colonial-era emergency regulation used by the British against Indian nationalists), the J&K Preventive Detention Act, the federal Unlawful Activities Prevention Act and, from 1978 on, the J&K Public Safety Act.

After Bakshi Ghulam Mohammed lost his premiership and fell out of favour with New Delhi, he was arrested in September 1964 and sent to the same prison in the Jammu region where Abdullah had been consigned eleven years earlier (although Bakshi was released after a few months on health grounds). The oppressive atmosphere was worst in the Kashmir Valley, but the other two regions, Jammu and Ladakh, were also trapped in the dysfunctional and dystopian system. Abdullah was right when he noted in 1968: 'The fact remains that Indian democracy stops short at Pathankot [the last major town in India's Punjab state before the Jammu region of Indian J&K]. Between Pathankot and the Banihal [the mountain pass that connects the Jammu region to the Valley] you may have some measure of democracy, but beyond Banihal there is none.'[49]

Wearing the martyr's halo, Abdullah haunted the official politics of Indian Jammu and Kashmir like the ghost of Banquo in Shakespeare's *Macbeth* throughout his twenty-two years in captivity. In his book on the early Kashmir conflict published in 1954, the UN official Josef Korbel mentioned Abdullah's near-iconic stature in the Kashmir Valley, while noting that it progressively diminished south of the Banihal Pass.[50] In the spring of 1954, my mother Krishna Chaudhuri (later Krishna Bose), a young Indian woman from Bengal, toured the Kashmir Valley for several weeks. She wrote sixty years later: 'I remember that during a *shikara* trip on the Dal Lake [in Srinagar] – the *shikara* is the distinctive boat of the waterways of Kashmir – the boatman sang Sheikh Abdullah's praises and bitterly criticized Bakshi Ghulam Mohammed'.[51]

On 10 August 1955, Abdullah's followers formed a new organisation called the Jammu and Kashmir Plebiscite Front, because the National Conference label had been usurped by the New Delhi-backed ruling clique. From then until its disbandment in 1975, the Plebiscite Front was the most popular organisation in Indian J&K, and commanded overwhelming support in the Kashmir Valley. Mir Qasim's 1992 memoir candidly says that the Plebiscite Front 'reduced the [official] National Conference to a nonentity in Kashmir's politics'.[52] The Front's two top leaders were Mirza Afzal Beg, the sole minister in Abdullah's cabinet who stayed loyal, and Maulana Masoodi, the NC party's general secretary who also sided with Abdullah. Relentless repression made no difference to its popularity. On 23 August 1955, two weeks after its formation, the J&K government banned political rallies, and in November Afzal Beg, the Front's first president, was re-arrested. Three men who succeeded him in that position were all arrested in quick succession between then and September 1956.

Sheikh Abdullah was let out of prison on three occasions before being rearrested: for a year between April 1964 and May 1965, and for brief periods in 1958 and 1968. His short-lived public appearances triggered mass euphoria in the Valley. On 18 April 1964, Indian newspapers reported, 'Abdullah entered Srinagar and was greeted by a delirious crowd of 250,000 people. Srinagar was a blaze of colour [in spring] and everyone seemed to be out on the streets to give Abdullah a hero's welcome ... Addressing a gathering of 150,000 people on 20th April, Abdullah said that in 1947 he had challenged Pakistan's authority to annex Kashmir on grounds of religion and now he was challenging the Indian contention that the Kashmir question had been settled.' In March 1968, 'almost the entire population of Srinagar turned out to greet him' once again, the *Times of India* newspaper reported, and added that hundreds of thousands were chanting '*Sher-e-Kashmir zindabad* [Long live the Lion of Kashmir], we demand plebiscite'. A few days later, Abdullah declared at a rally of 100,000 people in Anantnag/

Islamabad that 'repression will never suppress the Kashmiri people's urge to be free'.[53] In 1969 the Plebiscite Front ran candidates as independents in elections to local bodies in Indian J&K and swept the Valley. In 1971 Shamim Ahmed Shamim, a prominent Kashmiri journalist and editor of *Aina* (Mirror), an Urdu paper, stood as a Plebiscite Front-backed independent candidate in India's parliamentary elections from the Srinagar constituency. He defeated Bakshi Ghulam Mohammed, who contested as the candidate of the Congress party – led by Nehru's daughter and political heir, Indira Gandhi – by a massive margin.

THE INTEGRATION OF INDIAN JAMMU AND KASHMIR INTO INDIA

In parallel with the institutionalisation of the police state, the integration of Indian Jammu and Kashmir with India proceeded purposefully from 1954.

Indian J&K's statutory autonomy had been proclaimed in 1950 by a constitutional order issued in the name of the president of India, the titular head of state. In May 1954, another constitutional order effectively superseded the previous one. The 1954 order extended New Delhi's legislative jurisdiction over Indian J&K to the majority of subjects on the Union List, far beyond the three in the 1947 Instrument of Accession. Indian J&K's financial and fiscal relationships with the 'Centre' (New Delhi) were placed on the same footing as those of other Indian states, and India's supreme court got full jurisdiction over Indian J&K. The extensive fundamental rights guaranteed to citizens by India's constitution were also extended to Indian J&K. But this was a mockery because of a caveat – those rights could be suspended at the discretion of the government of Indian J&K on grounds of security and no judicial reviews of such suspensions would be allowed.

Bakshi Ghulam Mohammed's government readily gave its consent to the wave of integration, as required by Article 370. In February 1954 Bakshi told a silent J&K Constituent Assembly – in the absence of a small minority of doggedly pro-Abdullah members, most of whom were in jail – that 'we irrevocably acceded to India more than six years ago and today we are fulfilling the formalities of our unbreakable bonds with India'. On the floor of India's parliament, Nehru welcomed Bakshi's statement as 'representing the wishes of the people of Kashmir'.[54] This was the beginning of the end of Article 370. The original version of Indian Jammu and Kashmir's special status and asymmetric autonomy within India effectively ended in 1954.

Around the same time, the geopolitics of the Cold War impacted the Kashmir dispute. Pakistan entered the orbit of the US as a participant in its strategy of 'containment' of the Soviet Union. In May 1954, Pakistan joined the US-sponsored South-East Asian Treaty Organization (SEATO, the Manila Pact), and it joined the Central Treaty Organization (CENTO, the Baghdad Pact) in September 1955. By contrast, India appeared intent on a neutral foreign policy which steered clear of the superpower rivalry engulfing the post-1945 world.

Pakistan's membership of the network of military alliances sponsored by the US led to a decisive shift in Soviet foreign policy vis-à-vis the subcontinent. In December 1955 the new Soviet leader after Stalin's demise, Nikita Khrushchev, visited India accompanied by Marshal Nikolai Bulganin, the chairman of the Soviet Union's council of ministers. The duo travelled to the Kashmir Valley, and in Srinagar, Khrushchev said:

> The people of Jammu and Kashmir want to work for the well-being of their beloved country, the Republic of India. The people of Kashmir do not want to become toys in the hands of imperialist powers. This is exactly what some powers are trying to do by supporting Pakistan on the so-called Kashmir question. It made us very sad when imperialist powers succeeded in bringing about the partition of India ... That Kashmir is one of the States of the Republic of India has already been decided by the people of Kashmir.

In his remarks in Srinagar, Bulganin referred to Kashmir as 'this northern part of India' and to its population as 'part of the Indian people' who, he said, felt 'deep joy' at being included in India.[55]

Fortified by superpower support, Nehru told India's parliament in March 1956 that a plebiscite was now 'beside the point'. In April, he made it public that he had offered Pakistan's prime minister a permanent, formal division of the ex-princely state along the 1949 Ceasefire Line a year earlier, in May

1955.[56] In Delhi, Balraj Puri, the activist from Jammu, met Nehru again and pleaded that pro-Abdullah elements be allowed some political space to operate. Nehru, according to Puri, agreed that Bakshi was a very unsavoury character but 'argued that India's case now revolved around him and . . . the Bakshi government had to be strengthened'. In 1954 the Praja Socialist Party (PSP), a leftist all-India party which was then the main opposition to Nehru's Congress government, had been prevented from opening an office in Srinagar by the Bakshi regime's thugs, who ran amok in the Valley throughout Bakshi's ten years in office (1953–63). Nehru's response was to accuse the PSP of 'joining hands with the enemies of the country'.[57]

In November 1956, the Indian J&K Constituent Assembly – set up five years earlier by Abdullah – was presented with a draft constitution for the Indian state of Jammu and Kashmir. This started from the premise that 'the State of Jammu and Kashmir is and shall be an integral part of the Union of India'.[58] The state constitution was quickly approved by sixty-seven of the Constituent Assembly's seventy-five members – 'the remaining members were either in gaol or had withdrawn from the proceedings'.[59] In a symbolic gesture of allegiance, it came into effect on 26 January 1957, the seventh anniversary of the proclamation of the constitution of the Republic of India. From prison, Abdullah wrote protest letters to Nehru and to G.M. Sadiq, his former colleague and the speaker of the J&K Constituent Assembly. He received no replies. On 24 January 1957, the UN Security Council passed a resolution which reiterated the 1948–51 UN resolutions and called for the Kashmir dispute to be settled 'in accordance with the will of the people expressed through the democratic method of a free and impartial plebiscite conducted under the auspices of the United Nations'.[60] This was the last time the Security Council intervened in the Kashmir dispute. In February 1957, the Soviet Union vetoed a further resolution for the first time, and did so regularly thereafter.

After enacting the state constitution, the J&K Constituent Assembly dissolved itself, and a legislative assembly was elected for the Indian state of Jammu and Kashmir. The official National Conference secured sixty-nine of the seventy-five seats, including all forty-three seats from the Kashmir Valley. The token opposition consisted of five Praja Parishad members elected from the Jammu region. In 1958 this assembly gave its consent to the deployment of Indian civil servants from outside the state in the administration of Indian J&K. By the time of the next assembly election in 1962, a bitter rift between the Bakshi and Sadiq factions of the ruling clique had been papered over through intervention from New Delhi, and the superficially reunited government party secured sixty-eight of the seventy-four seats. The Praja Parishad got three seats and the other three were filled by independents, one of whom was the chief of the Buddhist clergy of eastern Ladakh. But by this time the Bakshi regime was becoming an embarrassment for its sponsors in New Delhi. After the 1962 election, Nehru wrote to Bakshi: 'It would strengthen your position much more if you lost a few [more] seats to bonafide opponents'.[61] Bakshi managed to stave off a New Delhi-backed attempt to replace him with his rival, G.M. Sadiq, but in October 1963 he reluctantly stepped down as prime minister of Indian J&K in favour of one of his obscure ministers, Khwaja Shamsuddin.

THE SECOND KASHMIR WAR

Winters are usually quiet in the Kashmir Valley because of the bitter cold and frequently snowbound conditions. People huddle indoors hugging body-warming contraptions unique to the region – *kangris*, earthen pots encased in woven wicker, filled with charcoal embers that provide warmth under woollen *pherans*, long cloaks which are the traditional and unisex Kashmiri outer garment. But in the winter of 1963–64, the Valley exploded in protest, which began the countdown to the second India–Pakistan war over Kashmir in 1965.

The unrest started in late December of 1963, a week after the beginning of the long winter's harshest period – *chillai-kalan*, which lasts for forty days from the fourth week of December until the end of January or early February. It was triggered by the disappearance of the *moi-e-muqaddas* – the holy relic believed to be a hair of the Prophet – from Srinagar's Hazratbal shrine. The gleaming-white shrine, which rises like a vision off the shores of the Nageen Lake in a suburb of the city, is the most important spiritual centre of Kashmiri Islam (the mid-fifteenth-century shrine and mausoleum of Kashmir's patron-saint Sheikh Nooruddin Noorani, located in the town of Charar-e-Sharief 20 miles south-west of Srinagar, is second). The Hazratbal shrine had served as a political base for Sheikh Abdullah since the 1940s.

The missing relic reappeared just as mysteriously after a week. But 'in the meantime a central action committee led by Maulana Masoodi, the former general secretary of the National Conference [and now a top Plebiscite Front leader] had been formed for the relic's recovery and taken control of the city in a mass upsurge'.[62] The crisis committee's two other prominent figures were G.M. Karra, who had been the NC's Srinagar chief, and Maulvi Farooq, the pro-Pakistan *Mirwaiz* (head preacher) of Srinagar's Jama Masjid. Masoodi and Karra 'did wonderful work pacifying excited crowds in the critical days when a small mistake could have soaked the Valley in blood'.[63] The relic's reappearance – and subsequent authentication by Masoodi, a cleric – did not stanch the mood of rage across the Valley. It was not just that the public suspected the Indian-backed authorities of negligence – or worse, malfeasance – in the matter of the relic. The outpouring of anger was actually the release of ten years (since August 1953) of pent-up resentment against the Indian government and its local proxies, and the relentless repression of the police state.

The Valley continued to be convulsed by agitation and protest in the first months of 1964. In February an outbreak of violence against minority Hindus in East Pakistan (post-1971 Bangladesh) was followed by reprisals against minority Muslims in Calcutta (the capital of India's adjoining state of West Bengal), and this fuelled the Kashmir turmoil. Indian intelligence agencies reported to New Delhi that the Valley was in a state of uprising and the proxy government had completely lost control. In late February the obscure Shamsuddin was replaced as Indian J&K's prime minister by G.M. Sadiq. Then, in April, Sheikh Abdullah was released after eleven years of almost continuous incarceration, since it was believed that only his presence could calm things down. This was the context of Abdullah's triumphant return to Srinagar as hundreds of thousands flooded its streets and other places in the Valley. In late April, Abdullah went to Delhi to meet Nehru (who was ailing and died a few weeks later). In May, Abdullah was even allowed to travel to Pakistan, where he met General Ayub Khan, the country's military dictator.

The promise of a Srinagar Spring soon dissipated. Abdullah's release did have a calming effect, but the Indian government was deeply alarmed by his tough rhetoric. Addressing 150,000 elated supporters on 20 April, for example, Abdullah stressed that the Kashmir question was unresolved – in flat contradiction of the official Indian stance – and said: 'A solution must be found agreeable to both India and Pakistan with due regard to the sentiments of the people of Kashmir'.[64] The lion of Kashmir was clearly unbowed, and roaring. With an untamed Abdullah on the loose and Bakshi Ghulam Mohammed plotting intrigues from the sidelines – many members of the Indian J&K assembly from the fraudulent 1962 election were his men – the Sadiq government looked very shaky.

The backsliding took shape by late 1964. In December, India's home (interior) minister announced in the Indian parliament that J&K would be brought under the purview of the two most anti-federal clauses of India's constitution – Articles 356 and 357, which respectively empower the Union government to dismiss an elected state government and impose Central rule. A constitutional order to this effect was immediately promulgated from New Delhi. Then, on 3 January 1965, the working committee of the ruling National Conference (meaning the Sadiq clique, Mir Qasim being the party's general secretary) announced that it would dissolve its existence and merge into India's ruling Congress party as a provincial branch. On 10 January the Congress party's working committee accepted the merger offer.

In March 1965 the Indian J&K assembly passed a slew of amendments to the J&K constitution of 1957. The title and post of *sadr-e-riyasat* (ceremonial head of state), elected by assembly members, was abolished and replaced, as in other Indian states, by a governor appointed from New Delhi. The title of the head of J&K's government was changed from 'prime minister' to 'chief minister', as in other Indian states. Provision was made for direct election from Indian J&K to the Lok Sabha (House of the People), the popularly elected lower chamber of India's Parliament, replacing the practice of nomination by the J&K assembly.

These events marked the substantive end of Article 370 and its provision of special status and asymmetric autonomy for Indian J&K. After 1965, Article 370 remained in India's constitution – until 5 August 2019 – in a residual, hollowed-out form. Indeed by 1965, the Hindu nationalists' agenda of integration 'had emerged victorious'.[65]

The 'people of the Valley reacted with unprecedented anger' and their 'protests were again suppressed with brute force and large-scale arrests'.[66] In mid-January Abdullah made a vitriolic speech to a huge Plebiscite Front rally at the Hazratbal shrine, condemning the imposition of Articles 356 and 357 and the attempt to erase the name of Kashmir's historic political movement, the National Conference. 'Violence and arson took place in some parts of Srinagar', targeting shops and businesses owned by Pandits and other Hindus, as crowds returned home after the rally.[67] By March mass arrests of Plebiscite Front leaders and workers were taking place, and in May Abdullah himself was rearrested under the Defence of India Rules. The final countdown to the second India–Pakistan war over Kashmir had begun.

War between India and Pakistan had become likely since late 1962, when India suffered a crushing defeat in a brief but bitterly fought border war with China. For most of the 1950s, relations between India and the People's Republic of China were characterised by a superficial bonhomie, fed by Nehru's belief in Asian and anti-colonial solidarity and his desire for camaraderie with a neighbour which, like India, possessed a great civilisational inheritance. This rosy view of Sino-Indian entente (*hindi chini bhai bhai*, Indians and Chinese are brothers) unravelled rapidly from the late 1950s. In 1958, the Indians became aware of a road the Chinese had built across Aksai Chin – a barren high-altitude plateau on the north-eastern periphery of the former princely state – to connect Xinjiang with Tibet. The Tibet crisis of 1959 and the Dalai Lama's flight to India, where he was given refuge, caused further distrust.

The backdrop to these developments was the unresolved border between the Republic of India and the People's Republic of China. There were (and are) two flashpoints along its 2,500 miles: the Aksai Chin/Ladakh area bordering western Tibet in the western Himalayas, and the North-East Frontier Agency or NEFA region (later the Indian state of Arunachal

Pradesh, or 'Sunrise Province', but referred to by the Chinese as 'south Tibet') in the eastern Himalayas. In 1961, Nehru's government ordered a so-called forward policy of aggressive military patrolling and outpost construction in the most sensitive border areas. This eventually elicited a large-scale Chinese military offensive in both the disputed eastern and western sectors in October–November 1962.[68] The Indian forces virtually disintegrated in the eastern sector and suffered heavy losses in the western (Ladakh) sector. Having administered a hiding, the victorious Chinese then returned to their pre-offensive positions. In March 1963, shortly after the debacle and the total collapse of the Sino-Indian relationship – which was not to revive until the 1980s – Pakistan sealed its growing closeness with China by signing a boundary agreement which ceded a sizeable tract (Shaksgam) in Pakistan's Northern Areas (the Gilgit-Baltistan region of the ex-princely state) bordering Xinjiang to China.

After the late 1962 border war with China, India began a major rearmament and expansion of its military capabilities, which had been badly neglected since independence. On the other hand, Pakistan, as a US Cold War ally since the mid-1950s, had been and continued to be the recipient of copious American military hardware, which in the mid-1960s included the latest Patton battle tanks (India also received some American military equipment during and after the war with China, but not on any comparable scale). After 1962, Pakistan was simultaneously the beneficiary of American military supplies and Chinese political and diplomatic support, a unique position because the US regarded and treated the PRC as a rogue state in the international system until 1971. Meanwhile, the Kashmir dispute was clearly stalemated at the UN. As unrest gripped Indian J&K in 1964, Pakistan sensed an opportunity to change the territorial status quo in place since the end of the 1947–48 Kashmir war by using force. The iron was hot, in this thinking, and it was imperative to seize the moment and strike before India's rearmament and military modernisation programme progressed significantly. Ayub Khan and his fellow generals were still cautious about starting another war with India. The principal advocate of a military offensive in Kashmir was a civilian politician – Zulfiqar Ali Bhutto, the young and charismatic foreign minister, who had been instrumental in the 1963 border pact with China.

The Pakistani war-plan which took shape in 1965 had two elements, codenamed Operation Gibraltar and Operation Grand Slam. Operation Gibraltar was named after the eighth-century Muslim/Moorish conquest of Spain, which had the strait and rock of Gibraltar as its launchpad. Under Operation Gibraltar, several thousand armed men crossed the 1949 Ceasefire Line into Indian J&K in late July and early August of 1965. They were organised in nine separate task forces, each named after a legendary warrior in the annals of Islamic history. Six entered the Kashmir Valley, two the Jammu region, and one came into the Kargil-Drass area of western Ladakh, close to the Zojila Pass gateway to the Valley. The men were mostly drawn from the Azad Kashmir Regular Force, a paramilitary formation under the Pakistani army's operational command which originated during the fighting of late 1947 (the formation was integrated into the Pakistani army as its Azad Kashmir Regiment in 1972). Some soldiers of the Pakistani army's commando unit, the Special Service Group, were also involved.

The aim of Operation Gibraltar was to ignite a general uprising in the Valley and in Muslim-dominated parts of the Jammu region close to the Ceasefire Line. Its key assumption was that the Muslim population of Indian J&K would welcome and abet the operation. This did not materialise. The infiltrators were met with a mixture of bemusement and suspicion, some locals informed the Indian Army about their arrival and movements, and the non-Kashmiri-speaking men from Pakistan's 'Azad' Kashmir had difficulty communicating and blending in with the people of the Valley. The operation 'had taken for granted the fullest cooperation of the local Muslims but this was not forthcoming, at any rate not on the expected huge scale'.[69] Only one of the nine columns, which entered the Rajouri sector of the Jammu region, achieved any success in rousing the local populace and establishing a 'liberated' zone.[70] Once alerted, the Indian Army acted swiftly and decisively to combat and root out the infiltrators. In the process, Batamaloo, a neighbourhood of Srinagar, was razed by Indian firing and shelling after some infiltrators holed up there.

By the time the Pakistanis launched Operation Grand Slam on 1 September 1965, Operation Gibraltar had already failed miserably. Operation Grand Slam was a conventional thrust led by tanks towards the strategic border town of Akhnur in the Hindu-dominated south-western plains of Indian J&K's Jammu region. It aimed to cut off Indian forces further north in the hilly and mountainous areas abutting the Ceasefire Line. The offensive made advances into the area's Chhamb-Jaurian belt. But then the offensive stalled and the tables turned when on 6 September the Indian Army launched major tank-led thrusts into Pakistan, targeting the Pakistani Punjab cities of Sialkot (which is about 30 miles from Jammu city) and Lahore. The Pakistanis had not expected that – unlike in 1947–48 – the Indian government would broaden the hostilities beyond Jammu and Kashmir and had particularly underestimated the resolute leadership of Lal Bahadur Shastri, a soft-spoken and diminutive figure who had succeeded Nehru as prime minister. The imperative to counter the Indian offensives into Pakistani Punjab spelled the end of Pakistan's Kashmir operation. China openly sided with Pakistan but limited itself to issuing threatening statements against India. On 22 September 1965, the UN Security Council passed a resolution calling for an immediate ceasefire and the fighting ended. In January 1966, Ayub Khan and Shastri signed an agreement in Tashkent which committed their countries to withdraw to August 1965 lines and positions (in a dramatic final turn, Shastri died suddenly in Tashkent just after signing the agreement). The territorial status quo ante was fully restored and Pakistan's bid to seize as much as possible of Indian Jammu and Kashmir had come to nought.

In the aftermath of the 1965 war, the Kashmiri Pandit activist Prem Nath Bazaz observed: 'It is necessary to recognize the fact that by and large State [Indian J&K] Muslims are not very friendly towards India. An overwhelming majority of them are not happy under the present political set-up and desire to be done with it. But they are reluctant to bring about change through warfare and bloodshed.'[71] That reluctance would change a quarter-century later.

THE POLICE STATE REDUX

In 1966, as the dust settled on the 1965 war, Jaya Prakash Narayan, a prominent Indian opposition leader who had been active in India's freedom struggle, wrote to Indira Gandhi, Nehru's daughter and India's new prime minister: 'We profess democracy, but rule by force in Kashmir. We profess secularism, but let Hindu nationalism stampede us into establishing it by repression. Kashmir has distorted India's image in the world as nothing else has done. The problem exists not because Pakistan wants to grab Kashmir, but because there is deep and widespread discontent among the people.'[72]

But in Indian Jammu and Kashmir, it was soon back to politics as usual. In elections to its legislative assembly in 1967, the Congress party (the Sadiq–Qasim ruling group) won sixty of the seventy-five seats, including thirty-nine uncontested seats. Of the opposition candidates, 118 were disqualified from running, 55 for not taking a compulsory oath of allegiance to India and the rest with no reason given. For the first time, elections were concurrently held to fill six seats in the Indian parliament's Lok Sabha from Indian J&K – three from the Valley, two from Jammu, and one from Ladakh. The Congress party won five of the six seats, two uncontested (Anantnag in the Valley, and Ladakh). In the Jammu region, the leftist Praja Socialist Party and the Hindu nationalist Bharatiya Jana Sangh – both all-India opposition parties – 'severely criticized electoral irregularities'. The complaints common to the conduct of both the state and national elections were 'large-scale rejection of nomination papers [of opposition candidates], arrests of [opposition] polling agents, advance distribution of ballot papers to Congress workers, absence of opposition agents at time of counting, and use of official machinery to the advantage of the ruling party'.[73]

The one parliamentary seat where an opposition candidate prevailed was the Srinagar constituency of the Kashmir Valley. This winner was none other than the notorious Bakshi Ghulam Mohammed, Indian J&K's prime minister from 1953 to 1963. It is certain that 'Bakshi would not have won a free election at any point during his ten years in office'.[74] But now sidelined, he claimed to be running to save the identity of Kashmir's historic political party, the National Conference, since the Sadiq–Qasim group had forsaken that identity. Indian intelligence operatives were sent from Delhi with instructions that 'Bakshi had to be defeated in the national interest'.[75] But riding a groundswell of popular support, he won.

A piquant situation arose in December 1970, when the Plebiscite Front announced its intention to run in Indian parliamentary elections in March 1971 and the state elections due in 1972. Mir Qasim, who had just replaced his deceased mentor G.M. Sadiq as Indian J&K's chief minister, panicked. As he wrote in his 1992 memoir, 'if the elections were free and fair, the Front's victory was a foregone conclusion'.[76] Indira Gandhi was not amused at the prospect. On a visit to the city of Jammu on 23 December, the Indian prime minister said that attempts to enter legislative bodies with the intent of 'wrecking the constitution' would not be tolerated. Asked by local journalists how this could be prevented, she replied: 'Ways will be found'.[77]

On 8 January 1971, 'externment orders' were served on top Plebiscite Front leaders Afzal Beg and Ghulam Mohammad (G.M.) Shah, Sheikh Abdullah's son-in-law, requiring them to leave the territory of Indian J&K. During the night of 8–9 January, 'at least 350 officials and members of the Front were arrested under the [J&K] Preventive Detention Act in police raids'. On 12 January, the Union government in New Delhi declared the Plebiscite Front an illegal organisation under the federal Unlawful Activities Prevention Act (UAPA), as it had 'on diverse occasions by words, either spoken or written, and signs and visual representations, asserted a claim to determine whether or not Jammu and Kashmir will remain part of India'.[78] In the 1972 state elections, the Congress party got fifty-seven of the seventy-five assembly seats. Unlike the banned Plebiscite Front, the Indian J&K wing of Jama'at-i-Islami, the fundamentalist movement which has wings in Pakistan, Bangladesh and both Indian and Pakistani Kashmir, was allowed to run and won five seats. According to the grapevine, the staunchly pro-Pakistan group had assured the Qasim government that it would help oppose the Plebiscite Front.

The slippery slope to the inferno of violence that engulfed the Kashmir Valley from 1990 to the mid-2000s and spread to some parts of the Jammu region, can be traced to 1975. In that year, Sheikh Abdullah renounced his politics of resistance to power and surrendered abjectly to New Delhi. In November 1974 his faithful lieutenant Afzal Beg and a bureaucrat representing the government of India signed a brief agreement, subsequently known as the 'Delhi accord' and sometimes as the 'Indira–Abdullah accord'. The agreement said that 'the State of Jammu and Kashmir, which is a constituent unit of the Union of India shall, in its relation with the Union of India, continue to be governed by Article 370 of the Constitution of India'. The agreement, however, made no provision for the revocation of any of the 28 constitutional orders issued in the name of India's president since 1954 or the 262 Union laws made applicable to Indian J&K which had reduced its actual autonomy to a hollow shell. Instead, the agreement was categorical that 'the provisions of the Constitution of India already applied to the State of Jammu and Kashmir ... are unalterable'. A minor exception was made 'with a view to assuring freedom to the State of Jammu and Kashmir to have its own legislation on welfare measures, cultural matters, social security, personal laws and procedural laws'. For this purpose, it was 'agreed that the State Government can review laws made by Parliament or extended to the State after 1953 on any matter relatable to the Concurrent List' (the grey area of governance matters of shared jurisdiction between the Union and state governments in India) 'and may decide which of them, in its opinion, needs amendment or repeal'. The agreement said that any such suggestions made by the Indian J&K government would be 'sympathetically considered'. A committee was later set up to examine what could be done under this provision of the agreement, but its recommendations were never made public.

The 1975 agreement was especially careful to protect 'the appointment, powers, functions, duties, immunities and privileges of the Governor' of Indian J&K, since 1965 a direct appointee of New Delhi. It specified that 'no law made by the Legislature of the State of Jammu and Kashmir seeking to make any change' in the governor's role and prerogatives 'shall take effect' without the assent of the president of India (meaning the Union government, given the ceremonial nature of India's presidency). Abdullah accepted this agreement in February 1975, after his plea for the restoration of his 1947–53 'prime minister' title was flatly rejected. Mir Qasim then stepped down and faded into political oblivion, and Abdullah was reinstated as Indian J&K's chief minister. In March, both chambers of India's parliament approved the agreement – the only opposition came from the small Hindu nationalist contingent, who demanded the outright abrogation of Article 370 and objected to the rehabilitation of the notorious separatist Sheikh Abdullah. Abdullah then dissolved the Plebiscite Front, formed in 1955, and once again became the leader of the All Jammu and Kashmir National Conference. Of the usurpers of the NC mantle post-1953, Bakshi Ghulam Mohammed and G.M. Sadiq were dead and Mir Qasim had been made redundant by his employers.[79]

Abdullah may have calculated that after Pakistan's rout in the December 1971 India–Pakistan war – which birthed the sovereign state of Bangladesh from erstwhile East Pakistan – the strategic balance in the subcontinent had shifted decisively in India's favour. Indeed, in July 1972, Zulfiqar Ali Bhutto, now the leader of a defeated and truncated country, came to the north Indian hill resort of Simla and signed an agreement with Indira Gandhi. The Simla Agreement said that 'the basic issues and causes of conflicts which have bedevilled relations between the two countries for the last 25 years shall be resolved by peaceful means ... through *bilateral negotiations* or by other peaceful means *mutually* agreed upon between them' (emphases added). This indicated that the Kashmir conflict could be resolved 'bilaterally' between India and Pakistan – prior to this, Pakistan had always formally insisted that the only solution was a UN-administered plebiscite as per the Security Council resolutions of 1948–57.

The Simla Agreement also stipulated: 'In Jammu and Kashmir, the Line of Control resulting from the ceasefire of December 17, 1971, shall be respected by both sides without prejudice to the recognized position of either side. Neither side shall seek to alter it unilaterally, irrespective of mutual differences and legal interpretations. Both sides further undertake to refrain from the threat or use of force in violation of this Line.'[80] This meant that Pakistan had agreed, on paper at least, to the renaming of the Ceasefire Line (CFL) from the 1947–48 Kashmir war as a 'Line of Control' (LoC) which was not to be violated by force, as it had been in 1965 by the Pakistanis, mainly on Bhutto's urging.

There were other factors as well for Abdullah, and the Pakistani government, to reckon with. India was now fortified by a twenty-year treaty of friendship and cooperation with the Soviet Union signed in August 1971, which had enabled the decisive Indian military intervention in support of the Bangladesh liberation movement in December 1971. The Soviet–Indian pact neutralised attempts to prevent the Indian military intervention in Bangladesh by the US's Nixon administration and its newfound ally China, whose July 1971 rapprochement based on their shared antipathy to the Soviet Union had been vitally facilitated by Pakistan. Then, in May 1974, India announced its intention of becoming a nuclear power by testing its first atomic bomb in Pokhran in north-west India's Rajasthan desert – close to the border with Pakistan – in an operation codenamed 'Smiling Buddha'. Abdullah may also have been worn down by two decades of incarceration and his advancing age; he turned seventy in December 1975 and suffered a major heart attack in 1977. He probably realised that if he continued to resist New Delhi, he faced the bleak prospect of dying in prison or in forced exile from his homeland.

Abdullah returned to Srinagar amid wild celebration and acclaim. The ordinary people of the Kashmir Valley did not initially understand that he had capitulated unconditionally to New Delhi. They thought their lion was back in charge and the twenty-two-year reign of the jackals had come to an end. But the Plebiscite Front's hardened activists were appalled by the terms of the Delhi Accord. In 1995 I interviewed Abdul Qayyum Zargar, a courtly middle-aged man, in his hometown Doda. Doda is a town predominantly populated by Kashmiri-speaking Muslims in the north-east of the Jammu region, and is part of a swathe of mountainous territory just south of the Banihal Pass that has a mostly Kashmiri-speaking Muslim population. At the time of our conversation, the area was in the grip of a brutal conflict between insurgents – mostly locals, with a sprinkling of Pakistani radicals – and the Indian Army and federal paramilitary police. Twenty years earlier, Mr Zargar had been the private secretary of Afzal Beg, who signed the Delhi Accord on Abdullah's behalf. He recalled that the terms of the agreement caused consternation and anger among the Plebiscite Front's activists. It took tremendous persuasion, he said, to convince them not to openly oppose the agreement. That persuasion was a sentimental appeal – the aged Sheikh's personal prestige was at stake, and he had suffered much since 1953 in the cause of the *awaam* (people).

New state elections were not held in Indian J&K until mid-1977. When they were, the National Conference emerged with a clear majority in the assembly (forty-seven of seventy-six seats), built on a near-sweep of the Valley's forty-two constituencies. The outcome was almost identical in the next election in June 1983. The NC – now led after the Sheikh's death in September 1982 by his eldest son, Farooq Abdullah – again got forty-seven seats, including thirty-eight from the Valley and one-quarter (eight) of the Jammu region's thirty-two seats.

The 1977 and 1983 elections were the first in Indian J&K's history to be contested in any meaningful sense. All previous elections – in 1951, 1957, 1962, 1967 and 1972 – had been farces. The state governments in office from 1953 to 1975 had had no popular legitimacy. Compared to that, the NC governments elected in 1977 and then in 1983 did have discernible popular support. It had taken thirty years, since the accession of 1947, for a reasonably competitive election to take place in the Indian state of Jammu and Kashmir.

But it was an illusion that a new democratic order had dawned in Indian J&K. Sheikh Abdullah was a lion in winter, of emasculated authority and stature. As his term as chief minister (1977–82) progressed, it became clearer that the Delhi Accord had deeply diminished him in the eyes of many in the Kashmir Valley, and that he had lost the veneration he had commanded until 1975.

A generational divide became apparent. Older people generally still felt a visceral loyalty to Abdullah, and the NC (i.e. the disbanded Plebiscite Front) had a grassroots organisation throughout the Valley and some parts of the Jammu region which brought out the vote in both 1977 and 1983. But for many born after 1947, whose experience of Indian rule was the police state of 1953–75, Abdullah had sold out to the oppressor and been reduced like his predecessors to a puppet ruler. Around 1975, a group of young men in the Valley formed an organisation called the Jammu and Kashmir People's League to keep alive the 'self-determination' platform Abdullah had renounced. Its best-known figure subsequently was Shabir Shah (born 1953), from the Valley's southern Anantnag/Islamabad district, who spent almost all of the next twenty years – until late 1994 – in prison.

Through the 1980s, more and more young men born during the 1960s became activists opposed to the NC government and the Abdullah family. Many – including some who became pioneering insurgents in the end-1980s under the banner of the Jammu and Kashmir Liberation Front (JKLF), a movement seeking independence for the entire territory of the ex-princely state from both India and Pakistan – cut their political teeth in the student wing of Jama'at-i-Islami. But it was not just the youth. Maulana Masoodi, the veteran National Conference and Plebiscite Front leader, could not stomach Abdullah's capitulation and parted ways with him. Even Afzal Beg fell out with the Sheikh in 1978, and they were estranged until they died a few months apart in 1982.

The clearest indication that this was not a new democratic order, and that resentment was simmering and growing in the Valley, was that the police-state apparatus was not dismantled, or even controlled. Instead, it was fortified and strengthened. In April 1978 Abdullah's government enacted a draconian law called the Jammu and Kashmir Public Safety Act (PSA), which is being used today, more than forty years later, as the main 'legal' instrument to stifle all shades of political opposition in the Valley by India's Hindu nationalist government. The 1978 PSA was 'enacted by the Jammu and Kashmir State Legislature in the 29th year of the Republic of India . . . in the interest of the security of the State and public order'. Its text is chilling – it reads like a law made by a colonial power or a ruthless dictatorship. It provided for twelve months in detention without any recourse to a court of law for 'persons acting in any manner prejudicial to the maintenance of public order' and two years 'in the case of persons acting in any manner prejudicial to the security of the State'.[81]

Even so, there were eruptions. On 28 July 1980 the *Indian Express* newspaper reported on its front page: 'At least one person was killed and several injured, some seriously, when armed police resorted to firing and tear-gas shelling in various parts of Srinagar. The police chased away violent crowds which set on fire two places of worship [Hindu temples] and many vehicles of the Army and paramilitary forces.' The next day the newspaper reported a further six deaths on its front page: 'The Centre [New Delhi] is rushing additional units of the CRPF [Central Reserve Police Force, federal paramilitary police] to help the local authorities maintain law and order in the troubled areas of the state. According to [Indian] Home Ministry sources, the reinforcements were being sent in response to a SOS from the Chief Minister, Sheikh Abdullah.' On 18 August 1980 the paper, a national daily in India, reported another four deaths in police firing in Srinagar on its front page: 'Four persons were killed and two injured in Srinagar when police opened fire to disperse crowds ... The police had repeatedly asked the crowds not to throw stones, but when the warning went unheeded had to resort to firing.'[82]

Sheikh Abdullah died in September 1982, and hundreds of thousands of people joined his funeral procession. Less than a decade later, in the early 1990s, his grave on the shores of the Dal Lake close to the Hazratbal shrine had to be put under the guard of Indian paramilitary police to prevent its desecration, as a massive uprising for *azaadi* (freedom) from India gripped the Valley. In the summer of 2010, during large-scale *azaadi* demonstrations in the Valley, angry crowds repeatedly tried to storm his grave and mausoleum yet again. For the past three decades, almost no locals have visited the grave to pay their respects to the man who was Jammu and Kashmir's pre-eminent political figure for fifty years, from 1932 to 1982.

The portents were evident soon after the Sheikh's death. In October 1983 Srinagar's Sher-e-Kashmir stadium, named in his honour, hosted Indian J&K's first international cricket match. The Indian national team took on the West Indies, the world's top side at the time, in a one-day game. Three months earlier, in July 1983, the Indian team had unexpectedly made it to the final of the World Cup for one-day cricket and beaten the West Indies in the final to win the Cup in a game played at the Lord's stadium in London. On their return to India from England, the players were feted as national heroes. The Indian side that turned out in Srinagar included the all-rounder Kapil Dev, the captain of the World Cup-winning team, and Sunil Gavaskar, the legendary opening batsman. They were booed and jeered throughout the game – which they lost – by the large crowd. Gavaskar later wrote: 'Being hooted at is understandable, but this was incredible. There were many in the crowd shouting pro-Pakistan slogans, which confounded us because we were playing the West Indies and not Pakistan.' Young men in the crowd waved pictures of the Pakistani cricketer Imran Khan (Pakistan's prime minister since 2018). Every Indian setback during the match – they batted first – was met with 'applause that was astonishing and deafening'. When the West Indies came out to bat, the Indian fielders were ceaselessly taunted and subjected to a barrage of projectiles including half-eaten Kashmiri apples, bottles, stones and trash. The Indian players, Gavaskar recalled, were simply 'stunned' by the hostility. At dinner that evening Farooq Abdullah, the chief minister, apologised to the Indian team.[83] Throughout the 1980s, thousands of Pakistani flags would appear across the Valley on 14 August, Pakistan's independence day.

The situation turned grimmer in February 1984 when a Kashmiri called Maqbool Butt was hanged in Delhi's well-known Tihar Jail. Butt, 46, a native of the northern Kashmir Valley district of Kupwara, was a leading activist of the pro-independence Jammu and Kashmir Liberation Front, formed in the mid-1960s in Pakistani Kashmir. He had been sentenced to death in 1968 by an Indian J&K court for allegedly killing a police officer during a shootout, but escaped and went back across the Ceasefire Line to rejoin his comrades in Pakistani Kashmir. He was recaptured in 1976 while apparently trying to rob a bank in the Valley, and his 1968 death sentence was carried out in 1984, days after UK-based JKLF militants of 'Azad' Kashmir origin abducted and murdered a junior Indian diplomat in Birmingham in a botched attempt to secure Butt's release. Maqbool Butt became an iconic martyr (*shaheed*) for some of the Kashmir Valley's steadily growing legions of angry young men, and the fact that he held independence-seeking beliefs – he was opposed to both Indian and Pakistani control over their respective parts of the former princely state – contributed to the rise of JKLF in the late 1980s as the Valley's first armed insurgents.

The precarious state of affairs was fatally destabilised by Indira Gandhi in mid-1984. After taking over as Indian J&K's chief minister in the autumn of 1982, Farooq Abdullah started to hobnob with Indian opposition parties. This enraged the Indian prime minister, who viewed it as breaching an understanding she had had with his father that the National Conference would not be party to efforts to challenge her Congress party's primacy in India's politics. In retaliation, she campaigned energetically in the Jammu region in the mid-1983 state elections in Indian J&K, appealing directly to

Jammu Hindus' resentment of the relative political dominance of the Valley after 1947. The campaign paid off in the Jammu region, which has a Hindu majority, where the Congress party won almost three-fourths of the seats (twenty-three of thirty-two). But the NC still won a decisive majority of seats in the Indian J&K assembly (forty-seven of seventy-six) by taking thirty-eight of the Valley's forty-two seats, supplemented by eight seats in Jammu and one of Ladakh's two seats.

By the first half of 1984, Farooq Abdullah emerged as a major player in efforts by Indian opposition parties to create an all-India front to take on Mrs Gandhi's Congress party in the Indian general election due by the end of 1984. In the spring of 1984, Mrs Gandhi dispatched a trusted henchman as Indian J&K's governor. The appointee, Jagmohan, had earned notoriety a decade earlier as a heavy-handed administrator of Delhi during the 'Emergency' regime Mrs Gandhi clamped on India from June 1975 to January 1977, when civil liberties were suspended, the press muzzled, and mass arrests of opposition leaders took place. In June 1984, twelve of the forty-seven NC legislators revolted against Farooq Abdullah's leadership and quickly formed a new government with the support of the legislature's twenty-six Congress members. The leader of the renegades was G.M. Shah, Sheikh Abdullah's son-in-law and an organiser of the erstwhile Plebiscite Front, who had nursed ambitions of inheriting the Sheikh's mantle (Farooq, a political greenhorn, was anointed by the Sheikh as his successor in 1981). Jagmohan dismissed Farooq Abdullah from office, rejected his plea for a 'floor test' to ascertain where the numbers stood in the legislature, and denied his appeal for a fresh election. G.M. Shah became the new chief minister, and all of the other eleven renegades became ministers in his government. In 1985, Farooq Abdullah wrote that the plot to depose his government was 'hatched in 1 Safdarjung Road, New Delhi', the prime minister's residence, and 'directed by Mrs Gandhi'.[84]

It was a surreal rerun of the 1953 coup, with Indira Gandhi, Jagmohan, G.M. Shah and Farooq Abdullah in the roles of Jawaharlal Nehru, Karan Singh, Bakshi Ghulam Mohammed and Sheikh Abdullah. The night before the coup, large numbers of the Central Reserve Police Force, or CRPF, paramilitary police under the control of the Union government's home (interior) ministry, were airlifted into Srinagar to suppress protests, which was duly accomplished.

Indira Gandhi's intervention in Kashmir had two objectives, apart from punishing Farooq for insubordination. She wanted to reduce the small number of state governments run by India's opposition parties; in September 1984, the same modus operandi was used in an eventually failed attempt to topple an opposition government in the large south Indian state of Andhra Pradesh. But even more important, she had devised a strategy for winning re-election in end-1984 by presenting herself as the defender of India's unity against various secessionist threats. In June 1984, the same month as the Srinagar coup, she sent the Indian Army to assault the Golden Temple, Sikhism's holiest shrine located in the city of Amritsar in India's Punjab state, to eliminate a group of armed Sikh radicals who had taken over the shrine. The group had been nurtured by her Congress party before they got out of control. A bloody battle resulted, and a few months later, on the morning of 31 October 1984, Mrs Gandhi was assassinated in the garden of her Delhi residence by two Sikh members of her security detail, who were incensed by what they perceived as the desecration of the Golden Temple. Mrs Gandhi had also been portraying a student-led agitation ongoing since 1979 in Assam, the largest state in India's restive north-east region bordered by China, Myanmar, Bangladesh and Bhutan, as part of a grand conspiracy to break up India. The post-1975 National Conference was anything but secessionist, but the removal of Farooq Abdullah's government was nonetheless presented as part of a tough stance on 'national unity and integrity'.

In December 1984 the Congress party – now led by Indira Gandhi's elder son Rajiv, a political novice – benefited from a nationwide sympathy wave from Indira's assassination and won more than three-fourths of the seats in the Lok Sabha, the directly elected chamber of India's parliament.[85] The only exceptions to the Congress party's landslide victory were in the states of Andhra Pradesh, Punjab and Assam, and in the Kashmir Valley, where all three constituencies – Srinagar in the centre, Baramulla in the north and Anantnag in the south – returned pro-Farooq candidates with huge majorities.

G.M. Shah's twenty-one-month tenure as Indian J&K's chief minister was shambolic. He earned the sobriquet 'curfew chief minister' – for seventy-two of his first ninety days in office, the Kashmir Valley was under curfew to prevent protests. The real authority in Indian J&K was Governor Jagmohan. Jagmohan's authority became formal in March 1986, when a localised eruption of violence against Kashmiri Pandits in an area south of Srinagar provided a pretext for Shah's dismissal under Article 356 of the Indian constitution, which empowers New Delhi to dismiss a state govern-ment on grounds of a breakdown of law and order. Until November 1986, Jagmohan ran Indian J&K on behalf of New Delhi.

In November 1986, Farooq Abdullah made a disastrous blunder. He agreed to be reinstated as chief minister, pending fresh elections in March 1987, in return for becoming an ally of the Congress party. The turn of events evoked outrage in the Valley. This was the same Congress party whose governments had – under three dynastic prime ministers, Jawaharlal Nehru, Indira Gandhi and Rajiv Gandhi – been responsible for India's Kashmir policy as narrated in this chapter. With Farooq's *volte-face*, the National Conference forfeited the limited credibility it still had among its mass base. It was the political equivalent of *hara-kiri*.

In the 1983 state election, the NC and the Congress had contested as adversaries and between them won seventy-three of the seventy-six seats in the legislature (forty-seven and twenty-six). With the two now poised to contest in alliance – the NC in forty-five seats, mostly in the Valley, and Congress in thirty-one, mostly in the Jammu region – Indian Jammu and Kashmir faced the prospect of a government with no institutional opposition.

Over the winter of 1986–87, such an opposition took shape in the Kashmir Valley. A broad and heterogeneous spectrum of groups came together in an alliance called the Muslim United Front (MUF, Muttahida Muslim Mahaz). The MUF, a report in India's leading newsmagazine observed during the campaign, was an '*ad hoc* bloc' composed of diverse religious, civil society and political groups 'with no real unifying ideology'. One element was the funda-mentalist Jama'at-i-Islami, a party with a small popular following but a grass-roots organisational network across the Valley and contiguous Kashmiri Muslim-populated parts of the Jammu region. Another was the People's

Conference, a small party strong in the Valley's northern Kupwara district led by Abdul Ghani Lone, a former Congress politician. Yet another prominent MUF figure was the cleric Qazi Nissar, the popular *Mirwaiz* (chief preacher) of the southern part of the Valley, around the town of Anantnag/Islamabad. The Indian magazine found that the MUF base was as diverse as its leaders: 'educated youth, illiterate working-class people, and farmers who express anger with the Abdullahs' family rule, government corruption and lack of economic development'. It noted that 'the Valley is sharply divided between the party machine that brings out the traditional vote for the National Conference and hundreds of thousands who have entered politics as participants for the first time under the umbrella provided by the MUF'.[86] The hodgepodge opposition front generated mass enthusiasm across the Valley. One of the twelve renegade NC legislators of 1984, Khemlata Wakhloo, a Kashmiri Pandit woman, wrote in a subsequent memoir that there was a discernible 'wave' of support for the MUF.[87] Its campaign on the ground was especially energetic because it was run by an army of youth volunteers, mostly young men in their twenties.

Polling was held in Indian J&K on 23 March 1987. The Indian magazine reported 'rigging and strong-arm tactics all over the Valley', 'massive booth-capturing [forcible takeover of polling stations] by gangs', and 'entire ballot-boxes pre-stamped in favour of the National Conference'. Numerous citizens were 'simply not allowed to vote', the bureaucracy 'worked blatantly in favour of the NC–Congress alliance' and 'the police refused to listen to any complaint'. Once counting began, a pattern emerged of supervising officials 'stopping the counting as soon as they saw opposition candidates taking a lead'.[88] The NC–Congress alliance took an overwhelming majority: sixty-six of the seventy-six seats (NC candidates won in forty of the forty-five constituencies the party contested and Congress twenty-six of the thirty-one constituencies its candidates contested). MUF candidates got through in only four constituencies, including the northern Valley town of Sopore and the town of Anantnag/Islamabad in the Valley's south. Even according to the official tally of votes, however, the MUF polled one-third of the state-wide votes, which means that its vote share in the Kashmir Valley was much higher than one-third.

A microcosm of the events of 23 March 1987 played out in Amirakadal, a prestigious constituency covering Srinagar's downtown area and adjacent old neighbourhoods. Here the MUF candidate was Mohammad Yusuf Shah, 41, a schoolteacher and Jama'at-i-Islami member. Originally from a village called Soibugh in the Valley's Badgam district, adjoining Srinagar, it was Shah's third attempt to get elected to Indian J&K's legislature. The coordinator of Shah's campaign was Mohammad Yasin Malik, 20, a resident of the working-class Maisuma neighbourhood, a warren of narrow streets packed with old houses next to the city centre. Once counting began, it became clear that Shah was headed for an overwhelming victory, and celebrations broke out. The dejected NC candidate left the counting centre, only to be summoned back and declared the winner. As the crowd protested, police arrived in strength, dispersed them using force and arrested both Shah and Malik. Both men remained in prison until early 1988, held under the Jammu and Kashmir Public Safety Act for acting in a manner prejudicial to 'public order' and 'the security of the State'.

The police state swung into action as soon as the election concluded. In a sweeping crackdown across the Valley, hundreds of young men who had worked in the MUF campaign were picked up and detained – of course without any court appearance or recourse to legal aid – for up to a year. Many were tortured in custody. Yasin Malik recalled his experience in an interview to an Indian journalist two years later, in May 1989. He had crossed the LoC to Pakistani Kashmir after his release and had recently returned to Srinagar with a few comrades after acquiring weapons and training. Now committed to armed struggle against Indian rule, he had joined the pro-independence Jammu and Kashmir Liberation Front while in Pakistani Kashmir and become a key figure in an embryonic JKLF organisation in the Valley. After his 1987 arrest, he remembered, 'they called me a Pakistani bastard. I told them I want my rights; my vote was stolen. I am not pro-Pakistan but have lost faith in India.'[89] Yusuf Shah spoke to another Indian magazine in autumn 1992. By then – under the *nom de guerre* Syed Salahuddin – he was the chief of Hizb-ul Mujahideen, the largest pro-Pakistan insurgent group. He said his 1987 experience had convinced him that 'slaves have no vote in the so-called democratic set-up of India'.[90]

THE BEGINNINGS OF INSURGENCY

Farooq Abdullah's post-1987 government was a runaway train-wreck. Devoid of any popular legitimacy in the Kashmir Valley, the National Conference's erstwhile bastion, his government floundered about as a creeping insurrection took hold in the Valley. In June 1988 police fired on crowds in Srinagar protesting a rise in the electricity tariff and killed several people. Then on 31 July 1988, bombs exploded outside Srinagar's central telegraph office and at the Srinagar Club, a haunt of the local elite. The bombings were carried out by local youths returned from across the LoC but planned by Mohammad Rauf Kashmiri, a JKLF militant from the Pakistani side of the historic Poonch district who had infiltrated into the Valley. In September 1988 JKLF got its first 'martyr' when Aijaz Dar, a Srinagar youth, was shot dead during a failed attempt to assassinate a senior police officer. *Hartals* (general strikes) and 'black days' were observed in the Valley on 13 July 1988 (the date of the 1931 incident which marked the beginnings of mass politics in Kashmir), 15 August 1988 (India's independence day), 27 October 1988 (the date Indian troops arrived in Srinagar in 1947), 26 January 1989 (India's Republic Day), 11 February 1989 (the fifth anniversary of the execution in Delhi of the JKLF militant Maqbool Butt) and in April 1989, when the pro-Pakistan activist Shabir Shah's elderly father died in police custody. Farooq Abdullah, known for intemperate outbursts, responded with wild rhetoric. He declaimed that he had 'the backing of the Indian government' and threatened to raze particularly rebellious districts of his capital, break strikes by forcing markets and shops to open, and break the legs of protesters before burying them alive.[91]

In the second half of 1989, the situation deteriorated sharply as JKLF's small band of underground militants embarked on a series of targeted assassinations. The first victim, in August 1989, was Mohammad Yusuf Halwai, a National Conference official who had been particularly prominent in rigging the 1987 state election in Srinagar. He was publicly executed on a city street by masked gunmen. On the day of the killing, 'many shops in Srinagar were closed in protest against the opening of a session of the State Assembly and police clashed in some [city] districts with rock-throwing crowds'.[92] In September, Tika Lal Taploo, a Kashmiri Pandit and head of the Hindu nationalist BJP in the Kashmir Valley, was gunned down in Srinagar. In November, Neelkanth Ganjoo, also a Kashmiri Pandit and a judge of the J&K high court, was ambushed by three gun-wielding men and shot dead in downtown Srinagar. Twenty years earlier in 1968, Mr Ganjoo, then a judge in a lower court, had sentenced JKLF's Maqbool Butt to death. That sentence was upheld by India's supreme court in 1982 and carried out in 1984.

In the midst of all this, India's general election was held in November 1989. Rajiv Gandhi's Congress party was heavily defeated in this election and lost power, and this election, India's ninth since independence, signalled the end of the Congress's four-decade dominance of India's politics since 1947. In the Kashmir Valley, there was an en masse boycott of the election. In the Srinagar constituency, the National Conference candidate was elected unopposed to India's parliament as no other candidate filed papers – unopposed elections are virtually unheard of elsewhere in India, whether in state or national elections. In the other two parliamentary constituencies – Baramulla in the northern Valley and Anantnag in the southern Valley – NC candidates were elected with 94 per cent and 98 per cent respectively of the votes. The turnout in these two constituencies was 4 per cent, that too achieved by security forces stuffing ballot boxes at selected sites. Turnout was also abnormally low, just 38 per cent, in one of the Jammu region's two parliamentary constituencies, Udhampur, which has a large Muslim electorate including Kashmiri-speaking Muslims who live in areas contiguous to the Valley.

Over the winter of 1989–90, the Kashmir conflict entered a new phase. A bloodbath that would take tens of thousands of lives during the next fifteen years was about to ensue.

CHAPTER TWO

The Carnage

1990–2004

I N 1945, GEORGE Orwell wrote an essay titled 'Notes on Nationalism'. He defined nationalism as 'a habit of mind', of 'identifying oneself with a single nation, placing it beyond good and evil and recognizing no other duty than that of advancing its interests'. Nationalism, he stressed, should not be 'confused with patriotism'. Patriotism, he wrote, is about 'devotion to a particular place and a particular way of life, which one believes to be the best in the world but has no wish to force on other people. Patriotism is of its nature defensive'. But nationalism 'is inseparable from the desire for power . . . A nationalist is one who thinks solely, or mainly, in terms of competitive prestige. His thoughts always turn on victories, defeats, triumphs and humiliations. He sees history, especially contemporary history, as the endless rise and decline of great-power units. Nationalism is power hunger tempered by self-deception. As nearly as possible, no nationalist ever thinks, writes or talks about anything except the superiority of his own power unit.' And in this mentality, 'actions are held to be good or bad, not on their merits but according to who does them, and there is almost no kind of outrage – torture, the use of hostages, forced labour, mass deportations, imprisonment without trial, forgery, assassination, the bombing of civilians – which does not change its moral colour when it is committed by "our" side. The nationalist not only does not disapprove of atrocities committed by his own side, but he has a remarkable capacity for not even hearing about them.' Orwell concluded: 'There is no limit to the follies that can be swallowed if one is under the influence of feelings of this kind'.[1]

The carnage that engulfed Indian Jammu and Kashmir from 1990 until the mid-2000s is a grim lesson in the ruinous potential of nationalism, as Orwell defined it. Or rather, of *nationalisms* competing for supremacy – the state-led nationalisms of India and Pakistan and the state-seeking Kashmiri nationalism which has its epicentre among the Muslims of the Kashmir Valley.

There is a cemetery in the Eidgah neighbourhood of Srinagar's old city. It occupies part of a large plot of land which has been the main venue for the city's biannual Eid prayer congregations for many decades, and otherwise served as a local playground. The cemetery, however, is only three decades old. Burials began there in January 1990. When I first visited the site in the mid-1990s there were already several hundred graves there, in neat rows. The place naturally had a forlorn feel, but roses had been planted to brighten up the surroundings. A middle-aged man tending the plants looked at me in some surprise; he was clearly not used to a non-local visitor. Otherwise, the cemetery was eerily empty.

Since then, the Eidgah cemetery has gradually expanded to at least 2,000 graves, and the original fenced-off space has quadrupled. A fairly ornate entrance gate has been built, and on later visits I noticed a few families at the tombstones of their lost ones. But the inscription – in Urdu and English – at the entrance was already there on my first visit: 'Lest you forget, we have given our today for your tomorrow'. The Eidgah cemetery is a 'martyrs' graveyard'. Those interred there are mostly 'militants' (insurgents) who have fallen in the fight against Indian rule since 1990, including many of the most prominent figures in the Kashmir Valley's pantheon of martyrs. There are also important political leaders of the *azaadi* (freedom) movement, several of whom died by assassination, as well as ordinary people killed by Indian security forces.

When I entered, the first graves I saw were three arranged side by side. Two had the usual green-and-white tombstones inscribed in Urdu. They belong to two pioneering militants of the pro-independence Jammu and Kashmir Liberation Front (JKLF) – Ashfaq Majid Wani, killed on 30 March 1990 in Srinagar, and Abdul Hamid Sheikh, killed on 19 November 1992 in Srinagar. Their graves had slightly raised mounds of earth covered with white cloths. The equally simple tombstone at the top of the row was, however, black in colour, inscribed in white, and did not have the shrouded mound of earth. This is an empty grave meant for the remains of Maqbool Butt, the JKLF militant of the earlier generation whose hanging in Delhi's Tihar prison in 1984 inspired the young pioneers of the armed struggle that began in 1988–89 and spread like wildfire from 1990. Butt's body was not returned to his homeland, and he was buried somewhere in the compound of the Delhi prison. The inscription on his tombstone says that the people of Kashmir are in *intezaar* – waiting with longing – for his return. A JKLF flag – whose design resembles that of the Palestine Liberation Organization – stood in vigil over the trio, soaked and drooping from rain. Another pioneering militant lay close by – Mohammad Abdullah Bangroo of the pro-Pakistan Kashmiri insurgent group Hizb-ul Mujahideen, JKLF's rival in the armed struggle. He was killed in Srinagar on 18 June 1990.

Between 1990 and 2002, some 56,000 incidents of insurgency-related violence were recorded in the Indian state of Jammu and Kashmir. According to official Indian figures, more than 16,000 insurgents died during this period along with about 4,600 personnel of the Indian security forces (the regular Army, the paramilitary Central Reserve Police Force and Border Security Force, and J&K police) and about 13,500 civilians.[2] These figures understate the toll – for instance, they do not include the 'disappeared', mostly persons taken away by Indian forces and never seen again. The Srinagar-based Association of Parents of Disappeared Persons (APDP), founded in 1994, plausibly says that this number across the Kashmir Valley is about 8,000.[3] The large majority of the insurgent and civilian deaths occurred in the Valley, although there was also a high toll in some parts of the Jammu region in the late 1990s and early 2000s. The bulk of insurgent deaths – about four in five – were of natives of Indian J&K, mostly residents of the Kashmir Valley. The rest were Pakistani militants who entered the fight from the mid-1990s onwards. As the carnage unfolded, Srinagar's Eidgah graveyard was joined by hundreds of middle-sized and small martyrs' cemeteries which appeared in the Valley's towns and in numerous villages, as well as in some areas of the Jammu region.

THE INSURRECTION TAKES HOLD

The insurgency was launched in 1989 under the banner of the Jammu and Kashmir Liberation Front. JKLF was formed in Pakistan's 'Azad' Kashmir in late 1965, shortly after the failure of the Pakistani military operation in Indian J&K that brought on the second India–Pakistan war. It was known until 1977 as the Jammu and Kashmir National Liberation Front (JKNLF). The JKNLF was the militant offshoot of a 'Kashmir Independence Committee' (KIC) founded in the early 1960s in 'Azad' Kashmir by a handful of young activists who felt that an independent state free from both India and Pakistan was the best solution to the Kashmir dispute. The KIC mutated into the Azad Kashmir Plebiscite Front (Mahaz-e-Raishumari) in 1964. This was set up as the parallel organisation in the Pakistani territories of the erstwhile princely state of the Plebiscite Front active in Indian Jammu and Kashmir, which commanded mass support in the Kashmir Valley.

The two key JKNLF leaders were Amanullah Khan (1934–2016) and Maqbool Butt (1938–84). They complemented each other – Butt was primarily a man of action while Khan was both a political organiser and an ideologue. They also shared a connection to the northern part of the Kashmir Valley. Butt was from Trehgam, a large village in the Valley's northern Kupwara district close to the post-1948 Ceasefire Line (the Line of Control, or LoC, from 1972) between the Indian and Pakistani Kashmirs. Khan had been born in the Gilgit region in the far north of the princely state but grew up in the Kupwara district, where he completed his schooling. He then briefly attended college in Srinagar under the mentorship of Maulana Masoodi, the general secretary of the National Conference party, before moving to Pakistan in 1952.

The independentist JKNLF/JKLF was not able to make inroads or establish a network in the Kashmir Valley – until the end of the 1980s. When Butt infiltrated back into the Valley in 1966 with the intention of starting a guerrilla movement, he was quickly captured. Sentenced to death in 1968, he dramatically escaped from prison and returned to Pakistani Kashmir, but was again captured when he crossed back to the Valley in 1976. Around the same time, Amanullah Khan went to the United Kingdom to escape Pakistani persecution, where he stayed until he was deported to Pakistan in 1984. During his long sojourn in England, Khan was able to build a strong pro-JKLF network in Birmingham in the English Midlands and Bradford in north-west England. These two cities had a large population of working-class migrants from 'Azad' Kashmir's southern Mirpur district, who had been displaced from their homeland by the construction of a large dam – the Mangla dam, named after a local village – in the 1960s. They felt victimised by the Pakistani state and were receptive to Khan's message. But in the Kashmir Valley, the crucial arena of the conflict, JKLF had no presence through the 1970s and 1980s. In January 1971, Butt organised a PLO-style hijack of an Indian commercial flight between the cities of Srinagar and Jammu to Lahore in Pakistan. The hijackers were two brothers from a Srinagar family, both in their late teens, one of whom had been influenced by Butt during a visit to Pakistan. The incident had negligible impact in the Valley, where the Plebiscite Front's politics of mass-based, peaceful mobilisation was dominant. But it brought on severe repression of the pro-independence movement in Pakistani Kashmir after the Pakistani authorities declared the hijack to be an Indian conspiracy to defame Pakistan.

In 1970, Amanullah Khan published the seminal treatise of Kashmir's independence movement, a book titled *Free Kashmir*. He was immediately arrested by the Pakistani government and imprisoned until 1972 in distant Gilgit, his birthplace. In *Free Kashmir*, Khan advocated for a 'united, neutral, secular and federal republic' of Jammu and Kashmir encompassing the entire territory of the princely state which existed from March 1846 to October 1947. He wrote that the proposed republic must, of necessity, remain strictly neutral between India and Pakistan and cultivate cordial relations with both. A 'secular set-up' was similarly essential, Khan argued, to 'ensure freedom of faith and communal harmony' due to the presence of 'several religious groups' – Muslims, Hindus, Sikhs and Buddhists – in the population.

Moreover, Khan wrote, 'justice and equity demand that the State should be a federal one to afford full opportunities to the people of its different regions to administer their own areas and eliminate the chances of domination, economic and political, of any region over others'. Thus, Khan proposed that the free republic be constituted of three regions – Kashmir (the Valley), Jammu, and the frontier areas of Gilgit, Baltistan and Ladakh – with 'each enjoying maximum internal autonomy. Each Province can be sub-divided into districts and the districts will have their own internal arrangements [to accommodate intra-region heterogeneity, particularly strong in Jammu and the frontier areas]. At the centre, there should be a bicameral national Parliament, with the lower house having representation on the basis of population of the [three] provinces and the upper house equal representation [for each province].' For a socioeconomic programme, Khan endorsed the 'Naya [New] Kashmir' charter, 'adopted by the All Jammu and Kashmir National Conference in the 1940s [1944]' and premised on egalitarianism and social justice. The free state, he further said, must develop economic cooperation and trade with both India and Pakistan and welcome tourists from both countries and across the world. Finally, Khan wrote, 'the State will be a republic because democratic values form the very basis of Kashmiris' political struggle'.[4]

By the late 1980s, Amanullah Khan and his associates had established a JKLF network across Pakistan's 'Azad' Kashmir, from Muzaffarabad in the north to Poonch (Rawalakot/Bagh) in the centre and Mirpur in the south. The first groups of angry young men from the Kashmir Valley who travelled across the LoC in search of weapons and training in 1988–89 made contact with this network. They liaised mainly with Khan's deputy, Raja Mohammad Muzaffar. The Pakistani military and its Directorate of Inter-Services Intelligence (ISI), which had coordinated the US-backed mujahideen war in Afghanistan against the Soviet occupation and their Afghan allies through the 1980s, looked on with interest mixed with scepticism. In the words of General Asad Durrani, who was director-general of the Pakistani army's military intelligence (DG-MI) in 1988–89 and director-general of the ISI (DG-ISI) in 1990–91, 'when the uprising [in the Kashmir Valley] began, we were just marking time to see what happens'.[5]

What happened in 1990 – a popular insurrection against Indian rule in the Kashmir Valley – far exceeded the expectations of the Pakistanis, Amanullah Khan and his cohorts, and indeed the small group of young JKLF insurgents operating in Srinagar. The actual praxis of JKLF insurgency in the Valley was, however, quite different from Khan's sophisticated formulations of two decades earlier.

A twenty-minute video exists of an interview with JKLF's core group of young insurgents, conducted in Srinagar in early 1990. Six hooded men cuddling semi-automatic rifles sit indoors, against a backdrop of a rectangular curtain with typical Kashmiri embroidery adorned with the JKLF flag. A voice speaking English with a French-sounding accent conducts the interview. The respondent is a hooded man wearing a dark-coloured *pheran*, the traditional Kashmiri winter cloak. He appears to be Ashfaq Majid Wani, 23, who was the acknowledged leader of the JKLF group which launched the insurgency in the Valley. Wani died in a confrontation with Indian forces in a *mohalla* (neighbourhood) of Srinagar's old city on 30 March 1990. Only one of the other five men, all of whom are wearing Western-style jackets, interjects briefly – twice – during the interview.

Speaking animatedly in somewhat broken English in response to a series of pointed questions, Ashfaq Wani repeatedly denies that religion and politics are separable in the context of Kashmir (by which he means the Valley, his overwhelmingly Muslim native region). He rejects Iran-style clerical leadership but asserts that the struggle is rooted in the Kashmiris' Muslim faith and its objective is an 'Islamic democratic state' which will be based on a 'theo-democratic approach'. In saying so, he was simply repeating the faith-suffused idiom of popular politics in the Kashmir Valley since the 1930s (see Chapter 1), albeit in the new context of an armed struggle. Asked about non-Muslim citizens, he says they will have 'rights . . . with no discrimination', but will be welcome to move out if they so choose. Queried about whether Indian J&K's Jammu region might be granted 'special status' in the independent state due to its distinctive multi-ethnic and multi-religious character, he replies in an insular and arrogant vein sometimes found among Valley Kashmiris: 'There will be no special status'. Throughout the interview, he is repeatedly evasive when asked to lay out a detailed blueprint ('charter') of an independent state, which he says will be revealed 'in a short period of time'. There is no trace in his remarks of Amanullah Khan's framework. He keeps repeating that Indian forces must be expelled, and after that everything will fall in place. Ashfaq was young, catapulted into a position of leadership by extraordinary circumstances. But the nature of his responses was, in retrospect, a portent of the troubled trajectory of the radicalised *azaadi* movement through the 1990s and into the new century.[6]

In December 1989 the kidnapping of a young woman in Srinagar electrified India and made news internationally. She was Rubaiya Sayeed, a 23-year-old trainee doctor at the city's main hospital for women. Rubaiya Sayeed was abducted on her way home from work by several men who forced her into a car and sped away. The same afternoon, a local newspaper received a phone call. The caller said that Rubaiya was in the custody of JKLF and read out the names of jailed JKLF activists the organisation wanted released in return for her freedom.

Just a week earlier, Rubaiya's father, Mufti Mohammad Sayeed, had been appointed India's home (interior) minister, usually the second most important position in the cabinet after the prime minister. He was a long-time Congress politician in the Valley, who began his career in the late 1950s as a junior member of the G.M. Sadiq faction of the post-1953 ruling clique sponsored by the Indian government, which became the Indian J&K branch of the Congress party in 1965. Sayeed, a staunch opponent of the Abdullah family, became disillusioned with the Congress after it rehabilitated Farooq Abdullah as chief minister in late 1986, and in 1987 he joined a breakaway group of Congress dissidents opposed to Rajiv Gandhi. The breakaway group provided the focal point for a concerted opposition campaign that heavily defeated Rajiv's Congress party in India's general election in November 1989.

After five days of high drama that gripped India's attention, the home minister's daughter was released once five jailed JKLF militants were freed. To the astonishment of Indians, most of whom had no idea that the picturesque Kashmir Valley so many had visited as tourists was on the brink of uprising, thousands of Srinagar citizens – women, men and children – jubilantly celebrated the militants' release on the streets.

The Valley erupted in uprising in the second half of January 1990. On 19 January, Farooq Abdullah's lame-duck government was dismissed by New Delhi citing a breakdown of law and order (he claimed to have resigned first). Jagmohan, the controversial governor of Indian J&K who had left the post in July 1989 after five years, returned to take charge as Central rule was imposed. These developments were the trigger for the outbreak of huge demonstrations across the Valley calling for *azaadi* (freedom) from India. Hundreds of thousands took to the streets in Srinagar and other Valley towns.

The local police disappeared almost overnight. It fell to troopers of the Central Reserve Police Force (CRPF) – the paramilitary police force under the authority of the Indian government's home ministry long used to suppress unrest in Kashmir – to confront the insurrection. The CRPF's officers and men were all outsiders from various parts of India (especially north India) and overwhelmingly non-Muslims. Over three days, 21–23 January, around 300 demonstrators were shot dead by the CRPF in Srinagar alone.

A particularly infamous incident occurred on 21 January at the Gawkadal bridge, one of the old bridges across the Jhelum river, when the CRPF faced off against a large crowd trying to march towards Lal Chowk in the city centre. Farooq Wani, a participant, recounted his experience to a delegation of Indian human rights monitors:

I fell down on the road. I saw small boys being shot. I remained lying. Then I saw a paramilitary officer coming. I saw him pumping bullets into the bodies of injured people. A young boy trying to hide under the bridge was killed. As I lifted my head, a CRPF man shouted: 'He's still alive!' I pleaded: 'I'm a government employee, please don't shoot.' The officer shouted abuses at me and said *Islam mangta hai?* (you want Islam?) and fired at me. My back and hands were hit. Another paramilitary moved up to me and shouted: *Tu sala zinda hai, mara nahin hai?* (you bastard, you're not dead yet?). He left after kicking me. Then a truck was brought and all of us, dead and wounded, were piled into it. They loaded about 30–35 bodies. As there was no space for more, the officer ordered: *Baaki ko naale*

71

mein phek do (throw the rest into the stream). A tarpaulin was thrown over us. After driving for some time we stopped, and I heard voices speaking Kashmiri. One of the injured among us cried out. The tarpaulin was lifted and we saw a local policeman, who said: 'My God, there are living bodies here'. Three other people were still alive.[7]

Mr Wani survived with six bullet wounds. He heard later that the policeman who saved him had suffered a heart attack. On 25 January JKLF gunmen fired on Indian Air Force personnel at a bus stop in a modern part of the city, killing four IAF officers and injuring many others. Thereafter the Valley descended into a maelstrom of violence.

The insurrection was the result of four decades of Indian policies and actions since the 1950s. It had a cathartic quality, and a wave of euphoria swept the Valley. In March 1990, 300,000 people congregated in response to a JKLF call at the shrine and mausoleum of Sheikh Nooruddin Noorani, Kashmir's early fifteenth-century patron-saint, in the town of Charar-e-Sharief south-west of Srinagar. There they took a collective vow to fight for freedom. The young militants who had taken to the gun were feted as heroes. When Ashfaq Majid Wani died in an 'encounter' (gun-battle) with Indian forces at the end of March, 500,000 weeping, chanting mourners joined his funeral march in Srinagar. The turnout surpassed the 1982 funeral of Sheikh Abdullah (whose tomb near the Hazratbal shrine had to be placed under the guard of Indian paramilitary police to prevent its desecration). Almost everyone seemed to believe that 'freedom' was around the corner, or at least on the horizon, now that the people had risen after four decades of tyrannical rule by New Delhi and its succession of local stooges. The atmosphere was heady. A century earlier, in the 1890s, the British official Walter Lawrence had observed that 'the people of the valley have retained their peculiar nationality unimpaired' through a series of alien rulers over three centuries, since the Mughal conquest of the late sixteenth century.[8] Now they seemed to have found their own political agency, after being fought over by India and Pakistan since 1947. It was a watershed moment.

Typical of populations of long-term conflict zones, the Kashmir Valley's people have a high level of political awareness and keenly follow global developments, particularly other struggles for 'self-determination'. In 1989, the Soviet Union withdrew from Afghanistan, humbled and worn down by a decade of escalating resistance by the mujahideen fighters backed by the US and Pakistan. The limits to the might of a superpower – even if an unravelling one – were exposed in Kashmir's neighbourhood. Meanwhile, the Palestinian Territories had been in uprising against Israeli occupation since the end of 1987, and a repressive apparatus as strong as Israel's had been unable to curb that massive insurrection. The intifada raged on, and the example of defiant young Palestinians taking on Israeli tanks with stones and rocks touched a deep chord in the Valley, where stone-pelting had been a common form of protest since the 1950s. On the subcontinent's southern edge, the limits to India's military power were revealed when a large expeditionary force of the Indian Army sent to end Sri Lanka's civil war in autumn 1987 had to withdraw in spring 1990 after being fought to a standstill by a few thousand Tamil guerrillas. The Indian expeditionary force had lost almost 1,200 soldiers. Even the fall of the Berlin Wall in November 1989 became a reference point. 'We felt that if the Berlin Wall could be dismantled, so could the Line of Control', Hameeda Bano, a professor at Kashmir University, recalled in 1994.[9]

However, these expectations of imminent freedom were dangerously naïve. The Soviet retreat from Afghanistan and the Indian retreat from Sri Lanka marked the end of misguided military interventions in foreign lands. India was not going to contemplate any such course in Kashmir, the possession of which as an 'integral part' (*atut ang*) of India had been a cornerstone of the Indian republic's 'secular' and 'inclusive' identity since the 1950s. The French Fifth Republic under Charles de Gaulle did reluctantly give up the notion in the early 1960s that Algeria was a constitutive part of France, but Kashmir was vitally different in the Indian perspective, being the territory at the crux of the bitter antagonism with Pakistan. The Palestinian intifada compelled a section of the Israeli political elite to enter into a process of engagement with the PLO's dominant group led by Yasser Arafat in 1993. India's leadership would not contemplate any such course either. The response, supported by virtually the entire spectrum of Indian political opinion, was simply repression – of a scale and intensity that made the draconian police state of the previous four decades look positively benign.

India's leading newsmagazine reported from the Valley in April 1990 that the *azaadi* uprising had the support of 'workers, engineers, schoolteachers, shopkeepers, doctors, lawyers, even former MLAs [members of the Indian-sponsored J&K legislature] and the Jammu and Kashmir police' – in other words, the entire society.[10] The result, one of India's national dailies reported from the Valley at the same time, was that for the Indian forces tasked with fighting the insurrection 'the face of the Kashmiri has dissolved into a blurred, featureless mask. He has become a secessionist-terrorist-fundamentalist traitor.'[11] The stage was set for carnage to unfold.

The massacres of January 1990 were the first of many to occur during the first half of the 1990s. Almost every sizeable town in the Kashmir Valley was affected. Sometimes Indian security forces fired on demonstrators, at other times they ran amok and killed people indiscriminately in town centres and major markets after militant attacks. In early March of 1990, thirty-three people were killed and dozens more injured in firing on a demonstration near the Hazratbal shrine calling for the implementation of the decades-old UN resolutions on a Kashmir plebiscite. In May 1990 the pro-Pakistan *Mirwaiz* (head preacher) of Srinagar's Jama Masjid (Grand Mosque), Maulvi Farooq, was murdered in his Srinagar home by gunmen from the militant group Hizb-ul Mujahideen (also pro-Pakistan), who apparently suspected him of secret contacts with the Indian government. The CRPF then fired on his funeral procession, killing at least sixty people, including several women, and injuring scores of others. The town of Handwara in the northern Valley saw two large-scale killings in 1990, the first on 25 January by the paramilitary Border Security Force (BSF) in firing on demonstrators, and the second on 1 October when an Indian Army unit razed the town's market after being shot at by guerrillas. About fifty people died in the two incidents (I later came to know Handwara well, as it served as my base for field research in the northern Valley between the mid-1990s and mid-2000s).

By 1992 the unrest had spread from the Kashmir Valley to the Jammu region's Doda-Kishtwar zone, which lies just south of the Valley's Anantnag district and has a majority population of Kashmiri-speaking Muslims. In July 1992, Doda's market was razed by the CRPF in reprisal for a militant attack. The town of Doda is 80 per cent Kashmiri-speaking Muslim, but many of the shops belonged to local Hindus. By the time I visited the town in 1995, the market had been rebuilt with community donations raised through the town's mosque, whose gleaming-white minarets overlook the market. The town of Kishtwar – whose population is almost evenly split between Hindus and Kashmiri-speaking Muslims – was, however, in ferment and had recently seen a 20,000-strong demonstration after a 22-year-old local shopkeeper was tortured to death in BSF custody.

In January 1993 a BSF unit went on a shooting spree and burned down the entire market in Sopore, a large town in the northern Valley, after a JKLF ambush in the town killed one trooper. Fifty-seven people died, forty-eight of gunshot wounds and nine burnt to death in the arson (by the time I visited Sopore two years later in 1995, a few shops had reopened and their kindly owners served me tea with Kashmiri bread, but most of the market was still a charred hulk). In April 1993 the BSF went on a similar rampage in Srinagar's city centre which gutted a part of Lal Chowk, the city's iconic square crammed with shops like the adjoining Residency Road. At least sixteen civilians including one Hindu were killed. When I first visited the site a year later in 1994, the damage to Lal Chowk's buildings was very visible, and it remained so for several years afterwards. In October 1993 the BSF fired on a march in the town of Bijbehara, south of Srinagar. The 15,000-strong crowd, which had gathered after the weekly Friday prayer at the town's mosque, were protesting a siege of JKLF militants holed up in Srinagar's Hazratbal shrine by the Indian Army and paramilitary forces. At least thirty-seven demonstrators were killed.

In mid-1990 the Indian government declared the Kashmir Valley a 'disturbed area' subject to the Armed Forces Special Powers Act (AFSPA). The AFSPA is directly descended from the Armed Forces Special Powers Ordinance of 15 August 1942, used by the British to brutally suppress the 'Quit India' uprising launched in 1942 by the Indian National Congress under Mahatma Gandhi's leadership. The AFSPA was enacted by Nehru's government in 1958, initially covered an area adjoining Myanmar in India's north-east region affected by an ethnic Naga revolt against Indian rule, and was later extended to other parts of the region which also produced ethnic rebellions.

AFSPA defines armed forces as 'the military forces and air forces operating as land forces, and any other armed forces of the Union operating' in areas notified as 'disturbed'. It empowers officers of these forces to 'arrest, without warrant, any person . . . against whom a reasonable suspicion exists that he has committed, or is about to commit, a cognizable offence'. Such officers can 'enter and search, without warrant, any premises to make any such arrest . . . and may use such force as may be necessary to effect the arrest'. Any officer, if 'he is of the opinion that it is necessary to do so for the maintenance of public order, after giving such due warning as he may consider necessary, may fire upon or otherwise use force, even to the causing of death, against any person who is acting in contravention of any law or order for the time being in force in the disturbed area prohibiting the assembly of five or more persons' (this prohibition, Section 144 of India's criminal procedure code, is also descended from British-era regulations used against the Indian freedom movement). Lastly and crucially: 'No prosecution, suit or other legal proceedings shall be instituted, except with the previous [prior] sanction of the Central Government, against any person in respect of anything done or purported to be done in exercise of the powers conferred by this Act'.[12]

The application of AFSPA in 1990 to Indian Jammu and Kashmir – where it continues to be in force more than three decades later – gave the Indian Army as well as the BSF and CRPF (now referred to along with other similar formations as the Central Armed Police Forces, or CAPFs) carte blanche in Kashmir, and blanket protection from any accountability. The BSF led the counter-insurgency campaign in Srinagar and other towns, and in the countryside the Indian Army wielded absolute power. Neither was trained to combat an uprising-cum-insurgency – the army's remit was conventional war and the BSF was raised after the 1965 war with Pakistan to help secure India's land borders with its various neighbours in peacetime. The army and BSF personnel were almost all non-locals operating in a hostile environment; the J&K police did not revive until 1996.

The main instrument of these forces against the insurrection was the 'crackdown' – which is now referred to by the sanitised acronym CASO (cordon-and-search operation). It is rare to find anyone in the Kashmir Valley who has not experienced crackdowns. A large detachment of gun-toting troops would arrive in a fleet of jeeps and trucks and cordon off a neighbourhood (*mohalla*) in cities, or a village or a cluster of villages in rural areas. Often, a crackdown would occur during a period of prolonged curfew lasting days (sometimes weeks), which meant that the population was already confined indoors. Using loudspeakers, able-bodied men of all ages would be ordered to come out and gather in an open space such as a school playground or a park. There hundreds would squat in a huddle while the crackdown went ahead. This consisted of two elements, the first being an identification parade. The assembled men would be lined up in front of a vehicle in which one or more *mukhbirs* (informers) were seated, hooded to hide their identity. These were usually individuals picked up in earlier raids and broken through torture. Meanwhile, other soldiers conducted house-to-house searches for insurgents and weapons. As allegations of molestation of women during house searches proliferated, sometimes the women and children were also ordered to come out and gather in a group separately from the men. Theft and vandalism were common during house searches. A typical crackdown lasted an entire day and occasionally longer, even in freezing winter weather.

The crackdown was an experience in collective humiliation. But the dire risk was being identified – rightly or wrongly – as a militant or a supporter of militants by the hooded informer(s). Those men were taken away to be interrogated in detention centres which mushroomed in Srinagar and across the Valley. These detention sites became infamous for gruesome forms of torture. Many detainees never returned and simply joined the growing ranks of the 'disappeared'. Others did return, but often with permanently damaged bodies and lasting psychological problems. I have met many such survivors. They frequently said that the objective seemed to be not so much to extract information as to punish perceived disloyalty by inflicting agonising pain and humiliation.

Some detention-and-torture sites became known among the population by odd names given by those who ran them. 'Papa-1' was a sprawling late-1920s mansion overlooking Srinagar's Dal Lake built for the royal family of the erstwhile princely state. It was refurbished in the second half of the 2000s to be an official guesthouse but continues as a detention centre: Omar Abdullah, Sheikh Abdullah's grandson and chief minister of the Indian state of J&K from the end of 2008 to the end of 2014 was held there for seven months by India's Hindu nationalist government in 2019–20. 'Papa-2' was another stately pre-1947 building in the same elite enclave of Srinagar. In the second half of the 2000s it transitioned to becoming the residence, named 'Fairview', of the Kashmir Valley's other leading India-aligned political family, the Muftis. This family's legatee, Mufti Mohammad Sayeed's politician daughter Mehbooba Mufti, succeeded her deceased father as Indian J&K's chief minister in 2016 and held the post until mid-2018. She was taken into custody by India's Hindu nationalist government from that residence in August 2019 and held – under the J&K Public Safety Act enacted in 1978 by Sheikh Abdullah after his capitulation to Indian power – for fourteen months elsewhere in Srinagar, until October 2020. Another interrogation centre, 'Cargo', had previously been a transit warehouse for cargo arriving into Srinagar's airport. This facility is now Srinagar's cyber-police station, where activists, journalists and ordinary citizens are routinely summoned or brought for posts on internet sites and social media deemed to be seditious.

While thousands – dead and living – passed through these particularly well-known houses of horror during the 1990s, torture of detainees was routine in army bases and paramilitary camps across the Kashmir Valley.[13] According to an American journalist who covered the Kashmir Valley in the early 1990s, 'in interviews officers of the security forces stated that the use of torture was absolutely vital to obtain information on weapons caches, hideouts and insurgent groups' memberships, and the whereabouts of the leaders'.[14] In 1993, reports emerged of a 'catch-and-kill' policy of summary executions of captured insurgents in Srinagar and other Valley towns. A civilian official said: 'Yes, they're killing them. Perhaps because the jails are full, or they want to frighten the people.' A paramilitary commander asserted in April 1993: 'We don't have custodial deaths here [any more], we have alley deaths. If we have word of a militant, we will pick him up, take him to the next lane, and kill him.'[15]

The hyphenated word 'Kunan-Poshpora' is instantly recognised in the Kashmir Valley, and indeed by anyone with knowledge of the conflict since 1990. Kunan and Poshpora are actually two adjacent villages in the Valley's northern Kupwara district, in the district's Trehgam *tehsil* (sub-division) close to the LoC. Since 1991, they have been bracketed together, ever since a crackdown on the two hamlets during the night of 23–24 February 1991. Two decades later, five young Kashmiri women took it upon themselves to revisit and write a book about the events of that chilly winter night in Kunan-Poshpora, and its aftermath.[16]

At about 11 p.m. on 23 February, the sleeping villagers were woken by soldiers beating on and in some cases breaking down the doors of their houses. They were from the 68th Mountain Brigade, stationed nearby in the much larger village of Trehgam, of the Indian Army's 4th Rajputana Rifles (often referred to as 'RajRif' in India). According to a list of soldiers with their full names and ranks provided to a police inquiry by the army – which denied that any misconduct had occurred during the crackdown – there were 125 personnel in all involved in the nocturnal operation, commanded by a Colonel K.S. Dalal. There were eight other officers – four majors, two captains (one an army medic) and two second lieutenants. The raiding party was organised in four companies – Alpha (A), Bravo (B), Charlie (C) and Delta (D). The A and D groups were assigned to cordon off the two villages, and the men from B and C entered Kunan-Poshpora. The list mentions which of the 4 companies each of the 116 other ranks (non-officers) were part of. The colonel oversaw the operation inside Kunan-Poshpora and a Major R. Khullar led one of the two companies which entered the twin hamlets. The villagers, in their testimony, said that it felt like more than a few score soldiers entered Kunan-Poshpora. The soldiers left Kunan-Poshpora at 9 a.m. on 24 February, but the outer cordon remained in place for a few more days.

According to the villagers, two large barns (*kuthars*) were turned into makeshift interrogation centres, along with one house belonging to a villager. The male villagers were made to gather in front of these three sites – mostly the barns – where they squatted in the snow awaiting their turn. Through the night, many of the men said, they were tortured inside these premises. The methods they describe include some that were by then standard practice in the Valley and continued to be so through the 1990s and beyond. They say that they had their heads dunked over and over in buckets of ice-cold water, which in some cases had been sprinkled with red-hot chillies. Electric shocks were given to their genitals, they say – this was a very common technique in the repertoire of torture in the Valley. They also mention the well-known 'roller treatment' – where a heavy log of wood was placed across the legs of a detainee and two men sat on it and rolled it backwards and forwards. There was also much kicking with boots, they say, and severe beating administered with *lathis* (staves) along with a torrent of verbal abuse and threats. Some of the men crawled home on all fours in the morning as they were unable to stand or walk. Several men recall that they heard women's screams coming from houses during the night.

According to the testimonies of the female survivors of the raid, about forty women and girls were raped in their homes – in many cases by multiple attackers – during the night. Thirty-two women and girls who said they had been raped or gang-raped were examined in two batches in and shortly after mid-March – i.e. three to four weeks after the crackdown – in the nearest community medical centre in the Kupwara district. There was no woman doctor available and so the examinations were conducted by a male physician. He reported that all of them had abrasions and contusions on various parts of their bodies and at least one had bite marks on her face. A male villager also examined had a partially burnt penis, caused, according to the medical report, by electric shocks.

The thirty-two women examined ranged in age from 15 to 70 years old. One of the three minors among them was afflicted with polio. One adult woman was deaf and mute. Most were illiterate. It appears that a number of teenaged girls did not go for the belated medical examination because their families feared that would make it impossible for them to get married.

A significant number of the women who were examined were from the same households. One young married woman who was nine months pregnant was staying at her parents' house. She gave birth a few days later to a baby with a fractured arm. The woman's mother was also raped in an adjacent room, according to the mother's testimony, by one soldier after another until she passed out. Most of the houses in Kunan-Poshpora did not have electricity, but the soldiers carried battery-powered torches which they used to illuminate the older woman's body during the gang rape, the mother says. Many women reported that the soldiers stank of liquor and that some were still drinking from bottles. According to the testimonies, the soldiers generally ignored the crying children except for one howling toddler, who was thrown from a ground-floor window into the snow outside. The child was retrieved around dawn by Abdul Ghani, one of two constables from the Trehgam police station who had been asked by the raiding party to accompany them when they set off from Trehgam around 9 p.m. on 23 February. Ghani put the child on the house's verandah and went inside, where he found its mother naked and barely conscious. He told her the child was all right and covered the woman with a blanket he found in the house. He then went from house to house in the early morning hours, covering the women and girls he found there with blankets. Kunan-Poshpora had a bright, moonlit night on 23–24 February 1991.

That something very untoward had happened in Kunan-Poshpora was first revealed on 12 March by an Indian newspaper, whose Srinagar correspondent accessed a confidential communication from Kupwara's deputy commissioner (the head of the district bureaucracy) to senior civil and police officials in Srinagar, Jammu and Baramulla. The Kupwara DC sent this communication after visiting Kunan-Poshpora on 5 March and speaking with the villagers. The news was then picked up by the international press. In a report dated 13 March, a Brigadier H.K. Sharma, the commander of another army brigade stationed in the area, informed his superiors that he had visited Kunan-Poshpora on 10 March. His report stated that 'no rape could have taken place as alleged ... The charges are baseless, unfounded, mischievous and motivated and have been levelled for the following reasons: Defame the Army. Prevent further search and cordon to prevent inconvenience [to the locals]. Prevent search to provide protection to some suspected ANEs [anti-national elements].' The brigadier's report asserted that two AK-47 rifles with magazines and a loaded pistol had been found in 'specific houses' during the crackdown. If so, it is very curious that no one from those houses was taken into custody; indeed, not a single villager had been arrested. Wajahat Habibullah, the divisional commissioner of Kashmir (head of the Valley's civil administration) visited Kunan-Poshpora on 18 March. The Kupwara district official's urgent message had been addressed to him and copied to five others. Habibullah similarly reported to his superiors that 'having spoken to the officers concerned and the alleged victims, I am of the opinion that the allegation of mass rape cannot be sustained'. He suggested, nonetheless, that 'the unit [concerned] may make a determined bid to refurbish its image both in the eyes of the public and civil officialdom'.

But the two obscure hamlets in a remote part of the Kashmir Valley had got into the international media. In response, the Indian Army asked the Press Council of India to conduct an enquiry. The enquiry was led by B.G. Verghese, a senior journalist who had served on various Indian government bodies and was a family friend of the then Indian Army chief. Verghese travelled to Srinagar in May–June 1991 and was taken in a military helicopter to the northern Valley. However, he apparently did not visit Kunan-Poshpora. His report, based on an 'exhaustive investigation', concluded that the rape allegations were 'a massive hoax' and 'a tissue of lies'. The report was published by a New Delhi publisher with close ties to the Indian armed forces.[17]

As with the officers and men who conducted the Kunan-Poshpora operation, the identities of those who took 17-year-old Javaid Ahangar away from his home in Srinagar's working-class Batamaloo neighbourhood on the night of 17–18 August 1990 are known. An enquiry into his disappearance ordered in October 1991 by the Indian J&K high court's Srinagar bench found in March 1992 that the crackdown was led by Major S.N. Gupta, Captain Dinesh Sharma and Captain S.C. Katoch – all from the National Security Guards (NSG), an elite Indian Army unit. The judicial enquiry – very rare in the Kashmir Valley in the 1990s, or even later – was the result of multiple habeas corpus petitions filed by Javaid's mother, Parveena Ahangar. Mrs Ahangar did so in March 1991, after six months of frantic efforts to locate her son. The enquiry reported that one or more witnesses had seen Javaid being beaten at the entrance of the 'Papa-1' interrogation centre (the Hari Niwas Palace, Srinagar), and then being dragged towards Pari Mahal (Pavilion of Angels), a mid-seventeenth-century terraced garden and summer retreat of the Mughal suzerains of Kashmir. Pari Mahal, a beautiful site located on a hill overlooking the city, was also a known torture centre in the early and mid-1990s.

That was the last sighting of Javaid. Five weeks after he was taken away, his mother received word that he might be at the army hospital in the Badami Bagh cantonment on Srinagar's southern outskirts – the headquarters of the Indian Army's 15th Corps, which is stationed in the Valley. A sympathetic police officer arranged a police car and gate pass for her to visit the heavily secured cantonment on 25 September 1990. She visited a hospital ward 'full of boys groaning and writhing in pain', but her son was not there. After the enquiry report, a lengthy process ensued in the court of Srinagar's judicial magistrate. The court ordered the suspects to be produced for cross-examination. Major Gupta and Captain Sharma were brought to Srinagar but never appeared in court; they stayed at the Badami Bagh cantonment. Captain Katoch had terminal cancer and was excused. The public relations officer of the 15th Corps, a Colonel Joshi, did come to court and asked Mrs Ahangar if she wanted money, or a job.

On 25 June 1996, the Srinagar court asked India's home (interior) ministry in New Delhi for permission to charge the three officers. Because the Armed Forces Special Powers Act (AFSPA) is in force in Indian Jammu and Kashmir, the Indian home ministry's consent is required for any judicial prosecutions of personnel of the army and paramilitary forces. On 24 July 1996, the home ministry rejected the request. Mrs Ahangar's personal quest to find what had happened to her son ended there. But she found a larger mission in life as the chair of the Association of Parents of Disappeared Persons (APDP), which she formed in 1994 with the help of Parvez Imroz, a Srinagar lawyer. She says that she 'went to the villages, the forests and the mountains [of Kashmir] to find each one who has a sorrow like mine'.[18] She found thousands who share her grief. Mrs Ahangar, whom I met in Srinagar in 2017, is a modest but steely woman. In October 2020 her Srinagar home was raided yet again – by the National Investigation Agency (NIA), which is under the jurisdiction of India's home ministry, headed since May 2019 by Amit Shah, the closest associate of India's prime minister, Narendra Modi. The raid was part of a wider crackdown on civil society organisations and the Valley's major English daily, *Greater Kashmir*, purportedly to probe their finances.[19]

When the Valley erupted at the start of 1990, the insurgency was still limited. If the repression unleashed aimed to strangle the as yet nascent insurgency, it had the opposite effect. The steady trickle of young men going across the LoC to acquire weapons and training in 1988–89 turned into a flood from 1990. The insurgency spread like wildfire and engulfed the entire Valley. On just one day in early May 1991, seventy-two youths were killed by the Indian Army while trying to return from across the LoC (the melting of winter snows and the onset of summer makes the LoC easier to negotiate). The number of militants killed rose steadily – 550 in 1990, 844 in 1991, 819 in 1992, 1,310 in 1993, 1,596 in 1994. But the insurgency raged on. The insurgents who died were overwhelmingly natives of Indian J&K, and very largely from the Kashmir Valley. Of the 5,119 militants killed from 1990 to 1994, only 262 (5 per cent) were from across the LoC: 14 in 1990, 12 in 1991, 14 in 1992, 90 in 1993, 132 in 1994. In other words, while the weapons and training were being provided by the Pakistani military, mainly through the ISI, those fighting the Indian forces were almost all locals. Even as the presence of 'foreign militants' – almost all from Pakistani J&K or Pakistan itself – began to creep up from 1993, 93 per cent of insurgents killed in 1993 and 92 per cent in 1994 were still locals, as per official Indian figures. In 1995, 94 per cent of militants killed (1,247 of 1,332) were locals.[20] In autumn 1992 a leading Indian newsmagazine reported from the Valley that the counter-insurgency strategy had succeeded in 'eliminating militants in arithmetical progression and generating militants in geometrical progression', and that 'children no longer dream of becoming doctors or engineers – their ambition is to become *mujahids*'.[21]

When I began my fieldwork in Indian J&K in 1994, Srinagar was a 'bunker city'. Almost every street in every *mohalla* had a sandbagged bunker covered with wire netting (for protection against grenade attacks) manned by jittery paramilitary troopers, their guns peering out through firing slits. Troopers were stationed 10 yards apart on all major roads, fingers on triggers. Groups of troopers constantly patrolled every neighbourhood on foot, as well as in armoured vehicles. Checkpoints were numerous. The same was true of all other Valley towns. The Valley's sprawling capital turned into a ghost-city at dusk. The only presence on its eerily dark and silent streets were thousands of heavily armed troopers. In 1995, just two hotels were partially open in the whole of Srinagar, Ahdoo's in the city centre and Boulevard on the Dal Lake. I stayed at the Boulevard, on a lower floor. The hotel's two upper floors were still unusable. In June 1990 militants had fired rockets at the upper floors from boats on the Dal Lake, killing six and injuring nine CRPF troopers billeted there.[22] In 1996, returning close to midnight to the city centre after dinner at a friend's home in a suburb, Qamarwari, I passed through seven BSF checkpoints. The troopers were quite bemused to see me, as mine was the only civilian car on the streets. Army convoys with soldiers in full combat gear travelled constantly on major roads across the Valley, the lead vehicle sporting a mounted machine gun. The entire countryside was dotted with Army camps that had come up since 1990, and I often encountered checkpoints manned by suspicious and nervous soldiers.

THE INSURRECTION DECLINES

The wildfire spread of insurgency obscured, for a few years, growing problems in the *azaadi* struggle. The fundamental problem was the existence of two competing notions of *azaadi* (freedom) in the movement. JKLF's leadership in Pakistani J&K consisted of seasoned activists committed to the concept of an independent state across the territories of the former princely state. This commitment had been strengthened by the repression the pro-independence movement in Pakistan's 'Azad' (Free) Kashmir experienced at the hands of successive Pakistani governments – civilian and military – during the 1970s and 1980s. An 'Azad' Kashmir 'constitution' enacted in 1974 specified that 'no person or political party in Azad Jammu and Kashmir shall be permitted to propagate against or take part in activities prejudicial or detrimental to the ideology of the State's accession to Pakistan'.[23] All candidates standing for election to 'Azad' Kashmir's legislature have to sign an affidavit: 'I solemnly declare that I believe in the Ideology of Pakistan, the Ideology of [J&K] State's accession to Pakistan, and the integrity and sovereignty of Pakistan'.[24] This requirement meant that JKLF and smaller pro-independence groups boycotted the officially sanctioned sphere of politics. Instead, the Pakistani state relied on and promoted local stooges – much as the Indian state did in Indian J&K. One such long-serving politician, Sardar Abdul Qayyum Khan, declared as 'Azad' Kashmir's 'prime minister' in 1992: 'I look at Kashmir from Pakistan's point of view … the Kashmiris and Kashmir are not a separate geographical or historical entity, but part and parcel of Pakistan … I am opposed to the idea of an independent Kashmir.'[25]

Nonetheless, the Pakistani army's 'deep state' and JKLF did forge a relationship in the late 1980s. A steady stream of young men from the Kashmir Valley made contact with the JKLF organisation in Pakistani Kashmir from 1988. Once they went back with weapons and training, JKLF gained a foothold in the Valley. JKLF's leaders in Pakistani Kashmir were willing, indeed eager, to launch a guerrilla campaign in the Valley with these new recruits. At the time, JKLF was the only group unequivocally committed to a path of armed struggle in *maqbooza* (occupied) Kashmir across the LoC. General Zia-ul Haq, Pakistan's military ruler from 1977 to 1988, purportedly approved a plan for covert operations to foment rebellion in Indian J&K, especially in the seething Valley, prior to his death in a plane crash in August 1988. The purported plan is said to have been codenamed 'Operation Tupac' after Tupac Amaru, the leader of an eighteenth-century uprising of indigenous Peruvians against colonial Spain. JKLF was the instrument at hand for the implementation of such a strategy. For JKLF, on the other hand, it was difficult to launch a cross-border insurgency without the sanction and at least some support from the Pakistani army and its covert agencies.

The scale and intensity of the uprising that unfolded in the Kashmir Valley from early 1990 took both JKLF and the Pakistani military establishment by surprise. The latter sensed that the long-elusive opening to intervene in Indian J&K had at last materialised. In a fortuitous coincidence, the Soviets had just left Afghanistan and the Pakistani military's ISI agency, which had played a pivotal part in the mujahideen war there through the 1980s, was ideally placed to focus next on Kashmir, Pakistan's sacred but sadly unfulfilled national cause since 1947.

But because of JKLF's leading role, the insurrection took a distinctly independentist and not a pro-Pakistan character. This reflected the Valley's strongly developed cultural and political identity. I know from my field experience in Indian J&K over the past three decades that people in the Kashmir Valley cutting across social strata overwhelmingly aspire to independence, and those who wish to join Pakistan constitute a relatively small though committed minority. Such opinion surveys as are available have reported the same finding.[26] The Pakistani state has since its inception been hostile to distinct regional identities and aspirations, which stance led to the country's break-up in 1971 (when East Pakistan became sovereign Bangladesh) and has been the cause of long-term discontent in the Sindh, Balochistan and Khyber-Pakhtunkhwa provinces of the post-1971 rump Pakistan. The tone was set by Pakistan's founder M.A. Jinnah, who told citizens in a nationwide radio address in March 1948: 'I want you to be on your guard against this poison of provincialism that our enemies wish to inject into our State'.[27] In mid-2004, I attended a meeting in Sweden which discussed potential ways of addressing the Kashmir conflict through a peace process. The meeting was attended by very senior Indian and Pakistani civilian and military officials, all recently retired. A top-ranking Pakistani army officer who had retired from a distinguished career just a few years earlier (October 1998), who otherwise expressed very moderate views, strongly criticised the idea of an independent state of Jammu and Kashmir on the grounds that it would lead to further shrinkage of post-1971 Pakistan through the loss of 'Azad' Kashmir and the Northern Areas (Gilgit and Baltistan).

The relationship between JKLF and the Pakistani military's deep state rapidly unravelled in the early 1990s, as the ISI set about asserting Pakistani control over the insurgency in Indian Kashmir. This was done through a three-pronged strategy.

First, all assistance to JKLF was terminated. Second, defections from JKLF were engineered and the defectors encouraged to form splinter groups of a pro-Pakistan orientation. By 1991 at least two such splinter groups emerged: al-Umar Mujahideen and Ikhwan-ul-Muslimeen. Third and most important, a reliable proxy insurgent force was built up to replace JKLF as the dominant group in the armed struggle. A decade earlier in Afghanistan, the Pakistani military had chosen to support the most religiously orthodox of the seven major mujahideen groups: the Hezb-e-Islami led by Gulbuddin Hekmatyar. In Kashmir, the chosen proxy was Hizb-ul Mujahideen (HM), an insurgent group linked to the Indian J&K wing of Jama'at-i-Islami (JI), a Sunni fundamentalist movement formed in 1941 which has branches in Pakistan, Bangladesh and both Indian and Pakistani Kashmir.

JI, founded by Abul Ala Maududi, a cleric, had opposed the Pakistan movement led by Jinnah because a territorial Muslim nation-state in the subcontinent conflicted with its pan-Islamic concept of an indivisible *ummah* (global community of believers). But it then quickly adapted to the reality of Pakistan. JI in West Pakistan led the agitation for the persecution of Ahmadis (a sect deemed heretical) which began in 1953, and in 1971 its organisation in East Pakistan became the main collaborators of the Pakistani army's genocidal violence against the population supporting the Bangladesh independence movement. During the 1980s, JI in Pakistan became an important auxiliary of the Islamisation policies enforced by Zia-ul Haq's military regime, particularly in the field of education. The JI wing in Indian J&K had focused since the 1950s on indoctrination of the young, and in the 1970s and 1980s its network of schools in the Kashmir Valley achieved some success in building a cadre from the alumni of these schools.

But until the end of the 1980s, the JI in Indian J&K was sceptical of armed struggle against Indian rule. When JKLF militant Maqbool Butt was executed in a Delhi prison in 1984, the Indian J&K JI's mouthpiece *Azaan* (The Call) paid tribute to him but noted that, carried away by 'the overwhelming force of emotion', he had lost 'the capacity to distinguish between wrong and right'. In 1986 Syed Ali Shah Geelani (born 1929), a prominent JI leader in the Kashmir Valley, wrote that his movement's mission was 'to educate the people' and that 'an organized and peaceful struggle' was needed to implement 'the UN resolutions' on Kashmir (i.e. the plebiscite to choose Indian or Pakistani sovereignty).[28] In 1990, as uprising swept the Valley, the local JI dropped its pacific stance and switched to advocating *jehad* (holy war) to end Indian rule. In 1991, Geelani wrote from a jail in north India to Chandra Shekhar, who was briefly India's prime minister in the first half of

1991: 'Indians fought the British for freedom both at the political level and through armed struggle. Gandhi used non-violence . . . and Netaji Subhas Chandra Bose used the path of armed struggle.'[29] When I first met Geelani at his home in Srinagar's Hyderpora neighbourhood in 1995, he was emphatic that all of the former princely state should be part of Pakistan and said that the idea of independence risked dividing the Muslim majority of Jammu and Kashmir into opposing camps. He then kissed me on the forehead and presented me with an Arabic–English bilingual edition of the Holy Koran, produced in Saudi Arabia.

From 1991 HM enjoyed a meteoric rise in the Kashmir insurgency at the expense of JKLF. From 1990 to 1992 JKLF bore the brunt of Indian counter-insurgency. On the onset of insurgency, JKLF had been led in Srinagar by the four-man 'HAJY group', so called after the first letter of the given names of Hamid Sheikh, Ashfaq Wani, Javed Mir and Yasin Malik, all in their early to mid-twenties. Ashfaq Wani was killed at the end of March 1990 and Yasin Malik was captured in a wounded condition in early August of 1990. Malik was held in various prisons in India until May 1994. Hamid Sheikh was also captured; released by BSF intelligence in autumn 1992 to counter the growing power of HM, he was killed within weeks in Srinagar along with six comrades in an operation by the Indian Army, which apparently did not agree with the BSF's assessment of his potential usefulness. That left Javed Mir as the sole survivor of the HAJY group in the field.

JKLF had its moments even in decline. In February 1992, the parent JKLF organisation in Pakistani Kashmir organised a march to the LoC in solidarity with the struggle in Indian Kashmir. Some 30,000 people joined the march, which was fired on by Pakistani border troops close to the LoC, killing 21 marchers. When news of the killings reached Srinagar, '60,000 people defied curfew [orders] and gathered at the Hazratbal shrine', controlled by JKLF militants since 1990, to protest the Pakistani action against the independentists.[30] But by 1993 HM's ascendancy in the armed struggle was an established fact. In May 1993 Javed Mir bravely claimed: 'Gun-power is not the only thing that matters. The public are the most powerful weapon and they are on our side.'[31] It was an admission that JKLF was fading as an insurgent force, but he was right that it was JKLF's slogan *Kashmir banega khudmukhtar* (Kashmir will be sovereign) that commanded mass support, not HM's *Kashmir banega Pakistan* (Kashmir will be part of Pakistan) war cry. In autumn 1993, large demonstrations took place in the Valley in solidarity with JKLF militants besieged by Indian forces in the Hazratbal shrine, and several dozen died when the BSF fired on a march in the town of Bijbehera, south of Srinagar.

JKLF's decimation as a fighting force by 1994 was only in part due to the Indian counter-insurgency campaign. Starting in 1991, HM carried out an escalating campaign of killings of JKLF militants and a series of assassinations of prominent citizens known to be JKLF supporters. The most prominent case in the latter category was Dr Abdul Ahad Guru, a Srinagar cardiologist murdered in April 1993. HM was under the nominal command of Syed Mohammad Yusuf Shah, the JI activist who had contested the rigged 1987 elections to the Indian J&K state legislature from Srinagar's city-centre constituency (see Chapter 1). He had taken the *nom de guerre* Salahuddin, after the legendary twelfth-century Muslim commander who fought the Christian Crusaders, and was based across the LoC. The main commander of HM operations in the Valley was Abdul Majid Dar (1954–2003), a protégé of Pakistan's ISI. A native of the northern valley town of Sopore, he merged his small Islamist insurgent group into HM in 1991. JKLF, meanwhile, had been weakened by multiple splits engineered by the ISI. On his release after four years, Yasin Malik returned to Srinagar to a huge welcome in mid-1994 and declared a unilateral JKLF ceasefire. By that time, JKLF was largely spent as a fighting force and HM was indisputably the main insurgent group. Malik hoped his announcement would preserve what remained of the depleted JKLF cadre. When I first met him in January 1995, he told me that JKLF had lost another hundred or so cadres over the preceding six months to continuing attacks by both the Indian forces and HM militants. A senior journalist in Indian J&K estimated to me that about 300 JKLF members were hunted down and killed by Indian forces after the mid-1994 JKLF ceasefire, often acting on information about their identity and whereabouts provided by HM.[32] The JKLF militants eliminated directly by HM included Mohammad Yusuf alias Idrees Khan, the leader of the independentist group's militants in the autumn 1993 Hazratbal siege.

The other problem of the radicalised struggle for *azaadi* was an alarming proliferation in the early 1990s of armed groups operating in the Valley. The Valley's tendency to political factionalism played a role. For example, two factions of the People's League, a clandestine pro-Pakistan group formed in the mid-1970s, spawned separate insurgent formations – Muslim Jaanbaaz Force and Jehad Force – which were then uneasily united as al-Jehad. Young adherents of the People's Conference, a legal political party active since the late 1970s in the Valley's northern Kupwara district, formed their own insurgent group al-Barq (Thunderbolt). There were also a number of armed groups born of the JKLF splits engineered by the ISI. Beyond that, it was distinctly fashionable in the Valley of the early 1990s to become a 'freedom fighter'. With the Valley awash in lethal light weapons supplied from Pakistan, it was easy for a variety of freelancers, fantasists, adventurers and criminal types to gather a band of gunmen from their locality or extended family and float a *tanzeem*, an armed group. When I toured the Valley in 1994–95, I encountered a population embittered by Indian repression and atrocities but also increasingly fatigued by what was described as 'gun culture'. The heroic halo of the mujahideen was wearing off and the roving groups of gunmen were often regarded as a nuisance at best and a menace at worst. JKLF was almost finished as an insurgent force and HM did not have the same level of popular support. By mid-1994, the international press was reporting from the Valley that 'Kashmiris are sick of growing criminal tendencies among proliferating armed groups'.[33]

The *azaadi* uprising and the armed struggle had already had grave consequences for the Valley's main religious minority – the Kashmiri Pandits. In 1981, according to census figures, the Valley's population was just above 3,135,000, of whom 124,078 (4 per cent) were Hindus. The large majority of these Hindus were Pandits, the Brahmin community indigenous to the Valley. They share a common history over many centuries with Kashmiri Muslims, most of whom converted from Shaivite Hinduism to Islam under the influence of Sufi mystics around the cusp of the fourteenth and fifteenth centuries, and many more in the centuries since (see Chapter 1). The ethnicity, language (Kashmiri) and cultural traditions of the Valley's Muslims and Pandits are identical. As insurrection gripped the Kashmir Valley in early 1990, the bulk – about 100,000 people – of the Pandit population fled the Valley over a few weeks in February–March 1990 to the southern Indian J&K city of Jammu and further afield to cities such as Delhi. Many Pandits with ancestral origins in the Kashmir Valley already lived in various cities in India, and the community has long been prominent across a range of professions, from the arts to the military.

The large-scale flight of Kashmiri Pandits during the first months of the insurrection is a controversial episode of the post-1989 Kashmir conflict. Many Kashmiri Muslims purport to believe that the sudden, massive exodus of Pandits from towns and villages across the Valley was engineered by Indian J&K's Governor Jagmohan – who returned to hold that office for four months in 1990, from January to May – in order to defame the Valley's Muslims and enable the implementation of a no-holds-barred offensive on the *tehreek* (movement) against Indian authority. There is no compelling evidence for this claim. The counter-narrative – which has been hegemonic in India since the early 1990s – is that the Valley's Muslims collectively metamorphosed all of a sudden into fundamentalist fanatics, renounced their centuries-old syncretistic heritage and forced the Pandits to flee in a deliberate campaign of mass expulsion. This too is implausible.

JKLF's series of targeted assassinations that began in August 1989 (see Chapter 1) included a number of prominent Pandits. Tika Lal Taploo, the president of the Hindu nationalist BJP's Kashmir Valley unit, was killed in September 1989, followed in November by Neelkanth Ganjoo, the judge who had sentenced the JKLF pioneer Maqbool Butt to death in 1968 (the execution was carried out in 1984). As the Valley descended into mayhem in early 1990, Lassa Koul, the Pandit director of the Srinagar station of India's state-run television, was killed on 13 February 1990 by JKLF gunmen. The murders of such high-profile members of the community may have spread a wave of fear among Pandits at large. On 15 March 1990, by which time the Pandit exodus from the Valley was substantially complete, the All-India Kashmiri Pandit Conference, a community organisation, stated that thirty-two Pandits had been killed by militants since the previous autumn.[34] This plausible figure amounted to a third of about one hundred targeted killings by JKLF militants since autumn 1989. The sight of huge processions chanting slogans such as *Azaadi ka matlab kya? La Ilaha Illallah* (What is the meaning of freedom? There is no God but Allah), while in keeping with the Valley's longstanding tradition of faith-suffused protest, may have spurred further panic. There may also have been localised incidents of intimidation of Pandits, a community loyal to India.

Most of the Valley's Pandits held salaried jobs in Indian J&K's state government, or else worked in white-collar professions. But a sizeable number lived off small landholdings, especially fruit orchards. These rural Pandits were hit hardest by displacement. In 1995 I visited such Pandits living in refugee camps in Purkho and Misriwala, just outside the city of Jammu off the road to the town of Akhnur. They were living in tents and shacks in squalid conditions. They complained bitterly about the indifference of officialdom to their plight, and also about the blazing-hot summer weather of the Jammu plains, to which they were not accustomed, being from the Valley (in 2020, when I revisited the area, the ramshackle camps I remembered had become townships with concrete houses).

When I travelled in the Kashmir Valley in the mid-1990s, however, I was surprised to meet Pandits, in some cases whole families, living in towns and villages. Some had not joined the 1990 exodus, while others had recently returned from Jammu due to declining insurgency in their areas. They praised their Muslim neighbours and friends as supportive. Indeed, a diehard fraction of the Pandit community have held out in their Valley homeland for the past three decades. In July 2020 one such person, Kanth Ram Tikoo, passed away aged 112 in his village, Zainapora, in the Valley's south-western Shopian district. This area has a strong presence of militants, and deadly clashes with the Indian security forces are common. Tikoo, who headed the local farmers' cooperative until his retirement, was universally *abba* (father) to the villagers. His is one of three Pandit families in Zainapora. 'For the half-kilometre walk' from his home to the village's cremation ground, 'the cot bearing the body rested on the shoulders of mourners in skullcaps'. Tikoo's son Ramesh owns the village's pharmacy. 'I can't recall a single instance of anyone threatening us or our business,' he said at the funeral.[35]

In November 1991 a former Indian J&K state legislator and her husband, both Kashmiri Pandits, were abducted from their Srinagar home by members of a militant group calling itself Hizbullah. They were held for two months in various locations before being released. The couple wrote:

> During this time, we stayed for varying periods in 57 [Muslim] homes. All those people showered love and hospitality on us ... With their sympathy we were better able to cope ... We met a cross-section of people in the villages and a sizeable number of youths belonging to militant organizations. We talked with them about education, religion, social life, politics, *Kashmiriyat* [the values of Kashmiri identity], human emotions, and above all ways of building bridges and winning hearts. These interactions reinforced our faith in the values of love and goodness which are still deeply ingrained in the Kashmiri ethos.[36]

In August 1992, a young Pandit living in Delhi visited his parents in Srinagar for the first time since the beginning of the insurrection. He reported: 'Our *mohalla* [neighbourhood] had not changed except for two CRPF bunkers on the street. I was amazed at the friendliness and warmth with which I was greeted. Muslim neighbours turned up with *mithai* [sweets] to bless me as soon as word got out that I was in town, and invited me to their houses to celebrate with *sevion-ki-kheer* [vermicelli pudding]. There was not a single Muslim friend or acquaintance who did not greet me as they would have before the troubles began.' The *mohalla* experienced a crackdown during his stay and 'Hindu, Muslim and Sikh neighbours were united in their resentment against the security forces'.[37]

Both the Congress-led government of India (since mid-1991) and the increasingly influential Hindu nationalist movement highlighted the Pandit issue. In 1991 the Rashtriya Swayamsevak Sangh (RSS), the movement's parent organisation, published a book titled *Genocide of Hindus in Kashmir*.[38] It claimed among many other things that at least forty Hindu temples in the Kashmir Valley had been desecrated and destroyed by Muslim militants. In February 1993 journalists from India's leading newsmagazine sallied forth from Delhi to the Valley, armed with a list of twenty-three demolished temples supplied by the national headquarters of the BJP, the movement's political party. They found that twenty-one of the twenty-three temples were intact. They reported that 'even in villages where only one or two Pandit families are left, the temples are safe ... even in villages full of militants. The Pandit families have become custodians of the temples, encouraged by their Muslim neighbours to regularly offer prayers.' Two temples had sustained minor damage during unrest after a huge, organised Hindu nationalist mob razed a sixteenth-century mosque in the north Indian town of Ayodhya on 6 December 1992.[39]

Amid all the tragedy and torment that lacerated the Kashmir Valley during the 1990s, an incident that happened in January 1992 is scarcely remembered, even as a footnote. In December 1991, the Hindu nationalists decided to highlight the secessionist uprising in the Valley by undertaking a *Ekta Yatra* (Unity March) across India. The motorised march began from Kanyakumari, the southernmost point of India, on 21 December and aimed to culminate in Srinagar's central square, Lal Chowk, on India's forty-second Republic Day – 26 January 1992. In the lexicon of Indian nationalism, the phrase 'from Kashmir to Kanyakumari' is often used to describe the country's geographical spread. On 26 January 1992, it was announced, the marchers would raise India's national tricolour in Srinagar's Lal Chowk.

The march was led by Murli Manohar Joshi (born 1934), the BJP's national president. But its chief organiser, and the official *yatra* convenor, was Narendra Modi, a 41-year-old RSS veteran who had been seconded to work in the BJP in the late 1980s.

The marchers entered the Indian state of Jammu and Kashmir and made an overnight halt in the city of Jammu on 24–25 January. On the 25th they made it to the town of Udhampur, north of Jammu, where the Hindu-majority southern plains and foothills of the Jammu region give way to uplands with mixed Hindu–Muslim populations and then to Muslim-majority mountainous areas. At Udhampur – the location of the headquarters of the Indian Army's 16th Corps, which looks after the Jammu region – the march's leaders were put in a Soviet Antonov-32 turboprop military transport aircraft and two helicopters, and flown by the Indian Air Force over the snowclad Pir Panjal range to Srinagar. Srinagar was under curfew. The previous day, 24 January, a bomb planted in the city's police headquarters had injured the Kashmir Valley's police chief (a non-local Indian) and four other senior officers, and rockets had been fired at an Indian Airlines commercial flight as it landed in Srinagar. Joshi, Modi and their retinue spent the night at a BSF base near the airport. The next morning, they were driven to Lal Chowk in the city centre for a 'ceremony that lasted precisely 12 minutes' amid 'incessant firing' by militants holed up in adjacent residential neighbourhoods. Joshi brandished a national flag – which had been presented to him on 21 December in Kanyakumari – flanked by Narendra Modi, who cut a smart figure in a black jacket and closely trimmed black beard (which is now much longer and snowy-white). As their retinue 'raised feeble slogans', 'Joshi and yatra convenor Narendra Modi struggled with the flag ... [and] its pole snapped in two'. Joshi and Modi then made do with a flag provided by their escorts, before being spirited out of Srinagar and the Valley. India's leading newsmagazine reported the episode under the headline: 'An Odyssey in Futility'.[40]

A turning point in the insurrection arrived in June 1994. Qazi Nissar, the popular *Mirwaiz* (chief preacher) of the southern half of the Kashmir Valley, was murdered in his home near the town of Anantnag/Islamabad by gunmen widely believed by locals to be from HM. Qazi Nissar, who was in his early forties, was a respected Islamic theologian and had been one of the main figures of the Muslim United Front (MUF) in 1987 (see Chapter 1). A charismatic orator, he had a large following across the southern part of the Valley.

Qazi Nissar's killing was one in a growing spate of assassinations of prominent Kashmiris attributed to HM – the Pakistani ISI's favoured group in the Kashmir insurgency. The first assassination in May 1990 took the life of Maulvi Farooq, the *Mirwaiz* of the northern Valley, who was killed in his home in Srinagar. Other victims included the venerable cleric Maulana Masoodi, perhaps the Valley's most respected political leader from the 1940s to the 1970s (see Chapter 1). Masoodi was shot dead in his home in Ganderbal, a town north of Srinagar, in December 1990. He was 87. There were many other killings subsequently as HM asserted its dominance of the insurgency, including the cardiologist Dr Abdul Ahad Guru, killed in Srinagar in April 1993. Guru was known to have been a mentor to young JKLF militants, and Qazi Nissar had also been supportive of the independentist JKLF while publicly maintaining a non-partisan stance. Another well-known Srinagar physician affiliated to JKLF, Dr Mirajuddin Munshi, fled to the US in January 1994 after receiving HM death threats. HM's terror campaign, which many Valley Kashmiris suspected was being directed by its sponsors in the Pakistani military – who were at the time also building up the Taliban to take over Afghanistan – was not limited to the elite. During travels in the Valley in 1994–95, I heard many accounts from ordinary villagers that HM militants were trying to enforce Jama'at-i-Islami's orthodox creed on the Valley's Sufi belief system through intimidation and murderous violence. The word *zulm* (oppression), usually used to describe the conduct of the Indian security forces, was extended by some to HM's tactics.

By 1994, JKLF insurgents were on their last legs, and militants of the assortment of smaller groups – mostly of a pro-Pakistan orientation – also came under concerted attack from HM. HM seemed bent on establishing a monopoly of the armed struggle. Qazi Nissar, an outspoken individual, opposed the takeover of the *azaadi* movement by Pakistan's favoured group. Shortly before his murder, he 'accused HM of holding Kashmir to ransom, to hand over to Pakistan on a plate'. An 'unprecedented outburst of fury against pro-Pakistan insurgents erupted at his funeral' as 'more than 100,000' mourners shouted *Hiz-bul-Mujahideen Murdabad* (Death to Hizb-ul Mujahideen) and *Jo mangega Pakistan, usko milega kabristan* (those who want Pakistan will be sent to the graveyard), alongside the standard chant *Hum kya chahtey? Azaadi!* (what do we want? Freedom!)[41]

The last mass demonstrations of the Valley uprising that began in January 1990 occurred in May 1995. These did not recur until 2008. The May 1995 protests happened after the mid-fifteenth-century shrine and mausoleum of the Kashmir Valley's patron-saint, Sheikh Nooruddin Noorani alias Nund Rishi (see Chapter 1) – located in the Valley town of Charar-e-Sharief, about 20 miles south-west of Srinagar – burned down in a battle between the Indian Army and HM militants who had taken over the holy compound in March 1995. Most of the town of Charar-e-Sharief – hundreds of houses and shops – also burned down in the fire from the battle. When I arrived in the Valley shortly afterwards, anguished locals unanimously blamed the

Indian Army for the destruction of the shrine, the second holiest to Kashmiri Muslims after Srinagar's Hazratbal. It is not clear which side precipitated the conflagration, however. The leader of the HM insurgents who took over the shrine was a Pakistani *mehmaan* (guest) militant, Manzoor Ahmad alias Mast Gul, who escaped and turned up in Pakistan amid much acclaim.

In August 1995 a group of five tourists from Western countries who were trekking in the vicinity of Pahalgam, a resort in the south-east of the Valley, were abducted by a group which called itself al-Faran, probably a cover name for Harkat-ul-Ansar, an ISI-patronised outfit of Pakistani religious zealots who had entered the Valley. One of the abductees, a Norwegian man, was found beheaded. Another, a US citizen, managed to escape, and the other three men were never found. A commentary in spring 1995 presciently noted: 'In the Valley, Pakistan's heavy influence on the movement is deeply resented, especially among JKLF supporters. India clearly hopes to exploit the sentiment, once the Kashmiris find the fight is futile. In the long run, Pakistan's powerful intervention may prove to have undermined the very uprising it sought to fortify.'[42]

In 1995–96 a new word – 'renegades' – entered the Kashmir conflict's vocabulary. Even non-English-speakers used the term to denote insurgents who gave up the armed struggle and became auxiliaries of the Indian war on insurgency. During the boom years of insurgency (1990–93) the insurgent ranks had swelled with opportunists, criminals and numerous others with little political commitment but carried away by the fervour sweeping the Valley. As the armed struggle lost its sheen amid internecine warfare and realisation dawned that *azaadi* was more a slogan than an achievable aim, these types discovered that they had no stomach for a protracted fight against the vast and entrenched Indian forces. But they were steeped in the 'gun culture' that had enveloped the Valley since 1990, the fighting was far from over, and it was difficult to simply lay down arms and revert to civilian life in a hyper-militarised environment. The men who became renegades had mostly been JKLF insurgents at the beginning of the decade and later of smaller groups that formed as the JKLF insurgency fractured due to Pakistani-engineered splits, as well as the emergence of autonomous local militias in the absence of a central leadership. The renegades also included militants of pro-Pakistan *tanzeems* active during the first half of the 1990s, and some HM defectors.

This motley crew became what an international human rights organisation called 'India's secret army in Kashmir' in May 1996.[43] The renegades had a mix of motivations: survival and protection from HM attacks, revenge against HM, the lure of aggrandisement through robbery and extortion, and a simple addiction to the gun as a symbol of prestige and power. Some were genuinely disillusioned by what they saw as Pakistan's malign influence on the Kashmiri struggle. The gun-toting renegades came to be known also as 'counter-insurgents' and 'pro-India militants', and among working-class and rural folk as *Ikhwanis* – the first renegade militia that appeared in an area north of Srinagar in 1995 initially called itself Ikhwan-ul-Muslimoon and grew out of Ikhwan-ul-Muslimeen, a JKLF splinter of the early 1990s.

The first renegade concentrations emerged in 1995 – a 250-strong group in the hinterland of Pattan, a northern Valley town located between Srinagar and Baramulla, whom I encountered in July of that year, and a 200-strong group around the town of Anantnag/Islamabad in the southern Valley. More groups rapidly proliferated across the Valley, including a particularly violent gang around the town of Pampore just south of Srinagar, an area known for growing saffron, one of the Valley's famous products alongside apples, wooden furniture and handicrafts, and artisan-woven carpets and shawls. By 1996, renegades were prowling the suburbs of Srinagar and setting up roadblocks where they stopped vehicles and robbed passengers of money and valuables at gunpoint. At their peak in the later 1990s, the assortment of renegade groups operating in the Valley totalled several thousand men.

These ex-militants were allowed to do as they pleased by the Indian authorities and security forces, in return for their vitally useful collaboration in the counter-insurgency campaign. For the first time since the outbreak of insurgency, the Indian forces had local auxiliaries. Some renegades were absorbed into a newly created specialist counter-insurgency unit of the Indian J&K police, which was initially called the Special Task Force and later renamed as the Special Operations Group (SOG). The SOG, which includes Muslims, Hindus and Sikhs from the Valley and the Jammu region, has been notorious for the past twenty-five years for corruption and brutality. A much greater number of the turncoat militants were designated as special police officers (SPOs), given a monthly stipend and assigned to camps of the Rashtriya Rifles (National Rifles, RR) operating in their areas. The RR consists of troops drawn from regular Indian Army formations and has been conducting counter-insurgency operations in the interior areas of Indian J&K since 1994. There are 4 major RR commands, each of which has 10,000–12,000 soldiers assigned to counter-insurgency at any one time: Kilo Force in the northern Valley, Victor Force in the southern Valley, Delta Force in the Jammu region's mountainous Doda-Kishtwar zone, which lies just beyond the southern Valley's Anantnag district, and Romeo Force in the hilly, Muslim-majority Jammu districts of Poonch and Rajouri which abut the LoC with Pakistani Kashmir.

With the help of the renegades, the Indian forces were able to reassert control over most of the Kashmir Valley. Guerrilla activity moved out to remote, forested parts of the Valley, and in the late 1990s a new, deadly theatre of insurgency opened up in the Jammu region's Rajouri and Poonch districts (on which more below), in addition to the Doda-Kishtwar zone. Revisiting Srinagar in the late summer and early autumn of 1996, I was struck by the marked difference compared with a year or two earlier, when the city's neighbourhoods still teemed with militants. I noticed that the bunkers manned by paramilitary forces were fewer and had a somnolent air during daylight hours. The checkpoints too were fewer and less aggressive. There was even some pedestrian and automobile traffic in the city centre and its adjoining areas after dusk, unheard of since 1990. In the summer of 1997 thousands of middle-class Srinagar families tripped to Gulmarg, a resort 30 miles west of the city, for the first time since the late 1980s.

During the second half of the 1990s, the renegades sponsored by the Indian authorities fought a bloody intra-Kashmiri conflict with Hizb-ul-Mujahideen, the Pakistan-backed insurgent group. It was a classic proxy war. The renegades killed not just HM militants but hundreds of members of its affiliated political movement, the fundamentalist Jama'at-i-Islami, across the Kashmir Valley. The toll of JI cadre motivated a part of JI's leadership by the end of the 1990s to advocate a turn away from *jehad* – which the movement had embraced in 1990 – and a return to its original mission of teaching and indoctrination. It also led to a split in the early 2000s in HM's command structure, which severely weakened its fighting capability. But there were no winners in the intra-Kashmiri civil war. HM hit back hard against the renegades, and slaughtered entire families in some cases. By the early 2000s the renegades were a spent force. Of the leaders of the pioneering renegade groups, Ghulam Nabi Mir alias Naba Azad of Anantnag/Islamabad was assassinated in June 2001, and Mohammad Yusuf Parray alias Kuka Parray was killed in a September 2003 ambush in Hajin, his village north of Srinagar. The only long-term survivor of the top rene-gade leaders was Ghulam Mohammad Lone alias Papa Kishtwari, who terrorised Pampore in the second half of the 1990s. He died of a heart ailment in a Srinagar hospital in November 2020.

Taking advantage of the relative waning of insurgency, the government of India held elections to reconstitute an Indian J&K state legislature in September 1996. These elections produced a landslide victory for the National Conference party and retrieved the political career of Farooq Abdullah, who became chief minister once again. Voter turnout was substan-tial in the Jammu region, among both Hindus and Muslims (including Kashmiri-speaking Muslims), and in Ladakh. In the Valley, the picture was mixed. Polling was brisk in pockets dominated by the minority Shia and Gujjar communities, but was generally low elsewhere. Most people heeded a boycott call given by the All Parties Hurriyat [Freedom] Conference (APHC), an umbrella alliance of political and civil society groups advo-cating 'self-determination'. There were reports of army soldiers forcing people to vote in some rural areas, and the NC's victory – especially in the Kashmir Valley, where it won forty of the forty-six seats – owed more to the lack of competition than any other factor. An Indian journalist accompa-nying Farooq Abdullah on the campaign trail wrote that 'travelling with Abdullah is like travelling in a military column passing through enemy terri-tory' and that his typical audience consisted of 'about 150 villagers and close to 500 soldiers'.[44] Yet, that there was significant voting – including to a limited extent in the Kashmir Valley – showed weariness among the public with bloodletting with no end in sight. There was even some polling in

Soibugh, the home village in the Valley's central Badgam district of HM's Pakistan-based chief, Syed Salahuddin, which I visited just prior to the election. Although many across the Valley were dead set against voting, others told me that while they craved *azaadi*, they wanted a semblance of civilian government restored in the hope that it would be a buffer between them and the army and paramilitary forces. That hope was belied. The civilian NC government proved no more than a fig leaf, and total power remained with the enforcers of Indian authority.

In January 1997, Srinagar's Bar Association documented 218 custodial deaths in the Valley during 1996 – 120 civilians and 98 captured militants.[45] One of the civilians was a prominent lawyer, Jalil Andrabi, 36, a member of the independentist JKLF. Andrabi had made a nuisance of himself since the early 1990s by filing hundreds of habeas corpus petitions on behalf of families of disappeared persons. In 1994, the Indian J&K high court directed in response to a petition he filed that teams of doctors and lawyers be allowed to visit prisons and interrogation centres. In 1995, the court ruled in response to another petition he made that detainees should not be transferred to jails outside Indian J&K. These orders were simply ignored by the security apparatus.

In the early evening of 8 March 1996, Andrabi was stopped and abducted while driving home from the high court with his wife Rifat, a few months after I saw him for the last time over lunch in New York. Rifat described the incident to me in detail when I had lunch at their Srinagar home in August 1996. A temporary roadblock had been set up near their home by eight to ten uniformed RR soldiers led by an officer, who were accompanied by four or five renegades with covered faces. Rifat chased after their vehicles in a three-wheeled auto she hailed down, but could not keep up. On 27 March, Andrabi's body washed up in a burlap sack on the banks of the Jhelum river in Srinagar. It was decomposed and the autopsy determined that he had been killed within a few days of his abduction. There were gunshot injuries to his head as well as signs of blunt-force trauma to the face, and his eyes were gouged out.

Andrabi's murder – he was laid to rest in the Eidgah martyrs' cemetery in Srinagar – made international headlines, as his activism was globally known. By the time I spoke with Rifat, the identity of the RR officer –

Major Avtar Singh – had been uncovered by a police inquiry ordered by the high court. But he had gone missing. On 5 April, meanwhile, five corpses were found dumped by the Srinagar–Jammu highway. They were identified as the renegades who had been present at the temporary roadblock. In the next few years, there were purported sightings of Major Singh – who the police found had led the abductions of at least five other men subsequently found dead, or who disappeared without a trace – in an army cantonment in northern India, and then in Canada. But his whereabouts remained a mystery. When my mother, Krishna Bose MP, raised Andrabi's death in India's parliament in September 1996 she received a written reply which stated: 'Rashtriya Rifles categorically denies the allegation [made by Rifat Andrabi] ... Neither any member of Rashtriya Rifles was present at the spot [of the abduction] at around that time, nor did any member of them [sic] apprehend or receive him in custody.'[46]

Avtar Singh died in June 2012 at his home near Fresno, California, where he had apparently been living for several years. Just before his death, he called police to say that he had killed four people and was about to kill himself. Police found him dead from a gunshot wound in his living room. In other rooms, they found his wife and their three sons, aged 17, 15, and 3. The woman and the boys aged 17 and 3 were dead. All had gunshot wounds to the head. The 15-year-old had also been shot in the head but was still alive; he died a few days later. Singh had been on an Interpol wanted persons' list 'for the murder of human rights activist Jalil Andrabi'.[47]

In 1998, the number of militants slain fell below 1,000 for the first time since 1992 – official Indian statistics reported that 999 insurgents had been killed during 1998. After nearly a decade of insurgency and counter-insurgency, the armed conflict was essentially at a stalemate. The insurgency, and indeed the *azaadi* movement as a whole, no longer had the momentum and popular enthusiasm of the first half of the 1990s. But the Indian upper hand in the war of attrition was a relative one, and there was no end in sight to the violence. It was in this delicately poised context that India–Pakistan diplomacy made a dramatic appearance on the stage of the stalemated conflict in early 1999. That development, in turn, led to a roller-coaster chain of events which unfolded from 1999 to 2004.

NUCLEARISATION AND THE DIPLOMATIC OPENING

South Asia crossed the nuclear Rubicon in May 1998. In March 1998, a diverse coalition led by the Hindu nationalist BJP formed the government in New Delhi after a mid-term general election produced a hung parliament with BJP the single largest party (it won 181 of the 543 seats, exactly one-third). Atal Bihari Vajpayee (1924–2018), a Hindu nationalist veteran regarded as a relative moderate, became prime minister. Lal Krishna Advani (born 1927), a hardline Hindu nationalist, became the home (interior) minister, and George Fernandes (1930–2019), a veteran socialist and trade unionist, became the defence minister. Two months after the government took office, India detonated five nuclear devices – three on 11 May and a further two on 13 May – at its underground testing site near the village of Pokhran in Rajasthan's Thar desert, which shares a border with Pakistan.

This was not India's first nuclear test – Indira Gandhi's government had detonated a nuclear device at the Pokhran site in May 1974, in an operation codenamed 'Smiling Buddha'. That test had been motivated by a desire to match China's status since 1964 as a nuclear power, which the PRC achieved less than two years after the late 1962 Sino-Indian border war in which India was badly defeated. India's arrival as a nuclear state in 1974 enraged and alarmed Pakistan, which had been dismembered in the December 1971 Bangladesh war and feared that India would in due course pick off what was left of Pakistan. Zulfiqar Ali Bhutto, Pakistan's leader from 1972 to 1977 and the main instigator of the 1965 war with India, had said in 1965 that 'if India builds the atom bomb, Pakistanis will eat grass and leaves, even go hungry, but we will get one of our own'. In 1979, while awaiting execution by hanging at the age of 52 by his nemesis General Zia-ul Haq, who had seized power in a military coup in 1977, Bhutto wrote in his prison cell: 'My single most important achievement, which I believe will dominate the portrait of my public life, is an agreement I arrived at after an assiduous and tenacious endeavour spanning over eleven years of negotiations ... [This] agreement of mine, concluded in June 1976, will perhaps be my greatest achievement and contribution to the survival of our people and our nation.'[48] It seems that Bhutto was referring to the eleven years between his visit to

Beijing as foreign minister in May 1965, to secure diplomatic and practical support in the impending war against India, and his visit to Beijing as prime minister in June 1976, when he was the last foreign leader to be received by Mao Zedong just before the Chinese dictator's death. Bhutto appeared to be strongly hinting that during the latter visit, he made some sort of secret agreement with the PRC's leadership to help Pakistan's nuclear programme. In fact, China became the vital source of scientific expertise and materiel for Pakistan's nuclear programme over the next two decades – which was funded mainly by Saudi Arabia – supplemented by the global trafficking network run by the Pakistani nuclear scientist Abdul Qadeer (A.Q.) Khan in collusion with North Korea (a PRC client) and the Libyan regime of Muammar Gaddafi, another longstanding patron of Pakistan.[49]

The Indian nuclear tests of May 1998 triggered mass hysteria in Pakistan. On 28 May, Pakistan detonated five nuclear devices at its main testing complex in the Balochistan province. This was followed by a sixth detonation on 30 May at another site in the province, in order to reach parity with India's six explosions (including the 1974 'Smiling Buddha' test, known as Pokhran-1).

Prime Minister Vajpayee sent a letter to US President Clinton on 11 May. He wrote:

I would like to explain the rationale for the tests . . . We have an overt nuclear-weapon state [the PRC] on our borders, a state which committed armed aggression against India in 1962. Although our relations with that country have improved in the last decade or so, an atmosphere of distrust persists mainly due to the unresolved border problem. To add to the distrust, that country has materially helped another neighbour of ours to become a covert nuclear-weapon state. At the hands of this bitter neighbour [Pakistan], we have suffered three aggressions in the last 50 years. And for the last ten years we have been the victim of unremitting terrorism and militancy sponsored by it in several parts of our country, especially Punjab and Jammu & Kashmir . . . The series of tests are limited in number and pose no danger to any country with no inimical intentions towards India . . . We hope that you will show understanding of our concern for India's security.[50]

The US administration was not convinced, and felt acutely embarrassed that its vaunted intelligence services had failed to detect the Indian preparations for the tests. It promptly slapped a range of economic sanctions on India. But the government's move was hugely popular in India. In 2002 the Vajpayee-led coalition government made A.P.J. Abdul Kalam, a top Indian scientist involved with the nuclear programme, its candidate for India's ceremonial presidency. Kalam, a colourful but down-to-earth character, was elected amid acclaim to a five-year term and is easily the most popular president India has had since the post was inaugurated in 1950. The euphoric mood in India was mirrored in Pakistan, where flag-waving crowds celebrated the Pakistani tests in late May. The question was what effect the overt nuclearisation of the subcontinent would have on the bleeding Kashmir conflict.

In September 1998, Vajpayee met on the sidelines of the annual UN meetings in New York with his Pakistani counterpart, Mian Nawaz Sharif. Sharif, a business tycoon and moderate conservative from Pakistan's heartland Punjab province, had been promoted in Pakistani politics by General Zia during the 1980s. In February 1997, he had led his mainly Punjab-based party – Punjab has the majority of Pakistan's population – to a resounding victory in parliamentary elections against his rival Benazir Bhutto, Zulfiqar Bhutto's daughter and political legatee. Sharif hosted a lunch for Vajpayee in New York and suggested to the Indian prime minister that he visit Pakistan. Having demonstrated nuclear parity with India, Sharif apparently felt it was time to give diplomacy a chance. Vajpayee proved amenable – with India having recently gained a qualified upper hand over the Pakistan-supported Kashmir insurgency, he seems to have sensed a propitious moment to extend an olive branch to Pakistan's civilian leader. When the visit happened in February 1999 after a few months of secret preparations, it was a sensation.

Vajpayee travelled to Pakistan on the first run of a new bus service connecting Delhi to Lahore, the Pakistani Punjab city close to the Indian border. He was warmly received at the border between the Indian and Pakistani Punjabs by Nawaz Sharif. The Indian and Pakistani prime ministers signed a 'Lahore Declaration' visionary in intent: 'Sharing a vision of peace and stability' and 'recognizing that the nuclear dimension of the security environment of the two countries adds to their responsibility for avoidance of conflict', the Lahore Declaration pledged a 'composite and integrated dialogue process' on the basis of an 'agreed bilateral agenda' which would 'intensify efforts to resolve all issues, including the issue of Jammu and Kashmir'.[51] Visiting the Minar-e-Pakistan, a 1960s tower built on the site where the All-India Muslim League led by Jinnah passed its 'Lahore Resolution' calling for Pakistan in March 1940, Vajpayee wrote in the visitors' book on 21 February 1999: 'From this historic Minar-i-Pakistan, I wish to assure the people of Pakistan of my country's deep desire for lasting peace and friendship. I have said this before, and I say it again: A stable, secure and prosperous Pakistan is in India's interest. Let no one in Pakistan be in doubt about this. India sincerely wishes the people of Pakistan well.'[52]

Four months before Vajpayee's visit, Nawaz Sharif had forced the resignation of the Pakistan Army's chief, General Jehangir Karamat. General Karamat had drawn the assertive prime minister's ire by proposing a Turkey-style National Security Council with representation of civilian and military leaders to decide policy on sensitive matters of state. This would have formalised the military's powerful and often decisive de facto role in such matters. Sharif strongly objected and sought Karamat's resignation. Karamat chose not to go for a confrontation and resigned in early October of 1998. Sharif then appointed General Pervez Musharraf, the commander of one of the army's nine field corps, as the new army chief, superseding two corps commanders senior to him.

Musharraf immediately reshuffled the army hierarchy. He wanted to appoint his close associate General Aziz Khan as ISI chief but, overruled by Sharif, instead made him the chief of general staff (CGS) at Army headquarters in Rawalpindi. General Mahmud Ahmad was brought in as commander of the 10th Corps based in Rawalpindi, which is responsible for the entire Jammu and Kashmir front with India. A cabal of four officers – Lieutenant-Generals Musharraf, Khan and Ahmad, along with Major-General Javed Hassan, head of the Force Command Northern Areas (FCNA) based in Gilgit-Baltistan – then proceeded to plot and perpetrate a secret cross-LoC operation into Indian J&K's Ladakh region. That operation led in the summer of 1999 to what is known as the 'Kargil War' between

India and Pakistan, which spelled the end of the diplomatic opening engineered by Vajpayee and Sharif.

THE KARGIL WAR

Over the freezing winter of 1998–99, several thousand Pakistani soldiers crossed the Line of Control from Gilgit-Baltistan (then known as Pakistan's Northern Areas) into Indian J&K's Ladakh region. Most of the ingress was into the western Ladakh district of Kargil, and concentrated in a swathe north of the small town of Drass (10,800 feet), which lies in the west of the district shortly beyond the Zojila Pass (11,300 feet), the gateway to the Kashmir Valley. In this zone, the infiltrators penetrated up to 10 miles beyond the LoC and occupied a string of peaks and ridges overlooking the road running from the Valley to Leh, the main town in eastern Ladakh. There were other ingress points further east, extending into the Leh district.

The Pakistani soldiers were from the Northern Light Infantry (NLI), a paramilitary force under the operational command of the Pakistan Army's FCNA (just after the end of the Kargil War, NLI was made a full-fledged regiment of the Pakistan Army). The NLI soldiers were recruits from Gilgit-Baltistan, a vast high-Himalayan region, and naturally accustomed to the terrain and altitudes, and the officers leading the infiltrating units were regular Pakistan Army personnel. The equivalent of about six NLI battalions (4,500-plus men) crossed the LoC. They set up around 140 posts spanning a 110-mile stretch on the Indian side of the LoC, on barren peaks and ridgelines at altitudes of 15,000–18,000 feet dominating the valleys below. This uninhabited wilderness had had some Indian forward posts, which were withdrawn as usual in the late autumn until the following summer. Over the winter, the infiltrators occupied some of these vacated posts and set up many other vantage points. The large-scale ingress went entirely undetected until early May of 1999, when a six-man Indian Army reconnaissance patrol which had ventured out with the onset of summer in the upper reaches of the Kargil district lost radio contact and went missing – it was ambushed and its members killed. By the time Vajpayee visited Lahore in late February, the infiltration operation – codenamed Operation

Koh Paima (KP) – was substantially and perhaps fully complete. Musharraf pointedly refused to accompany Sharif to the border to greet the bus-borne Indian leader.

A Pakistan Army plan to infiltrate the LoC's Kargil sector had existed since the mid-1980s. It had been conceived as a retaliation to an Indian military operation (codenamed Operation Meghdoot or Sky-Messenger) which in 1984 took control of the Siachen glacier in the far north of the Ladakh region – at the tri-junction of India's Ladakh, Pakistan's Gilgit-Baltistan and China's Xinjiang province, and just west of the Karakoram Pass (18,694 feet above sea level). The Siachen glacier, which rises to 19,000 feet at its northernmost point, is shaped like an inverted triangle and has a horizontal length of 47 miles at its widest. In 1984 Indian troops took control of the glacier and all three of the passes located on its western Saltoro ridge into Gilgit-Baltistan, dominating Pakistani positions below the ridge. Since then, Siachen/Saltoro has been the world's highest battle-field, in which many more soldiers on both sides have perished from avalanches, frostbite and high-altitude sickness than from sporadic armed clashes. The Pakistanis viewed India's 1984 Siachen operation as a perfid-ious violation of the July 1972 Simla Agreement between the then leaders of the two countries, Indira Gandhi and Zulfiqar Ali Bhutto, which speci-fied that neither country would violate the LoC – the renamed Ceasefire Line from the 1947–48 Kashmir war. The Indian riposte is that when the two armies signed the agreement demarcating the serpentine, nearly 500-mile LoC in December 1972, the demarcation of the line as specified in maps only extended up to the southern end of the Saltoro ridge, a point known as NJ9842. The area further north was not demarcated, and the LoC was simply described as extending 'thence north to the glaciers'.

The choice of the Kargil sector as the site of a Pakistani counter-strike had several reasons. The Kargil district abuts the Kashmir Valley, the epicentre of the conflict since 1947. For almost all of the first India–Pakistan war over Kashmir that began in October 1947 and concluded at the end of 1948, the area, including the towns of Kargil and Drass and the Zojila Pass into the Valley, was under the control of Pakistani forces led by a formation called the Gilgit Scouts, the forerunner of the Northern Light Infantry.

They were evicted from the area by an Indian offensive in November 1948, which secured the road running from the Valley to eastern Ladakh and the frontier with Tibet (which came under the control of the communist PRC from 1950). In July–August 1965, one of the nine Pakistani columns that crossed into Indian Kashmir entered the Drass-Kargil area, where the arterial road running from the Kashmir Valley to eastern Ladakh – vital to Indian troop movements – lies close to the LoC (CFL until 1972).

But the Kargil plan was not acted upon – until late 1998. Preoccupied with supporting the American-backed mujahideen war on the Soviets in Afghanistan, Pakistan's military ruler General Zia-ul Haq decided against opening a second front against the Indians in Kashmir. Moreover, the top rung of the Pakistan Army in the 1980s was composed of men with vivid memories of the debacle of Operation Gibraltar, the 1965 cross-CFL infiltration led by the paramilitary Azad Kashmir Regular Force (incorporated into the Pakistan Army in 1972 as its Azad Kashmir Regiment), which failed to ignite an uprising in Indian Jammu and Kashmir.

In late 1998, the dormant Kargil plan was revived by the new leadership of the Pakistan Army headed by Pervez Musharraf. Musharraf, born in Delhi in 1943, had been a member of the Special Service Group (SSG), the Pakistan Army's commando unit established in 1956 under the tutelage of US special forces. The commando background may have predisposed him to adventurous behaviour. His closest associate in Operation Koh Paima, General Aziz Khan, had served as Zia-ul Haq's military secretary in the 1980s and directed ISI operations in both Afghanistan and Kashmir in the 1990s. Musharraf and his fellow plotters had drawn a lesson from the Indian and Pakistani nuclear tests of May 1998 that was completely different from that of the civilian government led by Nawaz Sharif. Sharif thought that nuclear parity provided an opening for diplomatic engagement with India, which had struggled with the Kashmir insurgency since 1990. Musharraf and his high-level army clique calculated that nuclear parity meant that India would not be able to respond to a sub-conventional limited war initiated by Pakistan in Kashmir by escalating the conflict to a conventional war, as had happened in 1965. There were other, deeper grievances at work, especially the dismemberment of Pakistan through Indian military intervention and the birth of Bangladesh in December 1971. 'If there is one event that cemented Pakistan's Islamic, anti-India narrative,' a Pakistani author writes, it is 'the loss of East Pakistan in 1971'.[53] According to another Pakistani writer, the author of an illuminating account of the Kargil War: 'Pakistan's 1971 surrender in East Pakistan had inflicted the deepest of cuts on the Pakistani psyche. For some, the shame and anger had lingered.'[54] But above all, Musharraf and his fellow plotters were concerned about the relative weakening of the insurgency in Indian Kashmir and determined to bring the conflict to renewed global attention.

Vajpayee and Sharif learned about Kargil around the same time. Sharif was briefed about the operation on 17 May 1999 at an ISI facility just outside Islamabad, Pakistan's capital. He was accompanied by senior ministers in his cabinet and top advisers. The army cabal of four led by Musharraf were present, along with the entire ISI brass.

The official Indian enquiry into the Kargil War is aptly titled *From Surprise to Reckoning*.[55] Vajpayee's coalition government had fallen in April 1999 after losing a confidence motion in parliament by a single vote, and he and his cabinet were serving in a caretaker capacity pending a fresh general election. In mid-May, neither the Indian government nor the military had yet realised the scale of the intrusion, and they were unclear about the identity of the infiltrators. Initially, the impression in India was that a wildcard cross-border operation by Pakistani religious militants, possibly supported by Afghan mercenaries, had taken place with the onset of summer. The Indians had no idea that thousands of well-equipped professional soldiers had dug in on mountain posts for several months. They were swiftly disabused. In the second half of May, hasty infantry assaults on some of the lower-lying peaks and ridges were repelled with heavy Indian casualties. In late May, the infiltrators shot down two low-flying Indian fighter jets – a MiG-27 and a MiG-21 – and a Mi-8 helicopter was blown out of the sky by a Stinger surface-to-air missile, the portable American weapon that had proved crucial to the Afghan mujahideen's fight against the Soviets during the second half of the 1980s.

Thereafter, the Indian counter-offensive changed tack. From early June, the Indians commenced a massive artillery bombardment of the peaks and ridges, using 155mm howitzers (the Bofors gun purchased from Sweden in an allegedly corrupt transaction in the second half of the 1980s), multi-barrelled rocket-launchers (MBRLs) and heavy mortars. Hundreds of thousands of shells were fired during June and into early July and pulverised the Pakistani units. At the same time, the Indian Air Force targeted the posts with laser-guided munitions launched by Mirage-2000 jets acquired from France, and other aerial bombing severely disrupted the posts' supply lines from Gilgit-Baltistan. Pakistan's armed forces could not bring their own artillery and air power to bear on the conflict, as that would expose the planners of the operation. The infiltrators hung on grimly to their heights, and follow-up infantry assaults were needed to take the posts. The first Indian successes in the critical Drass area came in the second week of June through close-range fighting including hand-to-hand combat, and were consolidated with further hard-won gains in the first week of July.

As the Kargil War became the focus of global newspaper headlines and television coverage, the Pakistanis devised a version of events which claimed that unspecified Kashmiri freedom fighters/mujahideen were taking on the Indian forces, with no knowledge or involvement whatsoever of the Pakistani military. The narrative fell apart in the second week of June, when the Indian government released a taped phone conversation between Musharraf and Aziz Khan, which took place during a visit by Musharraf to Beijing. On the tape, which was probably passed on by American intelligence services to the Indians, the two generals candidly discussed their operation and its progress. Yet the Pakistanis continued to propagate the mujahideen fiction. As the game unravelled in the first week of July, Musharraf said on 5 July: 'About 1500 to 2000 mujahideen are fighting courageously in Drass and Kargil. Pakistan will ask them to change their position and wait for their response.'[56] He eventually stopped dissembling and forthrightly declared in January 2002: 'We have fought four wars over the LoC'. He was referring to 1947–48, 1965, 1971 and 1999.[57]

The Kargil War erupted exactly a year after the Indian and Pakistani nuclear tests of May 1998. As the fighting intensified during June and it became clear that the Pakistan Army was responsible for the incursion, alarm spread in world capitals that the conflict between two nuclear-armed states with a history of fighting recurrently over Kashmir would escalate. In the first half of June, channels between the Pakistani civilian government and its Indian counterpart remained open, and high-level emissaries including ministers travelled between New Delhi and Islamabad, sometimes on commercial flights which continued to operate as usual. But there was no breakthrough, because the Pakistan Army's leadership was both in denial mode and outside the civilian government's control. In late June, General Anthony Zinni, the head of the United States Central Command (CENTCOM), visited Pakistan as an emissary of President Bill Clinton and told Musharraf in a meeting at the Pakistan Army's headquarters in Rawalpindi that Pakistani troops must be withdrawn immediately from the Indian side of the LoC.

Caught in a cleft stick, Nawaz Sharif dashed to Beijing at the end of June to seek support. Unlike in 1965 and 1971, when China made belligerent statements against India, he received none after meeting with the top Chinese leadership – President Jiang Zemin, Premier Zhu Rongji and Li Peng, chairman of the National People's Congress. The only Chinese public pronouncement on the crisis was a bland statement by its foreign ministry on 1 July, which called for de-escalation and dialogue. Running out of options, Sharif then invited himself to Washington, DC, where he was received by President Clinton in the White House on 4 July.

Clinton had just finished dealing with the Kosovo crisis of March–June 1999 when he was presented with the subcontinental flare-up. Sharif found him in an implacable mood. The meeting ended in a joint statement:

President Clinton and Prime Minister Sharif share the view that the current fighting in the Kargil region of Kashmir is dangerous and contains the seeds of a wider conflict. They also agreed that it is vital for peace in South Asia that the Line of Control in Kashmir is respected by both parties, in accordance with their 1972 Simla accord. It was agreed between the President and the Prime Minister that concrete steps will be taken for the restoration of the Line of Control, in accordance with the Simla Agreement . . . The Prime Minister and the President agreed that the bilateral dialogue begun in Lahore in February provides the best forum for resolving all issues dividing India and Pakistan, including Kashmir. The President said he would take a personal interest in encouraging an expeditious resumption and intensification of those bilateral efforts, once the sanctity of the Line of Control has been fully restored. The President reaffirmed his intent to pay an early visit to South Asia.[58]

The Kargil gambit had boomeranged on Pakistan. The statement – prepared by senior Clinton administration officials – emphasised the LoC, in tune with the longstanding Indian status-quoist position, *and* it emphasised the bilateral nature of the Kashmir conflict, also an Indian stance, ruling out any international intervention beyond American 'encouragement' of a bilateral peace process. Globally, Pakistan was widely regarded as having committed an act of reckless adventurism in a nuclearised subcontinent, while India was seen as restrained for limiting its response to just fighting back, hard, against the intruders. In the second week of July, the Pakistani units began withdrawing, and the process was completed in August. On 26 July, the Indian government declared that 'Operation Vijay' (Victory) – the name given to its counter-offensive – had ended in success. The Indian armed forces lost 527 personnel killed in action in the Kargil War. The Pakistani death toll is unknown, but was probably two to three times higher. The Musharraf clique's attempt to bring the Kashmir conflict to renewed global attention had ended in a political and diplomatic debacle for Pakistan.[59]

The aftershocks of the Kargil fiasco precipitated the return of Pakistan to full-fledged military rule. The Pakistani public had largely bought the tale of heroic mujahideen confronting the Indians put out by the army's propaganda machine and fed to the mass-circulated Urdu press. Sharif was blamed for selling out the freedom fighters, capitulating to American pressure and handing the Indians an undeserved victory. An assortment of Pakistan's opposition parties hit the streets in agitations against Sharif, who was in any case becoming unpopular because of his growing authoritarianism. In early October, the simmering tension between the beleaguered Sharif government and the army came to a head. Sharif tried to dismiss Musharraf as army chief, and the army reacted by deposing Sharif in a swiftly executed coup. Musharraf became Pakistan's ruler until his own fall from power in 2008.

The Kargil War ended in India's favour, and the Vajpayee government synchronised its military and diplomatic strategies exceptionally well. Almost simultaneously with the military coup in Pakistan on 12 October 1999, India finished its mid-term general election, and Vajpayee took office on 13 October 1999 at the head of another BJP-led coalition government, which lasted its full term until mid-2004 (the BJP won 181 of the 543 seats in parliament on its own, the same one-third share as in the previous mid-term election in February 1998).

The end of the Kargil War marked the beginning of a new, deadly phase of the Kashmir insurgency which lasted until 2003 and brought India and Pakistan to the brink of war in 2002. And just as dramatically, that period of extreme turbulence yielded to an India–Pakistan thaw and the glimmers of a Kashmir peace process in 2003–4.

THE *FIDAYEEN* CAMPAIGN, THE 2002 CRISIS AND THE RETURN OF DIPLOMACY

The first half of the 2000s was the era of *fidayeen* warfare in Kashmir. The word, of Arabic origin, means 'those who sacrifice themselves'. The *fidayeen* offensive began as the Kargil War ended.

The first *fidayeen* attack in July 1999 set the template for the campaign. Two militants simply barged into a BSF camp in Bandipora, a northern Valley town, firing from assault rifles and lobbing grenades. Between then and the end of 2002, there were at least fifty-five *fidayeen* attacks in Indian J&K, most of which targeted army, paramilitary and police installations in the Kashmir Valley.

Most of the raids followed a uniform model. They were typically executed by two-man teams who forced their way into the targeted sites after shooting sentries. Once inside, they fired indiscriminately and lobbed grenades. A pattern emerged of the attackers engaging in prolonged fire-fights lasting from twenty-four to seventy-two hours with Indian forces once they infiltrated the targeted compounds. They came trained and prepared for such protracted encounters. In a typical incident, the duo would split up after forcing entry, move swiftly in the style of commandos to different parts of the premises, and sometimes stop firing for a time to conceal their exact location. They carried plentiful ammunition, as well as dry rations and mineral water. Thus equipped, they would hold out and try to inflict casualties until cornered and killed. There was no shortage of sites to target because of the hundreds of army, paramilitary and police camps across the Valley. Not all *fidayeen* raids were successful, but many were. The maximum number of *fidayeen* attacks in Indian J&K – twenty-nine – occurred in 2001. According to Indian figures, 161 army, paramilitary and police personnel died in these attacks between July 1999 and late 2002 (the army alone lost 82 men) and 90 *fidayeen* were killed.[60]

The *fidayeen* campaign of the early 2000s marked a major change in the tactics of the insurgency. During the first half of the 1990s, thousands of insurgents active in the field operated in Srinagar and dominated many rural areas of the Valley. By the middle of the decade, that phase of the insurgency was spent, and by the end of the decade Hizb-ul Mujahideen, the favoured Kashmiri insurgent group of the Pakistani army and the ISI, was much diminished by the Indian counter-insurgency forces and their renegade auxiliaries. The Kargil operation was a response to this situation. Once that operation failed, the *fidayeen* were deployed to keep the pot boiling. In this offensive, relatively small numbers of highly trained militants conducted suicide attacks in targeted operations.

The bulk of the *fidayeen* attacks were the work of Lashkar-e-Taiba (Army of the Pious, LeT), the fighting arm of an ultra-orthodox Sunni movement headquartered near Lahore. The movement's most prominent face is Hafiz Muhammad Saeed (born 1950), a theologian who began his political life in Pakistan's Jama'at-i-Islami before founding LeT's parent organisation in the late 1980s. I first heard about LeT while travelling in 1995 in the Handwara *tehsil* (sub-division) of the northern Valley's Kupwara district, close to the LoC. Locals told me that fighters of a Pakistani group called Lashkar-e-Taiba had come from *us paar* (the other side) and set up camps in the forests of the area. But at that time, they kept a low profile and were barely known in the insurgency.

The rest of the *fidayeen* attacks were perpetrated by Jaish-e-Mohammad (Army of the Prophet, JeM), a militant group floated in early 2000 under the leadership of Maulana Masood Azhar (born 1968), a cleric from Bahawalpur in the southern part of Pakistan's Punjab province. JeM is descended from Harkat-ul-Ansar (HuA), a Pakistani jihadist group which first appeared on the margins of the insurgency in the Kashmir Valley in 1994–95. Azhar was caught in the Valley's southern Anantnag/Islamabad district in 1994. He was one of three men released by the Vajpayee government at the end of December 1999 – five months after the end of the Kargil War – after an Indian Airlines commercial flight from Kathmandu to Delhi was hijacked by a group of Pakistani terrorists and eventually flown to Kandahar in Afghanistan after stops in Amritsar (India), Lahore (Pakistan) and Dubai. The five hijackers demanded the release of Masood Azhar, Ahmed Omar Saeed Sheikh (born 1973), a British national of Pakistani descent and HuA member who had been arrested in northern India in 1994 on kidnapping charges, and Mushtaq Zargar alias Latram, a onetime JKLF militant from Srinagar who formed al-Umar Mujahideen, an ISI-sponsored breakaway group, in 1991 and was captured by Indian forces in 1992. The three men were flown by the Indian government to Kandahar – the de facto capital of Afghanistan's Pakistan-backed Taliban government – and all of the 186 passengers and crew were freed except for one young man, an Indian who had been stabbed to death by the hijackers. Ahmed Omar Saeed Sheikh, who studied at the London School of Economics as an undergraduate in 1992–93 before being radical-ised during a trip in the summer of 1993 to deliver relief supplies to Bosnian Muslims caught up in the 1992–95 war in Bosnia-Hercegovina, was later arrested again and sentenced to death in Pakistan for his role in the January 2002 kidnapping and murder in Karachi of Daniel Pearl, an American jour-nalist. Pearl, who was working for the *Wall Street Journal*, was beheaded by the top al-Qaeda terrorist Khalid Sheikh Mohammed. Masood Azhar formed JeM as HuA's successor in early 2000 after his release in Kandahar and return to Pakistan. JeM became the Pakistani ISI's second frontline organisation, after LeT, in the *fidayeen* campaign in Kashmir.

For its first two years, the *fidayeen* offensive concentrated on security-force bases in the Valley. Between late 1999 and the end of 2000 there were three attempts to penetrate the headquarters of the Indian Army's 15th Corps located in Badami Bagh, a sprawling cantonment on Srinagar's southern outskirts. The 15th Corps, known as the Chinar Corps, is responsible for the Valley. The first time, *fidayeen* on foot attacked the cantonment. On the second occasion in May 2000, Afaq Shah, a 17-year-old schoolboy from Khanyar, a neighbourhood in Srinagar's old city, detonated a car-bomb at the cantonment's main entrance, killing himself and eight soldiers. He had been recruited by JeM. In December 2000 another JeM car-bomber – Mohammed Bilal, 24, a British national of Pakistani descent from Manchester in England – targeted the cantonment. There was a major raid on the Srinagar headquarters of the Special Operations Group (SOG), the J&K police's specialist counter-insurgency force. Army and paramilitary camps across the Valley came under attack. In September 2000, for example, on a day I happened to be in the Valley, two *fidayeen* attacked a Rashtriya Rifles (RR) camp in the town of Beerwah in the Badgam district, close to Srinagar. They killed an army major and thirteen soldiers before being eliminated.

The *fidayeen* duos often consisted of one local and one Pakistani militant. One of the Beerwah raiders was Pakistani, the other a Kashmiri-speaking Muslim from a highland area of the Jammu region's Udhampur district. In November 2002, a CRPF camp in Srinagar's city centre came under attack. LeT identified the two *fidayeen* who killed six troopers and injured nine others as 'Abu Younis' from Pakistan and Reyaz Ahmad Khan, from the southern Valley town of Qazigund. In addition to army, paramilitary and police installations, a *fidayeen* attack targeted Srinagar's airport, which is used for both civil and military purposes. In October 2001, a JeM *fidayeen* squad broke into the compound of the Indian J&K state legislature in Srinagar. A militant from Peshawar, Pakistan, detonated a jeep-bomb at the heavily fortified entrance, and other militants entered the compound in the ensuing chaos. The attack killed thirty-eight persons, mostly local Muslim policemen on guard duty and Muslim employees of the legislature's secretariat.

The biggest *fidayeen* incident of all, however, did not occur in Kashmir. On the morning of 13 December 2001, a five-man squad managed to enter the compound of India's parliament building in New Delhi, riding in a white Ambassador car with a roof beacon, the typical vehicle used by senior officials at the time. They then tried to enter the building, a stately circular structure with 144 columns built under British rule in the 1920s. They almost succeeded and were very narrowly thwarted by alert stewards who closed the doorways just in time. The raiders opened fire from assault rifles and threw grenades, and were shot down in and around the building's central portico after a gun-battle that lasted forty-five minutes. Nine other men died – six security personnel, two stewards and a gardener who was tending the compound's lawns. Parliament was in session and hundreds of MPs including government ministers were in the building at the time. My mother, Krishna Bose MP, had attended the morning question-hour. She then got into her car at the central portico a few minutes before the attackers arrived and drove across the street to the main building's annexe, where her office as the chair of the parliamentary standing committee on external (foreign) affairs was located. She was locked down there for a few hours. Had the attackers managed to get inside the parliament building, unimaginable carnage would have resulted, making an India–Pakistan war all but certain. A calamity of massive proportions had been very narrowly averted.

While the identities of the five dead terrorists could not be ascertained, the Indian government was convinced that they were Pakistanis, and most probably members of JeM. The BBC reported seven years later that 'after the Delhi attack, a Pakistani [army] brigadier recalled Gen. Musharraf storming into ISI headquarters. "He walked into my office, having wrenched the door open. After running me down with a string of choice words, he said that either you rein in these mad dogs you have kept, or I will have them shot".'[61] Musharraf, who had appointed himself Pakistan's president earlier in 2001, formally declared LeT and JeM banned organisations in January 2002.

The Indians were not placated. Unlike in 1999, the Indian government downgraded diplomatic relations and suspended all travel links with Pakistan. It also ordered a massive military mobilisation. By mid-2002, 800,000 Indian Army troops led by armoured strike formations were positioned on India's frontier with Pakistan, on the entire border running from Pakistan's southern

Sindh province through Punjab to the LoC in Jammu and Kashmir. The Indian air force and navy also assumed positions primed to attack. The Pakistan military undertook a counter-mobilisation of similar proportions. The war clouds dissipated in late 2002, aided by American crisis diplomacy led by Richard Armitage, the deputy secretary of state in the George W. Bush administration. The Musharraf regime had emerged as the US's vital if uneasy ally in the 'global war on terror' after al-Qaeda's attacks of 11 September 2001 on New York and Washington and the subsequent US offensive to depose the Pakistan-backed Taliban government of Afghanistan. The Americans were desperate to avert an India–Pakistan war that would derail the war on al-Qaeda and its Afghan Taliban allies, and moreover disrupt planning for the impending invasion of Saddam Hussein's Iraq.

Post-Kargil, Vajpayee had continued his policy of trying to dampen down the armed conflict in Kashmir, but without success. In late July 2000 Hizb-ul Mujahideen announced a unilateral ceasefire. The HM commander behind the ceasefire was Abdul Majid Dar, known through the 1990s as a particular favourite of the ISI. Now he professed a change of heart: 'Even if this violence continues for another ten years, ultimately the parties will have to sit around a table and find a solution through talks. So it is better that a dialogue begins now, so that further bloodshed is stopped.'[62] By this time, though, the *fidayeen* campaign was well underway, HM had weakened under the onslaught of the Indian security forces and their renegade allies, and HM's leading role in the insurgency had been taken over by the Pakistani groups LeT and JeM. On 3 August, a delegation representing Dar met in a convivial atmosphere in Srinagar with senior Indian officials led by the top bureaucrat of the Indian government's home (interior) ministry. But a few days later, the HM leadership based in Muzaffarabad, in Pakistani Kashmir, withdrew the ceasefire and claimed responsibility for a car-bomb attack in Srinagar's city centre. In 2001 Dar and his Valley-based supporters were purged from HM, and in March 2003 Dar was assassinated at his home in the northern Valley town of Sopore. On 2 August 2000, a week after the ceasefire declared by HM's Dar faction, the Pakistani religious radicals now driving the insurgency attacked an annual summer pilgrimage undertaken by Hindus from across India to a cave shrine (Amarnath) of the deity Shiva located in the mountains of the south-eastern part of the Valley. The attack, probably the work of LeT, killed thirty-two people – twenty-one pilgrims, seven local Muslims and four Indian security personnel (a year later in July 2001, another attack on the pilgrimage killed thirteen people: eight pilgrims, three local Muslims and two Indian security personnel). Seemingly undeterred, on 19 November 2000 Vajpayee announced that Indian security forces would refrain from launching offensive operations against militants during the holy month of Ramzan (27 November–27 December 2000). The gesture went unrequited and the *fidayeen* campaign escalated sharply in 2001.

Vajpayee then took a bold gamble and in mid-2001 invited Musharraf for a summit in India. Musharraf was then an international pariah, a self-declared president who had seized power through a coup from a democratically elected government. When President Clinton made the visit to the subcontinent – in March 2000 – that he had promised to Nawaz Sharif in July 1999, he spent several days in India. He made a stopover at Islamabad airport that lasted a few hours on his return journey, during which he lectured Musharraf and his fellow generals on the virtues of democracy. It was a terrible snub for a country which had been a US ally since the mid-1950s.[63] Musharraf accepted Vajpayee's surprise invitation, and the summit took place in July 2001 in Agra, the city in north India famous for the seventeenth-century Taj Mahal. The summit was inconclusive and ended without the kind of joint statement of good intent that Vajpayee and Sharif had issued in Lahore in February 1999, but Vajpayee had made the point that he wished to engage with Pakistan.

Vajpayee's persistence against all odds with Pakistan is counter-intuitive, given his political background as a lifelong Hindu nationalist. It seems that his early political socialisation in the RSS had been tempered by four decades as a parliamentarian – he was first elected to India's parliament in 1957 and gained renown as an orator, resolute but never rabid. He also had experience of global geopolitics, having served with quiet distinction as India's external affairs (foreign) minister in a non-Congress coalition government from 1977 to 1979. It appears that as prime minister in his middle to late seventies, he wished to cut a statesman-like figure, and his

Kashmir policy until the end of his premiership in mid-2004 – when he unexpectedly lost the Indian general election – suggests that he understood both the gravity and the complexity of the Kashmir problem and possibly wanted a Kashmir settlement to be his legacy. Such a settlement, and legacy, was impossible without engagement with Pakistan. In June 2001 he and my mother, Krishna Bose, were admitted to the same hospital in Mumbai for knee-replacement surgery. In her tribute to Vajpayee's memory upon his death in August 2018, she wrote:

> During the days of recuperation, he was on the floor just above mine. He would sometimes call me to his room. When I arrived in my wheelchair he would, propped up in bed, initiate discussions on various matters. The Agra summit with Musharraf was imminent and we discussed that most of all. I realized from our conversations that he badly wanted to do something about the bleeding sore of Kashmir and had therefore reached out to the Musharraf regime at considerable political risk, just two years after his bus diplomacy to Lahore had been answered with the Kargil incursion.[64]

Until 2003, it seemed that all of Vajpayee's risk-taking was in vain. While the *fidayeen* offensive gripped the Valley post-Kargil, the Pakistani jihadist groups opened up a new theatre of operations in the Jammu region. Until the late 1990s, the only part of the Jammu region where the insurgency made a significant impact was the sprawling, mountainous Doda district (since divided into two districts, Doda and Kishtwar) which lies just southeast of the Valley. Doda and Kishtwar, which together have a population of about 700,000, are both religiously mixed districts with Muslim majorities (Doda is 54 per cent Muslim and 46 per cent Hindu, Kishtwar 58 per cent Muslim and 41 per cent Hindu). The Muslims of Doda-Kishtwar are mostly Kashmiri-speaking, ethnolinguistically identical to the Valley's majority population (when I first visited Doda-Kishtwar in the mid-1990s, it was described to me as 'an extension of the Valley', albeit with very large Hindu minorities). The large presence of Kashmiri Muslims, combined with rugged terrain and proximity to the southern Valley, resulted in a significant level of insurgency in Doda-Kishtwar through the 1990s.

But the other area of the Jammu region with a mainly Muslim population – the hilly districts of Poonch and Rajouri lying south-west of the Valley along the LoC with Pakistan's 'Azad' Kashmir – remained largely undisturbed despite having Muslim majorities (90 per cent of Poonch's 500,000 people and 63 per cent of Rajouri's 700,000 people are Muslim – much of the latter district's sizeable Hindu population are descendants of refugees from 'Azad' Kashmir districts, particularly the town of Kotli which lies directly across the LoC). This was partly because of their ethnolinguistic composition, which is very different from the Valley's. Kashmiris are a small, single-digit percentage of the Rajouri-Poonch Muslims, who very largely belong to other ethnic communities: Gujjars, Bakerwals, Rajputs and Pathans. Gujjars – some of whom are referred to as 'Bakerwals', rearers of goats and sheep – are traditionally pastoral nomads and form the single largest group. They are also found in the Valley but are numerically dominant in Poonch-Rajouri. The principal languages in these districts are Pahari (a hill dialect of Punjabi) and Gojri – not Kashmiri as in the Valley or Dogri as in the Jammu region's southern Hindu-dominated plains and foothills. The distinct ethnolinguistic character of Poonch-Rajouri contributed to its Muslims mostly keeping aloof from the insurgency sweeping the Valley. They were also cautious because Poonch and Rajouri were fiercely contested during the 1947–48 and 1965 wars, and in 1965 some of the local Muslims – many of whom have relatives across what was then still just a Ceasefire Line – were brutally treated by the Indian Army for suspect loyalties. From 1990, the Poonch-Rajouri sector became a major infiltration route for guerrillas. The entire stretch along the LoC is riddled with *galis* (literally, alleys) – hilly tracts with tall forests or scrub jungle which became infiltration corridors. The Indian Army's brigades guarding that terrain are named after *galis*: BG (Bhimber Gali) Brigade, JWG (Jharan Wali Gali) Brigade, and so on. But until the late 1990s the infiltrating guerrillas simply passed through en route to the Valley, or the Doda-Kishtwar zone.

That changed at the turn of the century. When I toured Rajouri and Poonch in September 2000, just over a year after the end of the Kargil War, the two LoC districts had become the new hotspot of the Kashmir insurgency. The RR's Romeo Force, the Indian Army troops assigned to counter-insurgency in Rajouri-Poonch whom I periodically encountered on narrow mountain roads cratered by landmine and IED (improvised explosive device) explosions, were having a very tough time. Their principal adversaries were only a few hundred albeit highly trained Pakistani militants equipped with PK general-purpose machine guns, sniper rifles, shoulder-fired rocket-launchers, mines and IEDs of various types, plastic explosives, binoculars and night-vision devices, and the latest radio sets for communication. As in 1947–48 and 1965, they did have some local recruits and support networks. According to the Romeo Force commander, his soldiers killed 166 insurgents in the 6-month period between 15 March and 15 September of 2000, of whom 54 per cent were 'foreigners' (i.e. militants from Pakistan or 'Azad' Kashmir).[65] This proportion of non-local militants was almost double the proportion of 'foreign' militants slain in Indian J&K as a whole during 2000: 436 of 1,520 militant fatalities (29 per cent). The fighting in Rajouri-Poonch worsened in 2001. In the 10-month period between 1 January and 31 October of 2001, the Romeo Force killed 572 insurgents.[66]

The year 2001 was the bloodiest year of fighting in the Kashmir insurgency. As many as 2,020 militants were killed across Indian J&K during the year, of whom 622 (31 per cent) were foreigners, i.e. Pakistanis, along with 536 personnel of the Indian security forces and 919 civilians. That nearly 70 per cent of slain insurgents were still native to Indian J&K showed that the problem was not reducible simply to 'cross-border terrorism', as Indian rhetoric claimed. Indeed, as per official Indian figures, the proportion of foreign militants killed never reached one-third of the total insurgent fatalities in any of the fifteen years in which guerrilla war raged in Indian J&K, 1990–2004. The highest proportion of slain foreign militants was 32 per cent in 1998 (319 of 999 insurgent deaths) and the lowest was 1.4 per cent in 1991 (12 of 844).[67]

In retrospect, the fallout of the 13 December 2001 attack on India's parliament in New Delhi marked the beginning of the end of the post-Kargil *fidayeen* offensive in Indian J&K. *Fidayeen* attacks in the Kashmir Valley fell off sharply in 2002 compared to 2001 or even 2000, as the Musharraf regime came under severe pressure on two fronts: diplomatically from the US administration and militarily from the Indian build-up on Pakistan's borders. From 2003, *fidayeen* attacks in the Kashmir Valley declined to sporadic incidents, and ceased more or less entirely in the second half of the 2000s.

But 2002 was still a difficult and turbulent year. On 21 May 2002 Abdul Ghani Lone, a onetime establishment politician turned prominent self-determination proponent, was shot dead in Srinagar, aged 70. Lone's assassins were gunmen from a small pro-Pakistan group who struck when he was speaking at the Eidgah graveyard at a commemoration of the assassination of Maulvi Farooq, the *Mirwaiz* (chief preacher) of the city's biggest mosque, who had been killed by HM militants twelve years earlier, on 21 May 1990. Rajouri-Poonch continued to be convulsed by violence. On a typical day, 28 April 2002, twelve guerrillas were killed, six while trying to infiltrate through Bhimber Gali and another six in the interior.[68] The previous day, 27 April, nine HM militants were killed near the LoC in the Nowgam sector of the Kashmir Valley's northern Kupwara district: eight were youths from Kupwara villages and one a Pakistani.[69] The Surankote *tehsil* (sub-division) of the Poonch district was a particular hotspot. In November 2001, eleven Indian Army personnel including a major had died in an ambush in a village there. In July 2002 seven guerrillas and three army personnel, again including a major, died in gun-battles in the Surankote area. In September 2002 militants threw bombs and opened fire at the bus stand in the town of Surankote, killing eight BSF personnel, three local police and two civilians; two attackers also died in the battle.[70] Two decades on, I vividly remember the war-torn atmosphere of Poonch-Rajouri in the early 2000s.

With more than a million Indian and Pakistani soldiers mobilised along the borders in 2002, however, the greatest danger lay in the spread of terrorist attacks to the Hindu-majority southern half of the Jammu region. In May 2002, three Pakistani gunmen who had infiltrated from across the border opened fire in a bus and then raided a compound near the city of Jammu housing families of Indian soldiers, killing eighteen family members of Indian Army personnel, ten other civilians and three soldiers. Then in July 2002, gunmen from LeT attacked a shantytown of labourer families on the outskirts of Jammu city and killed twenty-nine Hindus before fleeing.

In early August of 2002, the annual Amarnath pilgrimage in the mountains of the southern Valley was attacked for the third consecutive year and nine pilgrims were killed. In November 2002, two LeT gunmen opened fire in the bustling market in Jammu's old city and then entered a popular Hindu temple in the neighbourhood; a dozen civilians were killed and many others injured. This was the second attack on the locality and the temple in 2002 – a previous raid by two gunmen in March 2002 had killed seven people, including three policemen. The spate of raids was clearly designed to ignite an India–Pakistan war.[71]

The large-scale killings of Hindu civilians escalated a trend visible since the late 1990s. Before then, such attacks were rare. In August 1993, gunmen stopped a bus on a mountain road near the town of Kishtwar, separated Hindus from Muslims and massacred sixteen Hindu passengers. Maulana Farooq Hussain Kitchloo, the pro-independence imam of Kishtwar's mosque, quickly denounced the killings over the mosque's loudspeakers and announced a *hartal* (general strike) in protest, helping forestall the obvious incitement to inter-group violence in a town with almost equal numbers of Muslims and Hindus. At the time, this was an isolated atrocity. But such massacres became more frequent from the late 1990s, when the Pakistani zealot groups took on a major role in the insurgency. In January 1998, twenty-six Kashmiri Pandits were massacred in a village called Wandhama, north of Srinagar. The gunmen wore Indian Army fatigues and pretended to be soldiers before opening fire on the villagers; this impersonation recurred in subsequent incidents. In April 1998, militants raided two villages in a remote highland area of the Jammu region's Udhampur district and beheaded twenty-six Hindu men, women and children. In June 1998, gunmen ambushed a *baraat* (marriage procession) in a village in the Doda district and killed twenty-five Hindus. In August 1998, thirty-five Hindus were killed in a remote area, bordering the Doda district, of the Indian state of Himachal Pradesh. The Doda killings led to Hindus temporarily abandoning many mountain villages to seek shelter in the nearest towns. 'Village Defence Committees' (VDCs), ragtag militia comprised of Hindu villagers set up under the authority of the Indian security forces in both Rajouri-Poonch and Doda-Kishtwar, were not effective in countering the heavily armed insurgents. Then, just before President Clinton arrived in India in March 2000, gunmen wearing Indian Army uniforms raided Chittisinghpora, a Sikh village in the Valley's southern Anantnag district. They ordered thirty-six male villagers to gather near the shrine (*gurdwara*) and then opened fire, killing thirty-five men. The sole survivor, who was injured in the shooting, recounted that the group of killers addressed each other by Hindu first names and shouted Indian nationalist and Hindu religious slogans. A few days later, the army's local RR unit killed five Muslim men in a nearby village and claimed they were the killers, but they turned out to be innocent civilians.

Amid the mayhem of 2002, elections were held to constitute a fresh Indian J&K state legislature in September 2002. They were due, as the legislature constituted in September 1996 was about to finish its six-year term. The elections sparked a deadly but transient upsurge in militant attacks in the Valley and Rajouri-Poonch and were boycotted by the Hurriyat Conference, the umbrella forum of some two dozen political and civil society groups advocating for 'self-determination'. There were numerous reports of army troops forcing people to vote in the Valley's rural areas. But there was also a degree of genuine polling across the Valley. This was mostly triggered by the appearance of a new local party, the Jammu and Kashmir People's Democratic Party (PDP), as an alternative to the Abdullah family's unpopular National Conference government.

The PDP was launched in July 1999, as the Kargil War wound down, by Mufti Mohammad Sayeed (1936–2016), a veteran Valley politician. He had been a senior leader of India's Congress party in the Valley until the late 1980s and a staunch supporter of Indian J&K's integration with the rest of the country. Mufti became India's home (interior) minister from December 1989 to November 1990, and it was the JKLF kidnapping of his daughter Rubaiya in December 1989, recounted earlier, that first brought the simmering crisis in the Valley into international headlines. After a decade of carnage, Mufti reinvented himself in 1999 as a pro-people politician seeking an end to the bloodletting through India–Pakistan dialogue. His party's main face was his politician daughter Mehbooba Mufti (born 1960), who had gained some popularity in the Valley by campaigning against human rights abuses by the security forces. The PDP won sixteen of the Valley's forty-six seats (mostly in the southern Valley) and formed a coalition government with the Congress party, which did very well in the Jammu region, and a few smaller parties and independents. Under an agreement with the Congress, Mufti became Indian J&K's chief minister for the first three years of the legislature's six-year term.

The pincer offensive on the Musharraf regime – on the diplomatic front by the Americans and the military front by the Indians – led to the 'mad dogs' (Musharraf's December 2001 phrase) of the post-Kargil insurgency being leashed, though they were not kennelled. In April 2003, Vajpayee made a visit to Srinagar and addressed a public meeting flanked by Mufti Sayeed, the chief minister. Four weeks before the visit, at midnight on 23–24 March 2003, a group of heavily armed men wearing Indian Army fatigues appeared in Nadimarg, a mixed village of Muslims and Hindus in the Valley's southern Pulwama district. The gunmen, most probably from Lashkar-e-Taiba, rounded up the village's Kashmiri Pandits, who had lived undisturbed until then. The Pandits – eleven men, eleven women and two little boys – were lined up and gunned down. The oldest of the twenty-four victims was a 65-year-old man, the youngest a boy of 2. Vajpayee was not deterred from the pursuit of his strategy of diplomacy and engagement. On 22 April 2003, he reported on his Srinagar trip to the Lok Sabha, the directly elected lower chamber of India's parliament:

> I went to Jammu & Kashmir on a two-day visit on 18–19 April . . . In my public rally . . . I assured the people of Jammu & Kashmir that we wish to resolve all issues – both domestic and external – through talks. I stressed that the gun can solve no problem, brotherhood can. Issues can be resolved if we move forward guided by three principles: *Insaaniyat* (humanity), *Jamhooriyat* (democracy), and *Kashmiriyat* (Kashmir's age-old legacy of Hindu–Muslim amity). In my speech, I spoke of extending our hand of friendship to Pakistan. At the same time, I also said that this hand of friendship should be extended by both sides. Both countries should resolve that we need to live together in peace.[72]

Vajpayee, an accomplished poet in Hindi, dropped the usual Sanskritic Hindi of his speeches in favour of the Urdu words *insaaniyat* and *jamhooriyat*.

Musharraf, no poet, had meanwhile outlined his own principles for a peace process. In January 2002 and again in September 2002, he said: 'The first step should be the resumption of peaceful dialogue. The second should be to accept Kashmir as a central issue [a subtle but significant departure from the standard Pakistani formulation: "the core issue"]. The third is to negate any solution that is not acceptable to both countries. The fourth is to apply what remains of a solution according to the wishes of Kashmiris.'[73]

In November 2003, the Indian and Pakistani armies agreed a ceasefire on the entire border in Jammu and Kashmir: the 500-mile Line of Control, another 125 miles to its south that straddles the south-western part of Indian J&K's Jammu region and Pakistan's Punjab province, and the barren area to the LoC's north which ends at the Siachen glacier. The agreement provided a respite to hundreds of thousands of villagers on both sides of the militarised border from the firing and shelling that had turned their lives into a long nightmare since 1990. In January 2004, Vajpayee travelled to Pakistan's capital Islamabad to attend a summit of South Asian premiers – the South Asian Association for Regional Cooperation (SAARC) of seven countries: India, Pakistan, Bangladesh, Sri Lanka, Nepal, Bhutan and the Maldives (an eighth member, Afghanistan, has since joined the grouping, which remains a pale shadow of its highly developed counterparts like ASEAN and the EU). At that regional summit, he sealed the India–Pakistan thaw by shaking hands with Musharraf. In December 2003, Musharraf had narrowly escaped two assassination attempts in the space of a fortnight. The Jaish-e-Mohammad (JeM) group active in the Kashmir insurgency since 2000 was involved in the attacks, plotted by an al-Qaeda network in Pakistan which included several junior officers of Pakistan's armed forces.[74] After his return from Pakistan, Vajpayee met with some of the Hurriyat Conference's leading figures from the Kashmir Valley in New Delhi as a goodwill gesture.

When I returned to the Kashmir Valley in the summer of 2004, I sensed – for the first time since I started going there in 1994 – a cautious undercurrent of hope and optimism among its people, traumatised and exhausted by fifteen years of carnage. The carnage was over, but a very uncertain future beckoned.

CHAPTER THREE

The Stone Pelters

2005–19

THE ITALIAN PHILOSOPHER Giorgio Agamben has written about the 'state of exception' as 'a paradigm of contemporary government'. As a leading modern example, he cites 'the case of the Nazi State. No sooner did Hitler take power than, on 28 February 1933, he proclaimed the Decree for the Protection of the People and the State, which suspended the articles of the Weimar Constitution concerning personal liberties.' The decree, Agamben notes, 'was never repealed, so from the juridical stand-point the entire Third Reich can be considered a state of exception that lasted twelve years'. 'Since then,' Agamben writes, 'the creation of a perma-nent state of emergency has become one of the practices of contemporary states, including so-called democratic ones,' as 'the state power's response to internal conflicts.' This 'transformation of a provisional and exceptional measure into a technique of government' enables 'the elimination of not just political adversaries but of entire categories of citizens who for some reason cannot be integrated into the political system'. Under a state-of-exception regime, 'the law employs the exception – that is, the suspension of the law – as its means of referring to and encompassing life'.[1]

The root cause of the Kashmir conflict is the India–Pakistan antagonism and their competing claims to rightful ownership of Kashmir. But the main factor driving the conflict for the past seven decades has been the permanent state-of-exception regime in force in Indian Jammu and Kashmir, in a particularly draconian form in the Kashmir Valley. In 1954, the extensive fundamental rights of citizens guaranteed by the Indian constitution (1950) were made applicable to Indian J&K as one of the first measures of its integration with India, but with a vital escape clause – those rights could be suspended at the discretion of Indian J&K authorities on grounds of security. From the 1950s to the 1970s, Indian J&K was ruled under a raft of emergency laws – the Defence of India Rules inherited from the British, the J&K Public Security Act, the J&K Preventive Detention Act, and the federal Unlawful Activities Prevention Act. In 1978 the J&K Public Safety Act was enacted (see Chapter 1), and the PSA continues to be the main legal instrument of the police state in Indian Jammu and Kashmir more than four decades later. In 1990, upon the eruption of insurgency, the Armed Forces Special Powers Act was made applicable to Indian Jammu and Kashmir. Continuously in force since then, AFSPA gives virtually unlimited powers of search, arrest and use of lethal force to the Indian Army and paramilitary forces, and blanket protection from any prosecution to their personnel (see Chapter 2).

This apparatus of repression and coercion continued undiluted and unreformed after the fifteen years of carnage described in the previous chapter subsided from the mid-2000s and insurgency declined to negligible levels by the end of the decade. During the same period, a tentative India–Pakistan intergovernmental process ongoing since 2004 to find a compromise solution to the Kashmir conflict fizzled out in 2007 and collapsed completely in 2008. The result was that the interlude of cautious hope between 2004 and 2007 yielded to a long period of renewed turmoil which properly took hold from 2010. That new phase of the Kashmir conflict came to be symbolised not by the gun-wielding insurgent – armed militancy did not revive significantly – but by the stone-pelter. Mass stone-pelting at the enforcers of the state-of-exception regime revived a decades-old tradition of protest in the Valley, which had been temporarily displaced by the Kalashnikov-carrying insurgents from 1990 to the mid-2000s. Major stone-pelting uprisings led by a new generation of youth born in the 1990s broke out in the

Kashmir Valley in 2010 and again in 2016, and during the decade the stone replaced the AK-47s wielded by the previous generation as the weapon of everyday struggle.

A GLIMMER OF PEACE

Uri is a small town nestled in mountains on the western edge of the Kashmir Valley. The town has a mix of Kashmiris and Gujjars – traditionally a community of livestock-herders and seasonal nomads who are found in parts of both the Valley and the Jammu region – and is a centre of trading in walnuts, one of the Valley's signature products. The villages in Uri's hinterland are mostly populated by Gujjars, and the dominant tongues are Pahari (a highland dialect of Punjabi) and Gojri, rather than Kashmiri, which is the mother tongue of the vast majority in the Valley. The Gujjars in both the Valley and the Jammu region to its south were not drawn into the insurgency of the 1990s and early 2000s on the large scale of the Kashmiri-speaking Muslims, though some Gujjar youths did become insurgents and others living on the LoC in both the Valley and the Rajouri-Poonch sector of the Jammu region helped infiltrating insurgents by acting as guides. The Uri area has several hundred Hindu (Kashmiri Pandit) families, as well as a sprinkling of Sikh residents.

Uri has been on the frontline of the India–Pakistan conflict over Kashmir since the late 1940s. It sits astride the former 'Jhelum Road' – built at the end of the nineteenth century and so known because it follows the course of the Jhelum river – which until 1947 was the otherwise isolated Kashmir Valley's main link to the outside world. The Jhelum Road ran from Srinagar through the town of Muzaffarabad – the capital of Pakistan's 'Azad' Kashmir territory after 1947 – to Rawalpindi, the old city in pre-partition north-west Punjab which is now known mainly for housing the GHQ (general headquarters) of the Pakistan Army and the neighbouring custom-built capital city of Pakistan, Islamabad. The arterial road was the Valley's main transport and trade route and connected it with the districts of the North-West Frontier Province and west Punjab (which became part of Pakistan from August 1947) contiguous to the 1846–1947 princely state of Jammu and Kashmir.

In October 1947, the Pakistan-sponsored motorised assault force which entered the princely state from the NWFP (Chapter 1) used the Jhelum Road. They first seized Muzaffarabad and then passed through Uri – a distance of about 40 miles from Muzaffarabad – before continuing on the same road to take Baramulla, the major town of the northern Valley, and penetrated into the outskirts of Srinagar. The Indian fightback recounted in Chapter 1 retook Baramulla on 8 November 1947 and Uri on 14 November, and pushed the raiders back to the Valley's periphery. The Ceasefire Line of January 1949, renamed the Line of Control in July 1972, is 6 miles west of the town of Uri. Uri has a particularly strategic location because it is just 50 miles north as the crow flies of the town of Poonch, which is in the north-western corner of Indian J&K's Jammu region. The greater part of the princely state's Poonch district, however, lies in Pakistan's 'Azad' Kashmir, and the towns of Poonch and Uri are separated by a bulge which includes the Haji Pir Pass (8,700 feet), taken by the Indian Army in the 1965 Kashmir war but returned to Pakistan as part of the reciprocal restoration of the pre-war territorial status quo ante by the Tashkent agreement of January 1966 between the leaders of India and Pakistan. Until 1947, the Uri *tehsil* (sub-district administrative division) was part of the Muzaffarabad district of the princely state, and the former *tehsil* has been bisected by the CFL/ LoC since then.

As a frontline town, Uri features recurrently in the headlines of the Kashmir conflict. In September 2016, at a time when the Kashmir Valley was in the throes of a massive stone-pelting uprising against Indian authority, the headquarters of the Indian Army brigade in the Uri sector was pene- trated in a pre-dawn raid by four gunmen who infiltrated the LoC through the Haji Pir Pass. The attackers, probably from the Pakistani Jaish-e- Mohammad (JeM) jihadist group, killed nineteen Indian soldiers sleeping in tents before being killed themselves. A week later, the Indian government headed by Narendra Modi, a hardline Hindu nationalist, claimed it had conducted retaliatory commando strikes against terrorist bases across the LoC. In November 2020, a spike in cross-LoC shelling killed three Indian Army soldiers and four civilians in Uri's villages and reawakened memories among the latter of the years prior to 2004, when life along the LoC – before the ceasefire agreement of November 2003 between the Indian and Pakistani armies (Chapter 2) – was a living nightmare for villagers on both sides of the Line.

In the spring of 2005, however, Uri was for once the focus of non-belligerent activity amid the thaw in India–Pakistan relations achieved in 2003–4 by Vajpayee and Musharraf. On the LoC, Indian Army engineers worked round the clock to reconstruct a long-derelict wooden bridge across the Jhelum leading into Pakistani J&K. Two octogenarians in Srinagar recalled fond memories of driving eighteen-seater Ford and Chevrolet buses across that bridge on the daily Jhelum Road service that ran until the autumn of 1947 from Srinagar to Muzaffarabad (a distance of just over 100 miles) and on to Rawalpindi. The buses carried passengers, cargo and mail.[2] Since then, the area around the bridge had become a heavily mined no-man's land: 'Not long ago, this area was a minefield; soldiers in bunkers on either side, exchanging bullets and shells. Today they exchange pleasant-ries as bulldozers roll and men work. Hundreds of men are working on a war footing to rebuild the final 1,300-foot stretch of road to the bridge – defusing mines, clearing undergrowth and building a complex for immigra-tion and customs, a bank and other travel facilities.'[3] The bonhomie cooled somewhat when the Indians painted the restored bridge in the colours of India's national flag (saffron, white and green), but they repainted it in a neutral shade after the Pakistanis protested. The restored bridge was named Aman Setu: 'friendship bridge'.

In April 2005 a fortnightly bus service commenced on the Srinagar–Muzaffarabad route, crossing the LoC at Uri. Most of the early passengers were people from divided families, with relatives and in some cases ancestral properties on the other side. Passengers from Srinagar disembarked just before the bridge and walked across to board another bus waiting on the Pakistani side, and those from Muzaffarabad followed the same procedure in reverse. Just after the bus service began, Musharraf visited Delhi and met with India's prime minister, Manmohan Singh. The two leaders issued a joint statement that they had 'decided to increase the frequency of the bus service and also decided that trucks would be allowed to use the route to promote trade'.[4] In Washington, DC, Condoleezza Rice, the US secretary of state, said that the US was 'very impressed with what India and Pakistan have achieved. It is quite remarkable where they have reached. They have opened the bus service in Kashmir, which would have been unthinkable a few years ago. They are looking at broader economic ties.'[5]

Meanwhile, however, a rather different drama was also unfolding in relative obscurity along the LoC in the spring of 2005. From 2002 to 2004 the Indian Army had worked on a war footing to build a sophisticated fencing system covering 734 kilometres of the 742-kilometre LoC, most of which traverses hilly or mountainous terrain. The LoC fence consists of 'two or three rows of concertina wire three metres or ten feet high, electrified and connected to a network of motion sensors, thermal imaging devices and alarms acquired from the United States and Israel'[6] (Israel was of course engaged at the same time in building its security/separation barrier with the West Bank, as the second Palestinian intifada of 2000–05 raged). In 2005 exceptionally heavy late-winter snowfall obliterated the LoC fencing on many stretches and damaged it in other places. Even as global attention focused on the opening of the LoC at Uri, the army was engaged in a massive effort to repair the collapsed fencing in anticipation of the summer 'infiltration season' from across the LoC. Although that activity was on the decline due to the India–Pakistan thaw and the Musharraf regime's curtailment of the Lashkar-e-Taiba and Jaish-e-Mohammad groups, combined with war-fatigue in Indian J&K, insurgents did try to exploit the gaps in the fencing system over the summer, sparking gunfights with the army.[7]

The Srinagar–Muzaffarabad bus service was disrupted by a calamity of nature six months after its inauguration. On the morning of Saturday 8 October 2005, a severe earthquake centred on Muzaffarabad hit the northern part of Pakistan's 'Azad' Kashmir territory. At least seventy-five thousand people were killed in that area, and several hundred thousand rendered homeless just before the onset of winter. The quake also caused major loss of life and destruction in areas of the NWFP (now known as the Khyber-Pakhtunkhwa province) bordering the epicentre in the Muzaffarabad district. Across the LoC, the Kashmir Valley escaped the worst, but there was significant loss of life and damage in its western and northern parts closest to the epicentre; about 1,500 people died. The town of Uri suffered extensive damage and the quake collapsed the bridge across the Jhelum. The bridge was speedily rebuilt by army engineers and reopened in February 2006. But in 2006 passenger traffic on the bus route declined to a trickle, mainly because of frustrating bureaucratic and security procedures on both sides. Inaugurating the rebuilt bridge in late February, Ghulam Nabi Azad, Indian J&K's chief minister and a Congress party leader, said that 440 people from the Pakistani side and 391 from the Indian side had used the bus service since it began. He announced that an agreement to allow goods traffic on the route had just been reached and trucks would start rolling from April 2006 – a full year after Musharraf and Singh had reached an in-principle agreement on the matter.[8] This did happen and in June 2006 a second cross-LoC bus and trucking route commenced further south, between the town of Poonch in Indian J&K and Rawalakot, an 'Azad' Kashmir town 25 miles away (both towns were part of the princely state's Poonch district, divided since the 1947–48 war). Passenger numbers and the trade in goods both remained at anaemic levels, however.

The emphasis on opening up the LoC was sudden and unexpected. Since the mid-1950s, Indian leaders have ideally wanted to convert the Ceasefire Line from the 1947–48 Kashmir war (as the LoC was known from 1949 to 1972) into an extension of the *de jure* India–Pakistan international border – which would settle the dispute over Jammu and Kashmir on terms very favourable to India. As recounted in Chapter 1, India's prime minister Jawaharlal Nehru privately proposed that solution to the dispute to his Pakistani counterpart Mohammad Ali Bogra in May 1955 and made the offer public knowledge in April 1956. But no Pakistani leader or government can agree to a one-dimensional 'solution' to the Kashmir dispute that seals the territorial status quo, which heavily favours India – as told in Chapter 1, the Indian side contains about 70 per cent of the population of the erstwhile princely state of Jammu and Kashmir and the bulk of its territories, including almost the whole of the Kashmir Valley and most of the Jammu region.

Until the 1965 war, the CFL was in fact a relatively soft border on the ground. Residents living on or close to the CFL on both sides could go back and forth with permits readily issued by local authorities, to visit relatives or attend to land and property on the other side. But following the cross-CFL armed infiltration by the Pakistanis which triggered the 1965 war (Chapter 1), that era ended and the CFL became a tightly secured 'hard' border. In 1972, visiting India as the leader of a defeated, rump Pakistan following the Indian-backed emergence of sovereign Bangladesh (the former East Pakistan), Zulfiqar Ali Bhutto did agree to the renaming of the CFL as the Line of Control to impart a degree of juridical stability to the de facto border in Jammu and Kashmir, but *pending* a final settlement of the Kashmir dispute: 'The basic issues and causes of conflicts which have bedevilled relations . . . for the past twenty-five years shall be resolved by peaceful means . . . through bilateral negotiations or by other peaceful means mutually agreed'. The July 1972 agreement signed in Simla, a north Indian hill town, further stated that 'both Governments agree that their respective Heads will meet again at a mutually convenient time in the future and that, in the meanwhile, the representatives of the two sides will meet to discuss further the modalities and arrangements for a durable peace and normalisation of relations'.[9] That envisioned Kashmir peace process of course never materialised.

Once a large-scale insurgency fuelled by cross-LoC support and infiltration began in Indian J&K from 1990 (Chapter 2), the Indian status-quoist position hardened. Securing the LoC militarily and making it as impregnable as possible became the top Indian priority, and the fencing system built between 2002 and 2004 reflected that imperative. Pakistan, meanwhile, remained as revisionist as ever in its approach to the LoC. Musharraf bluntly stated in January 2002 that 'we have fought four wars over the LoC' (1947–48, 1965, 1971 and the Kargil War of 1999) and reiterated that Pakistan would never agree to formally accept the LoC as an extension of the India–Pakistan international frontier. Queried again on the proposition in September 2002, he tersely replied: '*Main bewkoof nahin hoon*' (I am not an idiot).[10] The actual but unstated Pakistani desire down the decades has almost certainly been a redrawing of the CFL/LoC to expand the Pakistani portion of Jammu and Kashmir, with a particular eye on the Kashmir Valley – that goal motivated the failed 'Operation Gibraltar' strike into Indian J&K in 1965 (Chapter 1) and the Kargil misadventure of 1999 (Chapter 2).

The sizeable pro-independence populations on both sides of the LoC – a 2009 opinion survey reported, plausibly, in light of my own field experience, that the vast majority in the Kashmir Valley and almost half the people in Pakistan's 'Azad' Kashmir wish to be independent of both India and Pakistan[11] – have their own distinct perspective on the LoC that can be described as *abolitionist*. Their ideal scenario is that the LoC be abolished altogether to enable a united, independent state of Jammu and Kashmir. The rigid Indian status-quoist stance is unacceptable to the Pakistanis and the Kashmir independentists, the Pakistani revisionist approach is unacceptable to the Indians and unpalatable for the Kashmir independentists, and the abolitionist desire of the independentists is unacceptable to both India and Pakistan.

In a book titled *Kashmir: Roots of Conflict, Paths to Peace* which was published in late 2003, I noted that 'the "cross-border" dimension of the Kashmir conflict is inevitable because history, international law, regional geopolitics and local religious, ethnic and political ties all spill across the boundary called the LoC'. I argued that:

A longer-term Kashmir settlement necessitates that the LoC be transformed – from an iron curtain of barbed wire, bunkers, trenches and hostile militaries to a linen curtain between self-governing Indian and Pakistani regions of Jammu and Kashmir. *Realpolitik* dictates that the border will be permanent (albeit probably under a different name), but it must be transcended without being abolished in order to meet the aspirations of those, on both sides of the line, who do not like the LoC, either in principle or in its present trajectory. This means that self-rule frameworks in Indian J&K and [Pakistan's] 'Azad' J&K must be complemented by cross-border links between the regions under Indian and Pakistani sovereignty. This will connect the large pro-independence population in areas under Indian sovereignty with their compatriots across the frontier (and vice versa), and the smaller but still significant pro-Pakistan segment to their preferred state, and vice versa (had a pro-India segment existed in Pakistani-controlled Kashmir, it would also have had the effect of connecting them to their preferred state, and vice versa). In the longer run, such cross-border linkages are the solution to the problem of 'cross-border terrorism'.[12]

As concrete measures, in 2003 I suggested the establishment of an inter-ministerial council of the Indian J&K and 'Azad' J&K governments to develop cross-border cooperation on trade and commerce, waterways, transportation, protection of the environment, agriculture and horticulture, cultural matters and tourism. I also suggested the establishment of a forum to bring together elected legislators from the two sides for consultation and deliberations. In the Kashmir case study of my later book *Contested Lands: Israel–Palestine, Kashmir, Bosnia, Cyprus, and Sri Lanka* (2007), I reiterated that 'the best compromise between the contradictory positions on the LoC is to transform the character of the line – into a soft border between self-governing entities in Indian and Pakistani Kashmir, a bridge of cooperation rather than an iron wall of antagonism'.[13] My proposed solution to the LoC conundrum cited the 1998 settlement to the Northern Ireland conflict, which combined devolution from London to a power-sharing Northern Ireland government consisting of representatives of the Unionist (British) and Nationalist (Irish) communities with institutionalised cross-border linkages between Northern Ireland and the Republic of Ireland. I drew also on a 2000 essay by Strobe Talbott, published when he was the US deputy secretary of state, which argued that tackling conflicts with intersecting internal and international dimensions requires making 'a virtue out of porous borders and intertwined economies and cultures' through 'cross-border economic development and political cooperation'. Talbott argued that such avenues to peace had been opened up by 'globalization and its sub-phenomenon, regionalization' and that 'the most successful states' of the twenty-first century would be those 'that harness these forces and facts of life rather than deny them'.[14]

The concept of a soft, permeable LoC appeared and took centre stage in the incipient Kashmir peace process that emerged in 2005–6 from the India–Pakistan thaw of 2003–4. The form it took – a bus service or two that made for good photo-optics, a handful of trucks travelling back and forth – was different from the long-term cross-border institutions I had suggested as one pillar of a necessarily multi-pillared Kashmir settlement. This was instant coffee rather than the rigorously brewed variety, fast food rather than the properly marinated version. Still, the opening of the LoC did send a powerful symbolic message of peace and cooperation and could be regarded as baby steps towards an eventual transformation of the line from barrier to bridge. At a practical level, it helped consolidate the November 2003 LoC ceasefire agreement between the two armies. After the earthquake of October 2005 devastated the northern part of 'Azad' Kashmir, the Indian government offered to send military helicopters to aid in search-and-rescue missions, but baulked when the Pakistanis requested that they be deployed without their Indian crews. But there was some solidarity in the air. A month after the quake, five points were opened on the LoC for transit of relief supplies. As an international donor conference for the survivors convened in Islamabad, a few villagers from a remote community on the Indian side of the LoC crossed a precarious suspension bridge at one such point, over a fast-flowing mountain river called the Kishanganga, to enquire after the fate of relatives on the other side. That would have been impossible two years earlier. The donor conference raised $5.8 billion, including an Indian contribution of $25 million. In an emotional speech, Musharraf appealed to India to settle the Kashmir conflict 'once and for all' and said that would be 'the best donation'.[15]

There were sinister indications of a backlash to the relative cordiality of intergovernmental relations. At the end of October 2005, three bomb blasts hit New Delhi on the eve of Diwali, the festival of lights. One was left on a motorbike parked in a congested area outside the city's railway station. Another was left in a bag on a bus, and the third was a car-bomb that exploded in a major market packed with Diwali shoppers. Sixty-two people were killed, two-thirds in the market, and more than two hundred injured. An obscure jihadist group based in Pakistan claimed responsibility, but the Indians suspected Lashkar-e-Taiba were the real perpetrators (LeT's parent organisation was at the same time heavily engaged in earthquake relief operations in the Muzaffarabad district). The climax of repeated mass-casualty terror attacks in Indian cities, timed to undermine the India–Pakistan *détente* at crucial junctures, would come in Mumbai three years later in November 2008.

There was a bigger problem with the way the tentative Kashmir peace process unfolded in 2005–6. From the time I started to try and formulate a framework for a Kashmir settlement at the end of the 1990s, I emphasised that the Kashmir conflict is defined by multiple intersecting and mutually reinforcing dimensions.[16] So in *Kashmir: Roots of Conflict, Paths to Peace* (2003), I argued that 'the Kashmir conflict has multiple dimensions and is defined by the complex intersection of an international dispute with sources of conflict internal to the disputed territory and its Indian and Pakistani parts. Any approach to resolving this multi-layered conflict must necessarily involve multiple, but connected and mutually reinforcing, tracks or axes of engagement and dialogue.'[17] In *Contested Lands* (2007), I reiterated that 'the architecture of a viable Kashmir settlement consists of several interlocking elements'.[18]

In 2003 I identified five necessary tracks or axes of dialogue and engagement. These were: the overarching New Delhi–Islamabad axis (a substantive and sustained India–Pakistan intergovernmental process); the New Delhi–Srinagar axis (mending the relationship between Indian authority and the Kashmir Valley, toxic since 1953 and more or less ruptured since 1990, through structured outreach to representatives of independentist and pro-Pakistan politics, as well as to society at large); the Srinagar–Jammu axis (systematic engagement between political and civil society leaders of the Valley and the Jammu region of Indian J&K, which is socioculturally and politically distinct from the Valley and has an overall Hindu majority); the Islamabad–Muzaffarabad axis (a process of rapprochement parallel to Indian J&K between the Pakistani state and dissident groups in 'Azad' Kashmir, especially the persecuted advocates of independentist politics); and finally, the Srinagar–Muzaffarabad axis (addressing the contentious LoC problem).

In 2003, I argued that while the lasting solution to the LoC problem lay in developing 'institutional links between the two Kashmirs [Indian and Pakistani] along with a soft border that permits the movement of citizens', that 'would be the *final* [emphasis added] element of the institutional architecture of an overall settlement'.[19] Such a permanently transformed Jammu and Kashmir border, the linen curtain, would require functioning governments in Indian J&K and Pakistani J&K endowed with reasonable autonomy, based on power-sharing for an initial transitional period between representatives of the basic segments of political opinion: pro-independence, pro-India and pro-Pakistan on the Indian side, and pro-Pakistan and pro-independence on the Pakistani side. I noted that autonomy did not necessarily mean reversion to the pre-1954 status and powers of Indian J&K (Chapter 1), especially since that 'raises complex constitutional questions pertaining to centre-state relations in India and is a sensitive issue in ... Indian politics', and thought it 'likely that some aspects of Indian J&K's post-1953 integration into the Indian Union, even if [effected] under authoritarian conditions, will endure'.[20]

I used the Urdu word *khudmukhtari*, which I translated as 'self-rule' rather than the conventional meaning of independence or sovereignty, to describe the restoration of dignity and voice to the people, especially those of the Kashmir Valley. (The term 'self-rule' got picked up and incorporated into the rhetoric of the People's Democratic Party or PDP, the mainly Valley-based party in Indian J&K formed in 1999 which sought to balance acceptance of Indian sovereignty with support for redressal of popular aspirations. Mufti Mohammad Sayeed, the PDP leader, became Indian J&K's chief minister in November 2002 at the head of a coalition government and held the post until November 2005.) I also stressed that any Indian J&K 'self-rule' framework must recognise the distinct character of the populous Jammu region, and especially the concerns of Hindus who dominate its southern half, by institutionally guaranteeing 'autonomy within autonomy', reinforced further through an upper house of the Indian J&K legislature constituted as a chamber of the regions: Kashmir Valley, Jammu and Ladakh.

A coherent and serious Kashmir peace process thus needed robust development of the critical New Delhi–Srinagar track, as well as the Srinagar–Jammu track. It also needed purposeful progress on the New Delhi–Islamabad track. None of this happened. The result was that when five years of India–Pakistan diplomacy collapsed in 2008, the only takeaway of the Kashmir peace effort was the symbolic 2005–6 opening of the LoC, the two heavily regulated bus and truck routes running from Srinagar to Muzaffarabad and Poonch to Rawalakot. Instead of the building up of the needed multi-pillared settlement, all that had emerged was a single, stunted pillar. The focus on LoC symbolism had, effectively, put the cart before the horse.

In a November 2005 commentary, I observed that 'the current India–Pakistan *détente* is going nowhere slowly'.[21] In *Contested Lands* (2007), I argued that the 'gradualist and piecemeal approach runs the risk of generating a peace process that is little more than a series of disconnected loose ends [and] . . . may simply stack up the odds of eventual failure'. I noted that there had been no progress on any Kashmir-specific issues in the 'composite integrated dialogue' between the two countries, such as de-escalating the military confrontation in the Siachen glacier area north of the LoC, or resolving disagreement over a hydro-electric project on the Chenab river in the northern part of Indian J&K's Jammu region. Thus, I noted, 'the intergovernmental process moves at a glacial pace . . . the key New Delhi–Islamabad track is stalled and concurrently there is little, if any progress on the other vital front: mending and reconstituting the New Delhi–Srinagar relationship'.[22]

As India's prime minister from mid-2004 onwards, Manmohan Singh did continue the practice Vajpayee began of granting audiences in Delhi to 'separatist' figures from the Kashmir Valley, mainly leaders of a non-hawkish faction of the Hurriyat Conference, the umbrella forum of groups advocating 'self-determination'. In February 2006, Singh also met in Delhi with Yasin Malik, the main leader of the independentist JKLF in the Kashmir Valley. Malik was a survivor of the nucleus of angry young men who started the insurgency in the Valley from 1989. Captured in August 1990, he had been imprisoned until mid-1994 and rearrested several times since then. He renounced violence after the mid-1990s, and in 2004–5 JKLF conducted a mass-contact campaign across the Valley which produced 1.5 million signatures to a memorandum calling on India and Pakistan to include Kashmiris in their nascent peace process (the campaign made no attempt to reach out to the Jammu region, or to Ladakh, a sign of both the insular mentality typical of Valley politicians and the habitual reluctance of Kashmir independentists to engage with other points of view). All of these meetings essentially remained photo-op sessions, however, and the ice was not really broken. When Singh's government tried to convene a roundtable of political parties and groups from Indian J&K in 2006, it was shunned by all of the Valley's independentist and pro-Pakistan factions, who apparently mistrusted the government's intentions and doubted its seriousness. The peace process had no momentum.

Manmohan Singh also continued Vajpayee's policy of running secret, high-level lines of communication with Pakistan. Before, during and after the 1999 Kargil War, Vajpayee's back-channel interlocutors with Pakistan – initially Nawaz Sharif's civilian government and then Musharraf's military regime – were Brajesh Mishra, his national security adviser and a retired diplomat, and R.K. Mishra (no relation), formerly a left-wing journalist. From 2004 to 2007, Singh's back-channel emissaries to the Musharraf regime were J.N. Dixit, his national security adviser who died at the beginning of 2005, and subsequently Satinder Lambah, a retired diplomat born in pre-partition Peshawar who had been India's high commissioner (ambassador) to Pakistan from 1992 to 1995. According to an article published in March 2009 in the *New Yorker* magazine by a senior American journalist, Singh's emissaries (mainly Lambah) had some two dozen meetings between the second half of 2004 and early 2007 in hotels in Bangkok, Dubai and London with Tariq Aziz, a bureaucrat and long-time friend of Musharraf's who was made the secretary-general of Pakistan's national security council in 2002.

The discussions focused on finding shared parameters for a Kashmir settlement. The secret dialogue eventually produced a 'non-paper' (an unofficial document with no author attribution) outlining such a settlement, which Musharraf apparently put to the Pakistan Army's leadership in meetings at its Rawalpindi headquarters in early 2007 (the foreign minister, a civilian, also attended). The non-paper apparently had four elements: a soft LoC, gradual reduction of military forces deployed on both sides, self-governance arrangements in both Indian and Pakistani Kashmir, and a joint India–Pakistan mechanism to supervise the settlement. Musharraf spoke in these terms in an interview to an Indian television channel in December 2006. There was apparently discussion of a visit by Singh to Pakistan in the spring of 2007, during which it would be announced that the broad parameters of a Kashmir settlement had been agreed.[23] Singh, a Sikh, had been born in 1932 in a village in north-western Punjab which became part of Pakistan in 1947, whereupon he came to India with his family as a refugee. But the visit did not materialise. It could be that Singh preferred to err on the side of caution, though it was also reported that the Pakistanis requested a delay 'so that Musharraf could regain his political balance' from an eruption of domestic turmoil.[24]

Thereafter, the back-channel trail went cold as the Musharraf regime rapidly unravelled. It began in spring 2007 with an ugly conflict between Musharraf and the country's supreme court, which generated an urban agitation against his regime by lawyers, quickly joined by activists of the political parties sidelined since the coup of October 1999. Musharraf declared in response that he intended to stay in power for another five years. The crisis deepened from July 2007 when Musharraf ordered an army assault on Lal Masjid, a radical mosque in Islamabad with close links to both the Afghan Taliban and al-Qaeda, whose members had kidnapped seven Chinese women and men running a massage parlour in the Pakistani capital that they suspected to be a front for prostitution. Militants armed to the teeth holed up in the heavily fortified mosque compound, which also housed a seminary for women and was laced with bunkers, tunnels and underground chambers, fought back fiercely against the Pakistan Army's Special Services Group (the elite commando force in which Musharraf had himself been a soldier). The assault killed at least 103 persons as per the official death toll – including a number of women militants as well as Afghans and 12 Uighur radicals from China's Xinjiang province – and three times that number according to media reports.[25]

Pakistan then entered a spiral of violence pitting the army and other security forces against radical Islamists. A spate of suicide attacks (47) took place in the remaining months of 2007, and the armed groups confronting the Pakistan Army in FATA (the Federally Administered Tribal Areas bordering Afghanistan) coalesced into the Tehreek-i-Taliban-Pakistan (Taliban Movement of Pakistan, TTP), which by April 2009 controlled territory 60 miles from Islamabad. Pakistan's two top civilian politicians, Nawaz Sharif and Benazir Bhutto, sensed an opportunity to return from exile – in Saudi Arabia and Dubai, respectively. Sharif, Musharraf's *bête noire*, tried to return in September 2007 and was deported back to Saudi Arabia (he successfully returned to Pakistan in November). Bhutto, Zulfiqar Ali Bhutto's daughter and political successor and like Sharif a former two-time prime minister (1988–90 and 1993–96), returned in October after a deal with Musharraf and was assassinated by a suicide bomber just two months later. In November, Musharraf tried to cope with the growing anarchy by declaring emergency rule and suspending the constitution, which made him even more unpopular. In February 2008, parliamentary elections resulted in the deceased Bhutto's Pakistan People's Party (PPP) and Sharif's Pakistan Muslim League-Nawaz (PML-N) emerging as the two largest parties, and they formed a coalition government led by a PPP prime minister which lasted through 2008. By now, Musharraf was living on borrowed time. He had relinquished his position as army chief in November 2007. In August 2008, he resigned as president (self-appointed in June 2001) under pressure from the PPP and PML-N and left the country for exile in London in November 2008. Asif Ali Zardari, Benazir Bhutto's widower, succeeded Musharraf as president.

Had Manmohan Singh's visit to Pakistan happened in spring 2007, a declaration on the broad parameters of a future Kashmir settlement would possibly have been issued by him and Musharraf. Whether that would have led to peace in Kashmir after sixty years of conflict is a counterfactual question which is impossible to answer. By 2007 Musharraf's lack of democratic legitimacy had caught up with his regime and a joint declaration might have been seen in Pakistan – including in its military – as capitulation on Kashmir by a weakening dictator in the twilight of his rule. On the other hand, a declaration outlining a Kashmir settlement framework signed by an incumbent army chief would have set a remarkably positive precedent because the Pakistan Army, the country's bedrock institution, is usually seen as the greatest obstacle to a compromise on Kashmir with India. That Musharraf, the mastermind of the 1999 Kargil War, had turned peacemaker would have signalled an unequivocal turn away from Pakistan's history of waging war (in 1947–48, 1965 and 1999) in the cause of Kashmir and of supporting insurgency through sponsorship of increasingly radical groups from 1988 to 2003.

Singh, for his part, must have had his own worries and doubts. In contrast to Vajpayee, he was a political lightweight who owed his premiership to the favour of Sonia Gandhi – the Italian-born daughter-in-law of Indira Gandhi and widow of her older son Rajiv Gandhi – who took over as leader of the Congress party in 1998 and became the chairperson of the Congress-led alliance of parties which formed a coalition government in mid-2004. The RSS, the core organisation of India's Hindu nationalist movement, bitterly disliked Vajpayee's dovishness on Kashmir and his willingness to engage with Pakistan but could not stop him because he was the only Hindu nationalist leader acceptable as prime minister to the other parties in the BJP-led coalition governments of 1998–2004. Singh, on the other hand, was no political leader at all. He was an economist and career technocrat who became India's finance minister amid an economic crisis in 1991 and largely disappeared from public view once the Congress party lost power in 1996. Unlike Vajpayee, whose lifelong Hindu nationalist credentials made him less vulnerable to being accused of appeasing Kashmir 'separatists' and cavorting with the Pakistani enemy, Singh would have worried about being attacked from the right by the BJP – the main opposition party now led, after Vajpayee's retirement from politics post-2004, by L.K. Advani, a considerably more hardline figure. India's status-quoist position on Kashmir may also have been a factor in Singh's circumspection. With insurgency progressively dwindling in Indian J&K from 2004 onwards, the urgency of seeking diplomatic engagement with Pakistan of the Vajpayee years had also dwindled, and Singh never demonstrated the level of personal commitment to the Kashmir problem that the (possibly) legacy-seeking Vajpayee did.

Indeed, the Vajpayee–Musharraf combination may have been the best bet for an India–Pakistan breakthrough on Kashmir, had Vajpayee been re-elected to lead a coalition government in mid-2004. But that was not to be. The window of opportunity to forge a Kashmir peace, born of the bloodbath in Indian J&K from 1990 to 2004 and the India–Pakistan crises of 1999 and 2002, shut decisively in 2008. A new era of unrest and turmoil began in the festering Kashmir Valley, symbolised by the stone-pelter.

THE 2008 CRISIS IN KASHMIR

Stone-pelting is a hallowed political tradition in the Kashmir Valley. Javed Mir emerged in 1989–90 as one of the four young men leading the independentist JKLF's insurgency in Srinagar. In a 2017 interview, he recalled:

> In 1979, when I entered the freedom movement, I was a hardcore stone-pelter. I was a stone-pelter from 1979 to 1987 before picking up the gun along with Yasin Malik, Hamid Sheikh, Ashfaq Wani and others. Stone-pelting is nothing new. It was there before the armed struggle. Whenever movements like *moi-e-muqaddas* occurred in Kashmir [the 1963–64 Valley uprising triggered by the disappearance of the Prophet's hair from Srinagar's Hazratbal shrine, described in Chapter 1], the people resorted to stone-pelting.[26]

Indeed, while photographic images of rebellion in the Valley from 1990 onward became dominated by hooded gunmen brandishing Kalashnikov rifles, those until 1989 – before the outbreak of large-scale insurgency – are typically of mobs of neighbourhood youths throwing stones and rocks at the local police and the Indian government's Central Reserve Police Force (CRPF).

In the past decade, hundreds of stone-pelters – who are mostly males in their teens and twenties – have like Mir and his comrades in the late 1980s become militants, i.e. gun-wielding guerrillas. But there is no simple or linear relationship between a stone-pelting background and becoming a guerrilla. Stone-pelting is a mass phenomenon, and in the period since 2010 only a relative handful of the tens if not hundreds of thousands who have hit the streets and lobbed stones have gone on to become gunmen. There have also been many cases in recent years of young men without a stone-pelting background – or sometimes even any evident interest in the struggle for *azaadi* (freedom) – suddenly taking to the gun to fight Indian rule. But after being displaced by assault rifles and grenades as the weapons of resistance from 1990 until the mid-2000s, the Valley's tradition of stone-pelting made a strong comeback – especially since 2010, when a stone-pelting uprising convulsed the Valley during the four summer months, June to September. When another massive stone-pelting uprising broke out in July 2016, young women and teenaged girls joined their male counterparts in some places.

Many older, otherwise genteel citizens of the Valley – women as well as men – privately admit that while they don't make a habit of pelting projectiles at the enforcers of Indian authority, they too have thrown the occasional stone, the weapon of everyday protest, in order to vent their feelings.

In October 2002 the People's Democratic Party – the mainly Valley-based party founded in 1999 to seek reform of the coercion-intensive Indian framework of exercising authority – formed a coalition government following elections to the legislature of Indian J&K with the Congress party and small local parties and independent legislators. The programme of the coalition government read:

> The goal of the coalition government is to heal the physical, psycho-logical and emotional wounds inflicted by fourteen years of militancy, to restore the rule of law in Jammu & Kashmir state, to complete the revival of the political process begun by the recently concluded [Indian J&K] elections, and to request the Government of India to initiate and hold sincerely and seriously wide-ranging consultations and dialogue, without conditions, with members of the legislature and other segments of public opinion [primarily a reference to independentist and pro-Pakistan groups, which boycotted the elections] in all three regions of the state [Jammu, Kashmir and Ladakh] to evolve a broad-based consensus for the restoration of peace with honour in the state.[27]

That, of course, did not materialise during the 2004–7 window of opportunity. Instead, Indian J&K, and the Kashmir Valley in particular, continued to be ruled – even as insurgency declined to negligible levels by the late 2000s – under what Agamben calls 'the state of exception': a permanent emergency institutionalised as the technique of government where the law deploys the exception, i.e., the suspension of the rule of law, as its means of controlling an insubordinate population. The state of exception has a long lineage in Indian Jammu and Kashmir, described in Chapters 1 and 2 and briefly at the beginning of this chapter. In its populist manifesto for the autumn 2002 state election, the PDP promised to work to remove Indian J&K from the purview of AFSPA, disband the Special Operations Group

(SOG), the counter-insurgency arm of the J&K police, and set up a commission to investigate the thousands of disappearances since 1990. In March 2015, the Srinagar-based Association of Parents of Disappeared Persons (APDP) requested the PDP leader Mufti Mohammad Sayeed, who had just assumed office as Indian J&K's chief minister for the second time (his first term was November 2002–November 2005), 'to set up an independent commission to probe cases of forced disappearances and unmarked graves in the state'.[28] In 2009, APDP had published a report on 940 unmarked graves located in the Uri area of the Valley.[29] In August 2019, Indian J&K's state status in the Indian Union was revoked by the Hindu nationalist government in New Delhi, and the J&K state human rights commission – which had a general mandate to probe complaints and recommend compensation – consequently ceased to exist along with a range of other institutions. At the time, it had a docket of 10,500 cases, of which 2,600 were being actively investigated.[30]

As long as India–Pakistan parleys offering some hope of a better future were on, the lid could be kept on the simmering cauldron of unredressed rage in the Kashmir Valley. By 2008, it was clear that the parleys had not led anywhere, and the cauldron boiled over.

The Kashmir Valley has been overwhelmingly Muslim since the late fourteenth century, when most of its people converted to Islam under the influence of Sufi mystics (Chapter 1). Until then, the region's dominant tradition was Hinduism of the Shaivite school, which worships the deity Shiva as the Supreme Being. In the mid-nineteenth century, Muslim shepherds discovered an ice formation inside a cave in the mountains of the south-eastern part of the Valley, which came to be regarded as a long-lost manifestation of Shiva mentioned in ancient texts. Since then, the cave shrine, Amarnath, located at an altitude of 12,750 feet, has been a famous Hindu pilgrimage site. Hundreds of thousands from across India come to the Valley every July to undertake the annual summer pilgrimage, the Amarnath *yatra* (journey). The pilgrimage continued with reduced numbers through the insurgency-hit 1990s. In 1996 there was a natural disaster when unseasonal blizzards killed almost 250 pilgrims. For three consecutive years, 2000 to 2002, the pilgrimage – heavily guarded by the Indian Army and paramilitary forces – was attacked by gunmen, probably from the Pakistani Lashkar-e-Taiba group. The deadliest attack in 2000 killed thirty-two people – twenty-one Hindu pilgrims, seven local Muslims accompanying the pilgrims with horses and provisions, and four security personnel. In all, the three attacks killed almost sixty, a mix of pilgrims, local Muslims and soldiers on guard duty.

There are two routes to the cave shrine. The approach from the north, via a hamlet called Baltal, is shorter but very steep. So most pilgrims do the five-day trek from the south which starts at the small town of Pahalgam, nestled in the verdant valley framed by tall peaks of a boulder-strewn stream called the Lidder, which flows down from a glacier.

In May 2008, the government of Indian J&K – a coalition of the PDP and the Congress party, headed since November 2005 as chief minister by Ghulam Nabi Azad, a Congress politician who is a Kashmiri-speaking Muslim from the Jammu region's Doda district – decided to transfer 800 *kanals* (100 acres) of land consisting of pine and birch forests on the Baltal route leading to Amarnath to the Shri Amarnathji Shrine Board, a religious trust which has jurisdiction over the pilgrimage. The ostensible purpose was to facilitate greater access for pilgrims from the northern approach. The decision sparked protests in the Valley in June, and at least six demonstrators were killed in police and CRPF firing. After protests intensified in late June, the government rescinded its land transfer order in early July. That triggered a counter-agitation during July in the Hindu-dominated southern districts of the Jammu region, led by the local wing of the RSS (the parent organisation of India's Hindu nationalist movement), demanding restoration of the land to the religious trust. Tens of thousands rallied and marched in the counter-agitation. The agitation caused disruption to the arterial Jammu–Srinagar road which is the Valley's main link to the outside world via the Banihal Pass.

In response to the 'blockade' to the south, the Valley's fruit-growers' association announced that it would instead sell its produce across the LoC. In the second week of August, tens of thousands joined a *Chalo Muzaffarabad* (let's go to Muzaffarabad) march which started from Srinagar and passed through the northern Valley towns of Sopore and Baramulla en route to the

Uri crossing point. The march was stopped by the police and CRPF on the Baramulla–Uri road and about fifteen demonstrators were killed by gunfire. The marchers were led by two middle-aged men: Shabir Shah (born 1953) and Sheikh Abdul Aziz (born 1952). Both men had been among the founding members of the People's League, a pro-Pakistan youth group formed in the mid-1970s in the Valley. Shah had been imprisoned almost continuously until the mid-1990s, and had been in and out of jail since then. Aziz became a guerrilla chieftain in 1990 and led al-Jehad, a pro-Pakistan insurgent group. Captured in September 1993, he was jailed until 2000 and then spent time in and out of prison between 2001 and 2004. He was allowed to visit Pakistan in 2005, where he kissed the ground upon landing at Lahore airport. On 11 August 2008, Aziz was seriously injured while leading the march to the LoC and died in hospital in Srinagar later that day. He was laid to rest in Srinagar's Eidgah martyrs' cemetery the next day, 12 August, when around a dozen more people were killed by police, CRPF and army firing on protesters across the Valley. On 16 August, several hundred thousand people gathered from across the Valley in Aziz's home-town Pampore, just south of Srinagar, to mourn his death.

The snowballing conflict over a parcel of forest land was puzzling. Most Kashmiri Muslims regard the Amarnath cave shrine as a marker of their heritage, and the pilgrimage has long been an integral part of the Valley's calendar. Besides, the annual event is the main source of income for thousands of poor Muslim families in the Pahalgam area who provide food, provisions and horses to the pilgrims. On the other hand, Hindus living in the Jammu region's southern districts, about 200 miles south of Amarnath, have no particular connection to the holy site or the pilgrimage.

The sudden conflagration was a sign that elements intent on religious polarisation had been emboldened by the failure of the India–Pakistan talks on Kashmir to produce progress, let alone a breakthrough (unbeknownst to them, the back-channel too had fizzled out). Cadres of the fundamentalist Jama'at-i-Islami had been lying low in the Valley for ten years, since the bloody onslaught on them by 'renegade' militants sponsored by the Indian security apparatus during the second half of the 1990s (Chapter 2). They now re-emerged with a vengeance and played a leading part in organising the Amarnath protests, while ceding the most visible roles to non-JI figures like Shabir Shah and Sheikh Abdul Aziz. On the other side, the RSS seized the opportunity to mobilise Jammu Hindus in an emotive religious cause, and confrontation. Here another calculation was at work. The six-yearly election to the Indian J&K legislature was due in autumn 2008, and the BJP, the Hindu nationalist movement's political party, stood to gain from instigating Jammu Hindus on the Amarnath issue. The PDP–Congress coalition government collapsed in July, a few months before the end of its term, after the PDP withdrew from it citing the Congress chief minister's mishandling of the Amarnath matter.

The renewed unrest in Indian J&K was accompanied by sinister developments elsewhere. On the morning of 7 July 2008, a suicide bomber driving a Toyota Camry tailed diplomatic vehicles carrying staff to work at the Indian embassy in Kabul to the embassy compound's gate. The explosive-packed car was detonated at the gate. Fifty-eight people were killed on the busy street lined with Afghan government buildings and embassies, mostly local civilians and Afghan security personnel. Four Indians died – an army brigadier serving as the defence attaché and the embassy's press counsellor, who were about to enter the compound, and two security personnel from the Indo-Tibetan Border Police (ITBP), an elite paramilitary force, who were posted at the gate. An Afghan employee of the mission also died.

Ever since the US ousted the Pakistan-sponsored Taliban regime in October 2001, after the 9/11 attacks, India had been cultivating ties with the post-Taliban government by opening consulates in Herat, Mazar-e-Sharif, Jalalabad and Kandahar and providing generous assistance to Afghan infrastructure and development projects, some involving Indians working on the ground. By 2008 the Indian aid to Afghanistan topped $1 billion. The concerted Indian effort to secure influence in Afghanistan greatly upset the Pakistani military establishment, whose view is that Afghanistan should be its sphere of influence and provide 'strategic depth' in any full-blown war with India – effectively a backyard. There had been minor attacks on Indian facilities and personnel already, but the Kabul attack was of a different order. At the end of July, the US government made it public that its investigations had concluded that the Pakistani military's ISI agency was behind the attack, which had been executed by the Haqqani network, an Afghan group with close ISI ties since the 1980s.[31] The attack happened a month before Musharraf gave up on his last-ditch bid to cling to power and resigned as Pakistan's president, before leaving for exile in London.

Then in the early evening of 26 July 2008, twenty-one small bombs exploded in the space of seventy minutes in Ahmedabad, the largest city of India's western Gujarat state. Many of the bombs were placed on buses serving the evening rush hour, and two of the later blasts were detonated outside the A&E sections of city hospitals just as injured people were being brought in by ambulances. Fifty-six people were killed and over two hundred injured. A hitherto unknown group called 'Indian Mujahideen' claimed responsibility, although Harkat-ul-Jehad-i-Islami, a Pakistani militant group with a record of involvement in the Kashmir insurgency, also did so. Prime Minister Manmohan Singh rushed to Ahmedabad and inspected some of the blast sites accompanied by Narendra Modi, Gujarat's BJP chief minister. Ahmedabad had been targeted before. In autumn 2002, two young men armed with assault rifles and grenades stormed a major Hindu temple and cultural centre in the city in a textbook Kashmir-style *fidayeen* raid. They killed twenty-seven visitors, two police officers and two elite army commandos in a fourteen-hour battle. That attack was seen as retribution for a large-scale pogrom led by Hindu nationalist groups which killed over a thousand Muslims in Gujarat in March 2002, a few months after Modi became the state's chief minister. The pogrom happened after an arson attack on a train in the state killed fifty-nine Hindu nationalist activists.

I recall meeting Manmohan Singh at his official residence in New Delhi in August 2008. I accompanied my mother, Krishna Bose, who was making a courtesy call on the prime minister. Singh asked me what I thought of the tumult in Indian J&K. Since there were several other people present, I replied cautiously that both sides were at fault and the situation needed to be defused expeditiously. My actual view was contained in a commentary titled 'Kashmir: Missed Chances for Peace' published on the BBC's website on 22 August 2008: 'In late 2003, a ceasefire on the LoC took hold and since 2004, relations between India and Pakistan have seen a thaw. But four years later, it is clear that the thaw has not developed into a serious peace process, and that a settlement to the Kashmir dispute is nowhere on the horizon.' Acknowledging the 'symbolic breakthrough' of the two cross-LoC routes opened to limited traffic of people and goods in 2005–6, I noted that 'subsequently, there was no progress in the India–Pakistan dialogue on substantive aspects of the Kashmir problem, even on relatively peripheral issues such as ... the Siachen glacier on the northern fringes of the territory'. I argued that though 'the paralyzed nature of the talks seemed bearable because insurgency ... ebbed during these years', 'in fact the past few years of relative calm represent a major missed opportunity to engage all communities and factions in Kashmir in a genuine and credible – as distinct from an illusory and vacuous – peace process'. I concluded that 'a "let sleeping dogs lie" approach is unwise. Without peace processes leading to political settlements, such flashpoints remain a breeding ground for recurring crises ... The lesson? Frozen conflicts don't stay frozen, and windows of opportunity to make real progress towards solutions don't come often. Stalling on such opportunities can be perilous.'[32] Just how perilous would be revealed merely three months later, in Mumbai in November 2008.

The RSS-led agitation in the southern Jammu districts was called off at the end of August after talks with the Indian government. When I arrived in the Kashmir Valley in September after visiting the city of Jammu, I found that the situation there had subsided as well, though people were seething at the loss of lives. They compared the firing on protesters in the Valley to the restraint shown towards the agitators in Jammu. I was invited to accompany a march organised by the independentist JKLF from Srinagar to the shrine and mausoleum of Sheikh Nooruddin Noorani, the Valley's patron-saint, in the town of Charar-e-Sharief, a distance of about 20 miles. The original mid-fifteenth-century shrine and mausoleum, which burned down along with most of the town in a battle between the Indian Army and insurgents in 1995 (Chapter 2), had been meticulously reconstructed in a twenty-first-century replica. It is the second most important spiritual site for Kashmiri Muslims after Srinagar's Hazratbal shrine.

The march was led by Yasin Malik, JKLF's main leader in the Valley and a pioneering insurgent of 1989–90 who renounced violence in 1994 (he has been held in Delhi's Tihar Jail since early 2019). It began with a couple of hundred people and about a dozen vehicles from Srinagar's old Maisuma neighbourhood – where Malik's house is located, next to Lal Chowk and the city centre. The march gradually swelled to many thousands of participants and hundreds of vehicles as it wound its way through the Srinagar suburbs of Chanapora and Natipora and entered the Badgam district. Hundreds of young men walked alongside the vehicles chanting *Hum kya chahtey? Azaadi!* (What do we want? Freedom!) and *Goli maaro, azaadi! Danda maaro, azaadi! Zor se bolo, azaadi!* (Shoot us, beat us, we will still say, freedom! Say it louder, freedom!). Women, old and young, came out along the route in Badgam to clap and cheer the marchers. The atmosphere was one of measured defiance, not anger, and had a rather festive quality. At Charar-e-Sharief, the townspeople warmly greeted and mingled with the marchers. I spent a sunny and warm autumn afternoon chatting on the rebuilt shrine-mausoleum's grounds with locals and young marchers wearing 'JKLF' bandannas. A mass prayer for Kashmir's salvation was offered, with hundreds of women in colourful headscarves praying in their own enclosure alongside the men.

When Manmohan Singh visited the restive Valley in the second week of October, his experience was different. An Indian newspaper reported: 'Residents of the Kashmir Valley on Saturday observed a "civil curfew" to protest Dr Manmohan Singh's visit. In Srinagar, transport was off the roads and shops, markets and petrol pumps were closed. On Friday, two persons were killed and 75 others including 34 security personnel injured in clashes in the city. According to reports from district towns, a complete shutdown was observed in Anantnag, Bandipora, Baramulla, Badgam, Ganderbal, Kulgam, Kupwara, Pulwama and Shopian.'[33]

MUMBAI AND THE END OF THE PEACE OPENING

In the early evening of 26 November 2008, I was at the theatre in London's Covent Garden. We had just taken our seats when I received a call from my mother, Krishna Bose, in Kolkata (formerly Calcutta). She told me that a major terrorist attack was underway in Mumbai (formerly Bombay), the metropolis that is India's financial nerve centre.

Mumbai had been targeted in mass-casualty attacks before, most recently on 11 July 2006 when seven bombs planted on the city's commuter train network exploded in the space of eleven minutes during the evening rush hour. The high-explosive devices made with RDX and ammonium nitrate were packed in pressure cookers to enhance their lethality in crowded compartments. The timed bombs were planted on rush-hour trains running from a city-centre station to the western suburbs. The toll was huge: 209 people died and 714 were injured in the explosions, which came 8 months after buses, a bustling market and congested public areas had been targeted in the pre-Diwali bombings in New Delhi at the end of October 2005, killing 62 people. Culpability for the July 2006 Mumbai bombings was never ascertained, though a claim suspected to be from a front for Lashkar-e-Taiba – which often uses pseudonyms – was made on 14 July. At the time of the 2006 attacks, India–Pakistan relations were still in a promising phase, and the second cross-LoC route between Poonch and Rawalakot had just been opened.

When I returned home from the theatre to live coverage of Mumbai on every television channel, I realised this attack was different. Gunmen were rampaging across a series of high-profile locations in downtown (south) Mumbai, firing indiscriminately from assault rifles and tossing grenades. They had targeted two luxury hotels, a trendy café, a Jewish cultural centre and the city's main railway terminus. It was clear that there were multiple groups of attackers, operating in two-man teams. The nature of the attacks, and the duo format, rang a very familiar bell to a student of the Kashmir conflict and specifically its phase of *fidayeen* warfare waged intensely by radical Pakistani groups from 1999 to 2003 (Chapter 2), and sporadically thereafter.

The next morning, 27 November, I wrote a piece on the unfolding attacks which was published later that day on the BBC's website. I wrote:

Frontal attacks, usually carried out by two-man teams firing semi-automatic rifles and lobbing grenades, were the favoured tactic of the insurgency in Indian Kashmir between 1999 and 2003. Scores of such attacks were carried out by so-called 'fidayeen' squads in Indian Kashmir during that period. The fidayeen technique, a rudimentary form of 'shock-and-awe' warfare, was introduced into Kashmir by Pakistani radical organizations that entered the Kashmir insurgency from the mid-1990s. The large majority of fidayeen attacks in Kashmir were perpetrated by one such organization, Lashkar-e-Taiba, headquartered in Pakistan and founded and led by Pakistani religious radicals. LeT did over time recruit a handful of local Kashmiris as fidayeen cadre, but most of the attackers were Pakistani nationals who had crossed into Indian Kashmir. Fidayeen attacks have died down in Kashmir since India–Pakistan relations thawed from 2004 onward. But the deployment of exactly the same tactic in Mumbai shows that this technique has now found a new and even more dangerous theatre in which to operate.

I concluded that while 'it is tempting to label the attackers as "crazies"... it is more than likely that the masterminds are seasoned operatives and the foot-soldiers, young as they may have been, had undergone rigorous training for months, perhaps years'.[34]

The assault on Mumbai ended on the morning of 29 November, when attackers holed up in the city's Taj Mahal Hotel, opened in 1903, were killed by Indian commandos. A photograph of the building's imposing façade belching smoke from a fire set by the gunmen is the iconic image of the 'terrorist spectacular', as I called the attacks in the BBC article.

The Mumbai attacks killed 166 people: 141 Indians, 6 Americans, 4 Israelis, 3 Germans, and citizens of Australia, Canada, France, Italy, the United Kingdom, the Netherlands, Japan, Jordan, Malaysia, Mauritius, Mexico, Singapore and Thailand. The Indian dead included fifteen police officers and two army commandos. Nine of the ten terrorists were killed, but one was captured alive in a lightly wounded condition. He turned out to be Ajmal Kasab, 21, from a village in the central part of Pakistan's Punjab province. Born into a very poor family, he had been a juvenile delinquent and petty criminal before being recruited and indoctrinated by LeT one year before the attacks. He and the other members of the squad received rigorous training at multiple locations in Pakistan's 'Azad' Kashmir, in both the northern Muzaffarabad and the southern Mirpur districts. The training consisted of a series of increasingly challenging courses run by retired Pakistan Army officers who had joined LeT, and included commando tactics and marine warfare. Of the nine slain terrorists, eight were from towns and villages in Pakistani Punjab and one from the Khyber-Pakhtunkhwa province. They were all around Kasab's age. Kasab was caught on CCTV entering the railway terminus with his rifle clearly visible; he and his accomplice killed fifty-eight people there. He was executed by hanging in November 2012.

The ten men had set off for Mumbai by boat from an embarkation point near Karachi. In the Arabian Sea, they had intercepted an Indian fishing trawler, killed four of its five occupants and forced its captain to sail to Mumbai. On approaching Mumbai, they had abandoned the trawler after killing the captain and come ashore in two inflatable dinghies at about 8 p.m. on 26 November. They had been thoroughly briefed about the targets and carried GPS devices in addition to their weapons. The targets had been reconnoitred in 2007–8 by a man called Daood Gilani, son of a Pakistani father and an American mother, who performed the task under the pseudonym David Coleman Headley (Headley was his mother's maiden name). Gilani, a former drug-peddler, had been an on–off informant for the US Drug Enforcement Administration (DEA) for many years; unknown to his American handlers, he had been recruited by LeT in the early 2000s. On 28 November, with the attacks still in progress, a caller purporting to be Pranab Mukherjee, India's foreign minister, threatened President Asif Zardari of Pakistan with war. Zardari, who had assumed the presidency two months earlier after Musharraf quit, was panicked, and the Pakistani armed forces were put on high alert. The impersonator turned out to be Ahmed Omar Saeed Sheikh, the British-born terrorist who had been released from prison in India at the end of 1999 after the Kandahar hijack episode (Chapter 2). Arrested in February 2002 and sentenced to death later that year for his role in the kidnapping and murder by al-Qaeda of the American journalist Daniel Pearl in Karachi, he had made the call from his death-row prison cell in Pakistan.

It is improbable that an attack of this scope and magnitude could have been planned without the knowledge and collusion of elements in the Pakistani military's 'deep state'. Indeed, a serving ISI officer, 'Major Iqbal', seems to have been a key plotter along with the second-in-command of LeT, Zaki-ur Rehman Lakhvi, who hails from the same district of Pakistani Punjab as Ajmal Kasab. In 2002, Vajpayee's government ordered a full-scale military mobilisation on Pakistan's borders after the 13 December 2001 terrorist attack on India's parliament building in New Delhi recounted in Chapter 2. Singh's government chose not to escalate tensions in that manner. But the Mumbai atrocity was the death-knell of the slow-motion intergovernmental dialogue ongoing since 2004. That did not resume until 2010, and when it did it took the form of going through the motions. Any residual hope of an India–Pakistan modus vivendi on Kashmir ended in November 2008.

While international attention riveted on the terrorist attack in Mumbai, Indian Jammu and Kashmir was going through its six-yearly election to constitute a fresh state legislature and government. The election to eighty-seven single-member constituencies (forty-six in the Valley, thirty-seven in Jammu and four in Ladakh) had been delayed from the autumn due to the Amarnath disturbances, and was staggered over seven different days between mid-November and late December to allow maximum concentration of security forces in areas going to the polls. As many as 1,354 candidates including 517 independents ran, an average of 16 contestants per seat. Polling in sixteen constituencies, including six in the northern Valley, had already been completed when the terrorists struck Mumbai. In the first phase of polling, held on 17 November, there was a moderate to brisk turnout in the Valley's rural areas, as well as the Jammu region and Ladakh. This trend by and large continued in the five polling days after the Mumbai attacks: 30 November and 7, 13, 17 and 24 December.

By the time polling concluded, 60 per cent across Indian J&K had voted, and the percentage was even higher in some of the Valley's rural areas. The election boycott call given by the spectrum of pro-Pakistan and pro-independence groups was not particularly effective, except in the city of Srinagar and other Valley towns, although it must be noted that the boycott campaign was severely curbed by restrictions on public gatherings and the detention of leaders and key activists. In contrast to the 2002 state election, there was hardly any militant violence, nor were there reports of forced voting in villages by army troops as had happened in the 2002 and 1996 elections

(Chapter 2). The significant turnout in the Valley was driven by the lively rivalry between the National Conference and the People's Democratic Party, the two India-aligned political parties, as well as the capacity of some individual candidates to mobilise supporters at the grassroots level. There were even credible reports of cadres of the fundamentalist, pro-Pakistan Jama'at-i-Islami (JI) party canvassing support for PDP candidates in some rural constituencies, especially in the southern Valley, in order to defeat the NC.

The election threw up a 'hung' or fractured legislature, as expected. The NC once again emerged as the single largest party, winning in twenty-eight constituencies – the same number as in 2002 – mostly from the Valley. The PDP improved on its 2002 performance by winning in twenty-one constituencies, almost all from the Valley, up from sixteen in 2002. The Congress party slipped slightly from twenty in 2002 to seventeen wins, mostly from the Jammu region. The Hindu nationalist BJP, which had just one member in the 2002–8 legislature, got eleven seats, all in Hindu-dominated constituencies in the Jammu region, by riding on the Amarnath agitation. Since the NC and PDP could not come together, being sworn rivals, the Congress – the party leading the 2004–9 coalition government in New Delhi – held the trump card on which of the two to join in a coalition government in the state. The Congress's central leadership headed by Sonia Gandhi dumped the PDP, its coalition partner from 2002 to 2008, and chose the NC, possibly as payback for the PDP's decision to withdraw from the PDP–Congress state government in July 2008, during the Amarnath crisis (the reason given was that the NC, being the single largest party, was more deserving of support). The third-generation bearer of the Abdullah family's dynastic mantle, Farooq Abdullah's son Omar, 38, became Indian J&K's chief minister for the next six years, until late 2014.

The blowing over of the Amarnath crisis, and the unexpectedly respectable turnout in most of the Valley in the state election, probably induced a sense of complacency in the Indian government. That confidence would only have grown when the Congress party was re-elected to lead a coalition government in New Delhi for a second five-year term in May 2009. In the 2009 Indian general election, the Congress, the grand old party of India which had been in decline since the end of the 1980s, sharply increased its numbers in parliament, though still much short of a majority, as a BJP challenge led by the octogenarian veteran L.K. Advani failed to gain traction.

Any notion that India's Kashmir problem was under control was an illusion. The Valley was still a tinderbox, far from pacified. The end of hopes of a settlement with the failure of the India–Pakistan *détente*, coupled with the undiluted power of the police state and the military over the population, made for an explosive mix.

THE 2010 UPRISING

After the disturbances of 2008, the Kashmir Valley almost slipped into another summer of unrest in 2009, sparked by an incident at the end of May in a village in its south-western Shopian district. Neelofar Jan, a 22-year-old married woman with a small child, and her sister-in-law Aasiya Jan, 17, had gone out to tend the family orchard (the area is one of two in the Valley famous for producing apples, the other being around the northern town of Sopore). The two did not return home, and the next morning their bodies were found by a nearby rivulet. Rumours spread, first locally and then like wildfire across the Valley, that Neelofar and Aasiya had been raped and murdered by Indian Army personnel.

In the first week of June, the Valley was paralysed by a *hartal* (general strike) amid stone-throwing demonstrations. Syed Ali Shah Geelani (born 1929), the leading JI figure in the Valley, was especially active in spreading the protests. Police and CRPF action caused scores of serious injuries, though deaths were few. The authorities thwarted large marches by imposing curfews and placing the senior leaders of independentist and pro-Pakistan groups under house arrest or in outright detention. On 6 June, the state government appointed a retired judge to investigate the Shopian incident, who reported on 21 June that rape and murder had taken place. The government then suspended the two top police officers in the Shopian district, along with a mid-ranking and a junior officer, for negligence of duty and destruction of evidence; they were subsequently arrested as well. Two doctors who had done autopsies on the bodies were also charged with negligence and suspended from their government jobs. The protests subsided thereafter, but the episode revealed the Valley's volcanic reality, where a single incident could bring an eruption of large-scale unrest. The case was handed over to the Central Bureau of Investigation (CBI), the Indian government's premier investigative agency, which reported in December 2009 that the deaths were due to drowning, and charged thirteen people including six doctors and five lawyers for 'fabricating evidence of rape and murder'.[35] The CBI also exonerated the police officers of any negligence or wrongdoing. Shakeel Ahangar, Neelofar's husband and Aasiya's older brother, refuses to believe that his wife and sister could have drowned in an ankle-deep rivulet in an area they knew well.

The remote Machil sector on the Line of Control in the northern Valley's Kupwara district has been a route for guerrilla infiltration since 1990. In November 2020, for example, three guerrillas who penetrated the 'Anti-Infiltration Obstacle System' there were intercepted and killed in a gun-battle in which three Indian Army personnel, including an officer, died, along with a BSF soldier. Along with the Keran and Tangdhar sectors in the same district, Machil has been among the top dozen or so crossover points for the past three decades for insurgents infiltrating into Indian J&K along the 742-kilometre LoC and the 198-kilometre border south of the LoC between the south-western part of Indian J&K's Jammu region and Pakistan's Punjab province.

On 30 April 2010, the Indian Army briefed the media in Srinagar that three insurgents trying to infiltrate from Pakistani Kashmir had been intercepted and killed in the Machil sector:

Scuttling an infiltration bid, the army today gunned down three heavily armed militants near the LoC in Kupwara district of north Kashmir. The group made an abortive attempt to sneak in and were shot dead by troops in Machil sector, 150 kilometres from here [Srinagar] in the wee hours, the defence spokesman Lt-Col J.S. Brar said. Brar said security personnel observed the movement of the militants at about 3am and challenged the armed intruders, who opened fire. The troops retaliated and in the ensuing battle, the militants were killed. Five AK assault rifles and a pistol were recovered from them. He said the identity of the slain militants could not be ascertained immediately.[36]

They were Shahzad Ahmed Khan, 27, Riyaz Ahmad Lone, 20, and Mohammad Shafi Lone, 19, all from a village called Nadihal in the Rafiabad area of the northern Valley's Baramulla district, a three-hour drive from the place on the LoC where they died. Shahzad was a pushcart vendor in the market in Baramulla town, Riyaz a manual labourer, and Shafi a helper at an automobile repair shop in the small town of Sangrama, also in the Baramulla district. On 29 April, the three youths went in a rented vehicle to an army camp in the Machil sector. They were taken there by a man from their village, Bashir Ahmed Lone, who told them that he had arranged work for them as porters for the army, a common form of casual employment for villagers living on the LoC. The youths, living on the margins of subsistence, were attracted by the offer of a good daily wage. Bashir Lone was a former special police officer (SPO), the designation given in the second half of the 1990s to insurgents who surrendered and became auxiliaries of the Indian counter-insurgency campaign, and were usually attached to the nearest unit of the Rashtriya Rifles (RR), the army troops assigned to counter-insurgency. In 2010, he had a brother serving in the Special Operations Group (SOG), the specialist counter-insurgency arm of the J&K police. Bashir Lone had in early April visited and spent several hours at the Machil army camp – manned by soldiers from the 4th Rajputana Rifles, the regiment involved in the 1991 incident in the Kupwara villages of Kunan and Poshpora described in Chapter 2. After dropping the three youths off at the Machil army camp on 29 April, he and two accomplices – both also Kashmiri Muslims – shared out a cash payment of 150,000 Indian rupees received at the camp.

The families of the three young men raised an alarm when they went missing. They first confronted the ex-SPO, who told them he knew nothing, then filed a missing persons' report at their local police station on 10 May, and finally organised a sit-in on a major road to attract attention. On 28 May an Urdu newspaper, *Kashmir Uzma*, published photographs on its front page of the faces and upper bodies of the trio killed in the 30 April Machil 'encounter'. The photographs had been taken prior to the disposal of the corpses in a graveyard in the Machil area. The dead men in the photographs had beards and moustaches, and were dressed in Afghan-style clothes. The families said the youths were clean-shaven and had been wearing Western-style trousers and shirts with sweaters when they left home on 29 April. But that aside, they were easily recognised by the families as Shahzad, Riyaz and Shafi. The bodies were exhumed and brought back to Nadihal for reburial. A mob attacked the ex-SPO's house, who fled the village with his family before being arrested.[37]

An uproar ensued across the Valley over the Machil murders. The Valley was seething with fury when Manmohan Singh, the Indian prime minister, arrived in Srinagar on 7 June 2010 on a previously scheduled two-day visit. His major programme in the city was delivering the convocation speech at a university, during which he said: 'There are a handful of people [here] who don't want any political process for empowering people to succeed. This is the reason attempts to disturb the lives of people in the Valley continue from across the Line of Control. Our security agencies are forced to act in the wake of such incidents. Sometimes, innocent civilians have to suffer.'[38]

As Manmohan Singh departed for Delhi, stone-throwing crowds took to the streets in Srinagar and across the Valley. In the early evening of Friday 11 June, Tufail Ahmad Mattoo, a 17-year-old high school student, got caught up in a clash between stone-pelters and the security forces in old Srinagar's Rajouri Kadal area. Rajouri Kadal is one of the old city's protest flashpoints, and stone-pelting was often especially intense on Fridays, erupting after the afternoon prayer congregations in mosques. Tufail was walking home to Saidakadal in the old city's Rainawari area from a coaching class for medical school entrance examinations, when a police tear-gas shell hit his head and exploded. The impact split his skull open, and his brains fell out on the road.

Tufail's middle-class parents – I met his gracious father, Mohammad Ashraf Mattoo, in Srinagar in 2017 – wanted him to be buried in a family graveyard plot. That was not to be. On 12 June 2010, Tufail's bier was carried through the streets in a procession of thousands chanting slogans for *azaadi* (freedom) to the Eidgah martyrs' cemetery, where he was laid to rest.

Tufail Mattoo's death ignited a summer of rage in the Kashmir Valley.[39] Over the next four months, the Valley was convulsed by a massive stone-pelting uprising in which tens of thousands of teenaged boys and young men in their twenties and thirties confronted the police and CRPF every day, week after week, often defying curfew orders. By the time the volcanic eruption subsided around the end of September about 120 protesters were dead, the vast majority young stone-pelters shot by the police and CRPF and occasionally by the army when military convoys on the Valley's roads came under stone-pelting attack. At least 1,500 protesters were seriously injured, as were several hundred police and CRPF personnel.

The 2010 uprising was a transformational moment in the *azaadi* struggle, for two reasons. First, although the established leaders of various factions of the 'self-determination' movement tried to assert control and even proprietorship over the uprising by issuing directives and protest schedules, the uprising was and stayed largely spontaneous, driven by popular emotion. Second and even more important, I noted in a 2011 Al Jazeera commentary that the 2010 uprising of the stone-pelters marked the emergence of 'a new generation of resistance' in Kashmir. 'Unlike the previous generation who picked up the AK-47,' I added, 'this generation's weapon of choice is the stone, but the sense of grievance is equally intense.'[40]

In a BBC commentary published in September 2010, I argued that 'a combination of near-term, medium-term and long-term factors have come together to generate the most severe unrest seen in Kashmir since the early 1990s'. 'In the near term,' I wrote, 'the Congress party-led government that has been in power in New Delhi since mid-2004 has aggravated a festering problem by neglecting it' and 'over six years, shown no initiative to mend the fraught relationship with the people of the Kashmir Valley.' Moreover, 'Delhi's failure to grasp the nettle has been compounded by the indifferent performance of the [Indian J&K] state government elected at the end of 2008. The head of that government, Omar Abdullah, is the grandson of Sheikh Mohammad Abdullah, Kashmir's most important political leader from the 1930s until his death in 1982', but 'unlike his grandfather, is no man of the masses. He has been out of touch with the grassroots of even his own party, the National Conference' (the third-generation Abdullah, who was incarcerated by Narendra Modi's Hindu nationalist government from August 2019 to March 2020, mainly communicates through tweets, which have a following among Delhi-based liberal Indian media).

However, I argued, 'the renewed turmoil must be understood in a much longer time-frame'. In particular:

> The last twenty years have seen the brutalization of local society, particularly in the Kashmir Valley. An entire generation has grown up and come of age in an environment of repression and violence. This is the generation of 'stone-pelters', for whom the stone has replaced the AK-47s wielded by so many of the previous generation. Despite the sharp decline of insurgency to near-negligible levels, the Valley remains a police-state. The new generation are unwilling to put up with such a situation.

Yet, I argued, a perspective going back six and not two decades was needed to understand the twenty-first-century mutation of the conflict, since:

> The deep sense of oppression being vented by the stone-pelters goes back sixty years. Their grandparents' generation recall the 1950s and 1960s, when popular leaders – most notably Sheikh Abdullah himself – were cast into jail, harsh police methods used to muzzle dissent and elections doctored to install New Delhi's favoured clients in office. Their parents' generation grew up in the 1970s and 1980s, when any tentative liberalization of India's Kashmir policy relapsed into draconian control and election-rigging. By the mid-1980s, the [then] young generation was already a long way down the path to insurgency.[41]

The Indian government was apparently taken by surprise by the uprising and its ferocity. Its response was feeble and belated. Manmohan Singh took until mid-September to convene an all-party meeting in Delhi to discuss the crisis, by which time the death toll had reached 100. Following the meeting, a cross-party delegation of senior Indian politicians visited the Valley; a few literally knocked on the doors of pro-'self-determination' leaders and were rebuffed. As they visited the shut-down Valley, rioting erupted in the Muslim-dominated Jammu districts of Poonch and Rajouri after a Koran-burning incident in Florida on the anniversary of the 9/11 attacks in the US. Meanwhile, the BJP, the main opposition party, warned the Singh government against any move to dilute the Armed Forces Special Powers Act, in force in Indian J&K since 1990, in order to 'appease' the protesters. In October, Singh's government appointed a three-member panel consisting of Delhi-based persons – a (male) journalist, a (female) civil society activist and a (male and Muslim) academic who was then also serving in a formal role in the Indian government's bureaucracy – to act as its 'interlocutors' with Indian J&K's diverse sociocultural communities and political groups. The panel submitted a report in October 2011, which was made public by being uploaded on the Indian home (interior) ministry's website in May 2012. The report made a variety of tentatively worded suggestions, including looking at 'amendment' of the J&K Public Safety Act and 're-appraisal' of AFSPA. There was no follow-up on any of its ideas until May 2014, when the Congress party was almost obliterated in the Indian general election and the BJP led by Narendra Modi took office in New Delhi with a decisive parliamentary majority. In July 2014, the junior minister for home affairs in Modi's government told parliament that 'the government has taken no decisions on the report, and will welcome an informed debate on its contents'.[42]

Four years after the Machil murders, five military personnel, including two officers, were found guilty by an army court-martial, which sentenced them to life in prison. Colonel Dinesh Pathania, commanding officer of the Machil army camp in 2010, headed the list, and the other officer, who was likewise dismissed from service, had held the rank of captain. It is not known what their motive was, but it was probably a ploy to secure out-of-turn promotions, gallantry awards or – most likely – hefty cash prizes given for militant 'kills'. Wanted militants in Indian J&K are graded by the security apparatus according to assessments of their importance and the risk they pose, and award monies are greater the higher the grade of the eliminated militant. In the Machil case, the three innocent youths were being passed off as Pakistani infiltrators. When the verdict and the life sentences were made public in November 2014, their families welcomed the outcome despite the inordinate delay. But in July 2017 the armed forces tribunal's principal bench, which sits in Delhi and functions as an appeals court for military trials, suspended the court-martial's verdict and set all five convicts free on bail. The tribunal ruled that the court-martial had relied on 'circumstantial evidence'. One of the two army majors who represented the convicts as lawyers before the tribunal said that the men had been 'fighting for the nation', and the other claimed that 'it was not a case of fake encounter, but a fake trial'.[43] The families in Kashmir were stunned by the turn of events.

The acquittal of the accused killers in 2017 reinforced the climate of impunity entrenched in Kashmir since the early 1990s. In July 2020 an incident eerily similar to the 2010 Machil murders took place in the Valley's south-western Shopian district. On 16 July, three youths from the Jammu region's Rajouri district – Imtiyaz Ahmed and Abrar Ahmed, both in their early twenties, and Mohammad Ibrar, 16 – arrived in the Shopian district to look for work as seasonal labourers and rented a room in a village called Chowgam. The trio were cousins from adjacent villages in the Rajouri district – from where the Shopian district is easily accessible by a road opened in 2012 that descends into the Valley from the Pir Panjal Pass (11,500 feet) – and the fruit-picking season was about to begin in Shopian's extensive orchards. Chowgam has a camp of the Indian Army's 62nd Rashtriya Rifles (RR), troops assigned to counter-insurgency duties in the interiors of Indian Jammu and Kashmir.

The families in Rajouri could not contact the youths on their mobile phones from 18 July onwards, and on 9 August they made a missing persons' report at their local police station. Meanwhile, on 19 July, Brigadier Ajay Katoch, the RR commander in the sector, had briefed the media on a successful operation in a village called Amshipora, 6 miles from Chowgam:

On the night of 17–18 July, we received human intelligence of the presence of four to five unidentified terrorists in Amshipora. At 02:45 on 18 July, when the cordon party was laying the cordon, they came under heavy fire. At 05:30, after there was visibility, a search party moved into the target house, newly constructed. The search party came under fire from inside the house. In the ensuing action, three terrorists were neutralized. The bodies of the terrorists along with their arms and ammunition and IED [improvised explosive device] materials recovered were handed over to J&K police.

On 13 August, in response to the missing persons' report, a police team took DNA samples from the Rajouri families to match them with the Amshipora corpses. On 18 September, the army command in Srinagar issued a statement: 'The three unidentified terrorists killed in Op Amshipora were Imtiyaz Ahmed, Abrar Ahmed and Mohammad Ibrar, who hailed from Rajouri'. The statement further said that enquiries had 'brought out certain *prima facie* evidence which indicate that during the operation, powers vested under the Armed Forces Special Powers Act were exceeded ... Consequently, the competent disciplinary authority has directed to initiate proceedings under the Army Act against those found prima-facie answerable.'[44] In December, Indian media reported that the army enquiry had found an officer of the rank of major – whose name was not disclosed – 'culpable' in the case.[45]

The second term (2009–14) of the Congress-dominated coalition government headed by Manmohan Singh is almost universally regarded as shambolic. The government was dogged by growing popular perceptions that it tolerated high-level corruption and lacked direction and leadership. The perception of drift became focused on the figure of the prime minister, who came to be widely viewed as a weak leader excessively deferential to Sonia Gandhi, the Congress party's powerful president, and her son Rahul, the party's heir apparent. The perception, resulting in part from Singh's own sycophantic utterances, that his role was primarily keeping the chair warm for a dynastic succession was especially damaging to the prime minister's credibility. The government became very unpopular in its last two years (2012–14), and the backlash, due to the absence of any other alternative, propelled the BJP – fronted by a new leader, Narendra Modi, who promised purposeful leadership and a vision for India's progress – to power in May 2014. The Congress party was decimated; its leadership of two coalition governments since mid-2004 had temporarily obscured the reality that it had become organisationally shrivelled in large parts of the country due to its top-down, dynastic culture since the 1970s. The BJP won a narrow majority in parliament in May 2014, the first time any party had done so since the Congress's last resounding victory in December 1984.

The drift that defined the second Singh government was also true of its Kashmir policy – or lack thereof. The absence of political initiative was compounded by the government's projecting of a hardline stance on Kashmir in its last year and a half, most probably in an attempt to demonstrate muscular 'nationalist' credentials and play to the gallery as the 2014 election approached. In January 2013, the habitually soft-spoken prime minister resorted to tough rhetoric after an incident on the LoC in the Poonch district in which Pakistani troops killed two Indian soldiers, one of whom was found beheaded. As some Indian television channels called for revenge, Singh declared that 'after this barbaric act, there cannot be business as usual with Pakistan' and suspended a 2012 agreement which would have provided Pakistani visitors over 65 years old with visas on arrival in India. The BJP's leader in the Lok Sabha, the directly elected chamber of India's parliament, said that 'this has some echo of tough measures we have demanded'. The Indian Army's chief cut a different tone – he said the LoC is 'peaceful at large', barring 'localized incidents' which would be 'forcefully retaliated'.[46]

Although India's criminal laws allow for capital punishment, executions are very rare. In February 2013, such an execution took place when Mohammad Afzal Guru, a 43-year-old Kashmiri originally from the northern Valley town of Sopore, was hanged in Delhi's Tihar prison. Guru had been arrested in December 2001 along with two other men (one a cousin of his) and the cousin's wife for allegedly abetting the five gunmen – most likely from the Pakistani Jaish-e-Mohammad jihadist group – who attacked the Indian parliament in New Delhi on 13 December 2001 (Chapter 2). In December 2002 the three men were sentenced to death by a special anti-terrorism court, and the woman to five years in jail. In October 2003, the Delhi high court upheld the death sentences of Guru and his cousin but acquitted the other man and the cousin's wife. Then in August 2005, India's supreme court upheld Guru's death sentence but commuted the cousin's punishment to ten years in prison, to include time already served. Guru made a mercy petition to the president of India, and his sentence was kept in abeyance pending a decision.

In November 2012 Pranab Mukherjee, a senior Congress politician who had been elected to India's largely ceremonial presidency in July, asked India's home (interior) minister – also a senior Congress politician – for an opinion on Guru's case. The home minister recommended on 23 January 2013 that Guru be executed, and the president then rejected the mercy petition on 3 February. This sequence of events became known retrospectively, when it was announced on 9 February that Guru had been hanged that morning. His family in the Kashmir Valley learned about the execution like everyone else, through the official announcement relayed by the media. A formal notification sent by post and a letter Guru wrote to his wife as his last wish reached the family two and three days, respectively, after the execution. Curfew was imposed in the Valley on 9 February and cable TV and internet services suspended – even so, there were scattered stone-pelting protests.

The matter of Guru's guilt, and whether he deserved the death sentence, had generated a lively debate in India for several years. His hanging, and especially the fact that his family had not been privately informed and allowed to meet him one last time, inflamed public opinion in the Valley. Guru's execution happened almost exactly twenty-nine years after JKLF leader Maqbool Butt's hanging in the Tihar prison on 11 February 1984. Butt's hanging turned him into an iconic martyr for pro-independence people on both sides of the LoC and fuelled the growth of youth militancy in the Valley during the second half of the 1980s. Like Butt's, Guru's body was buried in the prison compound, and in death, Guru became a figure of reverence for the new, twenty-first-century generation of angry Kashmiri youth. The BJP chief minister of Gujarat, Narendra Modi, who was declared the party's prime ministerial candidate shortly afterwards in June 2013, tweeted 'better late than never'. Modi had been calling for Guru's death sentence to be carried out for some time.

Manmohan Singh's swan song in Kashmir was a visit he made to Indian J&K in June 2013, accompanied by Sonia Gandhi. It was his first visit to the state since June 2010, when his remarks in Srinagar set off mass rioting in the Valley. The Valley saw a surge in militant attacks after Guru's execution, and thirty members of the security forces died between February and June. After the 2010 uprising, a steady trickle of youths had moved from stone-pelting to taking up the gun to fight Indian rule. On the eve of Singh and Gandhi's visit, Hizb-ul Mujahideen militants shot two policemen dead in Srinagar's city centre, followed by an ambush in a city suburb on an army convoy that killed eight soldiers and wounded thirteen others. The latter incident was the biggest insurgent attack in over five years. Singh and Gandhi, accompanied by Omar Abdullah, laid the foundation stone of a hydroelectric power plant on the Chenab river in the Jammu region's mountainous Kishtwar district, just south of the Valley. Singh said: 'India is firmly united against terrorism. We won't let them succeed in their nefarious designs.' He noted that insurgency had 'shown a sharp decline and is the lowest in two decades' and added that the upsurge in attacks 'will not deter the security forces, who are engaged in bringing peace and order to the Kashmir Valley'. The Valley observed a total *hartal* (general strike) to protest the visit, and in Srinagar, 'security forces enforced curfew-like restrictions in the congested and volatile old city' to prevent demonstrations. 'We are confined in our homes every time a politician from Delhi visits our Kashmir,' a resident complained.[47]

NARENDRA MODI TAKES POWER

Narendra Modi, 63, took office as India's fourteenth prime minister on 26 May 2014. It was a remarkable coming in from the cold for a man dogged for twelve years by the long shadow of the Gujarat pogrom of 2002 (Modi was the western Indian state's chief minister from October 2001 to May 2014). In 2005, the US denied him a diplomatic visa on the eve of a planned visit on the basis of a 1998 federal law which bars foreign government officials guilty of 'particularly severe violations of religious freedom' and revoked an ordinary visa he already held. The United Kingdom, too, shunned contact with Modi's Gujarat government until 2012.

Modi invited the premiers of all member states of the South Asian Association for Regional Cooperation (SAARC) to his glittering swearing-in ceremony (inauguration) at New Delhi's Rashtrapati Bhavan – the Indian president's residence, built in the 1920s as the British viceroy's palace. SAARC consists of Pakistan, Bangladesh, Afghanistan, Sri Lanka, Nepal, Bhutan and the Maldives, in addition to India. Media attention and speculation focused on whether Pakistan's prime minister would accept. That prime minister was Nawaz Sharif, with whom Atal Bihari Vajpayee, India's first Hindu nationalist prime minister, had begun the ill-fated peace process with Pakistan in 1998–99 (Chapter 2). Sharif had returned from forced exile in Saudi Arabia in November 2007, towards the end of Musharraf's rule, and in May 2013 became prime minister for the third time after his party, Pakistan Muslim League (Nawaz), or PML-N – which is enduringly popular in Pakistan's most populous province, Punjab – won a narrow parliamentary majority. The mid-2013 election was the first time since Pakistan's formation in 1947 that an elected civilian government (headed since Musharraf's fall in 2008 by the Pakistan People's Party, PPP) completed its full term and a peaceful transition occurred to another civilian government after elections. Sharif attended Modi's inauguration bearing, he said, 'a message of peace'. Modi's gesture raised the intriguing possibility that, once in power, he might choose to distance himself from hardline Hindu nationalist politics and emulate Vajpayee's strategy of diplomacy with Pakistan and moderation on Kashmir. Vajpayee had used a summit of SAARC premiers in Islamabad in January 2004 to seal the *détente* with the Musharraf regime.

In Indian Jammu and Kashmir, the six-yearly state election was due to be held in late 2014. In September 2014, massive floods occurred there after a spell of torrential late-monsoon rainfall. Both sides of the LoC were affected, as was Pakistani Punjab. It was the most serious natural disaster since the October 2005 earthquake centred on Muzaffarabad which devastated the northern part of Pakistan's 'Azad' Kashmir. The Kashmir Valley was the worst-hit region. The Jhelum river burst its banks in Srinagar and several hundred thousand citizens had their homes flooded and neighbourhoods marooned. A few hundred villages in the Valley south of Srinagar were also underwater. In the Jammu region, the main problem was caused by landslides, which disrupted road connections. About 300 people died in Indian J&K. The inept response of the Indian J&K state government sealed the already unpromising electoral prospects of the National Conference-led government headed by Omar Abdullah, in office since the end of 2008.

The election to constitute a new eighty-seven-member Indian J&K state legislature was staggered over five days: 25 November (in fifteen constituencies), 2 December (eighteen), 9 December (sixteen), 14 December (eighteen) and 20 December (twenty). The overall turnout was 65 per cent, and higher than that in many rural areas of the Valley. The boycott call given by the

1. Jammu and Kashmir Liberation Front (JKLF) guerrillas, fighting for an independent state, mingle with the public in Srinagar, the Kashmir Valley's capital (August 1991). JKLF launched the insurgency that began in Indian Kashmir from 1989 and dominated the insurrection until 1993, during its most popular phase.

2. Indian soldiers firing artillery during the Kargil War (June 1999). The Kargil War was a fierce conflict fought between India and Pakistan from May to July of 1999 along a barren, mountainous stretch of the Line of Control (LoC) between Indian and Pakistani Kashmir, mostly in the Kargil district of Indian Kashmir's Ladakh region.

3. A Pakistani soldier on the Line of Control in the Neelum Valley (2004). The 742-kilometre LoC originated in January 1949, at the end of the first Kashmir war between India and Pakistan, as the Ceasefire Line (CFL) dividing the Indian and Pakistani parts of Jammu and Kashmir. It was renamed 'Line of Control' by an intergovernmental agreement in 1972, after the third India–Pakistan war. The LoC is probably the world's most militarised frontier.

4. Pakistani soldiers on a spur, at 18,655 feet, of the Siachen glacier (2005). The glacier lies in the far north of Jammu and Kashmir, beyond the northernmost point of the demarcated LoC and at the trijunction of (Indian) Ladakh, (Pakistani) Gilgit-Baltistan and China's Xinjiang province. Mostly controlled by Indian troops since 1984, it is the world's highest-altitude battlefield.

5. Stone-pelters face off with police in Srinagar (June 2008). Stone-pelting has been a common form of protest in the Kashmir Valley for at least six decades. It revived from the second half of the 2000s, after the decline of insurgency in Indian Kashmir.

6. Narendra Modi embraces Mufti Mohammad Sayeed, chief minister of Indian Jammu and Kashmir, at Sayeed's oath-taking ceremony (March 2015). The ceremony inaugurated a coalition government whose charter promised to address the grievances of the Kashmir Valley's people, and pave the way to a broader peace process to resolve the Kashmir conflict. In retrospect, it is clear that Modi's government had no intention of acting on the charter's commitments.

7. Indian Central Reserve Police Force (CRPF) personnel take a break in Srinagar during a stone-pelting uprising in the Kashmir Valley (August 2016). The 2016 uprising followed a massive stone-pelting outbreak in the Valley in 2010. About 120 protesters were killed in the 2010 uprising, and over 100 in 2016. Thousands were injured in both years.

8. Insha Mushtaq, blinded at fourteen by pellet-gun bullets during the 2016 protests, at her home in a Kashmir Valley village (May 2017). She is among hundreds of citizens blinded by pellet guns fired by security forces, and was hit in the face while standing at a window of her home. In 2018, Insha passed her tenth-grade exams. Due to her disability, she has given up her goal of becoming a doctor and chosen to pursue higher studies in music.

9. Riyaz Naikoo, an insurgent leader, addresses the crowd at the funeral of a slain comrade in the Kashmir Valley (July 2017). During the speech, Naikoo denounced al-Qaeda and Daesh. A schoolteacher of mathematics, Naikoo became an insurgent in 2012. He was killed by security forces in May 2020.

10. Thousands attend the funeral of a slain insurgent in the Kashmir Valley (August 2018). Since 1990, many insurgent funerals in the Valley have seen tens of thousands of mourners, and hundreds of thousands in a few cases. Since May 2020, such mass gatherings to mourn insurgents have been prevented by the Indian authorities, citing the Covid-19 risk.

11. Srinagar under lockdown (August 2019). From 5 August 2019, Indian Kashmir was placed under the most draconian lockdown seen in decades of turmoil to prevent protests against the Kashmir policy of India's Hindu nationalist government. The lockdown involved suspension of mobile phone and internet services for months, and mass arrests. It was severest in the Kashmir Valley.

12. Indian soldiers in Ladakh (February 2021). From May 2020, the Indian and Chinese militaries became embroiled in confrontations along the Line of Actual Control (LAC), Ladakh's de facto border with Aksai Chin and Tibet. Twenty Indian soldiers and an unknown number of Chinese soldiers were killed in a lethal clash in June 2020. The LAC crisis after six decades of calm adds a new dimension to the Kashmir conflict.

spectrum of 'self-determination'-seeking groups and their leaders was not effective except in the mostly urban Srinagar district, where only 28 per cent voted, and other Valley towns. A militant strike near Uri between the second and third polling days that killed eight army soldiers and three policemen failed to disrupt the election. The votes were counted on 23 December 2014.

The outcome, as in 2008 and 2002, was a 'hung' (fractured) legislature, but there were two significant changes. First, the National Conference party slipped to third position from the single-largest status it had achieved in 2002 and 2008. The twenty-eight constituencies it had won in both 2002 and 2008 halved to just fifteen. The PDP won the majority of the Valley's forty-six constituencies and emerged as the single largest party, with twenty-eight legislators. This represented steady progress for the reformist party founded in 1999, which had won sixteen seats in 2002 and twenty-one seats in 2008. The other change was the emergence of the BJP as the second largest party, with twenty-five seats, all won from mostly Hindu-dominated constituencies in the Jammu region. (The Jammu region has an overall Hindu majority of over 60 per cent. Hindus dominate the region's relatively populous southern plains and foothills, but six of the region's ten districts, in the less populous hilly and mountainous areas, have Muslim majorities.) The BJP swept the Hindu vote in the Jammu region riding on the still potent Modi wave of the mid-2014 Indian parliamentary election, and won two-thirds of the region's thirty-seven seats in the legislature. In July 2014 Amit Shah, Modi's closest associate from his long tenure in Gujarat politics and the manager of the BJP's successful national campaign in 2014, became the party's president. Shah led a high-decibel campaign for the Indian J&K state election labelled 'Mission 44', aimed at a BJP majority in the eighty-seven-seat legislature. The campaign more than doubled the eleven seats the BJP had won in the Jammu region in late 2008, on the momentum of the Amarnath agitation, though it fell far short of the 'Mission 44' rhetoric. The outcome was clear: the PDP was dominant in the Valley, and Jammu's Hindu majority had largely voted for the BJP.

A few days before the counting, I had been asked by an Indian newspaper to write an instant analysis of the outcome. In the piece, published in the early hours of 24 December, I argued that 'the fractured verdict' was natural given 'the heterogeneity of the state and its electorate' and that 'the outcome presents a historic opportunity to bridge two divides – the first between the Kashmir and Jammu regions and the second between the Kashmir Valley and the Indian Union'. Since the outcome made a coalition government inevitable, the question was its composition. While 'post-poll coalitions necessitated by hung legislatures are more easily formed between parties that are relatively compatible in ideological and programmatic terms', I noted that 'there is another variant of the post-poll coalition. This is known among political scientists as a "grand coalition" between the two largest parties, which are usually ideologically and programmatically distant from each other.' 'The prospect of such a grand coalition between the PDP, which has won the majority of the Valley's seats, and the BJP, which has won the majority of the Jammu region's seats,' I argued, 'presents a real opportunity to transcend the divide between the Kashmir and Jammu regions, and to begin mending the deep rift between the Valley and the Indian Union.' That was because of the PDP's identity as the establishment party closest to the *azaadi* sentiment prevalent in the Valley, and the BJP's traditional identity as the most hardline voice of Indian nationalism on Kashmir. While acknowledging that 'such a coalition will not be easy to negotiate – and to operate, if it comes to pass', I argued that 'the result has thrown up the tantalizing possibility of a *modus vivendi* between Indian nationalism and Kashmiri regionalism', which 'should not be wasted'.

'Such a coalition,' I pointed out, 'would mean a strong voice for Jammu's Hindu majority – who have often felt marginalized in the state's politics – at the heart of a power-sharing government with representatives of the Kashmir Valley.' I further noted that 'the obvious choice for chief minister in such an arrangement is Mufti Mohammad Sayeed', the PDP leader, due to his six decades of political experience, his efforts since 1999 to articulate the wounded Valley's grievances and aspirations, and also because 'he has been explicitly sensitive to the issue of inter-regional equality and amity, specifically the sense of grievance and inequality in Jammu, which is not limited to that region's Hindu majority but is shared by many of its Muslims'. I advocated that 'the defeated parties, especially the NC', which is Kashmir's historic party and has deep roots, should 'play the essential role of a constructive opposition', and expressed the 'hope that the political forces and leaders in the Valley [i.e. the spectrum of independentist and pro-Pakistan groups] who remain outside the ambit of electoral politics can be reached out to in the next few years'. As examples of grand coalitions, I pointed to the Christian Democrats (CDU/CSU) and the Social Democrats (SPD) in Germany from 1966 to 1969, 2005 to 2009 and 2013 onwards, and the 'historic compromise' in Italy in the 1970s between the Christian Democrats and the Communists. But above all, I highlighted the example of peace-building 'in Northern Ireland, the site of a violent conflict from the late 1960s to the late 1990s'. 'Since 2007,' I noted, 'Northern Ireland has been governed by a grand coalition in which the leading players are the Democratic Unionist Party (DUP), which is resolutely committed to Northern Ireland remaining a part of Britain, and Sinn Fein (SF), an Irish nationalist party whose declared aim is the unification of Northern Ireland with the Republic of Ireland.'[48]

Over the next two months (January–February 2015), I wrote several follow-up articles in Indian media advocating this way to break polarisation and stalemate and open up the path to a broader Kashmir peace process and settlement.[49]

A CYNICAL DECEPTION: THE PDP–BJP COALITION GOVERNMENT

On 1 March 2015 Mufti Mohammad Sayeed took office as Indian J&K's chief minister at the head of a PDP–BJP coalition government. The cere-mony took place in Jammu, Indian J&K's winter capital (Srinagar is the summer capital). Narendra Modi flew in from Delhi to witness the cere-mony. The enduring image of the event is of Modi clasping Sayeed in a bear-hug, standing behind a table decorated with equal-sized versions of the Indian national tricolour and Indian J&K's state flag. Hindu nationalists had objected to the state flag's existence for the previous sixty-five years, because India's states do not usually have their own flag. A BJP legislator from the Jammu region's southern, Hindu-dominated area became deputy chief minister and cabinet portfolios were divided between the two parties, the larger share going to the PDP.

The coalition agreement was based on a document called 'Agenda of Alliance', the result of two months of negotiations between PDP and BJP representatives. It addressed the two most contentious points: Article 370 of the Indian constitution, and the Armed Forces Special Powers Act. Article 370 guaranteed the special autonomous status of Indian Jammu and Kashmir in the Indian Union, and the Hindu nationalists had demanded its abrogation since the early 1950s. Although the substantive content of Indian J&K's autonomy had been largely hollowed out by 'integration' imposed from New Delhi during the 1950s and 1960s (Chapter 1), the token continuation of Article 370 continued to be a lightning rod for Hindu nationalist criticism and agitation. For the PDP, the virtually unlimited powers and immunity from judicial prosecution provided by AFSPA to the army and paramilitary forces in Kashmir had been a priority issue since the party's formation in 1999. While arguing for a PDP–BJP coalition government, I noted in January 2015 that a 'rollback' of AFSPA was 'overdue'.[50]

On Article 370, 'while recognizing the different positions of the parties', the agreement committed to maintain 'all the constitutional provisions pertaining to Kashmir including the special status'. On AFSPA, the agreement noted that 'the parties have historically held different views' but stated that because 'the [security] situation in the state has improved vastly, the coalition government will thoroughly review the security situation and the need for de-notifying disturbed areas', in order to 'enable the [Union] government to take a final view on the continuation of AFSPA in these areas'.

The ambition of the 'Agenda of Alliance' went much further. 'The purpose of this alliance,' the agreement read, 'is to catalyse reconciliation and confidence-building within and across the LoC, widen the ambit of democracy through inclusive politics, and create conditions to facilitate the resolution of all issues.' To that end, 'the coalition government will help initiate and facilitate a sustained and meaningful dialogue with all internal stakeholders irrespective of their ideological views [a reference to independentist and pro-Pakistan groups in Indian J&K], and seek to build a broad-based consensus on the resolution of all outstanding issues'. Moreover, 'as the [Union] government has recently initiated several steps to normalise the relationship with

Pakistan, the coalition government will seek to support and strengthen that approach', to 'be pursued by enhancing people-to-people contact across the LoC, encouraging civil society exchanges, and taking travel, commerce, trade and business across the LoC to the next level'.

In a BBC commentary published on 3 March 2015, I wrote that 'it is premature to say that this strategic bargain between Kashmiri Muslim regionalists and Hindu nationalists heralds a Kashmir Spring. But it is unmistakably the most hopeful development since the descent into violence a quarter-century ago. The challenge over the next few years is to convert symbolism into substance, and the promise into reality.'[51]

There was no movement subsequently on any of the progressive, even visionary, elements of the alliance charter. In June 2018, the charade of a coalition government came to an overdue end when the BJP withdrew from the government and Indian J&K was placed under 'Governor's rule' (effectively Central rule from New Delhi). In the three-year interregnum, much water – and blood – had flowed down the Jhelum.

There was a brief moment of illusory hope at the end of 2015. On 25 December 2015 Narendra Modi made a surprise visit lasting a few hours to Pakistan. He had gone on an official visit to Russia a few days earlier, and on the return leg of the trip he stopped in Kabul on 25 December. In Kabul he and Ashraf Ghani, the president of Afghanistan, jointly inaugurated a new building of the Afghan parliament, built over nearly a decade with Indian funding. Flying out from Kabul towards Delhi, Modi made a surprise touchdown in Lahore, the Pakistani Punjab city close to the Indian border where Nawaz Sharif and Vajpayee had issued the 'Lahore declaration' of February 1999. Sharif greeted Modi at Lahore airport and received birthday wishes in return – it was the Pakistani prime minister's sixty-sixth birthday – and the two then adjourned to the Sharif family's sprawling country estate near the city for a one-to-one conversation before Modi re-embarked for Delhi. At the time, it was thought that Modi made the surprise stopover in an attempt to reassure Pakistanis that they should not fear India's activities in Afghanistan – a tall order, given deep-rooted Pakistani paranoia on that issue – but perhaps also to restart a high-level dialogue with Pakistan's civilian head of government on Kashmir. During 2015 Sharif's national security adviser, Lt-Gen. (retired) Naseer Khan Janjua, and Modi's national security adviser, Ajit Doval, a former intelligence operative, had held talks in Bangkok.

In a sign of how much some elements in Pakistan fear even the most tentative moves towards India–Pakistan rapprochement, six gunmen, probably from Jaish-e-Mohammad, attacked an Indian Air Force base shortly after midnight on 1 January 2016. They were wearing Indian Army uniforms – a standard trope of *fidayeen* attackers in Indian J&K in the first half of the 2000s – and had apparently infiltrated across the border on 31 December. The air force base targeted was just outside Indian J&K, near the town of Pathankot, which is in India's Punjab state but very close to the border with the Jammu region. After scaling the base's outer wall, the attackers spread out across the sprawling base in typical commando style and kept their pursuers at bay by firing intermittently and setting off explosives. In addition to assault rifles, plentiful ammunition, and dry rations and water, they were carrying grenade-launchers and light mortars, likely with the intent of destroying air force planes and helicopters. They were not able to access the area where these were parked, but the incident went on for five days and the last surviving attacker was not killed until 5 January. Seven Indian military personnel died in the fighting and twenty-five others were injured.

Just as the Pathankot attack wound down, Mufti Mohammad Sayeed died in a hospital in New Delhi on 7 January 2016, five days before his eightieth birthday, after a brief illness of two weeks. The Indian J&K government was left leaderless for the next three months because his politician daughter and PDP's second-in-command, Mehbooba Mufti, apparently overcome by grief, went into seclusion and delayed taking over as chief minister until April.

THE 2016 UPRISING

In July 2016, the Kashmir Valley descended into a maelstrom of violence that lasted six months before tapering off in early 2017. The trigger was the death of Burhan Wani, a militant in his early twenties. Wani was a native of Tral, a mountainous area in the south-eastern Valley consisting of a small town and over one hundred villages and hamlets. Tral was a stronghold of the pro-Pakistan Hizb-ul Mujahideen insurgent group throughout the 1990s and into the early 2000s, and retained a residual HM presence after insurgency went into decline from the mid-2000s. Wani was born in the mid-1990s in one of Tral's villages to a schoolteacher father who went on to become the principal of the area's government-run higher secondary school, and a mother who has a postgraduate science degree. A good student who aspired to become a doctor, Wani dropped out of high school aged 16, shortly after the summer of stone-pelting rage that swept the Valley in 2010, and became a new-generation HM militant. His career as a guerrilla was rather curious. Although he was an active militant for almost six years and evaded capture by hiding out in the forested upper reaches of Tral, he is not known to have engaged in any significant operations against the Indian forces. That may explain the longevity of his guerrilla existence – six years is an unusually long time for a militant to survive on the run in Kashmir. When he was killed with two comrades on 8 July 2016 in a joint operation of the police's SOG and the army's RR in a village in the Kokernag area of the Valley's Anantnag/Islamabad district, located south of Tral, there were no casualties among the security forces. Burhan's death was preceded in April 2015 by that of his older brother Khalid, one of his four siblings. Khalid, 25, was intercepted by an army unit when he was returning to his village after delivering a home-cooked meal of rice and lamb to Burhan and three of his comrades in their mountain hideout and beaten to death. There were no bullet wounds on his body, but his face and skull were a mangled pulp.

During his guerrilla years, Burhan Wani became a household name in the Kashmir Valley – as a social-media celebrity. He used Facebook to post photographs of himself and his comrades, and audio and video clips in which he sermonised about armed struggle and resistance. The best-known photograph, from the summer of 2015, has Burhan at the centre of a group of eleven young men in combat fatigues, cradling assault rifles. The photograph, taken in a fruit orchard, powerfully conveys the camaraderie of the brothers-in-arms, all local Kashmiris born during the blood-drenched 1990s. All but one of the youths have their faces uncovered. Ten of these eleven youths were subsequently killed in encounters in southern Valley districts between October 2015 and May 2018 (the sole survivor surrendered in May 2016). They were just a few among hundreds of young militant recruits, and 'martyrs', in the southern Valley during the second half of the decade. The encounters often led to mass stone-pelting. As soon as word got out that a raid by the security forces was underway, people from the area's villages would approach the encounter site in large numbers and throw stones to try and divert their attention and help the militants escape. This usually did not save the trapped militants, but sometimes civilians would be shot dead by the forces, setting off further stone-pelting protests.

Burhan Wani's Facebook warfare fired the imagination of the Valley's young people, who came of age politically in the protests of 2010. On 9 July 2016 he was laid to rest next to his brother Khalid in their local graveyard in Tral. About 200,000 people attended the funeral, and hundreds of simultaneous prayers for the peace of his soul were held in urban neighbourhoods and villages across the Kashmir Valley. Militants appeared at the burial and fired a gun salute over the coffin.

Within days, the Valley erupted in a furious stone-pelting uprising which raged through July, August and September before gradually declining in intensity with the onset of winter. It was a reprise of 2010 – massive rioting, arson of government buildings, recurrent curfews and *hartals* (general strikes). A self-appointed 'joint resistance leadership' – headed by the independentist JKLF leader Yasin Malik, the octogenarian Jama'at-i-Islami veteran Syed Ali Shah Geelani and Mirwaiz Umar Farooq, the hereditary head cleric of Srinagar's Jama Masjid (Grand Mosque) – issued directives and proclamations but had little actual control of events, as hundreds of thousands rioted and clashed with security forces throughout the Valley. Many rural areas in the southern Valley districts became 'no-go' zones for the security forces as armed insurgents roamed freely. The disturbances spread to the Doda and Kishtwar districts of the Jammu region, which lie just south of the Valley and have large Kashmiri-speaking Muslim populations.

By the time the second volcanic eruption in six years subsided, about 100 Kashmiris were dead – mostly young male protesters – and 15,000 had suffered injuries. Five security personnel also died and four thousand were injured, the latter mostly by stone-pelting. There was one difference from 2010. The police and CRPF used hundreds of pellet guns, acquired since 2010 in anticipation of future uprisings, against the protesters. These guns, supposedly a non-lethal riot-control weapon, have cartridges which discharge several hundred tiny metal pellets over a few hundred feet when fired. The pellets are particularly deadly for the eyes. Hundreds of protesters, and some bystanders including children, became permanently blind after being hit by pellets in their eyes, and several thousand others suffered partial loss of eyesight. The use of pellet guns continues unabated. At the end of August 2020, Shias in Srinagar and Badgam districts took out processions on the tenth day of the month of Muharram, Ashura, which commemorates the martyrdom of Imam Hussein, the Prophet's grandson. A year earlier, in September 2019, a few dozen men in Srinagar who attempted a placard-protest against the Hindu nationalist government's Kashmir policy on the day of Ashura were simply beaten up and dragged away. In 2020, Ashura processions were banned citing Covid-19, but thousands of Shiite Kashmiris took to the streets anyway on one of their holiest days. The largest procession in Zadibal, a Shia neighbourhood of Srinagar, was broken up by police using tear-gas and pellet guns. More than one hundred people were injured, including seven youths who suffered serious eye injuries from pellets.

The Indian and Pakistani governments had held a vacuous meeting between their foreign secretaries – the career bureaucrats heading the respective diplomatic services – in April 2016. Even that token engagement ended with the new outbreak in Kashmir, as Sharif's government strongly criticised Indian repression. The Jaish-e-Mohammad terror group, closely linked to the Pakistani military's deep-state apparatus, pitched in with its suicide attack on an Indian Army camp in Uri that killed nineteen soldiers in September 2016 – mentioned earlier in this chapter – which elicited a counter-strike by Indian commandos against militant camps just across the LoC.

When I arrived in the Kashmir Valley in April 2017, the large-scale protests had subsided but the mood in the aftermath was sombre. There was a grim roster of daily fatalities as militants targeted fellow Kashmiri police personnel, the Indian Army fought militants in encounters and sporadic street clashes continued. My public interactions in the Valley were nothing but utterly civil, however. I gave a public lecture – not on the Kashmir conflict – at the Tagore Hall in Srinagar's Wazir Bagh neighbourhood in honour of Ved Bhasin (1929–2015), an iconic figure from Jammu who is regarded as the pioneer of modern print journalism in Indian Jammu and Kashmir. Srinagar's Tagore Hall, a 700-seat auditorium, has its own chequered history. It was inaugurated in 1961 to mark the birth centenary of Rabindranath Tagore (1861–1941), the poet, composer, writer and visual artist from Bengal – my own native region of India – who was awarded the Nobel Prize for Literature in 1913. Its premises became a billet for paramilitary troops in the 1990s before it was refurbished and restored to its original purpose of a performing arts venue in the second half of the 2000s. Hundreds of Srinagar citizens attended the event and the tea reception afterwards, and I could see that they enjoyed the superficial respite from the grimness and uncertainty of their daily lives.

On all of my previous visits to Indian J&K starting in 1994, I had done my research quietly and left. This time, because the Tagore Hall event was front-paged in all of the Kashmir Valley's English and Urdu newspapers, my presence became known. I had an interactive session with hundreds of students at the Central University of Kashmir, located on Srinagar's northern outskirts, and was interviewed for the campus's radio station by a female master's student sporting a magnificently colourful headscarf. I then travelled to Awantipora, a town south of Srinagar, for a smaller but still lively discussion with students at the Islamic University of Science and Technology, a young institution established in the second half of the 2000s. In private interactions, I noticed great anger at Mehbooba Mufti, the lame-duck chief minister. I was repeatedly told that the scions of the two leading political families of the Valley were shamefully stained by the blood of young Kashmiris: Omar Abdullah, who was chief minister at the time of the 2010 uprising, and Mehbooba Mufti, who had the same role in 2016. People wondered how Ms Mufti could live in her luxurious residence – converted from a notorious 1990s torture centre – in Srinagar's high-security zone overlooking the Dal Lake while hundreds of her fellow Kashmiris, blinded by pellet guns, suffered in silence with their families. When I referred to the 2015 'Agenda of Alliance' document as the political equivalent of toilet paper in my conversations with the students, no one laughed at the attempt at black humour.

When the comatose PDP–BJP coalition government expired with the BJP pulling out in June 2018, I noted in a BBC commentary that:

On paper, the March 2015 charter of the PDP–BJP coalition government represented both a vision and a roadmap for resolving the Kashmir conflict. The constructive potential of the coalition lay precisely in its 'unnatural' quality, because it signalled engagement between very different perspectives on the Kashmir conflict. But it remained just that – on paper ... In hindsight, any prospect of advancing the vision-cum-roadmap ended with the death of Mufti Mohammad Sayeed at the start of 2016. Sayeed, a wily veteran of both Kashmiri and Indian politics over six decades, may have tried in due course to hold the BJP to the letter and spirit of the charter, and pulled the plug if it did not. His daughter Mehbooba Mufti, who succeeded him, proved to be an unmitigated disaster as chief minister. She passively continued with the paralyzed, dysfunctional coalition government after renewed turmoil gripped the Valley from July 2016, until the BJP pulled the plug in June 2018.

'The timing of the BJP's move,' I wrote, 'may be explained by a decision to project an untrammelled mailed-fist in the restive and recalcitrant Valley in the countdown to India's general election in April–May 2019.'[52] That untrammelled mailed-fist was fully revealed in early August of 2019, two months after the Modi government returned to power for a second five-year term with a slightly enhanced parliamentary majority.

Modi's first public comments after the Valley erupted in July 2016 came after a month, at an all-party meeting his government convened in New Delhi on 12 August to discuss the crisis. He made no reference to the promises of the March 2015 'Agenda of Alliance' charter, which had remained completely unacted upon for nearly a year and a half. He instead talked about 'cross-border terrorism' and declared that 'Jammu and Kashmir defines our nationalism' – the standard rhetoric of past Indian leaders. Then in April 2017, Modi visited the Jammu region to inaugurate a new tunnel for motor traffic constructed in hilly terrain. Addressing a 100,000-strong rally of Jammu Hindus on the occasion, he advised the Kashmir Valley's youth to abjure 'terrorism' and seek 'progress through tourism', citing 'every Indian's dream of visiting Kashmir [at least] once'.[53] There was again no mention of the 2015 charter and its commitments.

Just after Modi's 2017 visit to Jammu, a gang of far-right extremists set upon and brutally assaulted a family of Bakerwals – Muslim nomadic pastoralists who breed livestock – who were travelling with their herd to summer pastures in the Jammu region. A girl aged nine was among several people seriously injured. The incident was one of a rash of often murderous attacks by self-proclaimed 'cow-protector' groups on Muslims that occurred across northern India during Modi's first term. Then in January 2018, another little Bakerwal girl, 8-year-old Asifa Bano, was kidnapped, drugged, gang-raped and murdered in a Hindu-majority district in southern Jammu. In June 2019, three of the perpetrators, including the ringleader, a temple priest, were sentenced to life in prison and three local police officers to jail terms for having tried to shield them and destroy evidence. After the incident came to light, the Jammu BJP and RSS agitated in favour of the accused, who were all Hindus, under the banner of a *Hindu Ekta Manch* (Hindu Unity Forum). Two BJP ministers in the coalition government – the minister for industries and the minister for forests – attended a protest supporting the accused men.

In retrospect – particularly post-5 August 2019 – it is clear that the coalition agreement Modi's BJP made with the PDP in early 2015 was an exercise in cynical deception, and its visionary-sounding charter a cruel hoax. The BJP's purpose was to get into Indian J&K's government, in line with the party strategy masterminded by Modi's closest associate, BJP president Amit Shah, of securing BJP governments in as many of India's states as possible – either on its own or through an expedient alliance with a local party. In April 2017, Modi at his side, Shah told a top-level party conference that the BJP aimed to dominate India 'from panchayat to parliament' (*panchayats* are elected bodies of grassroots governance in rural India) and that he would consider his task as party president complete only when 'every state' of India had a BJP government.[54] This conference took place two weeks after Modi's visit to the Jammu region.

The Modi–Shah duo were happy to let the PDP–BJP coalition government drift and then disintegrate, while they bided their time to unveil and implement their own blueprint of a solution to the Kashmir problem. That time came after Modi resoundingly won re-election in May 2019, capitalising on the Indian opposition's failure to put together a credible alternative. The chief executor of that brute-force blueprint was and is Amit Shah, who was appointed as India's all-powerful home (interior) minister in the second Modi government. In June 2018, I wrote:

> It is clear that Modi has decided not to emulate the diplomacy-based and healing-touch strategy Atal Bihari Vajpayee, India's first Hindu nationalist prime minister, doggedly pursued vis-à-vis Kashmir, and Pakistan, in the very difficult period between 1999 and 2004. The PDP–BJP coalition government of 2015–2018 is the newest addition to the overflowing dustbin of the Kashmir conflict's 70-year history. But – and this is the irony – the vision and roadmap articulated in the 2015 Agenda of Alliance represents the only feasible path to a better future. Such a future will need to bring together many unnatural partners in a pragmatic compromise.[55]

Initially, in the second half of 2018, the Hindu nationalists schemed to install an alternative, BJP-dominant government in Indian J&K – the mandate of the legislature elected at the end of 2014 had another two years to run, until the end of 2020 – by engineering defections from the twenty-eight-strong group of PDP legislators. This did not succeed and provoked a counter-move by the PDP. In November 2018, Mehbooba Mufti staked a claim to form a new government in alliance with the National Conference and the Congress (together, the three parties had a clear majority in the legislature). The BJP's goal was to install a government backed by PDP defectors and formally headed as chief minister by Sajjad Lone, the leader of a small party – with two legislators – based in the Valley's northern

Kupwara district (Sajjad Lone's father Abdul Ghani Lone, a prominent 'self-determination' proponent, was assassinated in Srinagar by pro-Pakistan gunmen in 2002). Following Mehbooba Mufti's move, Sajjad Lone too put in a claim to lead a government, but it was clear the BJP did not have the numbers to realise its game-plan. Indian J&K's governor, an appointee of the Modi government in New Delhi, then quickly dissolved the legislature – which had been kept in suspended animation since June – to prevent a PDP–NC–Congress coalition government from taking office, and Indian J&K entered a period of extended Central rule. Welcoming the governor's decision, the BJP's central office in New Delhi tweeted: 'J&K needs a firm administration to deal with terrorism, not a combination of terror-friendly parties'.[56] The statement was a forewarning of what was to unfold in Indian Jammu and Kashmir from August 2019.

THE FEBRUARY 2019 CRISIS

On 14 February 2019, a 78-vehicle CRPF convoy of 2,500 paramilitary troops was travelling in the Kashmir Valley towards Srinagar. The convoy had made a pre-dawn start from the city of Jammu, 190 miles to the south, in order to reach Srinagar before dusk. The convoy was of unusually large size because the Jammu–Srinagar highway had been closed for a few days due to snowfall and landslides, a common occurrence in winter. Around midday, the convoy crossed the Banihal Pass into the Valley, and at 3 p.m. passed Awantipora, a town on the highway. The town of Pampore, famous for the saffron fields in its vicinity, was next, followed by Srinagar. Between Awantipora and Pampore, a village called Lethipora spreads out on both sides of the highway, which follows the trajectory of the Jhelum river. The spot is 15 miles short of Srinagar. Pampore, Lethipora and Awantipora are all in the Valley's Pulwama district, immediately south of Srinagar.

As the convoy rumbled through Lethipora at 3.15 p.m., a small van came out of the side road off the highway and rammed into one of the buses in the convoy. The van detonated and the blast destroyed the bus, killing all the forty CRPF troopers travelling in it. Another thirty-five troopers riding in vehicles immediately front and behind were wounded. It was the single most deadly attack on Indian security forces in three decades of the Kashmir insurgency. They had not suffered such a major loss of life in any incident since 1990. The van carried a bomb weighing several hundred kilograms, made with a mix of RDX and ammonium nitrate.

The suicide bomber was Adil Ahmad Dar, in his early twenties, a native of a Pulwama village about 6 miles from Lethipora. He was a high-school dropout and worked as a labourer. The Pakistani jihadist group Jaish-e-Mohammad, active in the Kashmir insurgency since 2000, claimed responsibility and released a 'martyrdom video' the youth had made before the operation. In the video, he is clad in combat fatigues and cradles an assault rifle.

Adil Dar had been arrested six times between September 2016 and March 2018. The first arrest, in September 2016, was for stone-pelting. There was one further arrest for stone-pelting, and four on suspicion of being an OGW (overground worker) for militants, the term used by the security apparatus to describe persons who assist insurgents. He was released without being charged each time. Following the sixth arrest, he disappeared from his village on 19 March 2018 and was missing since then. The attack may have been planned for 9 February 2019, the sixth anniversary of the hanging of Afzal Guru in Delhi, and put off because of bad weather.

Jaish-e-Mohammad (Army of the Prophet), whose founder-leader is Maulana Masood Azhar, a radical Pakistani cleric, has a record of recruiting young Kashmiris for suicide operations. Its first suicide bombing, in May 2000, was carried out by Afaq Ahmad Shah, a 17-year-old schoolboy from Khanyar, a neighbourhood in Srinagar's old city. Afaq Shah detonated a car at the main entrance to the operational headquarters and cantonment in Srinagar's southern outskirts of the Indian Army's 15th Corps, which is stationed in the Valley, killing eight soldiers. On 31 December 2017, a centre for training CRPF commandos in Lethipora was penetrated by three Jaish militants, who killed five CRPF personnel – including two Kashmiri Muslims – and wounded three others in a gun-battle before being eliminated. Two of the three-member squad were local Kashmiris and the third a Pakistani. The youngest of the trio was Fardeen Ahmad Khanday, 16, a tenth-grade student from a village in Tral, the home turf of Burhan

Wani. The son of a police constable, Khanday left home and joined JeM in September 2017. He did not have a stone-pelting background but was upset since the March 2017 death in an encounter of a fellow villager, an HM militant who had been his Koran tutor. The attack in which he participated was probably triggered by the encounter death on 25 December 2017 of Noor Mohammad Tantray, a Kashmiri JeM militant active since the early 2000s. Tantray had been in hiding because he was easily identifiable due to a physical feature: he was a dwarf, 3 feet tall. Fardeen Khanday too made an eight-minute pre-martyrdom video in which he intoned in Kashmiri-accented Urdu: 'By the time this is released, I will be in heaven ... My friends and I have listened to the Koran's call and plunged into jihad. This will continue till the last occupying soldier leaves Kashmir.'[57]

Adil Dar's father Ghulam Hassan Dar, a farmer, said of himself and his wife Fahmeeda: 'We are in pain as the families of the soldiers are'. He blamed political leaders, saying that the Kashmir conflict 'should have been resolved through dialogue ... the sons of the common man die here, whether they are Indian soldiers or ours'.[58]

The 14 February 2019 attack sparked a furore across India, fuelled by some television channels calling for revenge. Outrage grew as funerals of the CRPF troopers started taking place in different parts of the country – the forty men hailed from sixteen different states across the length and breadth of India. On 24 February, hundreds of activists of independentist and pro-Pakistan political groups in the Valley were arrested, including JKLF leader Yasin Malik, and in March both JKLF and Jama'at-i-Islami were declared banned organisations by the Modi government under the federal Unlawful Activities Prevention Act (UAPA), enacted in 1967.

Then, on the night of 25–26 February, Mirage-2000 jets of the Indian Air Force bombed an alleged JeM training camp near Balakot, a town in Pakistan's Khyber-Pakhtunkhwa province close to the border with Pakistani 'Azad' Kashmir. Balakot had been very badly hit by the October 2005 earth-quake which had its epicentre in the northern part of 'Azad' Kashmir around Muzaffarabad. The Pakistanis did not detect the air raid and all the planes returned safely to India. The Indians claimed that a large number of terror-ists had been killed, and the Pakistanis denied any casualties, saying that an uninhabited wooded hill had been bombed. The aerial bombing, and that the targeted site was in Pakistan proper, albeit just beyond the 'Azad' Kashmir border, marked a significant escalation. On the morning of 27 February, the Pakistani air force crossed the LoC and conducted pinprick attacks in the Jammu region's Rajouri district, which abuts the LoC. Dogfights ensued on the LoC as Indian jets were scrambled in response. An Indian MiG-21 fighter was shot down and its pilot ejected on the Pakistani side of the LoC, where he was almost set upon by local villagers before being taken into custody by a Pakistan Army unit. The Pakistanis released the pilot on 1 March and he was escorted back into India at Wagah, the main border crossing point near Lahore. There was no further escalation of hostilities, but the flare-up was a stark reminder of the dangers of escalation posed by even a limited Kashmir insurgency, especially in the form of very deliberately timed attacks by *provocateur* groups like JeM.

The crisis came at a politically opportune time for the Modi government to escalate its rhetoric and flex some military muscle on the eve of India's general election in April–May 2019, which decisively returned Modi and the BJP to power with a slightly enhanced parliamentary majority.

Imran Khan, a famous Pakistani cricketer turned politician, had in August 2018 become Pakistan's prime minister following an election widely regarded as manipulated in his party's favour by the military elite, after Nawaz Sharif – distrusted by the army – was forced out of office on corruption charges in July 2017. As India went to the polls in April 2019, Khan mused to international journalists about the prospects of renewed talks with India on Kashmir: 'If the next Indian government is led by the opposition, it might be too scared to seek a settlement with Pakistan on Kashmir, fearing a backlash from the right. Perhaps if the BJP – a right-wing party – wins, some kind of settlement on Kashmir could be reached'.[59]

It is possible that this was also the cautious expectation of Imran Khan's patrons in the high echelons of the Pakistan Army.

He, and they, could not have been more wrong.

CHAPTER FOUR

The Hindu Nationalist Offensive

I N MID-2020 Minxin Pei, a scholar of China's one-party state, reflected on how the structure of power has changed in the People's Republic of China since Xi Jinping took over the leadership. 'Since taking power in 2012,' Pei wrote, 'Xi Jinping has replaced collective leadership with strongman rule. Before Xi, the regime displayed a degree of ideological flexibility and political pragmatism. It avoided [major] errors by relying on a consensus-based decision-making process. Such a regime was by no means perfect. Corruption was pervasive, and the government often delayed critical decisions and missed valuable opportunities.' But, according to Pei:

> The regime that preceded Xi's had one advantage: a built-in propensity for pragmatism and caution. In the last seven years, that system has been dismantled and replaced by a qualitatively different regime – marked by a high degree of ideological rigidity and punitive policies towards ethnic minorities and political dissenters. The centralization of power under Xi has created new fragilities. If the upside of strongman rule is the ability to make decisions quickly, the downside is that it greatly raises the odds of making costly blunders. The consensus-based decision-making of the

earlier era might have been slow and inefficient, but it prevented radical or risky ideas from becoming policy.[1]

This description of the evolution of China's authoritarian system since 2013 would apply, with minor modifications, to the trajectory of India's democracy since Narendra Modi took office as prime minister in mid-2014. For a quarter-century, from late 1989 until 2014, India was governed by a succession of coalition governments, as no party was able to win a majority in seven consecutive parliamentary elections. Then, in 2014, the Hindu nationalist Bharatiya Janata Party (BJP, 'Indian People's Party') won a narrow parliamentary majority under a new leader, Modi. Modi had until then been the chief minister of Gujarat, a mid-sized state in western India, since October 2001 and was known primarily for a large-scale pogrom of Gujarat's 10 per cent Muslim minority which occurred under his watch in 2002.[2] The Modi victory of 2014 was largely due to popular disillusionment with a coalition government led by the Congress party which had been in office since mid-2004.

In May 2019, Modi was re-elected to a second five-year term as the BJP won a slightly enhanced parliamentary majority, mainly because of the fractured and ineffective condition of the political opposition and the absence of a viable alternative. Upon winning re-election Modi appointed Amit Shah – his closest associate and BJP president from 2014 to 2019 – as India's home (interior) minister, the most powerful role in the cabinet. This both consolidated and formalised the status of Shah – a Modi associate in Gujarat's politics since the 1980s and a former junior minister of home affairs in Modi's Gujarat government – as the other member of the strongman duo which has been trying to assert total dominance of Indian politics since 2014 and recast India as a Hindu nationalist republic. The two men have been and remain intent on centralising decision-making power in their own hands to the greatest extent possible, and represent a particularly hardline tendency even within the Hindu nationalist movement, which was the far-right fringe of Indian politics until the end of the 1980s.[3] Emboldened by winning a second five-year term in mid-2019, the dynamic duo intensified their offensive against religious minorities (especially targeted at India's 200 million Muslims) and political opponents ongoing since 2014, and an openly authoritarian version of Hindu nationalism's ideological agenda was put into motion. As part of this intensified offensive to recast India as a *Hindu Rashtra*[4] (Hindu State), the Modi–Shah government made the radical and risky ideological view of the Hindu nationalist movement on Kashmir official policy in August 2019.

The territory of 'Kashmir' – a common shorthand for the large and internally heterogeneous area in the subcontinent's far north disputed between India and Pakistan since 1947 – came into being in the mid-nineteenth century and existed as an autonomous principality ('princely state') known as Jammu and Kashmir within Britain's Indian empire from 1846 to 1947 (Chapter 1). Since the end of the first India–Pakistan war over Kashmir in December 1948, the bulk of the lands and most of the population (at least 70 per cent, currently 14 million of a total of 20 million people) of the erstwhile princely state have been under Indian authority, in the Indian state of Jammu and Kashmir (J&K). The residual areas and population under Pakistan's authority lie across the January 1949 Ceasefire Line (CFL), which was renamed the Line of Control (LoC) by an India–Pakistan agreement in July 1972. Until August 2019, J&K was one of the twenty-nine states comprising the Indian Union and its only Muslim-majority one: 68 per cent Muslim, 28 per cent Hindu, 2 per cent Sikh and 1 per cent Buddhist, according to the Indian national census of 2011.

On Monday 5 August 2019, the government of India published a constitutional order, issued as per standard procedure in the name of India's president (a largely ceremonial post, occupied since July 2017 by an obscure ex-BJP politician). The order effectively revoked the autonomous status which was given to J&K at the time of the princely state's accession to India in October 1947 (Chapter 1) and subsequently incorporated into India's constitution (1950) as Article 370. The abrogation of Article 370 – seen by India's Hindu nationalist movement as undue 'appeasement' of J&K's Muslim majority – had been a consistent demand of the movement since the early 1950s. In reality, the extensive autonomy guaranteed to the Indian state of Jammu and Kashmir by Article 370 was stripped away through a series of measures to integrate J&K with the Indian Union which were imposed from New Delhi between 1954 and 1965 (Chapter 1). After 1965, there was not much left of J&K's asymmetric autonomy within the Indian Union beyond the largely symbolic – a J&K state flag, a J&K state constitution enacted in 1957 which was not much more than a sheaf of paper, and the continuing use of a penal code inherited from the princely-state era in J&K courts.

But even though J&K's special autonomy had been hollowed out by the mid-1960s and the state existed on more or less the same terms within the Indian Union as other states, the token continuation of Article 370 in the Indian constitution provided a propaganda weapon for the Hindu nationalists to campaign against the 'appeasement' of Muslims in the 'pseudo-secular' Indian republic. Every BJP manifesto for an Indian general election has featured the abrogation of Article 370 as an important goal, and commitment. So the formal revocation of Article 370 following the BJP's decisive victory in 2019 can be regarded as the fulfilment of a longstanding pledge.

Ghulam Mohammad Bhat, a middle-aged farmer who grows saffron in a village called Balhama located just south of Srinagar, the Kashmir Valley's capital city, and writes poetry under the pen name Madhosh Balhami, pithily expressed the blasé attitude of the Valley's people to the formal demise of Article 370: 'It was neither good nor bad. Narendra Modi just buried the rotted corpse.' Bhat alias Balhami is a scarred survivor of the brutal Kashmir conflict of the past three decades, like hundreds of thousands of his fellow Kashmiris. Arrested three times – in 1991, 1998 and 2000 – for reciting elegies at the funerals of Kashmiri insurgents slain in combat with Indian forces, he has experienced some of the Kashmir Valley's most notorious detention centres. In one called 'The Butchery', located inside the Indian Army's Valley headquarters situated on the southern outskirts of Srinagar close to his village, where he was taken in 1991, he was beaten 'with a bamboo cane until it broke into pieces'. In 1998 he was taken to 'Cargo', a detention centre operated in Srinagar by a specialist counter-insurgency wing of the Indian J&K police. There he composed a poem: 'Angels of death, are dancing in these cells'. At 1 p.m. on 15 March 2018, three young insurgents fleeing from Indian forces entered his house while he was writing poetry in his courtyard. He and his family fled the scene, and by the time the ensuing battle between the trapped insurgents and their pursuers ended thirteen hours later, his house was a pile of rubble and his most precious possession – a thousand hand-written poems composed over three decades – had been lost to fire.[5] This is a fairly typical Kashmiri story of life in a permanent war zone where people are focused on survival, not debates over an autonomy provision that had barely existed in practice for over five decades.

The Modi–Shah government's radical Kashmir initiative of August 2019, however, went far beyond burying the skeleton of Article 370. On the morning of 5 August, Amit Shah introduced a piece of legislation on the floor of parliament: the Jammu and Kashmir Reorganisation Bill, 2019. The legislation revoked the status of J&K as a constituent state of the Indian Union and dismembered it into two 'union territories' (UTs).

India's constitutional architecture is of a moderately decentralised polity. The country of 1.4 billion people is not a full-fledged federation like the US or Germany, but the extent of decentralisation goes beyond the devolution seen in the United Kingdom or Spain. The Indian Union is a hybrid of, and falls in the grey area between, the model of the unitary but devolved state (the UK and Spain, as examples) and the fully federal system of the USA or Germany.

The Indian Union is a union of its constituent *states* (Article 1.1 of the 1950 constitution), of which there were twenty-nine until J&K was stripped of that status in 2019. The states are the building blocks of India's polity, and statehood confers both symbolic status as a full member of the Union and significant statutory powers of self-governance, including the right to make state-specific laws on a wide range of matters. The political structure of India as the union of a gradually growing number of autonomous states evolved from the 1950s, and full statehood has been considered a major prize. In the twenty-first century alone, four new states have been carved out of the territory of existing states in response to longstanding demands for statehood pressed by communities within them, which increased the total number of states from twenty-five to twenty-nine. In the 1970s and 1980s there were at least seven cases of union territories being upgraded to states. Yet until August 2019, there wasn't a single case of the opposite: the downgrading of a state to a union territory, with the added twist of the liquidated state of J&K being divided into two union territories.

The union territories are a residual feature of India's political architecture. Before Indian J&K had its statehood abolished and was bifurcated into two union territories in August 2019, there were seven UTs – mostly small island and coastal enclaves as well as two cities, one of which is Delhi, the national capital. Of the seven, five are directly administered by the Union government through a New Delhi-appointed official called the lieutenant-governor. The other two – Delhi and Puducherry (formerly Pondicherry), an amalgam of four coastal enclaves in south India – have elected legislatures and ministerial executives with very limited powers, though they too have powerful lieutenant-governors and are subject to the Union government's overarching control. There are thus two types of union territories – those which are simply Union enclaves and those (Delhi and Puducherry) which have a limited measure of self-rule. But even the latter type, represented by Delhi and Puducherry, have governments which are not much more than glorified municipal authorities. They have only a fraction of the constitutional status and institutional powers of India's states, and the other UTs have virtually none.

The J&K Reorganisation Bill became law on 6 August 2019, after being passed by majorities in both chambers of the Indian parliament. In the Lok Sabha (House of the People), the popularly elected chamber of 543 members, the legislation passed with a two-thirds majority, powered by the BJP's own majority and the votes of its allied parties, plus support from some unaligned parties that got on the bandwagon to keep on the right side of the Modi government, which had just been re-elected to rule India until 2024. In the smaller, 250-member Rajya Sabha (House of the States), whose members are elected by legislators of the states' legislative assemblies, the BJP did not have an outright majority but mustered majority support with the help of allied and unaligned parties. In just two days, the Indian state of Jammu and Kashmir was liquidated and all of its institutions and laws became defunct overnight, with almost no serious parliamentary debate amid a surfeit of table-thumping triumphalism.

The J&K Reorganisation Act, which came into effect on 31 October 2019, carved two union territories out of the cadaver of the liquidated state.

One – the UT of Jammu and Kashmir – contains around 98 per cent of the erstwhile state's population and includes its two populous regions: the Kashmir Valley (about 8 million people) and the Jammu region to its south (about 6 million). The third region of the erstwhile state – Ladakh, a vast high-altitude desert which spreads east of the Valley to the frontiers of Tibet and Xinjiang – was made a separate union territory. Ladakh is very thinly populated and has about 300,000 people. The legislation stipulated that the UT of Ladakh would not have an elected assembly and executive (thus approximating the first and more common UT prototype), but that the UT of Jammu and Kashmir would (the Delhi/Puducherry prototype). In August 2019, Prime Minister Modi promised early elections to form such an assembly and a government – albeit with very limited powers – in the UT of Jammu and Kashmir. No election has materialised two years later.

The sheer radicalism of the new Kashmir policy unveiled by the Hindu nationalist government on 5 August 2019 was a major surprise and immediately made headlines across the world. Since Modi was re-elected to a second five-year term in May 2019, there had been speculation that his government would formally revoke Article 370, in keeping with the Hindu nationalist claim of almost seventy years that undue autonomy had encouraged separatism and secessionism in Indian Jammu and Kashmir. This claim is baseless – as Chapter 1 describes, that autonomy was rapidly hollowed out by integrative measures imposed from New Delhi between 1954 and 1965 and Article 370 reduced to a shell. I pointed out in a BBC op-ed published on 13 August 2019 that 'the actual cause of "separatism" in the state [Indian J&K] which [eventually] exploded in insurgency in 1990, was the de facto revocation of its autonomy in the 1950s and 1960s and the manner in which it was effected: through the collusion of puppet state governments installed by New Delhi and by turning the territory into a police-state ruled by draconian laws'.[6]

After Modi's re-election, there was also speculation that his government would revoke Article 35A of the Indian constitution, which pertained to the Indian state of Jammu and Kashmir. Article 35A was inserted into India's 1950 constitution in 1954, and restricted the right to own land and property in Indian J&K to permanent residents of the state, while also guaranteeing state residents priority access to government jobs. The guarantee continued a practice dating to the late 1920s, when the princely state ordered that 'state subjects' (domiciled residents) should receive preference in government jobs and land ownership after Kashmiri Pandits – the Valley's small Hindu minority – agitated against a prospective influx into the state of job-seekers from adjacent provinces of British-ruled India, particularly Punjab. Article 35A was intended as reassurance to the people of Indian J&K because the same presidential order (in 1954) which led to its insertion in the Indian constitution sharply rolled back Article 370 by extending the Indian Union government's legislative jurisdiction over Indian J&K to the majority of governance matters on the Union List, far beyond the three matters (external defence, foreign affairs, and currency and communications) originally specified by the accession agreement (October 1947) of the princely state to India, which formed the basis of Article 370. During Modi's first term as prime minister (2014–19), Hindu nationalist groups had been agitating against Article 35A, even though at least half-a-dozen other Indian states have very similar protections for native residents.

When the hammer wielded by Amit Shah descended on Indian Jammu and Kashmir on 5 August 2019, it obliterated not just Article 370 and Article 35A but Indian J&K's very existence as a state of the Indian Union. No BJP election manifesto had ever promised such a radical cure to the problem of Kashmir (though some Hindu nationalists had periodically agitated for the Jammu region, which has an overall Hindu majority, to be detached from the Valley and made a separate state of the Union). The erasure of Indian J&K's statehood was the political equivalent of an established academic being suddenly demoted from a full, permanent professorship to adjunct status on the faculty. The hammer-blow was compounded by Ladakh being hived off and turned into a separate union territory. A demand for Ladakh to be detached from the Indian state of J&K and made a union territory had existed since the end of the 1980s. But the demand – backed by the Hindu nationalists – was confined to the Buddhist community of Tibetan ethnicity who are numerically dominant in Ladakh's eastern Leh district, and was always strongly opposed by the Shia Muslims who are numerically dominant in the region's western Kargil district. According to the Indian national census of 2011, Muslims (46 per cent) outnumber Buddhists (40 per cent) in Ladakh's population.

THE HINDU NATIONALIST VIEW OF KASHMIR

The explanation for the Modi–Shah government's Kashmir policy can be located in the 'mission-and-vision' statement of the Rashtriya Swayamsevak Sangh (RSS, 'National Volunteer Organisation'), a hierarchically structured, all-male organisation which constitutes the core of post-independence India's Hindu nationalist movement. The RSS provides ideological direction and strategic guidance to a *sangh-parivar* (family of organisations) of which the BJP – the movement's political party – is one component. Narendra Modi, born in 1950, spent two decades, until the late 1980s, as a full-time RSS worker (*pracharak*, preacher or disseminator of Hindu nationalist ideology) before being seconded to work as a BJP organiser. The RSS's basic unit is the *shakha* (local branch); in 2017, 57,233 *shakhas* existed across India. Amit Shah (born in 1964) grew up participating in *shakhas* in his native state of Gujarat before becoming a leader of the RSS's student front in Ahmedabad, Gujarat's largest city, and then an activist of the BJP's youth wing.

The RSS's mission-and-vision statement describes a typical *shakha* meeting:

A saffron flag, called the *Bhagwa Dhwaj*, flutters in the middle of an open playground [saffron is the colour traditionally associated with Hinduism]. Youths, and boys of all ages, engage in indigenous [Indian] games. Uninhibited joy fills the air. There are [physical] exercises, *surya-namaskar* [saluting the sunrise] and sometimes training in skilfully wielding the *danda* [a stout wooden or bamboo stick]. All activities are totally disciplined. The physical-fitness programmes are followed by group singing of patriotic songs. Also forming part of the routine is the exposition and discussion of national events and problems. The day's activity culminates in the participants assembling in orderly rows in front of the flag at a single whistle of the group leader and reverentially reciting the prayer *Namaste Sada Vatsale Matrubhoome* – salutation to you, dear Motherland. The prayer verses, and the group leader's various commands, are all in Sanskrit [the classical language of ancient India]. The prayer concludes with a heartfelt utterance of the inspiring incantation *Bharat Mata Ki Jai* [Victory to Mother India].

The several million adult RSS members wear an identical uniform regardless of rank and age – in 2016 the longstanding uniform of khaki shorts, white shirt and black cap with laced black shoes was modified with the introduction of dark-brown trousers.

The RSS's mission-and-vision statement says that its 'goal [is] to attain *Param Vaibhav* – the pinnacle of glory – of the Hindu Rashtra' and predicts that 'the 21st century will be a century dominated by *Hindutva'* – the political ideology of Hindu nationalism. This ideology holds that the nearly 80 per cent of Indians who are census-classified as 'Hindu' by faith comprise an organic unity, and that Indian national identity is coterminous with being Hindu. The movement exists to inculcate that consciousness of unity by combating and neutralising deep fault-lines of caste, ethnicity, language, region and locality, and other divisive forms of identity and community. India is the country of Hindus thus defined and mobilised, not a mélange of diverse communities nor a melting pot of various influences down the ages. Since its first appearance as a political doctrine in the 1920s, the proponents of Hindutva have viewed the subcontinent's Muslims – three of ten Indians in pre-partition India and one of seven Indians today – as irreconcilable enemies of Hindudom who are undeserving of the status of fellow citizens. The six centuries of Muslim rulerships in India are seen as a long, dark night of enslavement of the Hindu nation as bad as, if not even worse than, the two centuries of British colonial rule.

The RSS's goal is to transform India into a giant version of its own self. In late 2019 Sunil Ambekar (born 1967), a top RSS official who became the organisation's *prachar pramukh* (chief of propaganda) in March 2021, published a book called *The RSS: Roadmaps for the 21st Century*. In the book's introduction, titled 'The Story of India's Future', Ambekar wrote that by 2047, the centenary of India's independence, 'the merger of the Sangh and Indian society would be as complete as the mixing of sugar in milk and just as the milk when stirred displays the characteristics of sugar, Indian society as a whole would start exhibiting the traits of the Sangh'. 'The Sangh's complete union with society,' he wrote, 'is conceived as the ultimate goal,' expressed through the RSS slogan *Sangh Samaj Banega* (the Sangh will become the society). Once this is achieved and the Sangh 'become[s] indistinguishable from Indian society' and 'coterminous with all of Indian society', 'the need for it [the RSS] to exist as a distinct entity would be obviated'. But until that time – when the RSS's belief system and world-view becomes that of India's – the RSS will exist and work towards that ultimate goal.[7] In March 2021, Dattatreya Hosabale, 67, a lifelong RSS activist, became the RSS's *sarkaryavah* (general secretary), the organisation's second-in-command and chief executive. As *sah-sarkaryavah* (assistant general secretary), he had explained in an interview to the Reuters news agency in 2015 that 'the RSS wants the BJP to win elections' not for its own sake but 'because only then can significant political, social and cultural changes take place in the country'.[8]

The RSS's mission-and-vision statement, which was written during the peak of the Kashmir insurgency in the 1990s, identifies Kashmir as a 'thrust-area' for the movement's work and objectives:

> The State of Jammu and Kashmir, with its oppressive Muslim-majority character, has been a headache for our country ever since Independence . . . The problem of Kashmir is in fact of our own making since . . . it has been conferred with a special status under Article 370 of the Constitution . . . The endless appeasement of the Muslim population by successive governments has been the bane of our Kashmir policy. Just as too much mollycoddling and lack of discipline spoil the child, so has Kashmir, a problem created by our own folly. With about one-third of the State territory illegally occupied by Pakistan, the alienated [Indian] area has virtually become a haven for subversives. The militants are taking advantage of the government's weakness, sure that the government dare not take ruthless action against them because of their privileged 'minority' tag.[9]

The Modi–Shah government's radical turn on Kashmir in August 2019 is based on this narrative of the conflict, and seeks to rectify the perceived follies of the past – mollycoddling, lack of discipline and appeasement – with unalloyed iron-fisted rule from New Delhi, where Hindu nationalists now reign. The liquidation not only of the (nominally) autonomous status of India's Jammu and Kashmir state but of the state itself, and its replacement by direct rule from New Delhi, is consistent with the kind of political structure Hindu nationalist doctrine holds that India as a whole should ideally have. This was expressed with the greatest clarity and candour by Madhav Sadashiv (M.S.) Golwalkar, who led the RSS from 1940 until his death in 1973. Revered as Shri-Guruji (The Great Guide) in the Hindu nationalist pantheon, Golwalkar published his magnum opus *Bunch of Thoughts* in the late 1960s. Since then, the lengthy treatise has been required reading for recruits to the middle and upper ranks of the RSS and is sometimes referred to as the Hindu nationalist 'Bible'. In it, Golwalkar wrote:

> The most important and effective step will be to bury for good all talk of a federal structure, to sweep away the existence of all autonomous and semi-autonomous states within Bharat [India] and proclaim: 'One Country! One State! One Legislature! One Executive!' with no trace of fragmentational [sic], regional, sectarian, linguistic or other types of pride being given scope for playing havoc with our integrated harmony. Let the Constitution be redrafted, so as to establish this Unitary form of Government![10]

In 2008, when he was Gujarat's chief minister, Narendra Modi published a book (in Gujarati) which consists of life sketches of sixteen men who have inspired him. All sixteen were RSS leaders or cadres, and the longest of the potted biographies is of Shri-Guruji, M.S. Golwalkar.

The liquidation of Indian J&K as a state of the Indian Union, which no one had anticipated prior to 5 August 2019, becomes perfectly intelligible in this ideological perspective. The demotion to union territory status served the practical purpose of bringing the ex-state under the rule of the Hindu nationalist government in New Delhi with no constraints or limitations whatsoever, and gave a *carte blanche* to the Union home (interior) ministry headed by Modi's chief enforcer, Amit Shah. But it also carried a deeper political message.

Apart from a far-right fringe among Jammu Hindus and the small Buddhist community who live on the remotest geographic fringe of the erstwhile state in eastern Ladakh, close to Tibet, most people in the Kashmir, Jammu and Ladakh regions of the liquidated Indian state of Jammu and Kashmir regarded that state to be an intrinsic part of their identity. The attachment cut across regional, social and political divides, and is a legacy of the princely state of Jammu and Kashmir that brought these regions and communities under one roof in the mid-nineteenth century and existed until 1947 (consciousness of this legacy exists on the Pakistani side of the LoC as well). In 2018, Indians were surveyed on whether they identified primarily with the nation as a whole, with their home state, or both equally. Overall, 36 per cent chose the national identity (Indian), 30 per cent their home state, and 27 per cent said they valued both identities equally (the remaining 7 per cent were not sure). In the Indian state of Jammu and Kashmir, the picture was strikingly different. There, 65 per cent chose the state (J&K) as the primary marker of their identity, and another 14 per cent said state and national identities were equally important. Only 16 per cent selected the national identity (Indian) as primary.[11] The erasure of the Indian state of Jammu and Kashmir from the political map of India was a very deliberate act, calculated to degrade the sense of self of most of the liquidated state's people, and represents a much deeper cut than the revocation of the hollowed-out shell of Article 370.

That degradation was compounded by the dismemberment of the dissolved Indian state of Jammu and Kashmir through the hiving off of Ladakh as a separate union territory. The Indian J&K state flag which officially ceased to exist in August 2019 had three white vertical lines on its red background to denote the state's three constituent regions: Jammu, Kashmir and Ladakh.

The dismemberment of Indian Jammu and Kashmir carried strong echoes of Hindu nationalist demands made in the early 2000s. In 2002, the Vishwa Hindu Parishad (VHP, 'World Hindu Council'), the RSS's religious affairs wing, demanded that Indian J&K be carved up into four parts. The VHP, formed in 1964, has been the most rabid face of India's Hindu nationalist movement and rose to prominence in the early 1990s as the spearhead of a campaign to demolish a sixteenth-century mosque in northern India said to have been built on the exact birthplace of Lord Ram, a deity of ancient Indian mythology (the mosque was razed in December 1992 in a frenzied attack by tens of thousands of Hindu nationalist militants). In June 2002, it was prominently reported in Indian media that:

> VHP demanded division of [Indian] Jammu & Kashmir into four parts, including a separate enclave with union territory status [in the Kashmir Valley] for resettling migrant Kashmiri Pandits [the Valley's small Hindu minority, most of whom left the Valley in early 1990 in circumstances discussed in Chapter 2]. Alleging neglect, discrimination, injustice and deeply rooted bias against Jammu and Ladakh by successive regimes in Srinagar, VHP's central board [further] demanded the carving out of a separate state [of India] comprising Jammu, Kathua, Udhampur, Doda, Poonch and Rajouri [the six districts making up the Jammu region]. VHP also demanded union territory status for Ladakh, and immediate abrogation of Article 370.[12]

A week later, the RSS leadership made a demand on similar lines: 'Close on the heels of the VHP demand for division of [Indian] Jammu & Kashmir into four parts, the RSS today sought trifurcation of the state – carving out the Kashmir Valley and Jammu as separate states, and Ladakh as a union territory. The resolution of the RSS national executive also demanded abrogation of Article 370.'[13]

The VHP and RSS demands were raised at a time when India and Pakistan appeared to be on the brink of war (Chapter 2) and were targeted at Atal Bihari Vajpayee, India's first Hindu nationalist prime minister, who headed a coalition government in New Delhi at the time. In contrast to Narendra Modi, Vajpayee doggedly pursued a Kashmir strategy based on moderation and diplomacy in very difficult circumstances between 1999 and 2004 (Chapter 2), which was greatly disliked by the RSS. Impending state elections in Indian J&K in autumn 2002 were another trigger for the rhetorical escalation. The BJP in Indian J&K hoped to gather the Jammu region's Hindu majority behind the demand for a separate Jammu state of the Indian Union. That flopped spectacularly, as the BJP won just one of the thirty-seven seats from the Jammu region in the autumn 2002 state election. The BJP manifesto for this state election also promised abrogation of Article 370, and the separation of Ladakh from the state and its reconstitution as a union territory.

Modi and Shah decided to detach Ladakh from Indian Jammu and Kashmir in August 2019, but did not separate the Jammu region from the Kashmir Valley. That may have been because six of the Jammu region's ten districts (up from six, as several new districts have been carved out of the previously existing districts for administrative convenience) have Muslim majorities, who would recoil at being made part of a separate UT formed from the Jammu region (the region's overall Hindu majority is concentrated in the four most populous districts in its southern plains and foothills, while the six Muslim-dominated districts in the hills and high mountains are more thinly populated). As the Hindu nationalist agenda of dividing Indian Jammu and Kashmir into three – or even four – parts remained incomplete, I noted in August 2019 that 'a further carve-up of [Indian] Jammu & Kashmir may be on the anvil, as advocated by the RSS and VHP in 2002'.[14]

Protests broke out in Ladakh's western Kargil district, where more than three-fourths of the population are Shia Muslims, against Ladakh's severance from Jammu and Kashmir and its reconstitution as a union territory. A joint action committee (JAC) of local political leaders across party lines, religious figures and civil society groups organised the protests. The Kargil district – where India and Pakistan fought a military conflict on the Indian side of the LoC in 1999 (Chapter 2) – observed a general strike on 6 August. There was a further two-day strike in late August and a three-day strike at the end of October, when the two UTs (Jammu and Kashmir, and Ladakh) formally came into existence. The Kargil JAC was able to take out several protest marches with thousands of people, unlike in the Kashmir Valley where a draconian lockdown was imposed from 5 August to prevent protests. The Kargil JAC's general secretary, Nasir Munshi, said: 'We never demanded a separate union territory. We never wanted the division of the state. The decision has been imposed on us and we will not accept it.'[15]

In August 2019, I noted that 'the reaction [to the Modi government's radical reset of India's Kashmir policy] among the Buddhists who dominate Leh, the eastern Ladakh district, as well as among Jammu Hindus, has been subdued owing to the loss of their rights given by Article 35A', which prevented people from outside the state from acquiring lands and property and gave locals privileged entitlement to government jobs.[16] That unease among Jammu Hindus and Ladakhi Buddhists – the only two communities in Indian J&K not rendered aghast by the hammer-and-axe attack launched from New Delhi on 5 August 2019 – has grown significantly since (on which there is more later in this chapter).

Both Kargil and Leh are thinly populated districts on the remote peripheries of the erstwhile Indian state of J&K, and their citizens had well-founded complaints of marginalisation and neglect going back decades. To address this, local governments were established in both districts to implement development projects and grassroots governance and provide an accessible layer of officialdom – first in Leh in 1995, and then in Kargil in 2003. These governments consist of councils of thirty members, of whom twenty-six are directly elected by the locals, and five-member executives drawn from the elected representatives. Reflecting the presence of a sizeable Buddhist minority in the Kargil district and a sizeable Muslim minority in the Leh district, the five-member executive in Leh typically has one Muslim and its counterpart in Kargil one Buddhist. The super-imposition of a union territory administration run by New Delhi's bureaucrats has badly undermined these elected local bodies. In May 2020 Chering Dorge, who lives in the town of Leh, resigned as the Ladakh region's BJP president. In October 2020, he explained why: 'The people running the union territory administration are not from Ladakh' and the elected local government has been rendered 'toothless'. He added: 'Earlier, like the people of the Kashmir and Jammu divisions, we Ladakhis were also protected by Article 35A. Now that protection is gone and we [too] are vulnerable to outsiders who come to buy our land and take our jobs.'[17]

On 15 August 2019, India's independence day, Narendra Modi delivered the customary prime minister's address to the nation from the Red Fort (Lal Qila), built by India's Mughal dynasty in the mid-seventeenth century in Delhi. He declared, the *Washington Post* reported, that 'the work that was not done in the last 70 years' – a decisive resolution of the Kashmir problem – 'has been accomplished in 70 days after my new government came to power' (Modi took office for his second term on 30 May 2019).[18] On 30 May 2020, Amit Shah published an op-ed in the *Times of India* newspaper on the first anniversary of the Modi government's second term. Titled 'Undoing six decades in six years' (since Modi first took power in May 2014), the article argued that 'historic decisions like the abolition of Articles 370 and 35A in Jammu & Kashmir' have 'rectified the historic mistakes after Independence'.[19]

In August 2019, I noted that 'this government's radical Kashmir initiative diverges from the authoritarian, centralist policies pursued by many previous Indian governments in two crucial respects'. First, earlier governments always relied on intermediaries: clients drawn from the Kashmir Valley's political elite. But Modi and Shah dispensed with those intermediaries and opted for an ultra-centralist approach. Second, New Delhi's repression in Indian Jammu and Kashmir from the 1950s onwards was always justified by the peculiar argument – mentioned and critiqued in Chapter 1 – that 'keeping Muslim-majority [Indian] J&K as part of India, by any means necessary, was essential to validating India's claim of being a "secular state". Modi and Shah, both hardline Hindu nationalists, have no use for such contorted rationales.'[20]

In retrospect, the first hint of the Kashmir policy unveiled by the Modi–Shah government on 5 August 2019 appeared two years earlier – in Prime Minister Modi's independence-day address on 15 August 2017. In that speech, Modi said that the Kashmir problem could only be tackled by warmly embracing Kashmiris (Hindi: *galay lagana*) disaffected with Indian authority. The speech's reference to Kashmir, made a year after the Kashmir Valley erupted in civil unrest in July 2016 which lasted six months before subsiding (Chapter 3), won praise for its generous and humanitarian tone. Modi repeated the same phrase – the need for a heartfelt embrace of Kashmiris – in his independence-day speech on 15 August 2018.

In September 2019, Modi reiterated the rhetoric during an election campaign speech for the BJP in the large western Indian state of Maharashtra

(Mumbai, formerly Bombay, is its capital), which was holding state elections in October: *'Humey naya Kashmir banana hai, har Kashmiri ko galay lagana hai'* (We have to make a new Kashmir, and embrace every Kashmiri).[21] 'From a rally in Maharashtra,' it was reported in Indian media, 'Prime Minister Narendra Modi reached out to the people of Jammu & Kashmir with a call to all Indians to help build a new Kashmir, embrace the people of the state [sic] who have suffered for decades and turn the Kashmir Valley into *jannat* – paradise or heaven – once again.'[22] Another report read: 'Prime Minister Narendra Modi said: "We want to create a paradise in Jammu & Kashmir once again, and hug every Kashmiri". He added that the people of Jammu & Kashmir want [economic] development and employment.'[23] The reference to development and employment is derived from a grandiose vision of 'New India' – developed and prosperous – that Modi has been promising to deliver since his first successful campaign to become India's leader in 2014. This 'development and employment' narrative – which claims that the Kashmir Valley and Indian J&K as a whole will be reborn as a twenty-first-century paradise through a flood of big-business investments, infrastructure improvements and mass tourism following its long-overdue full integration into India – has replaced the 'secularism' narrative previous Indian governments used to rhetorically bind Kashmir to India.

By September 2019, it was very clear what Modi's 'embrace' of Kashmiris really meant. The princely state of Jammu and Kashmir that existed from 1846 to 1947 has been the prime bone of contention between India and Pakistan since the subcontinent's partition in 1947. The Kashmir dispute sparked two India–Pakistan wars – in 1947–48 and 1965 – and the third war in 1971, triggered by the terminal crisis of Pakistan's unity and the blood-soaked birth of the sovereign state of Bangladesh from East Pakistan, also saw fighting on the Kashmir front (Chapter 1). India and Pakistan fought another border war in the Kargil sector of Ladakh in 1999 (Chapter 2). In 1990, the Kashmir Valley exploded in insurgency and insurrection against Indian authority, which subsequently spread to some parts of Indian J&K's Jammu region as well and cost tens of thousands of lives before subsiding from the mid-2000s (Chapter 2). After the insurgency waned, the Kashmir Valley was wracked by 'stone-pelting' uprisings against Indian authority, notably in 2010 and 2016–17 (Chapter 3). The sprawling territory disputed between India and Pakistan since 1947 has thus been the site of conventional wars, the brutal violence of protracted insurgency and counter-insurgency, and civil insurrection over seven decades. The locals could not be faulted for thinking they had seen it all.

The hammer-and-axe offensive on Indian Jammu and Kashmir that Modi and Shah unleashed on 5 August 2019 took repression to a surreal level and turned the Kashmir Valley, in particular, into a real-life approximation of the nightmarish worlds of George Orwell's *Nineteen Eighty-Four* and Franz Kafka's *The Trial*. In August 2019, I noted that 'what the BJP government has done is akin to what Serbia's Milosevic regime did in 1989 by unilaterally revoking Kosovo's autonomy and imposing a police-state on Kosovo's Albanian majority', but yet, 'the BJP government's approach to Kashmir goes beyond what Milosevic intended for the Kosovo Albanians: subjugation'.

Indeed, the Modi regime's vision of a *naya* (new) Kashmir which will once again be a *jannat*, or paradise, is far more ambitious. It entails making loyal Indians out of disloyal Kashmiris through a mixture of strict discipline and what is known in the People's Republic of China as 're-education', resulting in a psychological makeover. 'This approach,' I argued in August 2019, 'is [more] akin to China's policy towards the Uighurs of Xinjiang.' In January 2020 India's chief of defence staff (CDS), General Bipin Rawat, addressed the Raisina Dialogue, an international conference that takes place every winter in New Delhi. Referring to Indian Kashmir, he asserted that there 'girls and boys as young as ten or twelve are now being radicalized' and that 'people who have been completely radicalized need to be taken out separately, possibly taken into some deradicalization camps'.[24] Rawat had just finished his term as chief of the Indian Army and, instead of retiring, as is normal, been appointed as chief of defence staff, a new post overseeing all three wings of the Indian armed forces created at the initiative of the Modi government.

Towards the end of the sixteenth century, the forces of India's greatest Mughal monarch, Akbar, forayed north into the Himalayas and conquered the Kashmir Valley. Thereafter, the Mughal royals developed the habit of journeying there every summer – travelling along a route called the 'Mughal Road' through the Pir Panjal mountain range – to bask in its salubrious climate and lovely scenery, away from the punishing heat of the north Indian plains. Akbar's son and successor, Jahangir, was particularly enamoured of Kashmir and called the place a heaven on earth around 1619.[25] Exactly 400 years after that famous pronouncement by the ruler of Delhi, the current rulers, Narendra Modi and Amit Shah, turned the lost paradise – troubled and tortured since 1947 – into a veritable hell (*jahannam*) on earth.

A HELL ON EARTH

In 2020–21, the pandemic-hit world became acquainted with lockdowns and what they mean for normal life. The people of the Kashmir Valley have long been accustomed to lockdown conditions. In the three decades (since 1990) that the Valley has been an active war zone, they have recurrently experienced extended periods of curfew, thousands of counter-insurgency 'crackdowns' (a localised lockdown) and hundreds of protest *hartals* (general strikes). The precarity of everyday existence has over the decades become normalised in the Kashmir Valley, which even before 1990 was run – since the 1950s – as a police state, and was subjected to oppressive rule for a century before that, under the 1846–1947 princely state of Jammu and Kashmir. But seven months before the Covid-19 pandemic upended the world, the hardened population of the Valley – eight million people habituated over generations to the absence of normalcy – were hit with a lockdown that surpassed all their previous experiences.

The signal that the Modi government's move on Kashmir was imminent came on Friday 2 August. On that day, the home department of the government of Indian Jammu and Kashmir – run by bureaucrats acting for New Delhi, because the state had been under Central rule since June 2018, with no elected government in office – issued an 'Order' with the subject-line 'Security Advisory'. All visitors present in the Kashmir Valley were ordered to leave 'immediately'. At the time, the summer tourist season was in full swing. Since 2016, when large-scale and sustained protests engulfed the Valley from early July (Chapter 3), few tourists had visited the Valley, and a significant level of tourism resumed for the first time in several years in the summer of 2019. The tourism trade, particularly in the peak summer months, is the essential source of livelihood for hundreds of thousands of Valley families, from hotel-owners to the boatmen plying their distinctive *shikara* boats on Srinagar's Dal Lake. The holidaying tourists in the Valley in the summer of 2019 were as usual very largely people from various parts of India, plus some foreigners, mostly from Western countries.

But they were not the only visitors present in the Valley. The annual pilgrimage to Amarnath, a famous cave shrine of the Hindu deity Shiva located in a remote mountainous area in the eastern part of the Valley at an altitude of 12,750 feet, was in full swing. Thousands of pilgrims from across India were undertaking the journey on foot and horseback, accompanied as always by local Kashmiri Muslim guides. The Amarnath *yatra* (pilgrimage), which happens in July–August, had not been called off in much more dangerous times – in 1996, when an unseasonal blizzard in the insurgency-wracked Valley killed nearly 250 pilgrims, and in the early 2000s, when terrorist attacks in 3 consecutive years (2000–02) killed almost 60 people, including many local Kashmiri Muslims in addition to pilgrims and members of the Indian security forces guarding the *yatra* route and its wayside camps (Chapter 2). But the official directive issued on 2 August 2019 was unequivocal: 'Keeping in view the latest intelligence inputs of terror threats, with specific targeting of the Amarnath Yatra, and given the prevailing security situation in the Kashmir Valley, in the interest of safety and security of the tourists and the Amarnath Yatris, it is advised that they may curtail their stay in the Valley immediately'.[26] To reinforce the urgency, the commander of the Indian Army's 15th Corps, stationed in the Valley, held a press conference and reiterated the imminent risk of terror attacks.

A highly organised mass evacuation of all holidaymakers and pilgrims commenced immediately. On Saturday 3 August, 6,216 persons arrived at Srinagar's airport in response to the order for immediate departure. Of these, 5,829 left the Valley on 32 scheduled commercial flights, all full to capacity and mostly headed to Delhi. For the remaining persons, 387 in number, 4 Indian Air Force (IAF) transport aircraft were on hand and they were flown either to Jammu city, 200 miles to the south, or to Pathankot and Hindon, IAF bases in northern India. Hundreds of civilians travelling on military transport planes is unheard of in India, except in dire contingencies during wars. Those evacuated by air were around one-quarter of the approximately 25,000 tourists and pilgrims in the Kashmir Valley. Hundreds of buses had been dispatched to collect the rest from various places, and they were taken out of the Valley over the weekend along the highway leading south from Srinagar to Jammu. By Sunday 4 August, 'almost 95 percent' of the tourists and pilgrims had been evacuated according to the Valley's director of tourism, the majority 'ferried in buses and cars during the night'. They were joined by 1,400 students of the National Institute of Technology's (NIT) Srinagar campus, who departed the Valley on Saturday 'on special buses arranged by the administration'.[27] These students from various parts of India comprised over half of the Srinagar NIT's student body of 2,400 (the rest were locals). Some of the people subjected to the evacuation were frightened, many just baffled by the abruptness of it all, and yet others were unconvinced and resentful. 'I have been visiting Kashmir for many years and have never seen such irresponsible behaviour by the government,' a tourist from Delhi forced to cut short his holiday fumed.[28] Meanwhile, the *Hindustan Times* newspaper reported on Sunday 4 August that 'hundreds of non-local labourers [mostly working in construction] have also started leaving the Valley'.[29]

While tens of thousands of Indian citizens were being frog-marched out of Indian Jammu and Kashmir, tens of thousands of other Indians were arriving. They were not holidaymakers, pilgrims or students. During the week prior to Monday 5 August, 400 companies of Central Armed Police Forces (CAPFs) – paramilitary police under the authority of the Union government's home ministry – arrived in the Valley by road and airlift. These men were mainly from the Central Reserve Police Force (CRPF), the largest of the CAPFs. A company consists of 100–110 personnel, so between 40,000 and 45,000 paramilitary troopers arrived in the Valley. They reinforced the army troops and paramilitary and police personnel already present in Indian Jammu and Kashmir – several hundred thousand men if the numbers stationed on the borders (particularly the 500 miles of the LoC) and across the interiors are combined. From 1990 until the mid-2000s, the Valley and extensive areas of the Jammu region were gripped by insurgency and counter-insurgency (Chapter 2), and swamped with soldiers and police. But even after insurgency diminished sharply from the mid-2000s onwards (Chapter 3), first-time visitors would invariably be shocked by the scale of military, paramilitary and police deployment in the Valley. The visible increase of troopers on the streets beyond that 'normal' level fuelled mass trepidation and speculation about what was being planned. The revocation of Article 35A seemed certain, the abrogation of Article 370 probable, and the RSS-advocated 'trifurcation' of Indian J&K to carve out separate states in the Valley and the Jammu region and a UT from Ladakh looked possible.

On the morning of Monday 5 August, Srinagar – a city of 1.5 million – still bustled with crowds and traffic as markets and shops opened, children travelled to school and people tried to get to work. But as events unfolded in New Delhi, a deathly chill descended on the mid-summer day and the streets emptied out, while tens of thousands of heavily armed paramilitary troopers and police spread out across the city amid a ghostly urban landscape of shuttered and eerily silent neighbourhoods. By morning, citizens noticed that not only was the internet down and cable television inaccessible, but mobile phones were not working and even landlines had gone dead. So people had no way of finding out what exactly was transpiring in the Indian parliament, beyond the obvious that it must be something of grave magnitude. Darkness at noon – borrowing the title of Arthur Koestler's 1940 novel based on Russia under Stalinist terror in the second half of the 1930s – had descended on Kashmir.

The wave of repression unleashed by the new dispensation in Indian Jammu and Kashmir from 5 August 2019 relied on two main techniques. The first was a total lockdown to prevent protests, which was enforced most strictly in the Kashmir Valley and more loosely in the other two regions. The Valley lockdown was similar to the most draconian of the Covid-19 lockdowns the world saw in 2020–21, but with two very important differences.

First, all means for people to communicate beyond their urban neighbourhood or village were cut off. With no mobile (or even landline) telephone services, making a phone call or sending a text (SMS) message was impossible. Other everyday communication methods such as WhatsApp simply disappeared overnight – in December 2019, several million people lost their WhatsApp accounts because the application autodeleted accounts after four months of inactivity. There was no internet, so no way of sending or receiving e-mail. On 6 September, I received an e-mail from an acquaintance who had driven from Srinagar to the town of Kargil in western Ladakh – a journey of 125 miles along a mountain road that takes 5 to 6 hours and crosses the Zojila Pass at 11,300 feet into Ladakh. The e-mail read: 'Our internet service in Kashmir [Valley] is not working, I have come to Kargil to use the internet. I won't be online after tomorrow afternoon.'

A second feature makes the Kashmir lockdown of 2019–20 unique. Anyone who stepped out of their home could not go more than a few hundred yards, at the most, before encountering heavily armed soldiers in full combat gear. These uniformed, gun-toting men were stationed in every urban neighbourhood and every village. In Srinagar and other urban centres, whole neighbourhoods of tens of thousands of people were sealed off with concertina wire at all entry/exit points, while the soldiers kept watch. The combined effect of the snapping of all means of communication and the blanketing of populated areas with soldiers meant that every *mohalla* (urban neighbourhood) and village became an isolated island, and the Valley as a whole was cut off from the world outside. It was, effectively, home internment of millions of people.

Not all were fortunate enough to be confined to their homes with no communication with anyone else. Thousands were taken away from their homes to prison. The arrest and incarceration of thousands of people was the second technique of the Modi–Shah strategy. On 19 November 2019, the Modi government's junior minister for home affairs (Amit Shah's deputy) informed the Indian parliament, in response to a question, that 5,161 persons had been arrested in Indian Jammu and Kashmir since 5 August. At the parliament's next session in spring 2020 the home ministry stated, in response to another question, that 7,357 persons had been arrested in Indian J&K between 5 August 2019 and 29 February 2020. The ages of those arrested ranged from children – at least 144 minors, the youngest 9 years old – to octogenarians.

The vast majority of first-rung, second-rung and even third-rung leaders of Indian J&K's spectrum of pro-'self-determination' political factions – mostly from the Kashmir Valley – were already in prison since a wave of arrests targeted at those groups from February–March 2019 (Chapter 3). From 5 August, the arrests targeted prominent and mid-level leaders, as well as many local organisers, of the 'pro-India' political parties, especially the two largest – the Jammu & Kashmir National Conference (NC) and the Jammu & Kashmir People's Democratic Party (PDP). Those detained included three former chief ministers of the dissolved Indian state of Jammu and Kashmir – the father–son duo of Farooq Abdullah and Omar Abdullah (NC), scions of the leading Kashmiri political family, and Mehbooba Mufti (PDP), the daughter of another former chief minister, Mufti Mohammad Sayeed (who escaped incarceration because he died in January 2016). Other pro-India politicians detained included former cabinet ministers in the state government and members of the defunct Indian J&K state legislature. Some of them were imprisoned in the erstwhile state legislators' hostel in Srinagar, which was declared a 'sub-jail'.

But these members of the 'pro-India' political class constituted only a fraction of the thousands of arrests. Many leading figures of the Kashmiri intelligentsia and civil society were also arrested: lawyers, professors, business entrepreneurs and other professionals. Yet other detainees were people living in rural areas, respected and influential in their localities as community leaders. The midnight knock on the door came for residents of Srinagar's most affluent neighbourhoods and for residents of far-flung villages. Some of the captives were taken to well-known prisons such as the Srinagar Central Jail, and others to jails in the Jammu region. But many hundreds were airlifted out of Indian J&K to prisons in various cities in northern India, without the knowledge of their families. Hundreds of detainees were charged under the J&K Public Safety Act (PSA). The PSA was enacted in 1978 (Chapter 1) and provided for twelve months in detention without any recourse to a court of law for 'persons acting in any manner prejudicial to the maintenance of public order' and two years 'in the case of persons acting in any manner prejudicial to the security of the State'. As a state law, the PSA should by logic have lapsed with the liquidation of Indian Jammu and Kashmir as a state of the Indian Union, but it continues to stalk Indian J&K post-August 2019.

By February 2020, six months on, almost none of those swept up in the wave of detentions had been released except for a handful of minor politicians from pro-India parties who signed statements written by their captors agreeing to desist from political activity. A few relatively more prominent 'pro-India' politicians were moved from prison to house arrest after six months, subject to a ban on venturing out or even meeting with members of the public in their own homes. In the Jammu region, too, politicians from the entire range of legally recognised non-BJP parties – including India's withered Congress party, and a local party of Jammu Hindus opposed to the Hindu nationalists' sledgehammer onslaught – were prevented from engaging in any public activity and subjected to de facto house arrest.

In August and September, top leaders of Indian opposition parties who attempted to visit Indian J&K were sent back to Delhi on arrival at Srinagar and Jammu airports. On 31 August 2019, Krishna Bose, my mother, wrote an article in an Indian newspaper in which she recalled her visit to the Jammu, Kashmir and Ladakh regions in the summer of 2003, leading a delegation of Indian members of parliament. At the time, Indian J&K was just beginning to emerge from the bloodbath of insurgency and counter-insurgency that had consumed it from 1990 (Chapter 2). In Srinagar, she recalled, she met with both Mufti Mohammad Sayeed, the pro-India chief minister, and Mohammad Yasin Malik, chief of the pro-independence Jammu and Kashmir Liberation Front (JKLF) and a former guerrilla leader – who has been imprisoned in Delhi's Tihar Jail since early 2019 – at their respective residences. In the summer of 2019, she noted, Indian opposition MPs were being stopped from entering Indian Jammu and Kashmir by Indian security forces.[30]

The two techniques – the cruelly punitive mass lockdown and the sinister policy of targeted yet large-scale arrests – complemented each other. I call the first the strangulation technique, and the second the decapitation technique. The first technique aimed to strangle the possibility of spontaneous outbreaks of protest – large-scale or even localised – by imprisoning millions of people in their homes with no means to communicate with each other or with the outside world. The second technique aimed to reinforce the first by decapitating the political as well as civil society leadership – at both higher and local levels – who could articulate dissent and potentially organise protests.

The two-pronged strategy largely achieved its immediate objective – of suffocating protest and thus pre-empting the very real risk of an uprising that could become uncontrollable. The protests that did erupt were localised and sporadic. On the afternoon of Friday 9 August, 7,000–10,000 people marched in Soura, an inner suburb of Srinagar, after the weekly prayer congregation at a local mosque. A video of the protest the BBC authenticated and posted on its website shows the marchers scattering as women wail in the background, amid sounds of gunfire – first a number of individual gunshots and then staccato bursts. The video had footage of a demonstration, clearly at least several thousand strong, chanting 'India, go back' and 'Allahu Akbar' (God is Great), and of a man who seemed to be a mosque preacher leading a gathering of thousands assembled in an open grassy space in a chant that had previously reverberated in the Valley during the uprising against Indian rule in the early 1990s (Chapter 2): 'Hum kya chahtey? Azaadi' (What do we want? Freedom!) and 'Azaadi ka matlab kya? La Ilaha Illallah' (What is the meaning of freedom? There is no God but Allah).

For several months afterwards the residents of Anchar, a working-class enclave of about 15,000 in the Soura area, kept the police and paramilitary forces at bay by erecting barricades of tin sheeting and assorted other items. The youths of Anchar kept nightly vigil at the barricades, drinking kahwa (the distinctive Kashmiri tea flavoured with cinnamon, cardamom, saffron and almonds) around bonfires as winter set in. But the open show of defiance in Soura/Anchar remained exceptional. There were some other smaller, scattered protest marches in the Valley in August, which were quickly dispersed with use of force. In September, a few dozen men who tried to demonstrate with hand-written placards in Srinagar on the occasion of Ashura (an important religious observance for the Valley's Shia minority of about 15 per cent) were beaten up and hauled away; in October, a demonstration by a dozen elderly women wielding homemade placards in the city centre of Srinagar was broken up in minutes and the participants detained. Also in October, Ram Madhav, a Hindu nationalist leader entrusted with

Kashmir affairs, visited Srinagar and warned that there was yet plenty of space in jails in India.

Yet protest was not entirely suppressed. In January 2020 the Indian home ministry stated, in response to a right-to-information request made by a citizen, that of 1,999 stone-pelting incidents recorded in Indian J&K during 2019, 1,193 (60 per cent) had taken place after 5 August. Stone-pelting – which has a lineage going back many decades in Kashmir but became the main method of showing defiance of authority in the Valley from 2010, after the decline of insurgency to negligible levels (Chapter 3) – peaked during the year in August, when there were 658 incidents. There were 248 stone-pelting incidents in September and 203 in October, before falling to 84 in November.[31] In localised outbreaks of protest, people displayed a variety of flags, but the flag of 'Azad' (Free) Jammu and Kashmir, the nominally autonomous territory across the Line of Control which contains most of Pakistani Kashmir's population of about 6 million, was especially noticeable. There was no sign of the abolished flag of the liquidated Indian state of Jammu and Kashmir.

Instead of taking to the streets in the hundreds of thousands, or even millions – a scenario the government in New Delhi had clearly feared – the people of the Kashmir Valley chose circumspection over erupting in rage. That caution was probably due in part to the Valley's recent history – where tens of thousands have died violently since 1990, especially during the period between 1990 and the mid-2000s (Chapter 2) – and in part to the mature realisation that, after the watershed of 5 August 2019, a new phase had opened in the seven-decade Kashmir conflict and a long struggle lay ahead. The Valley took recourse to a continuous *hartal* (general strike) as the main form of protest. Grocery shops opened for a couple of hours in the mornings before downing shutters, public transport stayed off the roads, and parents disregarded calls by the authorities to send their children back to school. This situation persisted for three months until mid-November, when markets started to open to enable small businesses to make some money and citizens to stock up on essentials for the long winter. Schools stayed deserted – children studied from home or in makeshift community schools that sprang up in various localities – and reopened only in late February of 2020, only to close again after a fortnight as the Covid-19 pandemic struck.

The Hindu nationalist government's Kashmir policy was challenged almost immediately in India's supreme court. On 10 August 2019, two members of the Indian parliament elected from the Valley in the April–May 2019 general election petitioned the court to declare both the presidential order and the J&K Reorganisation Bill of 5 August as *ultra vires* of India's constitution, and made a strong case on procedural grounds. They sought an early hearing of the matter, given its gravity. That petition and a clutch of similar petitions have not been taken up by India's supreme court, whose judges otherwise take pride in their role of being the ultimate guardians of the law and the constitution of the world's largest democracy.

On the same day, 10 August, Anuradha Bhasin, executive editor of the *Kashmir Times*, Indian Jammu and Kashmir's oldest English-language daily newspaper (founded in 1964), filed an urgent petition before the supreme court citing a crisis of press freedom in the liquidated Indian state. The petition said that 'harsh curfew-like restrictions imposed through the heavy presence of police and paramilitary forces, using barricades and checkpoints, block the movement of journalists in the Kashmir Valley, which is excessive, disproportionate and a gross abuse of State power in violation of the rights and in derogation of the duty of the free press'. Ms Bhasin further stated that, being based in the city of Jammu – which is 190 miles south of Srinagar and Indian J&K's second largest city – she had been unable to contact her staff in Srinagar since 5 August because all landlines, mobile phone networks and the internet had been put out of operation.[32]

This petition did come up for a hearing in the supreme court in New Delhi – four months later, in January 2020 (by coincidence on a day I happened to be staying with Ms Bhasin and her family at their home in Jammu city). The court ruled that indefinite denial of internet access amounts to a violation of citizens' fundamental rights and asked the Indian government to 'review' its approach. A few days before this hearing, Syed Mujtaba, a Srinagar lawyer, complained to India's National Human Rights Commission (NHRC) that 'the internet ban in J&K is the longest ever imposed in modern [sic] history' and 'is *prima facie* violating fundamental rights', and asked the NHRC to urgently seek an explanation from the Indian government's ministry of home affairs.[33] At this time, in January

2020, thousands of Kashmiris from the Valley were braving snowy weather and packing like sardines into a daily train service – which had resumed in mid-November – from Srinagar to Banihal, a small town of 4,000 people which lies just south of the Valley, across the Pir Panjal range in the Jammu region. The reason for undertaking the two-hour journey was to access the internet, which had been restored in the Jammu region at the end of August. Banihal, a sleepy mountain town, heaved with people queueing every day at its half-dozen internet cafés, which did a roaring business along with the local eateries and hotels.[34] Meanwhile, in the first week of January 2020, the tourism department of the Indian union territory of Jammu and Kashmir took out multicoloured half-page advertisements in newspapers across India. The image featured a smiling skier on the slopes of Gulmarg – a famous resort of the Valley – against a backdrop of pine forests and snow-clad mountains. 'Kashmir Calling!' the advertisement read; 'Fall In Love Again' (the 'V' in 'Love' a heart emoji) and experience '*Jannat ka nazara*' (a glimpse of Paradise).[35]

The Valley's landline telephone network, disconnected on 5 August, was restored after six weeks, in mid-September. But all mobile services remained disabled except for the facility to make one-to-one voice calls, which was reinstated in mid-October. Under pressure amid a mounting international uproar, the Indian government's union territory administration announced at various points during January 2020 that government-run hospitals would be reconnected to the internet, one-to-one texting would be permitted, and fixed-line and mobile internet would be restored but initially only to a few hundred 'whitelisted' sites and restricted to 2G speeds on security grounds (the standard across India is 4G). In May 2020, the Indian supreme court belatedly heard a clutch of petitions asking for the restoration of 4G services and declined to intervene in the matter. An Indian newspaper editorial observed:

> The supreme court declining pleas for restoration of 4G services is disturbing, for several reasons. The continued denial of such services in the [India-wide Covid-19] lockdown constitutes a special injustice to a people deprived of fundamental freedoms since August 5, 2019. The 2G service

is not enough for children to access online classes, patients to consult doctors, businesses to conduct online transactions. But the supreme court's decision is also troubling because it appears to be part of a broader pattern of delay and evasion [on Kashmir-related matters since August 2019] ... By throwing the ball on internet access back to a government-led committee, and by its delay in taking up cases of *habeas corpus* in Kashmir, the court has given the executive a free pass ... The apex court is the custodian of fundamental liberties, and of the letter and spirit of the constitution. That it should be seen to display a lack of urgency where the executive needs to do some explaining is disappointing and dispiriting.[36]

Subsequently, in August 2020, the Indian government made a token concession of allowing 4G services in two of the twenty administrative districts in the UT of Jammu and Kashmir – one a small Valley district north of Srinagar, the other a Hindu-majority district in the southern part of the Jammu region. There was no rationale given for why these two districts had been chosen from the ten districts each in the Valley and Jammu regions. Finally, in February 2021, the UT administration announced that 4G services would be restored in all districts. 'Hoteliers, businesspersons and those connected with education in the Kashmir Valley and the Jammu region [especially] welcomed the decision,' though many initially thought it must be fake news. 'Is it really true?' asked Desh Ratan Dubey, a trader in Jammu city.[37]

The painfully gradual reinstation of essential communications provided some relief to the besieged population. But the economic damage done by the post-5 August lockdown – particularly the internet ban – was massive. The livelihoods of many hundreds of thousands of families were ruined as all sectors of the economy were crippled: tourism, transport and the trade in Kashmiri shawls, carpets and timber furniture among others. The cultivation of fruits, particularly apples, is a mainstay of the Kashmir Valley's economy, and the autumn apple-harvesting season – which provided income to thousands of seasonal workers who came to the Valley every year from across northern and eastern India since the waning of insurgency in the mid-2000s – was badly disrupted. The economies of the three regions of the liquidated Indian state of Jammu and Kashmir are interconnected and interdependent, and the situation in the Valley produced adverse effects on the other two regions – for example, on businesses in Jammu which transport Kashmiri apples in bulk to the Indian market or process and package walnuts grown in the Valley. In August 2019, it was announced that a 'global investors' summit' would be held in the cities of Srinagar and Jammu in mid-October, to generate a flood of Indian and international business investments in the newly created UT of Jammu and Kashmir which would turn Modi's developmental vision for the territory into a reality. The date was subsequently pushed back to late November. The mega-event failed to materialise.

The existential reality of Indian Jammu and Kashmir after 5 August 2019 had fatal consequences for lives, not just livelihoods. At the end of August Adil Akhzer, a Srinagar-based reporter for an Indian newspaper, wrote about the case of his younger sister, Aieman. Aieman, 26, had been admitted to the city's Lal Ded maternity hospital on 20 August to deliver her first child, and 'the wardrobe in her room [at home] was filled with baby clothes, diapers and milk powder'. On the evening of 23 August Akhzer went to the hospital, as he did every day after work to see his expectant sister – using his press credentials to pass through checkpoints on deserted 'roads blocked with spools of concertina wire and metal barricades' – and learned that the baby had died. The baby's heartbeat rate had dropped somewhat – not normally a fatal development – but the hospital's senior gynaecologist could not be called to urgently attend to Aieman because all phone lines were dead, and not even an online consultation was possible because there was no internet. The hospital sent a car to fetch the doctor, but by the time she arrived, 'she could only re-confirm that the baby was no more'. 'Our case was not the only one at the hospital,' Akhzer wrote, as 'there were many other stories of despair, agony and helplessness.' After burying the dead baby on 24 August, the journalist went to cover 'the [daily] official press briefing where the government spokesman Rohit Kansal said: "The situation is improving".'[38]

Mian Abdul Qayoom, the 76-year-old president of the Jammu & Kashmir High Court Bar Association, was taken away from his Srinagar home on the night of 4–5 August 2019. He was then taken by air to the main jail in the city of Agra in north India – the city of the seventeenth-century Taj Mahal. There he was put in a small cell along with two prominent Kashmiri business entrepreneurs: Mubeen Shah, 63, a diabetes patient, and Yasin Khan, 60. All three men had been taken away from their homes in Srinagar between midnight and 2 a.m. on 5 August 2019 by uniformed men who had no arrest warrants. Qayoom, a diabetic who has only one kidney, was charged after his detention in Srinagar under the J&K Public Safety Act of 1978. He is partially disabled and walks with a limp since being shot in his lawyer's chamber in Srinagar in 1995 by gunmen who were probably former insurgents turned government mercenaries known as 'renegades' (Chapter 2), and has had nine surgeries for his bullet wounds. Qayoom had a heart attack in the Agra prison in February 2020 and was moved to the Tihar Jail in Delhi on medical grounds. From the Delhi prison, the top lawyer appealed against his PSA detention twice and was turned down both times by the Jammu and Kashmir high court, which observed that he 'is like a live volcano' who has failed to 'declare and establish' that he has 'shunned his separatist ideology' – defined in the PSA charge-sheet as a belief that Jammu and Kashmir, on both sides of the LoC, is a territory subject to a continuing international dispute.[39]

Qayoom subsequently appealed to India's supreme court and was released in August 2020 after the government counsel did not argue in favour of his continued detention under PSA. He was luckier than Ghulam Mohammad Bhat, 62, who was detained in July 2019, charged under the PSA and subsequently taken to the Naini Jail in the northern Indian city of Allahabad (recently renamed 'Prayagraj' by the Hindu nationalists), where numerous Indian nationalists including independent India's first prime minister, Jawaharlal Nehru, were imprisoned under British rule. Bhat died there in December 2019. Bhat, who was from a village called Kulangam in the Handwara *tehsil* (sub-division) of the Kupwara district in the northern part of the Kashmir Valley, was a longstanding member of Jama'at-i-Islami (JI), a fundamentalist group which has wings in Pakistan, Bangladesh and both Indian and Pakistani Kashmir. Bhat's son, Mohammad Haneef, was abruptly taken from Kashmir to Allahabad in December 2019, where he was informed that his father had died. Bhat had no medical conditions except for an injured leg which had left him with a permanent limp, a result of torture in custody in 1993. The dead man's wife Zarifa said he had gone willingly to the local police station on being summoned in July 2019, after telling his family 'he hasn't committed any crime' and 'asking us to stay steadfast'.[40]

The PSA dragnet swept up virtually the entire political spectrum of the Kashmir Valley. JI, an avowedly pro-Pakistan tendency, represents one end of that spectrum. The other end is represented by parties which have long accepted the legitimacy of Indian authority: notably the National Conference (NC), which was established in the Valley in the late 1930s and in the mid-1970s abandoned its demand for a plebiscite or referendum to decide the status of the former princely state of Jammu and Kashmir (1846–1947), and the much newer People's Democratic Party (PDP), which was launched in 1999. Before 5 August 2019, it was unthinkable that leaders of these parties could be detained and imprisoned by an Indian government. Gowhar Geelani, a Valley-based Kashmiri journalist, overstated only a little when he wrote in August 2020 that these India-aligned elements 'are often wrongly referred to as the "mainstream" [of Kashmiri politics] by the Indian media, when the fact is that they represent a fringe as far as the popular political sentiment in the Valley is concerned'.[41] Indeed, the popular political sentiment in the Valley overwhelmingly favours being free of both India and Pakistan, so groups like JI on the one hand and NC and PDP on the other do represent the fringes in that sense. But both these fringes have punched much above their real weight because of backing from the state apparatuses of Pakistan and India (there are other complications: the populous Jammu region of Indian J&K is socially and politically much more complex than the Valley, and across the LoC, Pakistani Kashmir is sharply divided between independence supporters and Pakistan loyalists).

For seven decades until 2019, and especially in the last three decades since insurgency and uprising in the Valley erupted in 1990, the existence of a small Valley political elite with a limited following who have been willing to live and work with Indian authority had been crucial to the Kashmir strategy of Indian governments. The radically different Modi–Shah approach set in motion on 5 August 2019 dispensed brutally with these client Valley politicians. Farooq Abdullah, the octogenarian son and political heir of the NC founder Sheikh Mohammad Abdullah (1905–82), was placed under house arrest and charged under the PSA a month later, in September 2019. Farooq's son Omar Abdullah, also a former chief minister of the Indian state of Jammu and Kashmir liquidated and dismembered in August 2019, was taken into preventive detention and charged under the PSA in February 2020. So was Mehbooba Mufti, the PDP chief minister of Indian J&K from 2016 to 2018 and the daughter of Mufti Mohammad Sayeed, who was chief minister from 2002 to 2005 and again in 2015–16. The two Abdullahs were released from PSA detention in March 2020 and Mehbooba Mufti in October 2020. Even in their mass post-5 August 2019 misery, very many of their fellow Kashmiris gloated at their humiliation. Becoming PSA detainees – even if briefly compared to thousands of their fellow Kashmiris – was viewed as poetic justice, particularly for the Abdullahs, because the original PSA was enacted by a government headed by Sheikh Mohammad Abdullah in 1978.

The criminalisation and persecution of the erstwhile India loyalists in the Kashmir Valley had a clear and drastic objective: to make *all* forms of politics there defunct and, in effect, take the politics out of the Kashmir question and thereby make it a *non-question*. The fate of Naeem Akhtar, a senior PDP politician, is a chilling example of this strategy in action. Akhtar was a cabinet minister in a PDP–BJP coalition government that shambolically held office in the Indian state of Jammu and Kashmir from 2015 to 2018 (Chapter 3). He was Indian J&K's education minister from 2015 to 2017 and the minister for public works in 2017–18. Taken into preventive detention on 5 August 2019, he was charged under the PSA in February 2020. His PSA charge-sheet is a true blend of the Orwellian and the Kafkaesque. In July 2016, the Valley had plunged into a stone-pelting uprising (Chapter 3) which led to its educational institutions being shut until early 2017. One of the political leaders encouraging the agitation was Syed Ali Shah Geelani (born 1929), a top JI figure. In a public statement made as education minister in September 2016, Akhtar appealed to the young generation to ponder the damage being done to their education and future prospects. He advised them to read Geelani's autobiography *Wular Kinaray* (From the Wular's Bank, a reference to the Wular Lake in the northern part of the Kashmir Valley, where Geelani was born in a poor rural household), in which the pro-Pakistan leader emphasised the transformative impact of education on his life. In February 2020, Akhtar's PSA charge-sheet read: 'His radical leanings can be gathered from the statement dated 27/09/2016 when, as education minister, he advised people to read Geelani's book *Wular Kinaray*'. The charge-sheet also cited a statement Akhtar made in January 2019, in which he called BJP president Amit Shah's politics 'poison', as further evidence of radicalism.[42] Akhtar, 68, was released from PSA detention in June 2020 but rearrested in December and taken to the former J&K state legislators' hostel in Srinagar, designated as a jail for political detainees since August 2019. In January 2021, he was taken to hospital after he was found unconscious in his cell there, and returned to prison after three days of treatment. He was eventually released in June 2021.

The reign of terror that enveloped the Kashmir Valley from 5 August 2019 made global headlines. The festering Kashmir conflict had not received this level of attention since the tumultuous period of the early 2000s (Chapter 2). But the Valley's own journalists found themselves in dire straits. When the protracted insurgency began in the early 1990s, the Valley mainly had an Urdu press. The carnage in Indian Jammu and Kashmir for the next fifteen years (Chapter 2) brought the conflict sustained attention across the world. One consequence was the emergence of a lively English-language press in the Valley – newspapers, and in the new century web-based magazines founded by young Kashmiris. In August 2019, just as interest in Kashmir soared globally, the Valley's journalists found themselves without the essential means to work: no internet, no e-mail, no phone links. In November 2019, three months into the communications lockdown, the union territory administration's department of information opened a 'media facilitation centre' in Srinagar, where scores of journalists queued every day to use a handful of internet-connected computers under close watch of the authorities.

The partial return of means of communication in early 2020 provided some relief, but other problems soon emerged. In June 2020, the union territory's directorate of information and public relations (DIPR) published a fifty-three-page document laying down a new media policy. 'J&K has significant law and order and security considerations,' the document began, and 'it is extremely important that the efforts of anti-social and anti-national elements to disturb peace are thwarted.' To that end, 'DIPR shall examine the content of print, electronic and other forms of media for fake news, plagiarism and unethical or anti-national activities . . . any fake news will be proceeded against under IPC [Indian Penal Code] and cyber-laws' through 'a suitable coordination and information-sharing mechanism with the security agencies'.[43] An Indian newspaper commented, in an editorial titled 'The Ministry of Truth', that 'the J&K directorate of information and public relations may not have George Orwell's vocabulary but has managed to provide a remarkably clear picture of what they want – journalists and news organizations answerable not to their readers, not even to their editors, but to government bureaucrats and security officials with powers to decide what news is fake or "anti-national"'.[44]

The media policy announced in summer 2020 simply formalised official actions that had already been taking place in the Indian union territory of Jammu and Kashmir since the spring. In late March, the UT of J&K joined an India-wide total lockdown to contain the spread of Covid-19. The lockdown, which lasted ten weeks before being eased, was announced in an 8 p.m. television address by the prime minister, Narendra Modi, and came into effect four hours later at midnight (in November 2016, during his first term, Modi had announced in an 8 p.m. television address that his government had decided that 85 per cent of Indian banknotes would become invalid from midnight). Confined to her home in Srinagar, Masrat Zahra, a 26-year-old professional photojournalist, took to posting images she had taken of everyday life in the conflict-torn Valley since 2016 on her Facebook page; social media access had returned after seven months in early March, albeit restricted to 2G speeds on mobile devices. The images had already been published in various outlets including the *Washington Post*, TRT World and *Al Jazeera*. Just after mid-April, Srinagar's cyber-police station (which is housed in a former torture centre of the 1990s and early 2000s) registered a case against her under the federal Unlawful Activities Prevention Act (UAPA) and summoned her for questioning. The cyber-police said they had received information from 'reliable sources' that Zahra had been 'uploading anti-national posts with criminal intention' on her Facebook page, specifically 'photographs which can provoke the public to disturb law and order, that tantamount [sic] to glorify anti-national activities and dent the image of law-enforcing agencies, besides causing disaffection against the country'.[45]

The original UAPA was enacted by India's parliament in December 1967 and empowered its central government to declare 'unlawful' any 'associations' working for 'a cession of a part of the territory of India' and/or engaged in 'terrorist activities', and to punish members of such organisations under criminal laws.[46] It had been periodically invoked in the Indian state of Jammu and Kashmir since then, starting with the banning in January 1971 of the entirely peaceable J&K Plebiscite Front – by far the most popular political organisation in the Kashmir Valley at the time. On 2 August 2019, three days before the Modi government acted on Kashmir, the BJP-dominated Indian parliament passed an amendment to the law – tabled by the home minister, Amit Shah – that provided for individuals and not just members of suspect organisations to be arrested under the UAPA, which allows for detainees to be held for six months without being charged.

Zahra was interrogated but not arrested, probably because an outcry had already ensued in India and abroad. But as Gowhar Geelani, another Kashmiri journalist who had a UAPA case registered against him, wrote in an Indian newspaper in August 2020:

Journalism has been killed. Kashmir's leading opinion-makers and columnists, whose writing would [normally] feature in the many daily newspapers, are not able to express their views. Independent opinion has been criminalized. The [June 2020] media policy is [just] the proverbial final nail in the coffin. It gives unbridled powers to a clerk or a bureaucrat in the directorate of information and public relations ... Already dozens of journalists have been summoned and interrogated at police stations for normal reporting and cases under UAPA and the IPC [Indian Penal Code] have been registered against at least six prominent Kashmiri journalists.[47]

In October 2020, the offices of the Valley's most circulated English daily, *Greater Kashmir* – whose owners also publish a popular Urdu daily, *Kashmir*

Uzma – were raided by the National Investigation Agency (NIA), an arm of the Indian home ministry.

As Covid-19 gripped the world and overshadowed everything else, the Hindu nationalist laboratory experiment in Kashmir – directed by the Modi–Shah strongman duo based in New Delhi and executed on the ground by hand-picked bureaucrats – continued apace. On 31 March 2020, Shah's home ministry issued an order defining who would henceforth be regarded as 'domiciles' of the Indian union territory of J&K. The term superseded the category of 'permanent residents' of the Indian state of Jammu and Kashmir (descended from 'state subjects' of the princely-state era) who alone were entitled – under the abolished Article 35A of the Indian constitution – to hold government jobs and own land and property there until August 2019. The order of 31 March 2020 decreed that in addition to those who were permanent residents, anyone who had resided in the erstwhile Indian state of J&K for a total of fifteen years, any employees of a host of bodies of the Indian central government who had worked in the erstwhile state for a total of ten years, the children of such employees, and anyone who had studied in the erstwhile state for a total of seven years and took either their tenth-grade or twelfth-grade school examinations there would be eligible on application to become domiciles of the new union territory. The order also specified that of the four levels of government jobs, only the lowest level – such as recruitment as police constables, or as junior assistants in government departments – would be reserved for domiciles: the established permanent residents and the new entrants to the expanded domicile category combined. The three upper levels would be open to applicants from across India.

The order caused consternation and anger among the Jammu region's Hindus, who comprise nearly two-thirds of the population in that region – albeit concentrated in the region's south and numerically dominant in only four of its ten districts. The Jammu region's Hindus had largely voted for Modi's BJP in the Indian parliamentary elections of mid-2014 and mid-2019, and in the Indian J&K state assembly election at the end of 2014 (Chapter 3). Like their Muslim fellow citizens in the Jammu region, the Kashmir Valley and Ladakh, they had had no inkling that Modi and Shah would inaugurate a new phase of the Kashmir conflict in August 2019, and, also like their Muslim compatriots, they regarded the hollowed-out remnants of Article 370 with indifference. Yet while a strong undercurrent of resentment at the perceived domination of the Valley in the erstwhile state's polity had long existed among Jammu Hindus, they too felt shocked and disconcerted by the outright dissolution of the state and the reduction to union territory status of its rump, after Ladakh's severance from the state against the wishes of the Shia Muslims of the Kargil district.

I know the Jammu region – which is a multi-religious, multi-ethnic and multi-lingual mix and has a land area much bigger than the Valley's, though less populous – well since the mid-1990s, and ascertained through conversations with locals that this was the dominant feeling of its Hindus, except among a Hindu nationalist fringe, when I visited there again in early 2020. Above all, most of Jammu's Hindus were deeply uneasy about the implications of the revocation of Article 35A. Jobs at various levels of the government apparatus are the main source of employment in both the Kashmir Valley and the Jammu region – more so in Jammu, which does not attract tourists to the same degree as the Valley or have the Valley's extensive agriculture and horticulture. In February 2020 there were 84,000 vacancies in government posts in the newly created UT of Jammu and Kashmir, of which only 22,000 were at the lowest, fourth rung of employment.[48] The 31 March 2020 order from New Delhi meant that Jammu Hindus, along with other established permanent residents of the ex-state of J&K, would have to compete for even those low-level jobs with newly inducted 'domiciles', and for the other jobs they faced the prospect along with all other native residents of competing with – and being swamped by – applicants from across India.

'The notification of domicile rules for the newly created union territory of Jammu & Kashmir has the Jammu unit of the BJP worried and upset,' Indian media reported. 'We are facing a popular backlash and it will harm us,' a Jammu BJP leader who declined to be quoted by name said. Ram Madhav, a prominent BJP functionary who was its parent RSS organisation's national spokesman from 2003 to 2014 and was assigned to J&K affairs by the party from 2014, said that 'some issues regarding the domicile notification have been flagged' by the Jammu BJP and that since 'to an extent these fears are valid', Amit Shah had been 'apprised of the concerns'.[49] Harsh Dev Singh, leader of the Jammu and Kashmir National Panthers' Party (JKNPP), which has a base among poorer Hindus in the Jammu region, was more forthright. Singh, who was elected to three consecutive terms in Indian Jammu and Kashmir's legislature from 1996 to 2014 and served as Indian J&K's education minister from 2002 to 2008, called the notification 'an obnoxious piece of superimposed legislation' that had 'crushed the sentiments of the youth and trampled upon their aspirations'.[50] Singh then sat in a solo *dharna* (sit-in protest) on a potholed road in front of his party's office in Jammu city with placards fixed to his body which read: 'Revoke new domicile law of J&K', 'Betrayal of J&K youth unacceptable', 'Save jobs of J&K for J&K youth' and 'Anti-youth BJP *hai hai* [shame on you]'. An observer correctly noted that 'given the tough geographical terrain, remoteness, [economic] backwardness and the decades-old conflict, it will be very difficult for J&K candidates to compete [for jobs] with [external] candidates who have had far better educational infrastructure, coaching facilities, and a peaceful environment'.[51]

In a rare climbdown, the Modi government amended its 31 March order within seventy-two hours. On 3 April 2020, Shah's home ministry announced that all government jobs – and not just those at the lowest rung – would be limited to domiciles of the Indian union territory of J&K.[52] The amendment failed to mollify the Jammu region's Hindus, who pointed out that the new 'domicile' category includes vast numbers of people who are not natives of Indian Jammu and Kashmir. When the amended order was formally notified in May 2020, Harsh Dev Singh once again appeared outside his party's office in Jammu city and set fire to 'an effigy of the BJP-led central government' [sic] in protest. Singh observed that the amended order still 'includes outsiders within the ambit of the domicile law, which entitles them to avail the domicile certificate and enables them to encroach on government jobs in the UT [union territory]'. He argued that this is 'a cruel joke with the educated youth of [Indian] J&K, whose employment and empowerment formed the core of the BJP election manifestos [of 2014 and 2019]'.[53]

By September 2020, 1.85 million domicile certificates (DC) had been issued in the union territory. Of these, 72 per cent had been issued in the Jammu region (which has just over 40 per cent of the UT's population), and the rest in the Kashmir Valley (which has almost 60 per cent). Of the 1.85 million DCs issued, 1.63 million (89 per cent) had been given to persons who were already holders of permanent resident certificates (PRC) of the abolished Indian state of Jammu and Kashmir, i.e., native residents. Clearly, many more people had applied for DCs, which had replaced their PRCs, in the Jammu region compared to the Valley. But about 225,000 persons who had not held PRCs had also been granted domicile status. Some of these, totalling about 20,000, were long-term residents of the erstwhile state, mainly descendants of refugees who came from Pakistan to the Jammu region in late 1947 (unlike the much larger number of refugees who came to the Jammu region from the areas of the princely state of Jammu and Kashmir that came under Pakistani control, the refugees who came to the south-western part of the Jammu region from Pakistani Punjab were not automatically entitled to permanent resident status in Indian J&K). The UT administration claimed that the total number of DCs issued to applicants who were neither PRC holders nor long-term residents of Indian J&K was '30,445 . . . 1.64 percent of the certificates issued', but the actual number may be much higher.[54]

In the Kashmir Valley, people almost unanimously view the new 'domicile' category – whose eligibility criteria vastly expand the pool of people who would have previously qualified as permanent residents, entitled to government jobs – as a stratagem to effect 'demographic change' and specifically to dilute and ultimately eliminate the 'oppressive Muslim-majority character' of Indian J&K decried by the RSS in its mission-and-vision charter. This suspicion may be well founded. But the prospect of a demographic 'invasion' by non-natives applies more immediately to the Jammu region and especially to its southern Hindu-majority districts around the city of Jammu. Here the terrain is not mountainous as it is in most of the Jammu region, the population is largely non-Muslim and there is no powder-keg-like atmosphere of unrest as in the Valley. This southern part of the Jammu region, which in its western extremity has a 125-mile border with Pakistan's Punjab province, is also contiguous to India's Punjab state and is well connected by road, rail and air links to cities in northern India. The Hindus of the southern swathe of the Jammu region have more immediate reason than the Muslims of the Valley to be apprehensive of 'demographic change' caused by the Hindu nationalist government's Kashmir policy.

The fear of the fallout also haunts the Buddhists of eastern Ladakh, the other community apart from Jammu's Hindus used as pawns in the Hindu nationalist government's Kashmir game-plan. In September 2020, as the first anniversary of Ladakh becoming a union territory on 31 October 2019 approached, the Buddhists who are a two-thirds majority of the Leh district's population should have been in a celebratory mood. In August 2019, Modi and Shah had finally fulfilled their three-decade-long demand (since 1989), backed throughout by the RSS, for Ladakh to be detached from Indian Jammu and Kashmir and made a UT. Instead, the mood was sombre, and sullen. In early September, the Ladakh Autonomous Hill Development Council (LAHDC) for the Leh district, an elected body established in 1995 to exercise local autonomy and provide grassroots governance, passed two unanimous resolutions (western Ladakh's Kargil district, which has a three-fourths Shia Muslim majority, has a similar body, established in 2003). The sitting Leh council, elected by popular vote in 2015, had a decisive BJP majority (eighteen of the twenty-six councillors). The first resolution passed by the council called for the Leh district to be brought under the Indian constitution's Sixth Schedule, which allows self-government for areas inhabited by tribal peoples and would give the Leh council and its executive arm expanded legislative, judicial and fiscal powers (almost all of the Ladakh region's 300,000 people are classified as tribal communities). The second resolution called for the Leh council to be given complete jurisdiction over the following subjects: 'ownership and transfer of land, employment, natural resources, the environment, and the culture of the indigenous people of Ladakh [meaning the Buddhist-majority Leh district]'.[55]

The move by eastern Ladakh's Buddhists to protect their habitat and its identity was triggered by two factors. First, the elimination in August 2019 of Article 35A of the Indian constitution, which had protected access to government jobs and land ownership for locals in all three regions of the liquidated Indian state of J&K: Jammu, Kashmir and Ladakh. Second, the superimposition of a UT administration run by bureaucrats sent from New Delhi which had severely undermined the well-functioning Leh council and its executive (cabinet) of five members: four Buddhists and one Muslim. The Shia majority of the Kargil district were also chafing, for different reasons. They opposed the dissolution of the Indian state of Jammu and Kashmir and the reconstitution of Ladakh as a separate union territory, and were upset that the UT headquarters was situated in Leh, which is five to six hours' drive from the Kargil district.

The Leh council's move was sweetly timed. The five-yearly election to the Leh council was due in October 2020. 'After the September 19th notification of the poll,' the *Indian Express* newspaper reported on 27 September, 'representatives of twelve political parties' in the district, 'including BJP and Congress, and [local] Buddhist and Muslim religious organizations jointly called for a boycott' of the election unless the Modi–Shah government responded to its demands, and 'not a single nomination [paper] has been filed yet' by a candidate.[56] Three Buddhist leaders from Leh were then brought to New Delhi to meet with Amit Shah. After the meeting, the Indian home ministry announced that it would 'consider' the demands, and the boycott call was lifted. 'The Ladakhi leaders', for their part, stated that 'they had agreed to call off the boycott in light of the government's commitment, but also because they did not want to adversely affect national security at a time when the situation on the China border is tense'.[57] Since May 2020, the Indian and Chinese armed forces have been in a tense stand-off on eastern Ladakh's border with Tibet and Aksai Chin (a vast barren plateau claimed by India but controlled by China since the 1950s, Aksai Chin is wedged between Xinjiang and Tibet), and in June 2020 twenty Indian Army soldiers had been killed in a clash with the People's Liberation Army (PLA) on the Ladakh–Aksai Chin frontier.

The Leh election went ahead in late October of 2020, and 65 per cent of the district's electorate of 90,000 voted. The local BJP emerged victorious but with a reduced majority – fifteen of the twenty-six seats. It was pointed out by a business entrepreneur in the town of Leh that 'the BJP won in rural, far-flung areas' but not in the town, where both the constituencies were taken by opposition candidates: 'The urban and educated class in Leh didn't vote for the BJP because of the insecurities looming large over our identity, culture, and jobs'.[58] Indeed, in late July of 2020, both Ladakh districts observed a day's *hartal* (general strike) after Ladakhi job-seekers were told they were no longer eligible to apply for jobs in the Jammu & Kashmir Bank – an important public-sector employer in the undivided state – because Ladakh is now a separate entity. Modi and Shah had managed a face-saving 'victory' in the Buddhist heartland of eastern Ladakh, but only just. In the late September meeting in New Delhi, Shah promised to start talks with the Leh district's leaders on their demands within fifteen days of the election – i.e., November 2020 – in exchange for their participation in the election. Those talks have yet to begin.

The Hindu nationalist government's Kashmir strategy relies crucially on divide-and-rule, by exploiting the social and political heterogeneity of the pre-August 2019 Indian state of Jammu and Kashmir. This strategy seeks to pit Jammu Hindus against Kashmiri Muslims, and Ladakhi Buddhists against Ladakhi Muslims. The strategy put in motion on 5 August 2019 initially sought to manipulate the sentiments of the Jammu region's Hindus and Ladakh's Buddhists – who comprise local majorities in southern Jammu and eastern Ladakh respectively but are minorities in the broader geographic frame – by appearing to privilege them over their Muslim compatriots. But Jammu's Hindus and Ladakh's Buddhists learned the hard way that they had been taken for a ride, and that the Hindu nationalist government's Kashmir policy is indifferent to their concerns and harmful to their interests. Harsh Dev Singh, the fiery Jammu-based leader, noted in January 2020 that citizens in the Jammu region have been disenfranchised just as much as their compatriots in the Valley: 'Government in the UT has been outsourced to bureaucrats from outside the [former] state – both retired and in-service', and 'the Centre [New Delhi] seems hell-bent on proxy rule through these out-of-state bureaucrats'. He observed that 'the political process has been rendered defunct in the new UT' and 'opposition parties suppressed', and described the situation as a 'farce'.[59]

The divide-and-rule strategy extended to attempts to exploit ethnic differences and economic disparities among Indian J&K's Muslim population. In August 2019, the high-level RSS/BJP operative Ram Madhav addressed a gathering in Jammu city of leaders of the Gujjar-Bakerwal community, Muslims who traditionally practise nomadic pastoralism and are found in sizeable numbers in both the Jammu region and the Kashmir Valley. The Gujjars and their sub-group Bakerwals (literally: livestock-herders) are mostly poor people who inhabit remote highland areas and have an ethnolinguistic identity that is distinct from that of the much more numerous Kashmiri-speaking Muslims. Madhav promised them reserved seats – based on their long-recognised status as a tribal community – in a future token legislature of the New Delhi-governed UT of Jammu and Kashmir. In fact, Gujjar political notables have for decades exercised considerable weight in Indian J&K's politics and served as important ministers in its governments. 'Only the BJP can give you justice,' the J&K BJP president, who also attended, told the Gujjar-Bakerwal community leaders.[60]

A year later, in the late autumn of 2020, thousands of Gujjar-Bakerwal families in both the Valley and the Jammu region received eviction notices from the UT's forest department. The notices said that their homes, livestock-grazing pastures and apple orchards were all on illegally occupied government land. The families pleaded that they had been living on these lands for generations, and that no previous government had bothered them or tried to uproot them from their natural habitat. Community activists pointed out that after the abrogation of Article 370, India's Forest Rights Act (2006), which protects tribal peoples' right to their habitats, automatically applies to the Gujjars and Bakerwals of Indian J&K too. To no avail. A wave of raids by forest department officials and police on Gujjar and Bakerwal settlements occurred over the winter of 2020–21. In a typical raid, on a mountain village called Kanidajan in the Valley's central Badgam district in December 2020, one family of ten members had its fifty apple trees – their main source of livelihood – cut to stumps as they watched. In another mountain village, Lidroo in the Valley's southern Anantnag district, a young couple and their three small children had their hut-like dwelling razed as they watched. 'How can they suddenly make us homeless in the middle of winter? We have lived here for two centuries, where will we go?' asked the young father, a herder whose flock of sheep and goats graze on nearby pastures.[61]

On 1 September 2020, as the pace of issuing certificates of domicile status in the Indian union territory of Jammu and Kashmir gained rapid momentum, two senior officials of the UT's bureaucracy held a press conference at Srinagar's civil secretariat, an imposing but drab-coloured 1960s building which has the look of a Soviet secret police headquarters. The two men were Pawan Kotwal, principal secretary in the revenue department, and Rohit Kansal, the UT administration's spokesman. The press conference was apparently intended to assuage concerns that persons who were not previously permanent residents of the Indian state of J&K but were being granted domicile status under the vastly expanded eligibility criteria notified in spring 2020 would have the right to buy land locally, in addition to acquiring government jobs. 'The domicile certificate is for applying to jobs in Jammu & Kashmir. It does not confer the right to buy land,' they told reporters. They also said that new domiciles, who were not previously permanent residents, would not be included in the union territory's voters' list.[62]

Eight weeks later, on 27 October 2020, frontpage headlines in Indian newspapers read: 'Centre throws open J&K for land sale', 'Centre notifies new laws allowing anyone to buy land in J&K', and 'Now, outsiders can buy land in Jammu & Kashmir'. On 26 October 2020, the Indian home ministry in New Delhi issued an order, effective immediately, which opened up the purchase of land in the union territory of J&K to any Indian citizen or entity. There were to be no limitations whatsoever on the direct purchase of urban, non-agricultural land, whether for personal or commercial purposes: 'MHA [ministry of home affairs] officials said that post this notification, a domicile certificate will not be needed to buy land in Jammu & Kashmir. Non-agricultural land in municipal areas can now be bought by anyone. There is no domicile requirement after this notification.'[63] For agricultural land, the UT government is empowered to 'allow transfer of [such] land in favour of any person, institution or corporation [no domicile status necessary] for industrial or commercial or housing purposes, or agricultural purposes or any other public purpose' such as 'promotion of healthcare or senior secondary or higher or specialised education, as may be notified by the Government [of India] for the industrial and commercial development of the Union Territory'.[64] The only lands exempted were to be any deemed by the Indian Army to be a 'strategic area' needed for military purposes. It was reported that 'the Centre is likely to notify separate land laws for the UT of Ladakh soon'.[65] Omar Abdullah, a former chief minister of the Indian state of J&K who was imprisoned from August 2019 to March 2020, said that he suspected the notification had been deliberately delayed until just after the completion of the Leh council election – where the outgoing council had in September demanded full local jurisdiction over land ownership and transfer matters to protect the region's native residents and environment – to prevent the BJP's prospects from being fatally jeopardised in that election.

On 1 December 2020 Mohammad Yusuf Tarigami, a Valley politician who was elected in four consecutive elections (1996, 2002, 2008 and 2014) to the Indian J&K state legislature, petitioned India's supreme court to 'stay' (put in abeyance) the 26 October 2020 order. The petition argued that the Modi–Shah government's power to promulgate such orders is derived from the J&K Reorganisation Act of August 2019, 'which is itself unconstitutional' and the subject of many pending legal challenges – including one made by him – submitted to the supreme court in 2019. Therefore, the October 2020 order should be stayed until the supreme court determined whether the two dozen petitions challenging the constitutionality of the 5 August 2019 order revoking Article 370, and the legislation introduced the same day in India's parliament which liquidated and dismembered the Indian state of Jammu and Kashmir, were valid or not.[66] There was no response from the supreme court. After more than a year of futile appeals to India's apex judiciary, it was clear that divine intervention was more likely than judicial intervention.

In October 2020, the Hindu nationalist laboratory experiment in Indian Jammu and Kashmir took another turn. In August 2019, I noted that 'Mr Modi has promised the people [there] a glorious future of development and progress. He has also said that elections will be held soon to constitute a legislature for the [new] union territory of J&K. Any such election will likely be boycotted in the Kashmir Valley and by most Jammu Muslims, and produce a toothless union territory government led by the BJP.'[67] As explained earlier, union territory legislatures and their executive arm (cabinet) have very limited powers in the Indian system compared to the states that make up the Indian Union, and are little more than glorified municipal governments. In the post-August 2019 context of Indian J&K, any such government would be no more than a fig leaf for draconian Central rule, implemented by bureaucrats and enforced by the security apparatus.

But even such an election proved a bridge too far. Instead, the Modi–Shah government announced on 17 October 2020 that elections would be held to constitute 'district development councils' (DDCs) in the twenty administrative districts of the Indian union territory of Jammu and Kashmir – the Valley and the Jammu region each have ten such districts, of widely varying population sizes. Each district would be divided into fourteen electoral constituencies – no rationale was given for that number – and its inhabitants invited to elect a fourteen-member council that would oversee local development issues in the district, excluding areas under urban municipal bodies (such as the cities of Srinagar and Jammu). There would thus be 280 contests in all, to elect 10 councils of 14 members each in the Valley and the same in the Jammu region.

India has direct elections to 3 tiers of institutions: the national parliament (specifically its popularly elected chamber, the 'Lok Sabha', or House of the People, of 543 members), the legislative assemblies of the 28 states comprising the Indian Union (down from 29 since August 2019, when Indian J&K's statehood was revoked), and multi-level local bodies in rural areas (known as the *panchayat* system) along with municipal governments in urban centres. There is no provision for any other directly elected bodies. Naeem Akhtar, the former Indian J&K minister relentlessly persecuted since August 2019, observed immediately that 'the aim is total de-politicization. The aim is to sub-divide, overlap, create layer after layer [of bodies] so nobody knows who is in charge. The ultimate arbiters will be the bureaucrats and the security set-up.'[68]

After the elections were completed and the results declared in late December 2020, Haseeb Drabu, a former finance minister of the Indian state of Jammu and Kashmir, wrote that 'the obvious purpose is to change the political discourse [on the Kashmir question]: from autonomy, shared sovereignty and identity to local developmental and quotidian issues. A framework of disempowerment is being created in the garb of decentralization. Far from being proto-democratic bodies strengthening grassroots democracy, this is the atomization of electoral democracy.'[69] Indeed, the DDC framework made no provision for any inter-district – let alone interregional – coordination mechanism, making a nonsense of the purported 'development' agenda. In a rejoinder, the Hindu nationalist operative Ram Madhav wrote that 'the successful completion of the DDC elections in Jammu & Kashmir is indicative of the Narendra Modi government's resolve to return power to the people, and the resolve of the people of the UT to turn to democratic decentralization to achieve better governance and development'.[70] Modi himself argued in a speech that 'in a way, these elections fulfil Mahatma Gandhi's dream of *Gram Swaraj* [self-sufficient villages as the basic unit of a happy society]. We have worked day and night to strengthen grassroots democracy and democratic institutions [in the two union territories carved out of the Indian state of Jammu & Kashmir in August 2019]'.[71]

Modi and Shah had apparently calculated that the India-aligned political parties of Indian J&K – whose leaders and important local activists, arrested on a large scale in August 2019, had almost all been released by the autumn of 2020 – would stay in a deep sulk and boycott these elections. That would allow the BJP to run candidates virtually unopposed and pack the twenty DDCs with its own loyalists and recruits. They were taken by surprise when those parties, led by the National Conference (NC) and the People's Democratic Party (PDP), formed an alliance to contest the elections in order to deny the BJP a free run. Amit Shah vented his ire and referred to the alliance as a 'gang'.

The DDC elections were held in several phases during November– December 2020. Polling was brisk in the Jammu region, particularly in its four Hindu-dominated southern districts. In the Kashmir Valley, turnout varied from negligible to moderate levels. Of the 2.89 million votes cast, 1.98 million (almost 70 per cent) were in the Jammu region – which has slightly over 40 per cent of the union territory's population, the rest living in the Valley – and only 900,000 votes were polled in the Valley. Of the 278 DDC seats for which elections were completed (140 in Jammu, 138 in the Valley), the alliance of India-aligned J&K parties opposed to the BJP won 110, the BJP won 75 and independents won 50 seats. In the Kashmir Valley, the anti-BJP alliance won 84 of the 138 seats, independents won 31 and the BJP got just 3 seats. In the Jammu region, the BJP got 72 of the 140 seats, of which two-thirds (48) came from the four Hindu-dominated southern districts, and the anti-BJP alliance of J&K parties came second with 26 seats, almost all from Muslim-dominated and mixed Hindu–Muslim areas in the six Muslim-majority districts of the region. India's Congress party, which ran on its own, did poorly and won 26 of the 278 seats – 17 of 140 in the Jammu region and 9 of 138 in the Valley.

Two points are noteworthy about this peculiar election. First, in the Kashmir Valley, independent candidates won the single largest share (42 per cent) of the 900,000 votes polled, followed by the anti-BJP alliance (35 per cent), the Congress party (7 per cent), and the BJP (3 per cent). Second, in the Jammu region, the BJP won the single largest share of the votes, but still a rather modest 34 per cent in a region which is almost two-thirds Hindu. In the four southern districts which are overwhelmingly populated by Hindus (85–90 per cent), the BJP vote share was 47 per cent in Udhampur district, 46 per cent in Jammu district, 45 per cent in Samba district and 44 per cent in Kathua district.[72] This means that in the Jammu region as a whole, barely half of the Hindus who turned out to vote in this election supported the BJP.

A week after the bizarre DDC exercise drew to a close, Mushtaq Ahmad Wani, an apple-trader in his forties, furiously shovelled the earth in the graveyard of his village – Bellow, in the Valley's Pulwama district, just south of Srinagar – on a bitterly cold day in January 2021 as his wife Rafiqa, teen-aged daughter Zarqa and a clutch of fellow villagers looked on. Mr Wani was making the grave for his 16-year-old son Ather Mushtaq Wani, an eleventh-grade high school student who had been killed in a purported 'encounter' (gun-battle) with an Indian Army unit on the outskirts of Srinagar a few days earlier, during the night of 29–30 December 2020. Two other youths were killed along with Ather Wani in the encounter when the army unit closed in on a disused building in Lawaypora, a Srinagar suburb, where the trio were said to have been hiding. They were Aijaz Maqbool Ganaie, 20, a final-year undergraduate from Patrigam, a village close to Bellow, and Zubair Ahmad Lone, 23, who ran a construction business and was from Turkwangam, a village in the Valley's southern Shopian district. Ganaie's father is a head constable in the J&K police, and two of Lone's brothers are also in the police. The police statement on the encounter said that 'the [three] terrorists hurled grenades and fired indiscriminately on the troops, which was retaliated' and that an AK-47 rifle and two pistols, along with unspent ammunition, had been recovered from the encounter site.

When word of the encounter and the deaths reached the families on 30 December, they were aghast. All three families insisted that the youths were not 'militants' – the term used for insurgents. The police admitted that none of the three had any prior record or figured on any wanted lists, but claimed that they were 'radically inclined' and 'hardcore associates of terrorists (OGWs)'.[73] OGW stands for 'over ground worker' in the parlance of the security apparatus and denotes persons who secretly assist militants in various ways.

According to official counter-insurgency figures, 225 militants were killed during 2020 in Indian Jammu and Kashmir in 103 encounters: 207 in 90 encounters in the Kashmir Valley and 18 in 13 encounters in the Jammu region. The 103 successful encounters were among 9,500 cordon-and-search operations (CASOs) conducted by the security forces in Indian J&K in the course of the year.[74] Ather Wani, Aijaz Ganaie and Zubair Lone were killed in the last, 103rd encounter of 2020 and are listed as 223–225 on the roster of militants slain during 2020 (another 80 militants died in 2021, until mid-July).

Of the 225 militants killed during 2020, 67 died in the first 3 months of the year and 158 were slain during the subsequent 9 months – April–December 2020. The bodies of the 150-plus militants killed from April onwards were not returned to their families. This was a sharp departure from the established practice over three decades, since 1990, during which time the bodies of at least 20,000 Indian J&K militants killed in combat – the large majority natives of the Kashmir Valley – were always returned to their families for the burial rites. The exceptions were several thousand militants of Pakistani origin also slain over three decades who had infiltrated from across the border between Pakistani and Indian Kashmir. As they did not have families to claim their bodies they were usually buried in unmarked graves, mostly in remote locations in the northern part of the Kashmir Valley.

The change in policy – not returning the bodies of local militants to their families – was introduced after early April. On 4 April 2020, two funerals of four militants drew thousands of mourners in the southern Valley districts of Anantnag and Kulgam, and on 9 April thousands came to the funeral of a 23-year-old militant, Sajjad Nawab Dar, in a village called Saidpora near the northern Valley town of Sopore. The change of policy came to light in early May, when the body of Riyaz Ahmad Naikoo, a top guerrilla who was killed in Beighpora – his native village in the Awantipora *tehsil* (sub-division) of the Pulwama district, south of Srinagar – was not handed over to his family and was buried instead at a location in the northern Valley. Dilbag Singh, the police chief of Indian J&K, then told the media that 'the [Indian] ministry of home affairs, through a letter, has advised that bodies of militants not be returned. We are however allowing the family at burials.' He said that 'the home ministry directive cited Covid-19 and the flouting of social distancing at these funerals, and we are implementing that order', and added that the ministry had taken particular note of the huge funeral gathering near Sopore on 9 April 'in violation of the [India-wide] lockdown' to contain the coronavirus. Speaking on condition of anonymity, other senior security officials in the Valley said that 'the Centre [New Delhi] first sought such a policy shift in 2018 but all operating security forces advised against it' to avoid angering people further. But 'with the status of [Indian] J&K changing to a union territory directly under New Delhi's control, the decision was easily pushed through' in 2020, they said.[75] K. Vijay Kumar, a retired police officer who was appointed as the Indian home ministry's senior security adviser on Kashmir in December 2019, subsequently told India's *The Hindu* newspaper that the new policy 'not only stopped the spread of Covid-19 but also stopped the glamourising of terrorists and potential law-and-order problems'.[76]

Sonamarg (literally 'Golden Meadow') is an alpine valley 55 miles northeast of Srinagar, close to the Zojila Pass (11,300 feet) that connects the

Kashmir Valley to Ladakh. Perched at an altitude of 9,000 feet, Sonamarg is a scenically stunning place framed by snow-clad peaks, and one of Kashmir's major tourist sites. Since April 2020, a hilly slope in Sonamarg has become a cemetery, the resting place of over one hundred young Kashmiris killed in anti-militancy operations whose bodies were not returned to their families for burial. On the last day of 2020, Mushtaq Wani followed the police convoy which took Ather's body to that cemetery, to 'see his face one last time'. There he lowered his son's corpse into a pit dug by an earthmover machine. Since April 2020, many families have visited the Sonamarg cemetery to place flowers and inscribed the names of their loved ones on small boulders to mark their graves.

But Mushtaq Wani felt that his son, who he maintains was an innocent teenager killed in a 'fake encounter', deserves better. So when he returned to his village south of Srinagar, he set to work shovelling a proper grave – to be marked one day with a marble tombstone – as his family and neighbours looked on in bemusement. Then, standing knee-deep in the partially dug grave, he howled: 'I want my son's body'.[77]

The grave remains empty, of course. In February 2021, the police started a case under the federal Unlawful Activities Prevention Act (UAPA) against Mr Wani, five family members and the imam (preacher) of the village mosque in Bellow for shouting slogans demanding the return of Ather's body after the weekly Friday prayer congregation. Those arrested under the UAPA can be held for six months without a court appearance and face a standard jail term of seven years upon conviction by specially designated courts. Since 2 August 2019, when the Modi–Shah government used its majority to pass an amendment to the UAPA (which dates to 1967) in India's parliament, any individual(s), and not just members of unlawful organisations, can be booked under the law. Of the 2,364 persons arrested in Indian Jammu and Kashmir under UAPA between 2019 and July 2021, 1,100 remain in prison as of August 2021.

Mushtaq Wani was undaunted. 'I will continue to ask for it [Ather's body],' he said.[78]

CHAPTER FIVE

The 21st-Century Conflict

Kashmir can be conquered by the power of spiritual merit, but never by the force of soldiers.

Kalhana, *Rajatarangini* (The Flow of Kings), an epic
chronicle of Kashmir composed in Sanskrit, *c.* 1149[1]

The tragedies of the past have left a deep and profoundly regrettable legacy of suffering. We must never forget those who have died, or been injured, and their families. But we can best honour them through a fresh start, in which we firmly dedicate ourselves to the achievement of reconciliation, tolerance and mutual trust, and to the protection and vindication of the human rights of all ... We acknowledge the substantial differences between our continuing, and equally legitimate, political aspirations. However, we will endeavour to strive in every practical way towards rapprochement within the framework of democratic and agreed arrangements.

The Good Friday Agreement on Northern Ireland, April 1998[2]

An environment of peace and security is in the supreme national interest of both countries [India and Pakistan] and the resolution of all outstanding issues, including Jammu & Kashmir, is essential for this purpose.

The Lahore Declaration issued by Atal Bihari Vajpayee
and Nawaz Sharif, prime ministers of India and
Pakistan, February 1999[3]

THE VOLATILE FRONTIERS

Indian Jammu and Kashmir, the main arena of the twenty-first-century Kashmir conflict, has two borders with neighbouring countries: a western India–Pakistan border and an eastern India–China border.

The westerly de facto border is the Line of Control (LoC), descended from the Ceasefire Line (CFL) which emerged in January 1949 at the end of the first India–Pakistan war over Kashmir. The CFL was renamed the LoC by intergovernmental agreement in July 1972 (the 'Simla Agreement', Chapter 1), to 'be respected by both sides without prejudice to the recognized position [on the Kashmir dispute] of each side', pending a settlement of the dispute 'through bilateral negotiations or by other peaceful means mutually agreed' between India and Pakistan.[4] The serpentine LoC – produced by the 1947–48 India–Pakistan war and barely altered during the subsequent wars in 1965 and 1971 – meanders through mountainous terrain for nearly 500 miles. It separates the Jammu, Kashmir Valley and Ladakh regions on the Indian side of the LoC from the two parts of Pakistani Kashmir: 'Azad' Kashmir, a sliver of territory shaped like a long finger, and Gilgit-Baltistan, a vast but thinly populated high Himalayan region. The LoC's southern extremity is just west of the town of Akhnur in Indian J&K's Jammu region and its northern extremity is a point called NJ9842 located at the bottom of the Saltoro ridge, beyond which lies the Siachen glacier, where Indian troops took control in 1984 and have been embroiled ever since in a stand-off with the Pakistani military (Chapter 2). To the south of the LoC there is another 125-mile frontier between the southwestern part of Indian J&K's Jammu region and Pakistan's Punjab province. The Indians regard this stretch, which runs through plains on both sides, as part of the India–Pakistan international border (IB), while the Pakistanis call it a 'working boundary'. So the de facto India–Pakistan border in Kashmir is over 600 miles in all.

In December 1972 the Indian and Pakistani armies concluded a formal agreement which precisely demarcated the trajectory of the LoC, as well as the stretch to its south. In November 2003, at the beginning of a period of thaw in India–Pakistan relations (Chapter 2), the two armies reached a ceasefire agreement which applied to the entire length of the India–Pakistan Jammu and Kashmir border: the LoC, its southern extension, and the 'Actual Ground Position Line' (AGPL) in the barren Saltoro/Siachen sector to the north. The ceasefire agreement sharply reduced the firing and shelling duels which had made life miserable for many communities living close to the LoC (and its southern tail) on both sides of the border from 1990 – when insurgency erupted in Indian Jammu and Kashmir, centred on the Kashmir Valley – until the end of 2003. According to Indian Army figures, there were no cross-border firing and shelling incidents in 2004 and 2005, and just three in 2006. There were 21 such incidents in 2007, 77 in 2008, 28 in 2009, 44 in 2010, 62 in 2011, 114 in 2012, 347 in 2013, 583 in 2014 and 405 in 2015, climbing to 971 in 2017. But the dramatic spike came in 2019, when 3,479 cross-border firing and shelling incidents occurred – the majority from August onwards – on average 9 daily hostilities. That alarming figure was surpassed in 2020. In 2020, according to India's home ministry, there were 5,133 firing and shelling incidents on the LoC and its southern extension, in which 22 civilians and 24 Indian soldiers were killed and 197 persons injured. The Pakistani foreign office said that 28 civilians were killed and 257 injured on its side of the LoC.[5]

This is probably the world's most militarised frontier, where hundreds of thousands of soldiers embedded in trenches and bunkers face each other across electrified concertina-wire fencing and minefields. And it regressed in 2019–20 to pre-2004 levels of volatility (or worse) – though the infiltration of insurgents from across the LoC (and its southern tail) into Indian Jammu and Kashmir is now barely a trickle compared to the 1990–2003 period. The November 2003 ceasefire agreement unravelled in all but name. In late February 2021, the directors-general of military operations (DGMOs) of the Indian and Pakistani armies issued a joint statement committing to 'strict observance of all agreements, understandings and ceasefire along the Line of Control and all other sectors [of the border]'. This came after another 591 hostile-fire incidents in the first two months of 2021. An identical statement had been issued in May 2018, and people living in border communities were wary. Hostilities on the LoC did die down from the end of February, and civilians welcomed the respite but remained cautious and sceptical about how long it would last.[6] Reports subsequently emerged that the United Arab Emirates, and particularly the government of Abu Dhabi, had facilitated secret talks between Indian and Pakistani officials which led to the reiteration of the unravelled 2003 ceasefire. Yousef Al Otaiba, the UAE's ambassador in Washington, DC, stated that the UAE was indeed engaged in helping India and Pakistan to get to 'a healthy and functional relationship'. Manish Tewari, an Indian opposition parliamentarian, noted 'the dripping condescension' of the UAE diplomat's words. Tewari also pointed out that by accepting a third-party role for the UAE/Abu Dhabi in de-escalating tensions with Pakistan, Narendra Modi's government had abandoned the Indian stance established since the 1972 Simla Agreement with Pakistan that Kashmir is a strictly bilateral dispute in which no third-party involvement is permissible.[7]

The second, India–China border runs on a north–south axis along the eastern edge of the vast, high-altitude plateau of Ladakh, which was one of the three regions of the Indian state of Jammu and Kashmir abolished in August 2019 and replaced by two 'union territories' directly controlled from New Delhi. The two populous regions, the Kashmir Valley and Jammu – of about 8 and 6 million people respectively – became a union territory, and sparsely populated Ladakh, which has about 300,000 people, was declared a second, separate union territory (Chapter 4).

The eastern, Ladakh border of the erstwhile Indian state of J&K is known as the Line of Actual Control (LAC). The northern part of the LAC in the Ladakh sector abuts Aksai Chin, a barren plateau of 23,000 square miles perched at an altitude of 16,000 feet, and the southern part runs along Ladakh's boundary with the western frontier of China's Tibet Autonomous Region (TAR). Aksai Chin is wedged between China's Xinjiang Uighur Autonomous Region (XUAR) and Tibet. Historically bereft of human population apart from roving groups of nomads, Aksai Chin was a summer route for trading caravans journeying between Ladakh and Xinjiang, and Tibet and Xinjiang. This desolate wilderness came under the control of the People's Republic of China (PRC) from 1951, when People's Liberation Army (PLA) troops moved through the area en route to taking over Tibet. The PLA established a permanent presence in Aksai Chin and built a road running through the eastern part of the plateau to connect Xinjiang with Tibet. This road, opened in 1957 and currently part of China's National Highway 219, was regarded by Beijing until the 1980s, when air links expanded, as a strategically vital artery between China's two far-flung and politically restive regions. However, Indian governments have since the 1950s defined Aksai Chin as the north-eastern periphery of the princely state of Jammu and Kashmir that existed from 1846 to 1947, and regarded the plateau as part of Ladakh – and therefore India, due to the princely-state ruler's accession of his domain to India in October 1947 (Chapter 1).

The term 'actual control' originated in a letter sent in 1959 by Zhou Enlai, the PRC premier, to Jawaharlal Nehru, India's prime minister, regarding the India–China boundary question. The letter said that the boundary issue to be resolved consisted of 'the so-called McMahon Line in the east [Himalayas] and the line up to which each side exercises actual control in the west [Himalayas]'.[8] The McMahon Line refers to a demarcation between the territory of British India and south-eastern Tibet agreed by a British official and a Tibetan leader in 1914. The PRC does not recognise this agreement as it was made between India's colonial rulers and a Tibetan personage, at a time when China was in turmoil after the fall of the Qing dynasty and the 1911 republican revolution. China claims a large tract of territory (56,000 square miles), which it refers to as 'southern Tibet', south of the McMahon Line. The area – which includes a famous Buddhist monastery in Tawang, close to the disputed border – was administered as India's North-East Frontier Agency (NEFA) until 1972, when it was renamed Arunachal Pradesh (Sunrise Province) and given the status of an Indian union territory. Subsequently, in 1987, Arunachal Pradesh was upgraded to a full state of the Indian Union.

The Sino-Indian border dispute boiled over into a fierce border war in October–November 1962, when the Chinese launched large-scale offensives in both the western and eastern sectors. The refuge given to the fourteenth Dalai Lama and other Tibetan exiles by India from 1959 irritated China, but Mao Zedong's decision to escalate the confrontation was triggered by a 'forward policy' adopted by Nehru's government in November 1961 and implemented by the Indian Army during the spring and summer of 1962. Under the policy, small Indian detachments moved forward into the seam-zones with Chinese forces and established posts. Quoting Chinese sources, the American scholar M. Taylor Fravel writes that 'India occupied 3,000 square kilometres in the western [Tibet–Ladakh–Aksai Chin] sector by establishing 36 new posts, many near and sometimes behind Chinese posi-tions, and built 34 posts in the eastern [Tibet–NEFA] sector including several located north of the McMahon Line'.[9] The PLA's two-front offensive in autumn 1962 overwhelmed the Indian troops, who were outnumbered, poorly equipped and hampered by weak logistics and supply lines. On the eastern front, Indian forces practically disintegrated in the face of the blitzkrieg-like Chinese advance. On the western front, Indian resistance was tougher and there was intense, close-range fighting in a number of locations, but the Indians still suffered severe casualties and significant territorial losses in Ladakh. But it appeared that the Chinese leadership's aim was to teach India a bitter lesson, rather than seize territory. After demonstrating their superior military strength and having administered a hiding, the Chinese withdrew almost immediately to their pre-offensive positions. The Sino-Indian border dispute then went into a deep freeze, where it largely remained – until a dramatic resurgence on the Tibet–Ladakh–Aksai Chin frontier in 2020.

In 1960 and again in 1980, China's leaders indicated their view of an acceptable settlement of the border dispute. After holding talks in April 1960 with Nehru in New Delhi on the escalating dispute, Zhou Enlai told a press conference in the Indian capital that there should be 'reciprocal acceptance of the present realities in both sectors', i.e., Indian control of the NEFA tract (Arunachal Pradesh) and Chinese control of Aksai Chin. Nehru responded that 'if I give them Aksai Chin, I shall no longer be prime minister of India – I will not do it'.[10] Nehru seemingly felt that conceding Aksai Chin to China would compromise the Indian position on the domes-tically very sensitive matter of Jammu and Kashmir. The last ruler of the

1846–1947 princely state had legally acceded his entire dominion (which, in the Indian view, included Aksai Chin as its north-eastern periphery) to India in October 1947. So ceding Aksai Chin to China would amount to accepting China's occupation of a part – even if remote and unpopulated – of the historic entity of Jammu and Kashmir, in addition to the parts already under Pakistan's occupation since the late 1940s.

In 1980, three months after formally taking over as China's new leader, Deng Xiaoping revived the east–west territorial swap formula to settle the border dispute. On 22 June 1980, Indian newspaper headlines read: 'China offers new package deal to end border row: Line of Actual Control to form basis'. This was not in fact a 'new' proposition, but a restatement of what Zhou Enlai had floated in New Delhi twenty years earlier. In an interview given to the editor of an Indian military journal in Beijing during a visit by India's foreign secretary (the top career official of the diplomatic service) to the Chinese capital, Deng said: 'I think the border problem can be resolved in a package deal. While we can recognize the so-called McMahon Line, which is the present line of actual control in the eastern sector [Tibet–Arunachal Pradesh], India should recognize the *status quo* in the western sector [Ladakh–Aksai Chin]'. Deng added that if such a resolution was not acceptable to the Indians, 'this [border] problem should not hinder the development of relations between our two nations' and 'we can put it aside'. Asked about the Kashmir conflict, Deng said: 'This is a problem between India and Pakistan, and should be settled amicably'.[11] Deng's comment set the tone for a neutral-sounding Chinese posture on the Kashmir conflict which lasted for four decades – until August 2019. This was in sharp contrast to Chinese sabre-rattling on Pakistan's behalf just before and during the 1965 war the Pakistanis launched in a failed bid to seize territory in Indian Jammu and Kashmir (Chapter 1). The posture endured through the litmus test of the Kargil War the Pakistanis initiated on the LoC in 1999 (Chapter 2) in another ill-conceived attempt to challenge the territorial status quo in place in Jammu and Kashmir since 1949. In mid-1999, as the Pakistan Army's cross-LoC gambit in Kargil (western Ladakh) unravelled, the Chinese leadership rebuffed its close ally Pakistan's desperate pleas for diplomatic support.

Two days after Deng's 1980 interview, the Xinhua news agency ran an article on the Sino-Indian relationship. The article stressed 'the development of good neighbourly relations between China and India' and called for 'mutual understanding and concessions' on the boundary question, which it quoted Deng as saying could be resolved if both countries 'respect the present state of the border'. The article asserted that 'China has never asked for the return of all the territory illegally incorporated into India by the old [British] colonialists' – a reference to the McMahon Line and Arunachal Pradesh. As the American scholar John Garver writes, 'Deng was then engineering a fundamental reorientation of China's foreign relations, premised on the notion that the country's international conflicts should be reduced to create a more propitious environment for economic development'. The reorientation 'pointed towards improving relations with India', broken since the 1962 Sino-Indian war.[12] Through the 1960s and 1970s, China had materially supported insurgencies waged by rebel organisations of the Naga, Mizo and Manipuri ethnic communities in India's volatile north-east (a region wedged between China, Bangladesh, Bhutan and Myanmar) – and until East Pakistan became Bangladesh in end-1971, in collusion with Pakistan. When the Indian foreign minister, Atal Bihari Vajpayee – who was to lead India as its first Hindu nationalist prime minister from 1998 to 2004 – visited Beijing in 1979, Deng told him that 'such aid was a thing of the past'.[13]

The Indian response to Deng's 1980 overture was a measured but definite 'No'. In July 1980, P.V. Narasimha Rao, the Indian foreign minister – who would go on to serve as prime minister from 1991 to 1996 – told the Lok Sabha, the directly elected chamber of India's parliament: 'India has never accepted the premise on which it [Deng's overture] is based, namely that China is making a concession in the eastern sector by giving up territory which they allege is illegally incorporated into India. Nevertheless, we welcome the prospect of the eastern sector being settled without any particular difficulty.'[14] In other words, while a Chinese climbdown on Arunachal Pradesh was very welcome, a deal involving a swap with Aksai Chin/Ladakh based on the 'actual control' principle was out of the question. From 1985, China changed tack when, in intergovernmental talks with India on the boundary question, its representatives once again started raising the Chinese claim to 'south Tibet' (Arunachal Pradesh).

While any prospect of a big-bang settlement of the India–China boundary evaporated, India in the 1990s did accept the Chinese coinage – 'Line of Actual Control' – to refer to the trans-Himalayan frontier of 2,500 miles between Tibet and India, from Ladakh at the western end to Arunachal Pradesh in the east. During a visit to Beijing in September 1993 by P.V. Narasimha Rao, the Indian prime minister, an 'Agreement on the Maintenance of Peace and Tranquility along the Line of Actual Control in the India–China Border Areas' was signed. The agreement stated that 'pending an ultimate solution of the boundary question, the two countries shall strictly respect and observe the line of actual control between the two sides' and 'keep military forces in the areas along the line of actual control to a minimum level compatible with friendly and good-neighbourly relations'. The pact stipulated that 'the two sides agree that references to the line of actual control in this Agreement do not prejudice their respective positions on the boundary question'.[15]

This was followed by an 'Agreement on Confidence-Building Measures in the Military Field along the Line of Actual Control in the India–China Border Areas', which was signed in New Delhi in November 1996 to co-incide with a visit by Jiang Zemin, the first PRC president to visit India. The agreement committed the countries to 'avoid holding large-scale military exercises involving more than one division (approximately 15,000 troops) in close proximity of the line of actual control', and to 'give the other side prior notification if either side conducts a major military exercise involving more than one brigade (approximately 5,000 troops) in close proximity of the line of actual control'. The deployment along the LAC of 'combat tanks, artillery guns of 75mm. calibre and above, mortars of 120mm. calibre and above, surface-to-surface missiles and surface-to-air missiles' would be 'limited to mutually agreed ceilings'. The agreement further stipulated that 'both sides shall take adequate measures to ensure that air intrusions across the line of actual control do not take place' and, to that end, 'combat aircraft shall not fly within ten kilometres of the line of actual control'. Moreover, 'neither side shall open fire, cause bio-degradation, use hazardous chemicals, conduct blast operations or hunt with guns or explosives within two kilometres of the line of actual control'. Finally, 'if border personnel come in a face-to-face situation due to differences [conflicting interpretations] on the alignment of the line of actual control or for any other reason, they shall exercise self-restraint and take all necessary steps to avoid an escalation of the situation'.[16]

The India–Pakistan LoC in Kashmir (CFL until 1972) saw large-scale hostilities during the wars of 1965 and 1971, and localised fighting during the Kargil War of 1999. The LoC has also seen thousands of deadly encounters between the Indian Army and paramilitary border guards and insurgents crossing over from Pakistani Kashmir – particularly since 1990 and most of all during the period from 1990 to the mid-2000s. The India–China LAC, by contrast, has been remarkably calm since the border war fought in the late autumn of 1962. Until 2020, there were only two clashes which led to fatalities, both in the eastern Himalayas. In September 1967, a flare-up occurred at the Nathu-La mountain pass on the border of Tibet and Sikkim, then an autonomous principality of India which was subsequently incorporated into the Indian Union as its twenty-second state in 1975. Sikkim is a tiny but strategic territory wedged between Nepal and Bhutan, with south-central Tibet to its north and north-east and the populous Indian state of West Bengal to its south. The Nathu-La clash left thirty-two Chinese and sixty-five Indian soldiers dead but was a local outbreak that did not recur anywhere else, let alone signal a resurgence of large-scale hostilities. The only other fatal incident on the LAC occurred in 1975 when four patrolling Indian soldiers were ambushed and killed by the Chinese at Tulung-La, a mountain pass in the Tawang district on the Tibet–Arunachal Pradesh border. Another stand-off in 1986–87, also in the Tawang district, was defused without escalation, and there was no fighting or casualties.

Remarkably, the LAC in the west – the Tibet–Aksai Chin–Ladakh frontier – stayed free of any lethal incidents for almost six decades after 1962. This was despite a major problem the 1996 confidence-building agreement noted: the absence of 'a common understanding of the alignment of the line of actual control in the India–China border areas'. Unlike the LoC (and its southern tail), whose precise trajectory was demarcated by an agreement between the Indian and Pakistani armies concluded in December 1972, the LAC is not formally demarcated and therefore its exact location and course on the ground is open to different interpretations by the Indian and Chinese militaries. The problem is especially acute in the Tibet–Ladakh–Aksai Chin borderland, where the desolate terrain is vast and extremely rugged. Nonetheless, Indian Jammu and Kashmir's eastern border, the LAC in Ladakh with China, presented a tranquil contrast with its western border, the LoC with Pakistan.

That changed in mid-2020. With the onset of summer in May, Indian and Chinese soldiers became embroiled in a series of face-to-face confrontations on Ladakh's border with Aksai Chin and Tibet. In all cases, the Chinese seemed to be the proactive party, pushing into areas where the two sides have slightly different perceptions of where the LAC lies and preventing the Indians from patrolling grey areas where both sides had previously patrolled without incident or confrontation. It was as if the PLA was emulating the Indian 'forward policy' of 1962, ordered by Nehru's government, which led to the Sino-Indian war of that autumn. Heated verbal exchanges, fistfights and full-scale brawls broke out between groups of soldiers. In September, General V.P. Malik, who was the Indian Army chief at the time of the 1999 Kargil War with Pakistan, noted that 'along the LAC [in Ladakh], the PLA has now occupied many areas which were previously considered "disputed", that is, lying between Chinese and Indian perceptions of the LAC', and that 'the situation on the ground is indeed very tense and explosive'.[17]

The skirmishes took a deadly turn in mid-June. On the night of 15–16 June, Indian and Chinese soldiers engaged in a brutal fight at an altitude of 14,000 feet in the Galwan valley, located on the Aksai Chin–Ladakh LAC. The Galwan valley is named after Ghulam Rasool Galwan, a Ladakhi of Kashmiri descent who worked as a local guide for British and American explorers in the early twentieth century.[18] It is formed by a small river of the same name, freezing cold even in summer, which flows from Aksai Chin into Ladakh, where it joins the larger Shyok river, a tributary of the great Indus river which flows from Tibet through Ladakh into Gilgit-Baltistan and traverses the length of Pakistan before merging into the Arabian Sea near Karachi. During the autumn 1962 war, a Chinese battalion attacked and decimated a small Indian detachment deployed in the Galwan valley, which lost thirty-three men killed in action.

In the Galwan valley incident of June 2020, apparently no shots were fired because of the prohibition on using firearms on the LAC in the 1996 Sino-Indian confidence-building agreement. Instead, the soldiers fought with iron rods, clubs wrapped with razor wire or studded with protruding nails, knives, stones and rocks. Twenty Indian soldiers died, including the colonel commanding the detachment, and seventy-six were injured, eighteen seriously. About ten Indians were said by some reports to have been taken captive and released after a few days. Some of the soldiers were said to have been thrown to their deaths off a ridge, and others fell or were pushed into the rapidly flowing, ice-cold Galwan river and swept away. The Chinese refused to disclose their casualties, but several dozen may have been killed. In February 2021 the *People's Daily*, China's official newspaper, announced that the PRC's Central Military Commission had decided to confer posthumous bravery awards on a battalion commander and three rank-and-file PLA soldiers killed in the clash, and that Qi Fabao, a regimental commander who was seriously injured, had also been decorated. They were cited for 'defending the border' and 'China's national territorial sovereignty' against 'trespassing foreign military personnel'.[19] The gallantry award given posthumously to the dead Indian colonel, B. Santosh Babu, cited his courage 'in hand-to-hand combat with enemy soldiers, whom he valiantly resisted till his last breath despite being grievously injured, inspiring his troops'.[20] After the clash, the Chinese significantly reinforced and enhanced their strength in the Galwan valley.

The lethal Galwan encounter, instead of acting as a deterrent to further escalation, triggered a massive military build-up on both sides of the Ladakh LAC with Tibet and Aksai Chin. While military commanders met locally in inconclusive discussions, and the Indian defence minister met his Chinese counterpart in early September 2020 on the sidelines of a Shanghai Cooperation Organisation (SCO) meeting in Moscow, there was no sign of the coordinated, high-level political initiative from New Delhi and Beijing clearly needed to defuse the crisis. Over the summer, large Indian troop reinforcements travelled from the Kashmir Valley to the frontline in eastern Ladakh. By early autumn, the major flashpoint was clearly on and around Pangong Tso, a lake that straddles the Ladakh–Tibet frontier and begins

140 miles south-east of Leh, the main town in eastern Ladakh. The stunning blue-green lake, framed by mountains, is situated at an altitude of 14,000 feet and sprawls across the LAC like a horizontally placed finger. The lake is narrow, only 4 miles at its widest, but 83 miles long from west to east, of which one-third lies in Ladakh and two-thirds in Tibet. In autumn 1962, offensive Chinese thrusts on both banks of the lake had sent the Indians reeling. Face-offs and brawling began on the northern bank of Pangong Tso in May 2020, and over the summer both banks of the lake, north and south – the exact trajectory of the LAC which cuts vertically across the lake is slightly different in the Indian and Chinese versions – became heavily militarised.

Over the frozen winter of 2020–21, about 50,000 Indian troops dug in on the Ladakh LAC faced a similar number of Chinese soldiers massed on the LAC in Aksai Chin and Tibet. Both sides are supported by battle tanks, artillery guns and howitzers, and surface-to-surface and surface-to-air missile batteries. Numerous Chinese airbases located in Tibet and Xinjiang are on alert, as are numerous Indian airbases in Ladakh, the Kashmir Valley, the Jammu region and across northern India. Just as the November 2003 India–Pakistan ceasefire agreement on the LoC had been reduced to tatters and become effectively defunct by 2020, so have the 1993 and 1996 Sino-Indian agreements on the LAC, at least in the Ladakh–Aksai Chin–western Tibet sector.

When General Manoj Mukund Naravane took charge as the new Indian Army chief in January 2020, his first media interview focused on Pakistan. 'If Pakistan does not stop its policy of state-sponsored terrorism,' he said, 'we reserve the right to preemptively strike at the sources of the terror threat,' going beyond 'the resolute [cross-border] punitive response' already implemented in response to major terror attacks in the Kashmir Valley in September 2016 and February 2019 (Chapter 3).[21]

A year later in January 2021, General Naravane's comments at the customary press conference held by an incumbent army chief at the beginning of each year were much more defensive in tone. 'We are prepared to hold our ground in Ladakh for as long as it takes,' he said, and added: 'There is no doubt that Pakistan and China together form a potent threat, and there is an aspect of collusion [between them] that cannot be wished away, and is very much part of our strategic planning and calculus.'[22] In February, Naravane said that the Indian Army 'factors a two-and-a-half-front war' into its strategic planning, 'the half being internal security'.[23] This was almost certainly a reference to the internal situation in Indian Kashmir, particularly the Kashmir Valley. V.P. Malik, the ex-army chief, wrote in September 2020 that 'China and Pakistan are already engaged in a collusive threat vis-à-vis India' but:

> China is unlikely to bank on Pakistani collaboration and participation in any large-scale conflict with India. In the current scenario, a limited China–Pakistan military collaboration in the Karakoram Pass region [which straddles the northern edge of east Ladakh and Xinjiang, and is just east of the Siachen glacier and just west of Aksai Chin] cannot be ruled out. Its manifestations could be diversionary movements by Pakistan in the Siachen and Kargil sectors, and an intensification of proxy war in Jammu & Kashmir [the post-August 2019 union territory].[24]

Meanwhile, ten days after the Galwan incident, Admiral Arun Prakash, a former chief of the Indian Navy, wrote that 'Parliament should resolve, now, to ask the Government to establish with utmost urgency stable, viable and peaceful national boundaries all around so India can proceed, unhindered, with the vital tasks of nation-building and socioeconomic development'.[25]

THE CHINA FACTOR

China's appearance in the main frame of the Kashmir conflict elicited a variety of explanations. They ranged from the very general to the quite particular.

The Chinese escalation on the western sector of the LAC with India fits into a pattern of PRC belligerence towards many countries in Asia that has become pronounced since the Xi Jinping regime assumed power in late 2012. This aggressive twenty-first-century incarnation of the PRC may even have been latent in the 'twenty-character policy' Deng Xiaoping prescribed at the end of 1989 as the basis of a cautious and restrained approach to the world, at a time when the PRC elite coped with the international fallout of the Tiananmen Square massacre of June 1989, popular uprisings ended Soviet-backed one-party regimes across Eastern and Central Europe, and the Soviet Union itself unravelled: 'Observe things coolly, deal with things calmly, keep a firm footing, hide our capacities and bide our time, get some things done'.[26] China's maritime disputes – particularly but not only relating to the South China Sea – with Vietnam, the Philippines, Malaysia, Japan (the Senkaku islands), Indonesia and South Korea – are well known. But there are also several land border disputes, of which the one with India is by far the most prominent. Then there is the intensified revanchism under Xi towards democratic Taiwan, and the implementation of a hardline policy to integrate Hong Kong into the PRC. Clearly 'peaceful rise', the motto of China's Hu Jintao–Wen Jiabao leadership (2002–12), is a thing of the past, and hiding capacities and biding time is over. And unlike his predecessors in the post-Mao era, Xi Jinping intends to stay in power indefinitely and helm China's Asian and global strategies for at least another decade.

There are also very specific explanations of the LAC crisis. India has slowly but steadily been upgrading roads and airfields in eastern Ladakh over the past two decades. In 2008, India recommissioned a military airstrip at a spot called Daulat Beg Oldi (DBO), located at the foot of the Karakoram Pass (18,694 feet). The DBO airstrip, probably the world's highest at an altitude of 16,600 feet, occupies an especially strategic location: it is just south of the Xinjiang border, just west of Aksai Chin and just east of the Siachen glacier. This is effectively the trijunction of Pakistani, Indian and Chinese control in the area. The DBO airstrip was in use during the 1962 Sino-Indian war but fell into disuse from 1966, when an earthquake loosened the soil and made landings too risky. It was revived in the summer of 2008, when the Indian Air Force (IAF) landed an Antonov-32 plane there. The Antonov-32, a twin-engine turboprop plane, is an old but reliable means of transporting personnel and materiel that India acquired in large numbers from the Soviet Union in the 1980s. Then, in summer 2013, the IAF successfully landed the much larger and more modern C-130J Super Hercules at DBO, making the airstrip fully operational for twenty-first-century purposes.

In April 2019 the Border Roads Organisation (BRO), an arm of the Indian defence ministry, completed an all-weather road running north from Shyok – a village east of Leh, on the route to Pangong Tso – to Daulat Beg Oldi. The Shyok–DBO road, about 140 miles long, follows the course of the Shyok river and is equipped with 37 truss-bridges across that river – including one 1,410 feet long – and its tributaries. The road runs parallel and very close to the LAC for most of its length; the site of the June 2020 Galwan valley clash is just a few miles east of the road. There was speculation that the completion of this strategic road along the LAC, which significantly enhances Indian military logistics on the Aksai Chin frontier and provides a land route to the DBO airstrip, had, along with further construction of link roads connecting to Indian posts on the LAC, irked the Chinese and brought on their offensive behaviour.[27]

But offensive retaliation on this scale is unlikely to have been sparked by Indian road-building. The DBO airstrip has been operational since 2008, and the Chinese knew the road was coming – it was authorised by the Indian government in 2001. Before 2020, the Chinese used pinprick probes to show their disapproval of Indian activities on the LAC. In mid-April 2013, one month before a visit to India by Li Keqiang, the PRC's newly appointed premier, a fifty-strong PLA detachment set up camp in the Depsang Plain, an undulating upland framed by towering peaks which lies just south of Daulat Beg Oldi. The Indo-Tibetan Border Police (ITBP) responded by setting up a camp 1,000 feet away. The face-off ended after three weeks without further incident, when the Chinese withdrew and the Indian camp too was dismantled. This was followed by minor face-offs in the summer of 2014 at Chumar and Demchok, near the southern end of the Ladakh–Tibet LAC, and in summer 2015 at Burtse on the Ladakh–Aksai Chin LAC, all defused within a week to two weeks at the local level.

In contrast to the locally focused explanations of the Sino-Indian border crisis of 2020–21, a globalist view argued that the escalation had been engineered by China as a 'strategic trap', to divert Indian attention from 'where the real game is being played: in the Indian Ocean'.[28] This perspective missed two crucial and connected elements of the jigsaw puzzle: the longstanding China–Pakistan–India geostrategic triangle, and the new phase of the Kashmir conflict inaugurated by India's Hindu nationalist government in August 2019.

India has not attended either of the two Belt and Road Initiative (BRI) summits convened by China, in 2017 and 2019. The BRI, announced in 2013 as OBOR (One Belt, One Road), is the linchpin of the PRC's global strategy in the Xi era. The grand blueprint of expanding China's international influence drew on a 2012 paper by Wang Jisi, a senior academic, titled 'Westward: China's Rebalancing Geopolitical Strategy', and is commonly seen as the response to the Obama administrations' 'pivot to Asia', viewed by the PRC leadership as a strategy to contain China's power.[29] One of the routes of that westward march passes through the 375-mile border China has with Pakistan, which is entirely between Xinjiang and Gilgit-Baltistan, one of the two regions of Pakistani Kashmir. In 2017, India declined to participate in the first BRI summit on the grounds that the China–Pakistan Economic Corridor (CPEC) – which was announced during a visit by Xi Jinping to Pakistan in 2015 and is projected to run from Xinjiang to Gwadar, an Arabian Sea port in Pakistan's conflict-torn Balochistan province – passes through Gilgit-Baltistan, which India regards as a territory illegally occupied by Pakistan, along with the rest of Pakistani Kashmir. Although India did join the Asian Infrastructure Investment Bank launched by the PRC in 2016, it was again conspicuously absent from the second BRI summit in Beijing in April 2019. The summit, where Xi Jinping delivered the keynote address, was attended by thirty-seven heads of government, including two from South Asia – the prime ministers of Pakistan and Nepal. Imran Khan, the Pakistani prime minister, was one of seven heads of government who gave speeches at the event.

While India shuns the BRI, Pakistan sees CPEC as not just a lifeline but a stairway to economic salvation. Pakistan is, chronically, a borderline economic basket-case. Its Gross Domestic Product is barely one-eleventh of India's, it has a weak currency and a debt burden of at least $85 billion (the single largest creditor is the PRC), and it has taken twenty-three International Monetary Fund bailout loans during its existence as a country.[30] Its expectations of CPEC investment – worth $46 billion when announced in 2015, now upped to $62 billion – may be exaggerated. According to one informed observer, there is 'a large gap between the images conjured up of a vast flow of trucks, trains, oil and cables running from the Indian Ocean to northwest China' via the corridor 'and the reality of a disparate network of investments' in energy, rail and road projects 'in various regions of Pakistan'. Gwadar is not going to become 'a thriving port' in the near future, let alone an international hub, and in the short term 'the most tangible outcome will likely be a few new roads'. But, the commentator writes, 'the sheer scale of the initiative has one over-riding advantage. Whatever the failures, even a partial success could have transformative effects' for Pakistan.[31]

Pakistan's leaders, civilian and military, have long referred to the PRC as Pakistan's 'all-weather friend' – a reference to the US, seen as a fair-weather friend which exploits Pakistan's help when necessary but lets it down at critical junctures – and to Sino-Pakistani friendship as 'higher than the Himalayas, deeper than the Arabian Sea, sweeter than honey, and stronger than steel'. When Nawaz Sharif, then Pakistan's prime minister, referred to the relationship in these terms at Beijing's Great Hall of the People in 2013, Li Keqiang, somewhat embarrassed, responded: 'I greatly appreciate your great warmth and deep affection for the people of China'.[32] In fact, the extensive Sino-Pakistani relationship over the past five decades has been mostly about military-to-military ties, including vital assistance to Pakistan's nuclear-weapons programme.[33] There had been relatively little by way of economic ties in comparison – until CPEC, which both draws Pakistan deeply into China's orbit and makes Pakistan moderately important to the PRC's global ambitions in the twenty-first century. The Pakistan Army keeps tight control over CPEC and the chairman of Pakistan's CPEC Authority is Asim Saleem Bajwa, a retired lieutenant-general. Appointed in November 2019, he kept the post even after major corruption allegations – not directly connected to CPEC investment – emerged against him and his family in 2020.

India, on the other hand, has not only been keeping aloof from the BRI, but is a member of the 'Quad' (Quadrilateral Security Dialogue) along with the US, Japan and Australia. The Quad was formed in 2007 at the initiative of Shinzo Abe, Japan's prime minister, during his first short-lived premiership. India has longstanding close and cordial relations with Japan, China's historic foe in Asia. The Quad was revived in 2017 and promotes cooperation between its members in the 'Indo-Pacific', in a clear challenge to China's maritime ambitions. In November 2020, the Quad held joint naval exercises in both the Bay of Bengal and the Arabian Sea. In March 2021, a virtual Quad summit was held between US President Joe Biden and the prime ministers of the other three countries: India's Narendra Modi, Japan's Yoshihide Suga and Australia's Scott Morrison. Their joint statement asserted a commitment to a 'free and open Indo-Pacific anchored by democratic values, rooted in international law and unconstrained by coercion', and promised to 'counter threats to security and prosperity in the Indo-Pacific and beyond'.[34]

In 2017, the year the Quad was revived, India and China faced off in their most serious land-border incident in fifty years (since the Sikkim flare-up of 1967). The site was again in the eastern Himalayas – the Doklam plateau on Bhutan's western edge, located at the trijunction of Bhutan, India's Sikkim state and China's Tibet. The Doklam area is part of a swathe of territory in western Bhutan claimed by China. In mid-June, a PLA detachment came into the Doklam plateau with road-building equipment. Bhutan, a mountainous country of 800,000 people wedged between China and India, is a de facto Indian protectorate. It has a friendship treaty with India, which was updated in 2007 from the original 1949 version. The treaty enjoins the two countries to 'cooperate closely with each other on issues relating to their national interests' and to not 'allow the use of its territory for activities harmful to the national security and interest of the other'.[35] The Doklam plateau is just 60 miles north of India's 'chicken's neck', a corridor 15 miles wide in the northern part of the state of West Bengal which is the only land link between India's north-east and the rest of the country. Several hundred Indian soldiers crossed into Doklam from Sikkim and confronted the PLA's road-building detachment. The confrontation in the summer of 2017 continued for ten weeks, until late August, when both groups of soldiers withdrew from the area.

THE CHINA–PAKISTAN–INDIA TRIANGLE

The Pakistani government reacted to the Kashmir bombshell from New Delhi on 5 August 2019 with shock and anger. The prime minister, Imran

Khan, had said in April 2019 that he hoped that Narendra Modi, if re-elected to lead India, would engage with Pakistan during his second term for a Kashmir settlement (Chapter 3). Instead, the re-elected Hindu nationalist government unleashed its ideologically driven, radical approach to the Kashmir conflict (Chapter 4), brutally coercive and brazenly unilateralist. The co-architect and chief enforcer of that radical strategy, Modi's home (interior) minister Amit Shah, told the Indian parliament on 6 August that the return of 'PoK' (Pakistan-occupied Kashmir) to India was the only pending issue with Pakistan. Shah declared: 'Jammu and Kashmir is an integral part of India, let there be no doubt about it. [And] when I talk about Jammu and Kashmir, Pakistan-occupied Kashmir and Aksai Chin are included. Don't you consider PoK a part of Jammu and Kashmir? I will give my life for it [PoK]. We are ready to give our lives [to reclaim PoK and Aksai Chin].'[36] Most previous Indian governments regularly used the 'integral part' (Hindi: *atut ang*) phrase, mainly for the domestic audience, but did not altogether deny that a dispute with Pakistan over Kashmir remained in existence. This was to be resolved, in principle at least, 'through bilateral negotiations [between India and Pakistan] or other peaceful means mutually agreed' between the two countries – the language of the high-level intergovernmental agreement of July 1972 signed in the north Indian hill resort of Simla by the then prime ministers Zulfiqar Ali Bhutto and Indira Gandhi, which renamed the Ceasefire Line of 1949–72 between Indian and Pakistani Kashmir with a less precarious-sounding label: Line of Control.

Beyond voicing outrage, Imran Khan's government – in office since August 2018, after elections manipulated in his party's favour by the 'deep state', i.e., the Pakistan Army's high command and the intelligence services – was caught flat-footed and could not muster any coherent response. Going to war with India was not an option. The other possible path – to once again escalate sub-conventional warfare in Indian Kashmir by deploying cadres of Pakistani jihadist groups – was also fraught with risks and effectively a non-option. Since 2018, Pakistan has been on the 'grey list' of the Financial Action Task Force (FATF), an international watchdog body which monitors states suspected to be hubs of money-laundering and/or terrorism-financing. In October 2020, FATF stated that Pakistan is still not acting decisively against Lashkar-e-Taiba and Jaish-e-Mohammad – the two major Pakistani jihadist groups deployed by the deep state in the insurgency in Indian Kashmir since the late 1990s (Chapters 2 and 3) – and their leaders and front organisations. In February 2021, FATF retained Pakistan on its grey list. It noted that Pakistan had made 'significant progress' in addressing its concerns but had not yet taken decisive action against UN-designated terrorist groups, a reference to LeT and JeM.[37] A FATF blacklisting would have disastrous consequences for Pakistan's parlous economy by cutting off most foreign investment.

Pakistan's diplomacy also failed to mobilise the Islamic world against the strangling repression by the Hindu nationalist government in Indian Kashmir, particularly the Kashmir Valley (Chapter 4). Pakistan's relationship with its principal ally and benefactor in the Islamic world for several decades, Saudi Arabia, has declined in recent years, and its relationship with the Islamic Republic of Iran has always been uncomfortable. And on 24 August 2019, the United Arab Emirates conferred its highest honour, the Order of Zayed, on Prime Minister Modi in a glittering ceremony in Abu Dhabi (the award had been announced in April 2019). Pakistan's leaders could do little other than seethe in indignation. Pakistan has acquired a new diplomatic backer in the last few years in the person of Recep Tayyip Erdogan, Turkey's strongman president, but this is not sufficient to offset the lack of active support on Kashmir from key Islamic states.

Modi and Shah almost certainly anticipated that the Pakistani reaction to their new, iron-fisted Kashmir policy would verge on the hysterical, and that that reaction would help them to sell their policy to the Indian public. Kashmir has been Pakistan's sacred cause since 1947 (Chapter 1) and the plight of Kashmiri co-religionists in *maqbooza* (occupied) Kashmir across the LoC a national obsession. The obsession survived – indeed was deepened by – the failure of the Pakistani nation-state idea in 1971, when East Pakistan was lost and became Bangladesh with India's support. The selective preoccupation with the oppression of Kashmiris under Indian rule persists unabated, even though the praetorian Pakistani state too has repressed independentist groups in 'Azad' Kashmir and Gilgit-Baltistan for decades, and has since 2006 been committing abuses in the Balochistan province – in response to an independentist Baloch insurgency – which are on par with those of Indian forces during their counter-insurgency campaign in Indian Jammu and Kashmir between 1990 and the mid-2000s (Chapter 2). Modi and Shah were also almost certainly aware that various constraints and limitations meant that the Pakistanis would not be able to do much in response to their onslaught in Indian Kashmir, beyond raging and ranting.

It is almost as certain that the strongman duo in New Delhi did not anticipate the nature and severity of China's response. On 6 August 2019, the PRC's foreign ministry expressed 'serious concern' about the Indian government's new Kashmir policy, and criticised 'actions that unilaterally change the *status quo* and exacerbate tension'. The statement added that China's position on the Kashmir conflict was 'clear and consistent': 'We call on the two sides [India and Pakistan] to peacefully resolve the dispute through dialogue and consultation, and safeguard regional peace and stability'. But that was not all. The statement also invoked the Sino-Indian border dispute: 'China is always opposed to India's inclusion of Chinese territory in the western sector of the China–India boundary in its administrative jurisdiction. This firm and consistent position remains unchanged. Recently, India has continued to undermine China's territorial sovereignty by unilaterally changing its domestic law [on Indian J&K]. This is unacceptable.'[38]

China raised the Kashmir issue in the UN Security Council three times between August 2019 and August 2020 – in August 2019, January 2020 and again on the first anniversary of the Hindu nationalist government's move on Kashmir: 5 August 2020. By August 2020, Indian and Chinese forces were in confrontation along the LAC separating Ladakh from Tibet and Aksai Chin. The Chinese foreign ministry stated on 5 August 2020:

China closely follows the situation in the Kashmir region. Our position on the Kashmir issue is consistent and clear. First, the Kashmir issue is a dispute left over from history between Pakistan and India, which is an objective fact established by the UN Charter, relevant Security Council resolutions [of 1948–57, Chapter 1] and bilateral agreements between Pakistan and India [a reference to the 1972 Simla Agreement, possibly also the Lahore Declaration of 1999]. Second, any unilateral change to the *status quo* in the Kashmir region is illegal and invalid. Third, the Kashmir issue should be properly and peacefully resolved through dialogue and consultation between the parties concerned [India and Pakistan].[39]

By September 2020, Indian and Chinese forces were mobilised and massed on Ladakh's frontier with Aksai Chin and Tibet. On 29 September, the Chinese foreign ministry stated bluntly that 'China does not recognize the so-called [Indian] Union Territory of Ladakh', one of the two centrally ruled entities created by New Delhi in August 2019 by dissolving and dividing the Indian state of Jammu and Kashmir (Chapter 4).[40] Meanwhile, Indian media had reported in late June, two weeks after the deadly Galwan clash, that the escalation of hostilities on Pangong Tso, the lake on the Ladakh–Tibet border, started 'on 10th September last year [2019] when PLA troops started vehemently blocking Indian patrols' there, 'barely a month after' the Hindu nationalist government's decisive Kashmir move on 5 August 2019.[41]

China has always lurked in the background of the India–Pakistan Kashmir conflict, especially since the early 1960s, when the Sino-Indian relationship collapsed and the Sino-Pakistani relationship began to grow in tandem. In March 1963, as India reeled from the autumn 1962 war, China and Pakistan settled their own border dispute. The pact, signed in Peking by Marshal Chen Yi, the PRC's foreign minister, and Zulfiqar Ali Bhutto, Pakistan's foreign minister, 'agreed . . . to formally delimit and demarcate the boundary between China's Sinkiang and the contiguous areas the defence of which is under the actual control of Pakistan'. The settlement of Xinjiang's border with Gilgit-Baltistan involved a reciprocal swap of territory, which included the transfer by Pakistan to China of a slice (about 3,100 square miles) of Gilgit-Baltistan located just west of the Karakoram Pass and just north of the Siachen glacier – a desolate area called the Shaksgam tract. The 1963 pact stipulated that 'after the settlement of the Kashmir dispute between Pakistan and India, the sovereign authority concerned [in Jammu and Kashmir] will reopen negotiations with the Government of the People's Republic of China . . . to sign a formal Boundary Treaty to replace the present agreement' and, 'in the event of that sovereign authority being Pakistan', the agreement would be maintained without any change.[42] Indian governments have always held this agreement to be illegal, and a further encroachment by China on Indian territory beyond Aksai Chin, on the grounds that Gilgit-Baltistan, along with the rest of the Pakistani portion of the 1846–1947 princely state of Jammu and Kashmir, rightfully belongs to India as per the accession to India signed by the last princely ruler in October 1947. In this view, Pakistan and China do not have a legally valid land border at all, since the entire Sino-Pakistani frontier is between Xinjiang and Gilgit-Baltistan.

In 2020, China moved from lurking in the background to looming in the foreground of the India–Pakistan Kashmir conflict. This may be rooted in six decades of what the China scholar John Garver calls 'the Sino-Pakistani *entente cordiale*'. In his 2001 book on Sino-Indian rivalry, Garver wrote that 'there is a consensus among analysts who have studied the Sino-Pakistani relationship' that it has 'a truly special character'. That is because the relationship with Pakistan has been 'the most stable and durable element of China's foreign relations ... The Sino-Pakistani entente can be traced back to the heyday of Sino-Indian amity in the mid-1950s [when the slogan *Hindi Chini bhai bhai*, or Indians and Chinese are brothers, was propagated by Jawaharlal Nehru's government], deepened during the long period of Sino-Indian hostility [post-1962], and continued as China and India restored a level of comity in the 1990s [and beyond].'[43] An authoritative book on the twenty-first-century Sino-Pakistani relationship published in 2015 observed: 'Beijing can count its reliable friends on the fingers of one hand. The North Koreans have proved truculent and resentful, and are a standing risk to Chinese strategic interests in North-East Asia ... Authoritarian affinity and a common cause in resisting Western hegemony has not eradicated the deep-seated mutual suspicion in the Russia–China relationship ... Pakistan is the only friendship China has that has been tested out over decades.'[44]

Yet for four decades in the post-Mao era, China did assume a neutral-sounding posture in the India–Pakistan dispute over Kashmir, even rebuffing Pakistan's desperate pleas for diplomatic succour during the Kargil War of 1999. There is almost certainly a complex explanation for the shift in

2019–20, and that very contemporary context is outlined in the preceding pages. But the shift that began in August 2019 was abrupt indeed. Three months earlier, on 1 May 2019, the UN designated Maulana Masood Azhar, the founding leader of the Pakistani Jaish-e-Mohammad group, as a 'global terrorist' after China lifted a decade-long 'technical hold' on the designation, which had been requested by India in 2009 but blocked solely by China in the UN's Security Council ever since. The very belated Chinese climbdown came two and a half months after a suicide bombing claimed by Jaish-e-Mohammad killed forty Indian paramilitary soldiers in the Kashmir Valley in February 2019 (Chapter 3), the single deadliest attack on Indian forces in three decades of the Kashmir insurgency. I admit that when I wrote in August 2019 that 'the sheer radicalism of their [the Hindu nationalist government's] approach . . . may have reinvigorated the Kashmir conflict in a way the dynamic duo [Modi and Shah] will find difficult to manage going forward', China's entry from the backstage to the stage of the Kashmir conflict was not what I had in mind.[45]

That entry represents a cold-blooded strategy of realpolitik. China does not care in the least about the human, civil and political rights of Kashmiris and, unlike Pakistan, does not purport to do so. The Xi Jinping regime's mass persecution of the Uighurs of Xinjiang, its stance on Taiwan and its Hong Kong policy offer more than enough evidence about its nature. The precise strategic calculus behind China's new assertiveness on the matter of Kashmir is known only to its leaders, but that assertiveness is a fact, and it has come into play in response to the Hindu nationalist government's drastic move on Kashmir in August 2019.

The Hindu nationalist attempt to radically reset the Kashmir question has resulted in the regional geopolitics of the conflict becoming explicitly trilateral – India–Pakistan–China – at the beginning of the third decade of the twenty-first century. China initiated its military escalation in 2020 *only* on Ladakh's border with Tibet and Aksai Chin, and not in the eastern Himalayas, where it claims the Indian state of Arunachal Pradesh as part of Tibet and therefore of the PRC. But the *global* geopolitics of the reconfigured Kashmir conflict is likely to be quadrilateral. It was, after all, a decisive intervention by the US at the presidential level which ended the Kargil War in 1999, and high-level American diplomacy helped defuse the threat of a full-fledged India–Pakistan war in 2002 (Chapter 2).

THE UNITED STATES

In July 2019, President Donald J. Trump hosted Imran Khan at the White House. Sitting next to Khan, Trump said that three weeks earlier, during a conversation on the sidelines of a G-20 meeting in Osaka, Japan, Prime Minister Modi had asked him to 'mediate or arbitrate' the Kashmir dispute. Modi did not react, but his foreign minister told India's parliament that 'no such request' had been made. Trump and Modi next met in late August in Biarritz, France, on the sidelines of a summit of G-7 leaders. By that time, Indian Jammu and Kashmir had had its nominal autonomy abolished and its status as a state of the Indian Union revoked, and been divided into two centrally ruled 'union territories' by Modi's government. A draconian lock-down was being enforced across Indian J&K, amid large-scale detentions and with all means of telephonic and electronic communication cut to prevent protests (Chapter 4). Before meeting with Trump, Modi said: 'All issues between India and Pakistan are bilateral in nature, that is why we don't bother any other country about them. India and Pakistan were together before 1947 [sic] and I'm confident we can discuss our problems and solve them together.' Speaking after meeting with Modi, Trump said: 'We spoke last night about Kashmir, the prime minister really feels he has it under control. They speak with Pakistan and I'm sure they will be able to do something that is very good. I have a very good relationship with both the gentlemen [Modi and Khan], and I'm here, [but] I think they can do it themselves.'[46]

Modi continued to cultivate Trump thereafter. A month later, in late September 2019, the two leaders appeared together at a 50,000-strong rally of Indian-Americans held in Houston, Texas. They embraced and walked hand in hand at the event, headlined 'Howdy, Modi!' by the organisers: 'The loudest applause in the three-hour show was when Trump talked about "radical Islamic terrorism". The entire stadium gave him a standing ovation, Modi and his delegation included. The second loudest applause was when Modi talked about giving farewell to Article 370 [the Indian constitution's autonomy provision for Indian J&K]. After the applause, he asked the audience to give a standing ovation to India's lawmakers for passing the historic [Kashmir] legislation.'[47] Modi welcomed Trump as 'a very special person who needs no introduction. His name comes up in almost every conversation on global politics, his every word is followed by tens of millions.'[48] In his fifty-minute speech, Modi said that 'Article 370 kept the people of Jammu, Kashmir and Ladakh from progress. Terrorists were taking advantage of it. Now they [Kashmiris] have the same rights as all Indians.' He added that 'Pakistan has made hatred of India the centre of its agenda. They support and harbour terrorists. The time has come for a decisive fight against terrorism and those who support it.'[49]

Modi then chanted '*Ab ki baar, Trump Sarkar!*' (this time, a Trump Government) in reference to the unfolding campaign for the US presidential election due in autumn 2020 ('*Ab ki baar, Modi Sarkar!*' was the winning BJP campaign slogan in the Indian parliamentary election of 2014, and in 2016, a 'Hindu-American' group got Trump to say '*Ab ki baar, Trump Sarkar*' as part of the Trump campaign's outreach to Indian Americans). Modi then invited Trump to visit India. Trump did so in February 2020, in a visit styled '*Namaste*, Trump!' (*namaste/namaskar* is the traditional Indian greeting with the hands folded together). Donald and Melania Trump posed in front of the Taj Mahal in Agra during the visit. Their time in Delhi was marred by a large-scale outbreak of Hindu–Muslim violence in the Indian capital, triggered by a peaceful agitation by Muslims against a controversial amendment to India's citizenship laws pushed through parliament by Modi and Shah in December 2019. As the Trumps attended the dinner banquet hosted by India's president – a ceremonial post occupied by a BJP appointee – brutal killings and arson attacks engulfed parts of Delhi a few miles from the presidential palace. At least fifty-three people, mostly Muslim, died in the violence.

Trump, in the event, did not at any time endorse the Modi–Shah government's Kashmir policy launched on and from 5 August 2019. Instead, he kept repeating his offer to mediate between India and Pakistan. In January 2020, speaking on the eve of another meeting with Imran Khan at the World Economic Forum gathering in Davos, Switzerland, he said: 'We're talking about Kashmir and what's going on with Pakistan and India. We've been watching that and following it very, very closely. And if we can help, we certainly will be helping.' The Indian foreign ministry responded that 'India has always rejected any third-party role in its bilateral relationship with Pakistan, including several offers of mediation made by President Trump'.[50] Undeterred, Trump brought up the matter again during his visit to India a month later. In his press conference in riot-hit Delhi, he emphasised his 'good equation' with both Modi and Khan, and asserted that 'they [the Pakistanis] are working to control cross-border terrorism' targeting Indian Kashmir. Referring to his talks with Modi, he said 'we talked about it [Kashmir] a lot today. Anything I can do to mediate, help, I will do.'[51]

Modi makes a habit of cultivating fellow hard-right leaders and is especially close to Israel's Binyamin Netanyahu. But he failed to get Trump to endorse his Kashmir policy. The only international support his government received on Kashmir was from the far right in Europe. In late October 2019, a delegation of twenty-seven members of the European parliament (MEPs) flew into New Delhi and posed in a group photo with the prime minister. Twenty-three were then flown to Srinagar, the locked-down capital of the Kashmir Valley, its neighbourhoods barricaded with concertina wire and its streets patrolled by tens of thousands of security forces (four developed cold feet and dropped out once a controversy over the visit erupted in the media). In Srinagar, the visitors were put up in a luxury hotel and taken for a boat ride on the city's picturesque Dal Lake. Of the twenty-three MEPs, six each were from France's National Rally (formerly the National Front) and Poland's Law and Justice Party, four were from the United Kingdom's Brexit Party, two from the Alliance for Germany (AfD) party and one from Belgium's Vlaams Blok – all far-right parties. At the time, all shops and markets in Srinagar were closed as part of a 'civil curfew' in protest against Modi's government, except grocery stores, which opened for two hours every morning. When word of the visit got out, mosque loudspeakers announced 'no morning shopping' (a total strike), and clashes between stone-pelting protesters and the security forces broke out in 'about 40 locations' in and around Srinagar.[52]

At the other end of the American political spectrum, three of the candidates running for the Democratic presidential nomination – Bernie Sanders, Elizabeth Warren and Kamala Harris – publicly criticised the

Hindu nationalist government's Kashmir policy. Two weeks before the 'Howdy Modi' extravaganza in Houston in late September 2019, Harris was asked for her view of the post-5 August situation in Kashmir at a campaign event in that city. She responded that 'we are watching', 'we are all watching', and that it was important to 'remind people they are not alone' because 'the abuser convinces those that they abuse that nobody cares, nobody's listening, nobody's paying attention, and that's a tool of the abuser'. She then stated that it was imperative to reverse the 'decimation' of the US Department of State that had taken place under the Trump administration and revive 'a strong diplomatic corps' in order to conduct foreign policy coherently and effectively[53] (in fact, even under the Trump administration, State Department officials repeatedly expressed profound concern over the repression in Indian Kashmir, and called for the release of political detainees and the restoration of basic liberties). In December 2019 Pramila Jayapal, who represents the city and suburbs of Seattle in the US House of Representatives and is the first Indian-American woman elected to that body (she was born in India), introduced a bipartisan resolution in the House, 'urging the Republic of India to end mass detentions and restrictions on communications in Jammu and Kashmir and preserve religious freedom for all residents'. The resolution 'recognize[d] the dire security challenges faced by the Government of India in Jammu and Kashmir and the continuing threat of state-supported cross-border terrorism', but 'reject[ed] arbitrary detention, use of excessive force against civilians and suppression of peaceful expression of dissent as proportional responses to security challenges'.[54] Two weeks later, a diplomatic incident ensued during a visit to the US by S. Jaishankar, the Modi government's foreign minister. As part of his itinerary in Washington, DC, Jaishankar – a retired career diplomat who has been ambassador to China – was due to meet with Representative Eliot Engel, the chair of the House foreign affairs committee, and several other lawmakers. Jaishankar refused to go ahead with the meeting unless Jayapal was excluded from the group of lawmakers. Engel rejected the demand, and the meeting did not happen.[55] Harris tweeted: 'It is wrong for any foreign government to tell Congress which members are allowed in meetings on Capitol Hill. I stand with Representative Jayapal, and I'm glad her colleagues in the House did too.'[56]

The Biden–Harris 2020 campaign's charter included an 'agenda for Muslim-Americans'. While mostly focused on domestic issues, it made reference to five overseas cases under a section titled 'champion human rights and democracy globally'. It mentioned 'the forced detention of over a million Uighur Muslims in western China' as 'unconscionable' and 'appalling oppression'. It described 'atrocities against Burma's Rohingya minority' as 'abhorrent'. The reference to Kashmir had a milder tone: 'In Kashmir, the Indian government should take all necessary steps to restore rights for all the people of Kashmir. Restrictions on dissent such as preventing peaceful protests and shutting or slowing down the internet weaken democracy.' The document also promised to 'end Trump's blank check for Saudi Arabia's human rights abuses at home and abroad, and end the war in Yemen' (the Biden administration acted on Yemen within a fortnight of taking office). It further promised that 'Joe will actively engage Israelis and Palestinians alike to help them find ways to live together, and champion a two-state solution. He will continue to oppose Israeli settlement expansion, and has spoken out against annexation in the West Bank. He will restore economic and humanitarian assistance to the Palestinians' (the Biden administration acted on this last commitment within a fortnight of taking office).[57]

President Biden has a long record of promoting considerations of morality and justice in American foreign policy, and of supporting skilfully crafted solutions to complex, historically rooted conflicts. During the 1992–95 Bosnian War, by far Europe's bloodiest post-1945 conflict, he spoke up for the Bosnian Muslims – by no means blameless but still the main victims.[58] He has long been a resolute champion of the 1998 Good Friday Agreement, which ended the three-decade armed conflict in Northern Ireland, and reiterated that support strongly amid post-Brexit turbulence in 2021. But the complex geopolitical context of the contemporary Kashmir conflict is likely to test the Biden administration and its secretary of state, Antony Blinken. The Modi government and its policies are not at all to the Biden administration's taste (on which more below). But the Chinese military poised in strength on Ladakh's border represents a complication for the Biden administration's potential stance on Kashmir (apart from representing an opportunity for the Modi government to threat). In June 2021, at the Biden administration's behest, a NATO summit in Brussels described China as a 'systemic threat', and just prior to that, a summit of G-7 leaders held in England announced a 'Build Back Better for the World' (BBBW) initiative to counter China's BRI, also at the Biden administration's urging. At the same time, however, the Biden administration will be obliged to engage with Pakistan's concerns about the new Kashmir crisis created by the Hindu nationalist government since August 2019, if nothing else because Pakistani cooperation is necessary in Afghanistan, another fragile arena of conflict, rendered even more so by the withdrawal of American troops in September 2021. The quadrilateral geopolitics of the twenty-first-century Kashmir conflict – India–Pakistan–China–America – will play out not just during the tenure of the Biden administration, but over the rest of this decade.[59]

A FLAMMABLE CONFLICT

In its current condition, the Kashmir conflict is highly flammable. Its main arena, Indian Jammu and Kashmir, is bounded by two heavily militarised, volatile borders: the India–Pakistan LoC and the India–China LAC. In February 2021, after nine months of charged confrontation along the LAC, the Indian and Chinese defence ministries announced agreement on a slight pullback from the eyeball-to-eyeball stand-off on the Pangong Tso lake, where dozens of state-of-the-art battle tanks deployed by both sides a few hundred feet apart had been staring down the barrel at each other since the summer of 2020.[60] The agreement was reached after nine tortuous rounds of high-level army-to-army talks between June 2020 and January 2021. It amounted to no more than a slight (and localised) tactical pullback – which appeared to be to China's advantage in the contested lake area because it entailed Indian troops vacating a series of ridges and peaks on the lake's southern shore overlooking the Chinese side of the LAC that the Indians had seized in a lightning nocturnal operation at the end of August 2020, whereas the Chinese merely agreed to withdraw to their pre-May 2020 positions on the northern shore.

The tenuous Pangong Tso disengagement made no difference to the broader strategic reality that emerged in 2020 along Ladakh's border with Aksai Chin and Tibet – an ominous level of military mobilisation and confrontation which will not be defused even if similar localised agreements are reached regarding the other flashpoints along the LAC. General Naravane, the Indian Army's chief, was candid on this point two days after the Pangong Tso agreement was made public: 'The rising footprints of China in India's neighbourhood and its attempts to unilaterally alter the *status quo* on our disputed borders have created an environment of confrontation and mutual distrust'. He placed the LAC crisis in the broader context of 'Chinese belligerence in the Indo-Pacific, its hostility towards weaker nations and its relentless drive to create regional dependencies through initiatives like the BRI'.[61] That context and behaviour are undeniable, but the geopolitical fallout of the Hindu nationalist sledgehammer that descended on Indian Jammu and Kashmir in August 2019 means that Xi Jinping's PRC can now openly treat the Kashmir conflict as not simply 'a problem between India and Pakistan', as Deng Xiaoping characterised it in 1980. In April 2021, it was reported that continuing talks between senior military commanders on disengagement from a number of other friction points on the LAC had failed.[62]

In addition to this geopolitical vortex, Indian Jammu and Kashmir post-August 2019 is a simmering cauldron, with plenty of combustible potential. An incendiary escalation of the conflict could be triggered by one or some combination of three eventualities:

- Major insurgent strikes in Indian Jammu and Kashmir, along the lines of the 14 February 2019 suicide bombing near Srinagar that killed forty Indian paramilitary policemen and was claimed by the Pakistani jihadist group Jaish-e-Mohammad (Chapter 3).
- Large-scale deaths from Indian action against renewed protests in the Kashmir Valley.
- Mass-casualty terror attacks in India, along the lines of the November 2008 onslaught perpetrated by the Pakistani jihadist group Lashkar-e-Taiba on Mumbai (Chapter 3).

Each of these eventualities represents a grim scenario for escalation, in a period when India has a radical, hyper-nationalist government and Pakistan, politically unstable as always, seethes with frustration at that government's Kashmir policy. In late February 2021 India's deputy permanent representative to the UN told a Security Council meeting that 'a state would be compelled to undertake a pre-emptive strike [against another state] when confronted with an imminent armed attack by a non-state actor operating [from that state]', if 'the non-state actor has [already] repeatedly undertaken armed attacks against the [targeted] state, the host state is unwilling to address the threat posed by the non-state actor, or if the host state is actively supporting and sponsoring the attack by the non-state actor'. 'This state of affairs,' the Indian diplomat asserted, 'exonerates the affected state from the duty to respect, vis-à-vis the aggressor, the general obligation to refrain from the use of force.'[63]

The precariousness of the security situation in the Kashmir Valley can be gauged from an urgent advisory issued by the Indian J&K police on 13 February 2021 – the eve of the second anniversary of the 2019 suicide bombing which was carried out by a local Kashmiri recruit of the Jaish-e-Mohammad terror group – to all Indian Army formations and Central Armed Police Forces (CAPFs, paramilitary police under the authority of the Indian home ministry) deployed in the Valley. The advisory read:

> In view of imminent threat, a strict dry day [sic] shall be observed [on 14 February, the second anniversary of the attack] and no [military or paramilitary] convoy movement, repeat no convoy movement, should be allowed. All movement of administrative vehicles should also be restricted across [the] Valley. Movement of isolated vehicles, in particular, should be avoided at all costs. No movement of Army or CAPF vehicles on interior routes [in the Valley] to be allowed. No ROPs [road-opening parties] on the ground.[64]

The stark warning led to a piquant situation. Hundreds of thousands of soldiers were cooped up in their camps and barracks, and the Valley's main were eerily deserted to protect the army and CAPF personnel from suicide attacks. The 'interior routes' (network of side roads) too were free of this otherwise incessant flow of traffic, and the road-opening parties – foot patrols which check every morning for improvised explosive devices and any signs of insurgent activity – were also off-duty for fear of ambush. It was a strange confirmation of the solemn dictum of Kalhana, the twelfth-century chronicler, that Kashmir cannot be controlled 'by the force of soldiers'.

The Kashmiri journalist Gowhar Geelani wrote in August 2020 about the dilemma faced by the Valley's people since August 2019: 'In extreme fear, psychologists say, there are only three possibilities – flight, freeze, or fight. In Kashmir's case, it appears that during the past one year, people have been in the freeze mode. Many are uncertain how to respond [to the Hindu nationalist steamroller].'[65] This is certainly true, but the question is how long the 'freeze mode' will hold, and flight is not a feasible path out of torment for the great majority of the Valley's people. The Valley has a history of mass uprisings – in 1946, 1953, 1963–64, 1990, 2008, 2010 and 2016 – which, apart from the 1946 'Quit Kashmir' uprising against the rulers of the princely state (Chapter 1), broke out without much if any planning or leadership. The Valley's people have bitterly learned the virtues of caution and self-restraint, especially since the bloodbath of the 1990s and early 2000s (Chapter 2), but the tradition of protest has not gone away, as the outbreaks of 2010 and 2016 led by the young generation (Chapter 3) demonstrated. For all its ruthlessness and guile, it is not likely that the Hindu nationalist government in New Delhi will ultimately be any more successful than its predecessors in eradicating this tradition. In the tinderbox-like situation that prevails in the Valley, a single spark or a few sparks could light a prairie fire as has happened in the past, though the timing of such an eventuality is hard to predict.

A PEACE SETTLEMENT: URGENT NECESSITY, REMOTE POSSIBILITY

That the Kashmir conflict, now in its seventy-fifth year, desperately needs a peace process leading to a settlement is a very reasonable proposition. Two decades ago, the Lahore Declaration (1999) jointly issued by the

Nawaz Sharif, unambiguously acknowledged this imperative. They were not obvious peaceniks. Vajpayee (1924–2018) was a lifelong Hindu nationalist who practised moderation on Kashmir and pursued diplomatic engagement with Pakistan when he led a coalition government as India's prime minister from 1998 to 2004. Sharif (born 1949) was, and is, a moderate conservative with an enduring base of support in the Punjab, Pakistan's numerically and politically dominant province. The Lahore Declaration could not have said it with greater clarity: that resolving Kashmir 'is in the supreme national interest of both countries'.

Any process leading to such an outcome would need to take to heart Nelson Mandela's dictum that, as a matter of necessity, 'if you want to make peace with your enemy, you have to work with your enemy. You negotiate with your enemies, not your friends.'[66] And it would need to be based on a commitment to 'the protection and vindication of the human rights of all' and search for 'every practical way' to find 'rapprochement' between 'equally legitimate political aspirations'– the guiding principles of Northern Ireland's Good Friday Agreement of 1998.

The trans-LoC territory disputed between India and Pakistan is both sprawling and socially heterogeneous and contains people of three fundamentally different political orientations: Kashmir independentists and those who consider their national identity to be Indian or Pakistani. In autumn 2009, a broadly credible survey of public attitudes and preferences was conducted on both sides of the LoC by Ipsos-MORI, a polling agency, and published in mid-2010 by a London think-tank, the Royal Institute of International Affairs (Chatham House).[67] It found overwhelming support for the independentist position in the Kashmir Valley, but low levels of independentist support in the Jammu and Ladakh regions of Indian Jammu and Kashmir, where affinity with India dominated. Across the LoC, the survey covered almost all of 'Azad' Kashmir, the nominally autonomous region which contains three-fourths of Pakistani Kashmir's 6 million people (the rest are in Gilgit-Baltistan). There the survey reported a nearly vertical split in all the seven districts running from north to south – Muzaffarabad, Bagh, Poonch, Sudanhoti, Kotli, Mirpur and Bhimber (the thinly populated Neelum Valley in the far north was not covered) – between independentists and Pakistan loyalists. Overall, 50 per cent professed allegiance to Pakistan and 44 per cent supported the independentist stance. And if Pakistani Kashmir, which is nearly 100 per cent Muslim, is politically torn, Indian Kashmir and its 14 million people (8 million in the Valley, 6 million in Jammu and 300,000 in Ladakh) presents a much greater degree of sociopolitical complexity. Balraj Puri, an activist and writer who lived in the city of Jammu, summarised the multi-layered complexity of the now dissolved and dismembered Indian state of Jammu and Kashmir thus: 'A Muslim-majority state [68.3 per cent per the 2011 census] within a Hindu-majority country, a Hindu-majority region [Jammu] within the Muslim-majority state, Muslim-majority districts within the Hindu-majority region [currently six of Jammu's ten districts have Muslim majorities], Hindu-majority *tehsils* [administrative sub-divisions] within the Muslim-majority districts [of Jammu], and Muslim-majority villages within those Hindu-majority *tehsils*'.[68] The most telling microcosmic example of this complexity that I have come across is the mountainous district of Kishtwar in the far north-east of the Jammu region, just south of the Kashmir Valley. The Kishtwar district – part of the Jammu region, which is nearly two-thirds Hindu – is almost 60 per cent Muslim (and 40 per cent Hindu), and its epicentre, the town of Kishtwar, is split evenly between Kashmiri-speaking Muslims of a generally independentist orientation and Hindus who identify firmly with India.

A Kashmir peace process would require an exceptionally favourable constellation of circumstances. The Northern Ireland peace process of the 1990s was driven by the shared resolve of the governments of Britain and the Republic of Ireland to pursue and find a solution to the Northern Ireland problem. After 1998, the Good Friday Agreement proved difficult to fully implement until 2007 because of continuing schisms within Northern Ireland but survived primarily because the British and Irish governments stayed steadfast in their commitment to seeing it work. During the 1990s and subsequently the 2000s, there were no geopolitical obstacles to a Northern Ireland settlement. The sole global superpower, the US, strongly backed the peace process and then the agreement that emerged from it in 1998. The geopolitical context was advantageous in Europe in another crucial way. The 1990s and the turn of the millennium were the peak of the development of the European Union as a framework of regional integration and transnational cooperation. The framework helped foster a spirit of transnational partnership and popularised an elastic conception of state sovereignty compatible with porous frontiers and non-zero-sum national identities. The ethos vitally buttressed intergovernmental cooperation on the Northern Ireland conflict between Britain and the Republic of Ireland – both at the time longstanding member-states of the EU. That in turn aided the fashioning of a settlement based on devolution of power from London to Northern Ireland, power-sharing between the antagonistic communities within Northern Ireland, and institutionalised cross-border cooperation linking Northern Ireland, which remained under UK sovereignty in the new arrangements, with the Republic of Ireland. The settlement ended thirty years of armed conflict in Northern Ireland (late 1960s–late 1990s), and eventually power-sharing in Northern Ireland's government led by the 'extremes' of the pro-British and Irish nationalist camps came about from 2007 and lasted until 2017, and was restored again from 2020. That the Northern Ireland situation has been somewhat destabilised once again by the consequences of the United Kingdom's troubled exit from the European Union does not detract from these historic achievements.

Two decades after I first argued that the principles and the architecture of the Northern Ireland settlement provide a template that can be adapted to the Kashmir conflict's conditions, I can say with confidence that that approach remains the most plausible path to a substantive settlement of the Kashmir conflict.[69] For a few years (2004–7, Chapter 3), it seemed that such a settlement of the Kashmir conflict might be on the horizon. But the contrast between the proximate and geopolitical contexts of the Kashmir conflict in the early 2020s and Northern Ireland twenty years ago could not be starker, and makes any such endeavour a remote prospect in the immediate future.

Beyond the opportunities and obstacles posed by structural conditions, peacemaking calls for political agency: leaders endowed with a capacity for statecraft. Big, thorny and highly sensitive issues, of which the Kashmir conflict is surely one, require elites possessing both the will and the ability to make pragmatic judgements about what course of action best secures the long-term interests of their nations, or the communities they seek to represent.

The three-decade armed conflict in Northern Ireland, from the late 1960s to the end of the 1990s, threw up some remarkable political leaders of that calibre and mentality – most notably the moderate Irish nationalist John Hume, the more militant nationalist Gerry Adams, who was a guerrilla commander for over a decade in his early political life, and David Trimble, the unionist (pro-British) politician who played a crucial part in the making of the Good Friday Agreement. Hume and Trimble were jointly awarded the Nobel Peace Prize in late 1998. No comparable leadership exists on either side of the LoC in Kashmir. The erstwhile India-aligned political establishment of the Kashmir Valley, the local representatives of Indian authority for decades, had the shaky ground cut from under their feet in August 2019, when the Hindu nationalist government in New Delhi brutally dispensed with their services. The Valley's spectrum of groups advocating the cause of 'self-determination' are in a similar state of disorganisation. Chronically fragmented and lacking a concerted voice, most of their leaders and prominent activists are in Indian prisons. The sole figure with some popular standing – Syed Ali Shah Geelani, a pro-Pakistan Islamic fundamentalist – is in his early nineties and bedridden with age and illness in his Srinagar home. In Pakistani Kashmir, heavy-handed military control of 'Azad' Kashmir and Gilgit-Baltistan down the decades has created a class of client politicians whose limitations mirror those of their counterparts in Indian Kashmir. Independentist politics has popular currency in Pakistani Kashmir but is weakened by the absence of robust organisation and leadership, and the continual harassment and persecution of independentists by the Pakistani authorities.

The problem of the void of appropriate leadership in the Indian and Pakistani Kashmirs, however, pales in comparison with the problem in India and Pakistan. Pakistan is in the throes of yet another cycle of the conflict that has defined its existence since the 1960s – between military guardianship of the state and attempts by civilian politicians to challenge that supremacy. India, for its part, faces a truly historic moment of reckoning in the first half of the 2020s. The question is whether India's parliamentary-democratic and quasi-federal structure will survive or be overwhelmed and consigned to history by a Hindu nationalist government that seeks to impose authoritarian rule on the country while retaining the institutional trappings of democracy.

Since the end of the military regime headed by General Pervez Musharraf from 1999 to 2008, Pakistan has transitioned 'from military government to military governance', in the phrasing of the Pakistani scholar Ayesha Siddiqa.[70] In September 2020, eleven Pakistani opposition parties led by the Pakistan Muslim League-Nawaz (PML-N) and the Pakistan People's Party (PPP) formed an umbrella alliance called the Pakistan Democratic Movement (PDM) to challenge the government led by the ex-cricketer Imran Khan, whose party's narrow victory in national elections in July 2018 is widely attributed in Pakistan to crude manipulation in its favour by the high command of the Pakistan Army. Speaking from exile in London, Nawaz Sharif – most recently prime minister from 2013 to 2017, when he was forced out by the army – denounced the military as 'not a state within a state, but a state above the state'. The PDM's charter called for '[the] end of the military's interference in politics, new free and fair elections after election reforms with no role of armed forces and intelligence agencies, release of political prisoners, [and] withdrawal of [criminal] cases against journalists'.[71] Between October and December 2020, the PDM held a series of huge rallies in major cities across Pakistan – from Karachi in the south to Peshawar in the north, each attended by hundreds of thousands of people – to demand the resignation of the Imran Khan government. Addressing a rally in the Punjab city of Gujranwala by video-link in October, Sharif described Khan as a 'selected prime minister' and then targeted the Pakistan Army chief by name: 'General [Qamar Javed] Bajwa, you are the one who packed up our government when it was working well. You are the one responsible for rigging the 2018 election, curbs on the media, abduction, torture and harassment of journalists and forcing judges to give decisions of your choice.' At Peshawar in November, the PPP leader Bilawal Bhutto Zardari predicted the Khan government would collapse in 2021: 'The time is near when you, the people, will hold this selected government and its selectors responsible'. At Lahore in December, the star opposition politician, Sharif's daughter Maryam Nawaz, 'launched a frontal attack on the ISI [Inter-Services Intelligence] and the judiciary for ousting her father and imposing Khan'.[72]

At the final rally in Lahore, the PDM announced a 'long march' to Islamabad in February 2021 to topple Khan's government. This did not happen on schedule. The Pakistani scholar Farzana Shaikh commented in November 2020 that 'for a country as famously unpredictable as Pakistan, the regularity of its dispiriting pattern of politics can be hard to explain. Periodic waves of popular protest, each riding on the back of ever-higher expectations of democratic change, soon recede to expose an entrenched pattern of power which has remained broadly constant for seven decades.' She acknowledged, however, that Khan's government – whose term runs until July 2023 – is living on borrowed time and that the former cricketer can be expected to continue in office 'only as long as it takes to cobble together' an army-sponsored alternative.[73]

On strategic matters like Afghanistan and Kashmir, policy is controlled by the Pakistan Army's high command, and the ISI's perspective is usually critical. This has had major implications for the Kashmir conflict. In 1999, Pervez Musharraf and a small cabal of his fellow generals sabotaged the tentative opening to a Kashmir peace process created by Vajpayee's diplomatic outreach to Nawaz Sharif by launching the limited war in Kargil (Chapter 2). A few years after seizing power from Sharif in a coup, Musharraf turned dovish on Kashmir from the mid-2000s and repeatedly expressed his desire to negotiate a pragmatic Kashmir settlement with India. That window of opportunity closed in 2007–8 (Chapter 3). It is very doubtful, though, that Musharraf would have been able to 'sell' a Kashmir settlement with India in Pakistan because of his regime's lack of popular legitimacy, a problem that deepened over time and led to his fall in 2008. Pakistan's civil–military conundrum needs to be addressed, at least in relation to Kashmir policy, if history is not to repeat itself in the future. If sceptics like Shaikh are right, that may be a tall order, but given Pakistan's limited capacity to proactively influence the Kashmir conflict, a conjuncture where the military and civilian elites are both in favour of a negotiated Kashmir settlement is not inconceivable.

Pakistan's civil–military conundrum is a textbook example of a chronic problem, which has dogged its state for over sixty years. The existential threat to India's democracy posed by the rise of Hindu nationalism to dominant status in its politics since 2014 is a distinctly contemporary development. During the Modi government's first term (2014–19), India was on a slippery slope towards semi-authoritarian rule. It is now in free fall, ever since Modi was re-elected in May 2019 and his confidant Amit Shah, appointed as the home (interior) minister, emerged openly as the other member of a strongman duopoly exercising power in New Delhi. Unless the Hindu nationalist ascendancy can be checked, and then reversed through a decisive BJP defeat in the next Indian general election which is due in April–May 2024, there is no real prospect of a positive turnaround in Kashmir. Instead, India as a whole will become more and more like Indian Kashmir – ruled by repression and fear. In late June 2021, Modi and Shah suddenly summoned a roundtable meeting in New Delhi of leaders of the legal, recognised political parties present in Indian Jammu and Kashmir, with the ostensible purpose of restarting a political process in the paralysed union territory. The move, after two years of chaos and havoc wreaked by the strongman duo on Indian Kashmir (Chapter 4), lacks any credibility and is almost certainly a sleight of hand, possibly motivated by a new sense of nervousness about the popularity of their government. The Modi–Shah government has nothing to offer the Kashmir conflict except a variable mix of chicanery and repression. After engaging in chicanery from 2015 to 2018 (Chapter 3), and then unleashing unbridled repression from 2019 (Chapter 4), the duo may be scheming a fresh round of chicanery – which is not surprising, since the sledgehammer Hindu nationalist 'solution' to the Kashmir problem under implementation since August 2019 is a dangerous dead-end and an international embarrassment.

During its first term, the Modi government's main slogan was *sab kaa saath, sab kaa vikaas* (with all, for the development of all). The government launched several nationwide schemes that proved popular – such as *Swachh Bharat* (Clean India: a public hygiene and sanitation drive), *Ujjwala* (Brightness: an initiative to supply free cooking-gas cylinders to poor families) and *Jan Dhan Yojana* (People's Wealth Scheme: a plan to expand rural banking services). Alongside, a massive image-building exercise unfolded to imprint Modi in the public mind as India's man of destiny in the early twenty-first century, a messiah of progress. This assumed the proportions of a personality cult. In parallel, an insidious pattern of intimidation and violence became apparent. Groups of Hindu nationalist vigilantes perpetrated a spate of attacks on Muslims in BJP-ruled states, mostly in northern India, as part of a campaign against the consumption of beef, the cow being holy in Hindu orthodoxy. The campaign was a sham because cow slaughter is banned as a criminal offence in most of India's states and the only 'beef' that is available, in a few states, is buffalo and not cow meat. The vicious campaign took the form of attacks by small but well-organised mobs, and in a number of cases the victims were lynched. There was also a pattern of officially sponsored harassment of civil society organisations, rights advocacy groups and some universities considered unfriendly to Hindu nationalist politics.

The authoritarian creep evident during Modi's first term assumed the character of a full-blown ideological offensive once he was re-elected in May 2019 and Amit Shah, his closest associate, became the government's chief enforcer as home minister. The new, radical Kashmir policy – whose origins and motivations are described in Chapter 4 – became the re-elected government's flagship initiative and went into effect from August 2019.

The other major initiative was an amendment to India's citizenship laws, which Modi's government had been promoting since July 2016 and finally pushed through India's parliament in December 2019. The legislation promises to confer Indian citizenship on members of six designated religious communities – Hindus, Sikhs, Christians, Buddhists, Jains and Zoroastrians – who have over the decades moved to India from Bangladesh, Pakistan and Afghanistan and settled in India without legal status. The ostensible rationale is that such people are refugees from religious persecution in the three Muslim-dominated countries in India's neighbourhood.[74] Critics have pointed out that the humanitarian purpose of the law is incomplete without the inclusion of tens of thousands of Tamils (Hindu and Christian) who have taken refuge in India since the 1980s from violence in Buddhist-majority Sri Lanka, as well as the more recent Rohingya expellees from Myanmar and, indeed, Shias and especially Ahmadis (a sect considered heretical by orthodox Sunnis), who have faced violence and persecution in Pakistan for decades. The passage of the law – the Citizenship

Amendment Act (CAA) – sparked spirited but peaceful protests by Muslims waving the national tricolour flag in Indian cities, centred, to the government's embarrassment, on Delhi, the political capital. Fear spread among India's 200 million-plus Muslims that the law is the precursor to a National Register of Citizens (NRC) exercise that Amit Shah has been periodically threatening to implement to identify people illegally living in India ('termites', in his terminology) and which many Indian Muslims fear is a stratagem to target and disenfranchise them. The Biden–Harris campaign noted that 'Joe Biden has been disappointed by the ... passage of the Citizenship Amendment Act into law. These measures are inconsistent with India's long tradition of secularism and with sustaining a multiethnic and multireligious democracy.'[75] The latest salvo from the Hindu nationalists consists of a slew of laws enacted over the winter of 2020–21 by BJP-ruled states criminalising religious conversion for marriage. This stems from a longstanding theory of Hindu nationalist discourse ('love jihad') that Muslim men make a habit of seducing and marrying Hindu women in order to convert them. In fact, interfaith marriages of any kind are rare in India, and Hindu–Muslim unions even more so.

Narendra Modi and Amit Shah are simply the latter-day implementers of the ideological mission of Hindu nationalism, as defined by its pioneers. The single most influential figure of that pantheon is Madhav Sadashiv (M.S.) Golwalkar, who steered the Hindu nationalist movement in post-independence India as the RSS chief until his death in 1973. Golwalkar, whom Modi reveres, wrote in a seminal treatise of Hindu nationalism first published in the late 1930s: 'The non-Hindu people of Hindustan ... may stay in the country, wholly subordinated to the Hindu nation'.[76]

As explained in Chapter 4, the subcontinent's Muslims (until 1947) and India's Muslims (post-1947) have consistently been defined as the irreconcilable 'other' in Hindu nationalism's ideological framework. The Kashmiri Muslims, seen as an especially troublesome element of the enemy group, are naturally a top target now that the Hindu nationalists – marginal in India's politics until three decades ago – have the power to implement their ideological agenda. But, I argued in 2018, the Hindu nationalist movement's friend–enemy binary 'travels much beyond the Hindu–Muslim focus to include *anyone* who does not accept Hindu nationalism as the *only* authentic and legitimate ideology of Indian nationalism'.[77] So the second Modi government is defined by an Orwellian-Kafkaesque atmosphere in which a wide variety of citizens – from students to octogenarians – are being labelled as enemies of the state and arrested under a late nineteenth-century sedition law enacted by the British. The black law was used to persecute and imprison thousands of Indian anti-colonial patriots, including such famous figures as Bal Gangadhar Tilak and Mahatma Gandhi.

Indeed, under the Modi–Shah *raj*, democratic India increasingly resembles praetorian Pakistan in its hounding of independent media, the persecution of peaceful and democratic dissent and the strategic use of anti-corruption investigations against opposition politicians. There is an even deeper resemblance emerging at the institutional level, where a weakened and increasingly irrelevant parliament and a largely supine high judiciary fail to check and counter the abuse of executive power. On 15 August 2019, India's seventy-second independence day, the *Washington Post* aptly headlined its report from New Delhi: 'In Modi's move on Kashmir, a roadmap for his "New India"'. The report led me to point out the relatively obvious, that 'this is not just about Kashmir, it's about the future of India. Modi and his party are using Kashmir to advance their broader and ultimate agenda' – of turning India into a highly centralised and quasi-authoritarian state in which Hindu nationalism is the only game in town.[78]

In 2017, Amit Shah, then the BJP's national president, addressed a high-level party conference with Modi at his side. In his speech, Shah made clear the ultimate goal – that the BJP must dominate India 'from panchayat to parliament' (*panchayats* are elected local bodies in India's villages) and that 'every state' in India must have a BJP government.[79] If he fails, it will not be for lack of trying.

Yet the Hindu nationalist ascendancy in India's politics is not irreversible. A range of opposition parties continue to keep the BJP from power across a swathe of India's states, in all geographic regions of the country. If most of these disparate parties can coalesce into a coherent anti-BJP alternative, it is not implausible that the Hindu nationalist juggernaut will be stymied in 2024. In 2018, I noted that 'in fact the Hindu nationalists remain, even in the age of their ascendancy, a vocal, ideologically motivated and highly organized political minority'.[80]

The devastating second wave of Covid-19 that engulfed India from April 2021 onwards could mark the beginning of the end of the Modi era in Indian politics. The Hindu nationalists are certainly aware of the danger. As a nationwide uproar over the Modi government's incompetence and negligence in handling the pandemic gathered steam and the crisis in India dominated global headlines, Dattatreya Hosabale, the RSS's second-in-command and a close Modi ally, issued a public statement:

> In a large country like Bharat [India], problems can take gigantic proportions. It is also possible that destructive and anti-Bharat forces in society can take advantage of these adverse circumstances to create an atmosphere of negativity and mistrust in the country. The countrymen should be cautious of the conspiracies of these destructive forces. We request the media to contribute to maintaining positivity, hope and trust. Social media should also play a positive role, restrained and vigilant.[81]

The end of the Modi era would not in itself lead to a dramatic turnaround in Kashmir, in part because the BJP would remain in play as an opposition party and no doubt deploy its ultra-hardline Kashmir card against its opponents. But it would represent the proverbial glimmer of light at the end of a long and very dark tunnel. A better future in Kashmir hinges crucially, and in the first instance, on whether India's democratic and federalist structure can be saved from the Hindu nationalist onslaught. If it can, then the Hindu nationalists' attempt to erase Kashmir as a political question may turn out to have provided a clean slate for the crafting of a negotiated settlement.

The manifold adversities and uncertainties of Indian and Pakistani politics, combined with the complex geopolitical context, mean that the conjunction of favourable circumstances necessary for a Kashmir peace process is unlikely. But that does not mean the Kashmir conflict will simply lie dormant. To the contrary, it is rife with incendiary ingredients, and represents a clear and present danger to international peace and security in the early twenty-first century. If the crossroads at which the conflict presently stands does indeed lead to an escalation and major crisis, such a conflagration might pave the way to finally laying the conflict to rest through diplomacy and statecraft.

Endnotes

1. THE DISPUTE

1. In a letter to the Nawab of Bhopal, dated 9 July 1948. Quoted in Atul Mishra, *The Sovereign Lives of India and Pakistan* (New Delhi: Oxford University Press, 2021), p. 21.
2. *Speeches and Interviews of Sher-e-Kashmir Sheikh Mohammad Abdullah* (Srinagar: Jammu and Kashmir Plebiscite Front, 1968), Vol. 1, pp. 15–16 and Vol. 2, p. 13. The 'forces [which] have arisen' is a reference to India's then politically small but vocal Hindu nationalist movement.
3. On the princely states during the three decades of Indian mass mobilisation against the Raj, see Ian Copland, *The Princes of India in the Endgame of Empire, 1917–1947* (Cambridge: Cambridge University Press, 1997).
4. Jyoti Bhushan Dasgupta, *Jammu and Kashmir* (The Hague: Martinus Nijhoff, 1968), pp. 387–8.
5. C.E. Tyndale Biscoe, *Kashmir in Sunlight and Shade* (London: Seeley, Service and Co., 1922), p. 77.
6. Robert Thorp, *Cashmere Misgovernment* (Calcutta: Wyman Brothers, 1868); *Saturday Review*, 29 (19 March 1870).
7. Walter Lawrence, *The Valley of Kashmir* (London: Henry Frowde, 1895), pp. 2–3, 12, 284, 401. Nisbet's letter is quoted in Mridu Rai, *Hindu Rulers, Muslim Subjects: Islam, Rights, and the History of Kashmir* (Princeton: Princeton University Press, 2004), p. 174.
8. Tyndale Biscoe, *Kashmir in Sunlight and Shade*, pp. 79–80.
9. George N. Roerich, *Trails to Inmost Asia: Five Years of Exploration with the Roerich Central Asian Expedition* (New Haven: Yale University Press, 1931), pp. 4, 6.
10. Quoted in M.J. Akbar, *India, the Siege Within: Challenges to a Nation's Unity* (New Delhi: Roli Books, 2003), pp. 221–2.
11. Mohammad Ishaq Khan, *History of Srinagar, 1846–1947* (Srinagar: Cosmos, 1999), p. 193.
12. Quoted in Prem Nath Bazaz, *The History of the Struggle for Freedom in Kashmir* (Karachi: National Book Foundation, 1976), pp. 140–1.

13. Prem Nath Bazaz, *Inside Kashmir* (Mirpur: Verinag Publishers, 1987), pp. 252–3. The book was originally published from Srinagar in 1941.
14. Balraj Puri, '*Kashmiriyat*: The Vitality of Kashmiri Identity', *Contemporary South Asia*, 4, 1 (1995), pp. 56, 60–1. For a detailed treatment, see Mohammad Ishaq Khan, *Kashmir's Transition to Islam: The Role of Muslim Rishis* (Delhi: Manohar, 1994).
15. M.A. Stein, *Kalhana's Rajatarangini: A Chronicle of the Kings of Kashmir* (Mirpur: Verinag Publishers, 1991).
16. For a compilation, see T.N. Raina (ed. and trans.), *The Best of Mahjoor: Selections from Mahjoor's Kashmiri Poems* (Srinagar: Jammu & Kashmir Academy of Art, Culture and Languages, 1989).
17. Alastair Lamb, *Crisis in Kashmir, 1947 to 1966* (London: Routledge and Kegan Paul, 1966), p. 28.
18. Rai, *Hindu Rulers, Muslim Subjects*, p. 273.
19. Lamb, *Crisis in Kashmir*, p. 31.
20. Sumantra Bose, *Kashmir: Roots of Conflict, Paths to Peace* (Cambridge, MA and London: Harvard University Press, 2003), p. 22.
21. Dasgupta, *Jammu and Kashmir*, p. 70.
22. Quoted in Akbar, *India, the Siege Within*, p. 250.
23. Khan, *History of Srinagar*, p. 198.
24. Bose, *Kashmir*, p. 32.
25. Dasgupta, *Jammu and Kashmir*, pp. 95, 107.
26. Bose, *Kashmir*, pp. 34–8.
27. Dasgupta, *Jammu and Kashmir*, p. 113.
28. Dasgupta, *Jammu and Kashmir*, p. 109.
29. For the full text of the UNSC resolution of 21 April 1948 see Dasgupta, *Jammu and Kashmir*, pp. 395–8.
30. Sumantra Bose, *The Challenge in Kashmir: Democracy, Self-Determination and a Just Peace* (New Delhi, Thousand Oaks and London: Sage Publications, 1997), p. 17.
31. Prem Nath Bazaz, *Kashmir in Crucible* (New Delhi: Pamposh, 1967), pp. 136–7.
32. Saifuddin Soz, *Why Autonomy for Kashmir?* (New Delhi: Indian Centre for Asian Studies, 1995), pp. 121–39.
33. Dasgupta, *Jammu and Kashmir*, pp. 406–7.
34. Josef Korbel, *Danger in Kashmir* (Princeton: Princeton University Press, 1954). Korbel, a Czech diplomat of Jewish descent, is the father of Madeleine Albright, US secretary of state in the second Clinton administration.
35. Balraj Puri, *Kashmir: Towards Insurgency* (Delhi: Orient Longman, 1993), pp. 45–9.
36. Dasgupta, *Jammu and Kashmir*, pp. 188–9.
37. Rai, *Hindu Rulers, Muslim Subjects*, pp. 283–4.
38. Daniel Thorner, *The Agrarian Prospect in India* (Bombay: Allied Publishers, 1976), p. 50.
39. Wolf Ladjensky, 'Land Reform: Observations in Kashmir', in L.J. Walinsky (ed.), *Agrarian Reforms as Unfinished Business* (Oxford: Oxford University Press, 1977), pp. 179–80.
40. Soz, *Why Autonomy for Kashmir*, p. 128.
41. On the RSS, see Walter Andersen and Shridhar Damle, *The Brotherhood in Saffron: The Rashtriya Swayamsevak Sangh and Hindu Revivalism* (New Delhi: Penguin Books, 2019).
42. Dasgupta, *Jammu and Kashmir*, p. 195.
43. Dasgupta, *Jammu and Kashmir*, p. 196.
44. A.G. Noorani, *The Kashmir Question* (Bombay: Manaktalas, 1964), p. 61.
45. Noorani, *The Kashmir Question*, p. 101.
46. Dasgupta, *Jammu and Kashmir*, p. 194.
47. Bose, *Kashmir*, p. 66.
48. Syed Mir Qasim, *My Life and Times* (Delhi: Allied Publishers, 1992), pp. 68–70. Anantnag is the ancient as well as the official name of the town, the largest in the southern part of the Valley, but Kashmiris call it Islamabad.

49. *Speeches and Interviews of Sher-e-Kashmir Sheikh Mohammad Abdullah*, Vol. 2, p. 13.
50. Korbel, *Danger in Kashmir*, p. 149.
51. Krishna Bose, *Lost Addresses: A Memoir of India, 1934–1955* (New Delhi: Niyogi Books, 2015, translated from Bengali by Sumantra Bose), p. 165. Krishna Bose (1930–2020) is my mother.
52. Qasim, *My Life and Times*, p. 106.
53. Dasgupta, *Jammu and Kashmir*, p. 323; Sumantra Bose, *Transforming India: Challenges to the World's Largest Democracy* (Cambridge, MA and London: Harvard University Press, 2013), p. 255.
54. Korbel, *Danger in Kashmir*, p. 246; Dasgupta, *Jammu and Kashmir*, pp. 212–13.
55. R.K. Jain (ed.), *Soviet–South Asian Relations: Volume 1, 1947–1978* (Atlantic Highlands, NJ: Humanities Press, 1979), pp. 15–20.
56. Dasgupta, *Jammu and Kashmir*, pp. 222–4.
57. Puri, *Kashmir: Towards Insurgency*, pp. 45–9.
58. Noorani, *The Kashmir Question*, p. 73.
59. Dasgupta, *Jammu and Kashmir*, p. 226.
60. Dasgupta, *Jammu and Kashmir*, p. 408.
61. Akbar, *India, the Siege Within*, p. 258.
62. Dasgupta, *Jammu and Kashmir*, pp. 308–9.
63. Bazaz, *Kashmir in Crucible*, p. 100.
64. Dasgupta, *Jammu and Kashmir*, p. 323.
65. Reeta C. Tremblay, 'Jammu: Autonomy within an autonomous Kashmir?', in Raju G.C. Thomas (ed.), *Perspectives on Kashmir* (Boulder: Westview Press, 1992), p. 164.
66. Puri, *Kashmir: Towards Insurgency*, pp. 31–2.
67. Dasgupta, *Jammu and Kashmir*, p. 333.
68. Neville Maxwell, *India's China War* (London: Jonathan Cape, 1970); John Garver, *Protracted Contest: Sino-Indian Rivalry in the Twentieth Century* (Seattle: University of Washington Press, 2001), Chapters 3 and 7.
69. Bazaz, *Kashmir in Crucible*, pp. 100–4.
70. This battle-group was commanded by Malik Munawar Khan Awan, a Pakistani army major who had fought on the India–Burma frontier during World War II as a soldier of the Indian National Army (INA), an anti-colonial army raised with Japanese support from Indian prisoners-of-war in South-East Asia to fight for India's liberation from British rule. The INA was led from 1943 to 1945 by the legendary Indian nationalist Subhas Chandra Bose.
71. Bazaz, *Kashmir in Crucible*, pp. 99–100.
72. Akbar, *India, the Siege Within*, p. 267.
73. Shaheen Akhtar, 'Elections in Indian-Held Kashmir, 1951–1999', *Regional Studies*, 18, 3 (2000), p. 37.
74. Alastair Lamb, *Kashmir: A Disputed Legacy, 1946–1990* (Karachi: Oxford University Press, 1992), pp. 209–10.
75. Puri, *Kashmir: Towards Insurgency*, p. 49.
76. Qasim, *My Life and Times*, p. 132.
77. Akhtar, 'Elections in Indian-Held Kashmir', p. 87.
78. Akhtar, 'Elections in Indian-Held Kashmir', pp. 38–9.
79. For the full text of the Delhi accord, see Qasim, *My Life and Times*, pp. 138–40.
80. P.R. Chari and Pervaiz Iqbal Cheema, *The Simla Agreement, 1972: Its Wasted Promise* (Delhi: Manohar, 2001), pp. 204–6.
81. 'Jammu and Kashmir Public Safety Act (PSA), 1978', http://jkhome.nic.in/psa001.pdf (accessed 21 October 2020).
82. 'Firing to quell mob violence in Srinagar', *Indian Express*, 28 July 1980; 'Pakistani among six dead in Srinagar', *Indian Express*, 29 July 1980; 'Four killed as police fire on Srinagar mobs', *Indian Express*, 18 August 1980.

83. Abhishek Mukherjee, 'India face hostility from Srinagar crowd and West Indies', *Cricket Country*, 12 October 2016, https://www.cricketcountry.com/articles/india-face-hostility-from-srinagar-crowd-and-west-indies-277580 (accessed 21 October 2020).
84. Farooq Abdullah, *My Dismissal* (New Delhi: Vikas, 1985), pp. 1–2.
85. Indira Gandhi's younger son Sanjay, the key figure of the 1975–76 Emergency regime, had been her chosen political heir. He was killed in June 1980 when a small plane he was flying for recreation crashed in Delhi, leaving the previously apolitical Rajiv to pick up the dynastic mantle.
86. Inderjit Badhwar, 'Testing the accord', *India Today*, 31 March 1987, p. 26.
87. Khemlata Wakhloo, *Kashmir: Behind the White Curtain, 1972–1991* (Delhi: Konark Publishers, 1992), p. 321.
88. Inderjit Badhwar, 'A tarnished triumph', *India Today*, 15 April 1987, pp. 40–3.
89. 'Kashmir: Valley of Tears', *India Today*, 31 May 1989.
90. *Illustrated Weekly of India*, 10–16 October 1992, p. 4.
91. Puri, *Kashmir: Towards Insurgency*, pp. 56–7; 'Kashmir: Valley of Tears', *India Today*, 31 May 1989.
92. 'Senior NC member killed', *Free Press Kashmir*, 21 August 1989.

2. THE CARNAGE

1. George Orwell, *Notes on Nationalism* (London: Penguin Books, 2018), pp. 1–31. The essay was first published in *Polemic*, No. 1 (October 1945).
2. '16,000 terrorists killed over thirteen years', *Kashmir Times*, 5 December 2002, p. 1.
3. Association of Parents of Disappeared Persons (APDP), https://apdpkashmir.com/ (accessed 27 October 2020). The APDP is led by Parveena Ahangar. Her son Javaid Ahmed Ahangar, 17, was taken away from their home in Srinagar's Batamaloo neighbourhood by an elite Indian Army unit during a night raid in August 1990. He was last seen at one of 1990s Srinagar's notorious torture centres, a mansion built in the late 1920s for the princely state's ruling family.
4. Amanullah Khan, *Free Kashmir* (Karachi: Central Printing Press, 1970), pp. 139–49.
5. A.S. Dulat, Asad Durrani and Aditya Sinha, *The Spy Chronicles: RAW, ISI and the Illusion of Peace* (New Delhi: HarperCollins India, 2018), p. 97. RAW is the acronym of the Research and Analysis Wing, India's equivalent of the American Central Intelligence Agency (CIA).
6. https://www.youtube.com/watch?v=jKw2gi4WHEM (accessed 21 October 2020).
7. Tapan Bose et al., 'India's Kashmir War', in Asghar Ali Engineer (ed.), *Secular Crown on Fire: The Kashmir Problem* (Delhi: Ajanta Publications, 1991), pp. 229–30.
8. Lawrence, *The Valley of Kashmir*, p. 203.
9. Hameeda Bano, quoted in Victoria Schofield, *Kashmir in Conflict* (London: I.B. Tauris, 1996), p. 231.
10. *India Today*, 30 April 1990, p. 13.
11. Ayesha Kagal, 'Accidental terrorists', *Times of India*, 29 April 1990, p. 1.
12. 'The Armed Forces (Special Powers) Act, 1958', http://legislative.gov.in/sites/default/files/A1958-28.pdf (accessed 31 October 2020).
13. International and Indian human rights organisations alike documented the situation during the first half of the 1990s in Indian J&K. Amnesty International's report *India: Torture and Deaths in Custody in Jammu and Kashmir* (London: Amnesty International, 1995) details 715 cases of deaths under torture and summary executions between 1990 and 1994. See also Asia Watch, *Kashmir under Siege* (New York: Human Rights Watch, 1991); Asia Watch-Physicians for Human Rights, *Rape in Kashmir: A Crime of War* (New York: Human Rights Watch, 1993); Asia Watch-Physicians for Human Rights, *The Human Rights Crisis in Kashmir: A Pattern of Impunity* (New York: Human Rights Watch, 1993); Fédération Internationale des Ligues des Droits de l'Homme, *Kashmir: A*

People Terrorized (Paris: FIDH, 1993); Saqina Hasan, Primila Lewis, Nandita Haksar and Suhasini Mulay, *Kashmir Imprisoned* (Delhi: Committee for Initiative on Kashmir, 1990), which reports on conditions for women in the Kashmir Valley; Committee for Initiative on Kashmir, *Kashmir: A Land Ruled by the Gun* (Delhi: CIK, 1991); Tapan Bose et al., 'India's Kashmir War', pp. 224–70; People's Union for Civil Liberties, 'Report on Kashmir Situation', in Engineer (ed.), *Secular Crown on Fire*, pp. 210–23.

14. Edward Desmond, 'The Insurgency in Kashmir, 1989–91', *Contemporary South Asia*, 4, 1 (1995), p. 13.

15. A.G. Noorani, 'The Tortured and the Damned: Human Rights in Kashmir', *Frontline*, 28 January 1994, pp. 44–8. A 1993 report by the Institute of Kashmir Studies, Srinagar, details 118 cases of summary executions.

16. Essar Batool, Ifrah Butt, Samreena Mushtaq, Munaza Rashid and Natasha Rather, *Do You Remember Kunan Poshpora?* (New Delhi: Zubaan Books, 2016).

17. B.G. Verghese et al., *Crisis and Credibility: Report of the Press Council of India* (New Delhi: Lancer International, 1991).

18. Goldie Osuri and Iffat Fatima, 'A Provisional Biography of a Journey Towards Justice for the Enforced Disappeared', *APDP*, 27 January 2020, https://apdpkashmir.com/a-provisional-biography-of-the-association-of-parents-of-disappeared-persons-kashmir/ (accessed 31 October 2020).

19. 'NIA raids activists and journalists in J&K, triggers outrage', *Indian Express*, 29 October 2020, p. 1.

20. 'Fact Sheet on Jammu & Kashmir', 20 May 2002, https://mea.gov.in/in-focus-article.htm?18987/Fact+Sheet+on+Jammu+amp+Kashmir (accessed 3 November 2020).

21. *Illustrated Weekly of India*, 10–16 October 1992, p. 6.

22. Ghulam Nabi Khayal, 'Kashmiri militants kill 6 troops in rocket attack', *UPI*, 19 June 1990, https://www.upi.com/Archives/1990/06/19/Kashmiri-militants-kill-6-troops-in-rocket-attack/2738645768000/ (accessed 3 November 2020).

23. Afzal Khan Tahir, 'Human Rights Violations in Pakistan-Occupied Kashmir: A Memorandum of the Jammu and Kashmir People's National Party', 15 September 1993, p. 2.

24. Anam Zakaria, *Between the Great Divide: A Journey into Pakistan-Administered Kashmir* (New Delhi: HarperCollins India, 2018), p. 223.

25. *In Search of Freedom*, Vol. 5 (Muzaffarabad: Press and Publications Department, Prime Minister's Secretariat, 1992), pp. 175–200.

26. For example, *Kashmir: Paths to Peace* (London: Chatham House, 2010).

27. Madiha Afzal, *Pakistan under Siege: Extremism, Society, and the State* (Washington, DC: Brookings Institution Press, 2018), p. 36.

28. Yoginder Sikand, 'The Emergence and Development of the Jama'at-i-Islami of Jammu and Kashmir, 1940s–1990', *Modern Asian Studies*, 36, 3 (2002), pp. 746–8.

29. Yoginder Sikand, 'Jihad, Islam and Kashmir: Syed Ali Shah Geelani's political project', *Economic and Political Weekly*, 45, 40 (2 October 2010), p. 127.

30. *India Today*, 29 February 1992, p. 15 and 15 March 1992, pp. 30–2.

31. *India Today*, 31 May 1993, p. 27.

32. Ved Bhasin (1929–2015), founding editor of the *Kashmir Times* newspaper published from Jammu and Srinagar.

33. John Rettie and Ghulam Nabi Khayal, 'Kashmiris round on pro-Pakistan groups', *The Guardian*, 22 June 1994, p. 11.

34. Tapan Bose et al., 'India's Kashmir War', p. 261.

35. M. Saleem Pandit, '112-year-old Kashmiri Pandit's funeral bridges Valley divide', *Times of India*, 24 July 2020, https://timesofindia.indiatimes.com/city/srinagar/112-yr-old-kashmiri-pandits-funeral-bridges-valley-divide/articleshow/77135419.cms (accessed 5 November 2020).

36. Khemlata Wakhloo and O.N. Wakhloo, *Kidnapped: 45 Days with Militants in Kashmir* (Delhi: Konark Publishers, 1993), p. 396.

37. Amitabh Mattoo, *Illustrated Weekly of India*, 10–16 October 1992, p. 10.
38. Rashtriya Swayamsevak Sangh, *Genocide of Hindus in Kashmir* (Delhi: Suruchi Prakashan, 1991).
39. *India Today*, 28 February 1992, pp. 22–5.
40. Kaveree Bamzai, Harinder Baweja and Dilip Awasthi, 'An odyssey in futility', *India Today*, 15 February 1992, https://www.indiatoday.in/magazine/special-report/story/19920215-bjp-flag-hoisting-ceremony-in-srinagar-turns-out-to-be-a-damp-squib-militancy-gets-a-boost-765818-2013-06-24 (accessed 7 November 2020).
41. Rettie and Khayal, 'Kashmiris round on pro-Pakistan groups'.
42. Desmond, 'The Insurgency in Kashmir', pp. 11–12.
43. Human Rights Watch, *India's Secret Army in Kashmir* (New York: Human Rights Watch, 1996).
44. Sankarshan Thakur, 'Only guns, no roses in bloom yet', *The Telegraph*, 15 September 1996, p. 1.
45. Amnesty International, 'INDIA: Jammu and Kashmir: Remembering Jalil Andrabi', March 1997, https://www.amnesty.org/download/Documents/160000/asa200101997en.pdf (accessed 9 November 2020).
46. 'Written Answers', 11 September 1996, https://eparlib.nic.in/bitstream/123456789/33271/1/11_II_11091996_p29_p30_T23.pdf (accessed 9 November 2020).
47. Sydney Lupkin, 'California man wanted for 1996 murder kills family, self', *ABC News*, 10 June 2012, https://abcnews.go.com/US/california-man-wanted-murder-india-kills-wife-children/story?id=16533835#.T9QICbDrrVU (accessed 9 November 2020).
48. Andrew Small, *The China–Pakistan Axis: Asia's New Geopolitics* (London: Hurst and Co., 2015), pp. 31–2.
49. Small, *The China–Pakistan Axis*, pp. 27–46.
50. A.B. Vajpayee, 'Nuclear anxiety; Indian's letter to Clinton on the Nuclear Testing', *New York Times*, 13 May 1998, https://www.nytimes.com/1998/05/13/world/nuclear-anxiety-indian-s-letter-to-clinton-on-the-nuclear-testing.html (accessed 10 November 2020).
51. Bose, *Kashmir*, p. 140.
52. Ironically, 21 February is commemorated in Bangladesh – the former East Pakistan – as 'Language Day'. On 21 February 1952, large student-led protests erupted in Dhaka (then Dacca) against the Pakistani government's imposition of Urdu as the national language of Pakistan, a policy strongly advocated by Jinnah shortly after Pakistan's formation. The protesters in the overwhelmingly Bengali-speaking eastern wing of Pakistan saw this as an assault on their heritage and culture. Police fired and killed five university students. In retrospect, the events of 21 February 1952 in Dhaka are seen as the beginning of the end of Pakistan, which failed to complete twenty-five years as a united country.
53. Afzal, *Pakistan Under Siege*, p. 38.
54. Nasim Zehra, *From Kargil to the Coup: Events that Shook Pakistan* (Lahore: Sang-e-Meel Publications, 2018), p. 92.
55. *From Surprise to Reckoning: The Kargil Review Committee Report* (New Delhi: Sage Publications, 2000).
56. Zehra, *From Kargil to the Coup*, p. 336.
57. 'Musharraf: Pakistan cannot accept LoC as the border', *Indian Express*, 18 January 2002, p. 1.
58. Zehra, *From Kargil to the Coup*, pp. 313–14.
59. The Kargil War is discussed in depth in Peter R. Lavoy (ed.), *Asymmetric Warfare in South Asia: The Causes and Consequences of the Kargil Conflict* (Cambridge: Cambridge University Press, 2009).
60. *Kashmir Times*, 1 December 2002, p. 1.
61. 'Mumbai: A Pakistan militant link?', *BBC News*, 28 November 2008, http://news.bbc.co.uk/2/hi/south_asia/7753863.stm (accessed 14 November 2020).

62. *Kashmir Times*, 23 August 2000, p. 1.
63. The groundwork for Clinton's March 2000 visit to India had been laid by a continuous dialogue since June 1998 between Strobe Talbott, the US deputy secretary of state, and Jaswant Singh, who became the external affairs (foreign) minister in Vajpayee's cabinet in December 1998. See Strobe Talbott, *Engaging India: Diplomacy, Democracy, and the Bomb* (Washington, DC: Brookings Institution Press, 2004). Aside from growing bonhomie with the Indian government, the Americans were frustrated with the Pakistanis' failure to help them apprehend Osama bin Laden through their Taliban client regime in Afghanistan.
64. Krishna Bose, 'Vajpayee, as I knew him', *The Wire*, 25 December 2018, https://thewire.in/politics/tmc-atal-bihari-vajpayee-nda-krishna-bose (accessed 14 November 2020).
65. *Daily Excelsior* (Jammu), 19 September 2000, p. 1. For a detailed account of the fighting in Rajouri-Poonch from 2000 to 2002, see Bose, *Kashmir*, pp. 147–58.
66. '572 ultras killed so far in Rajouri-Poonch this year', *Hindustan Times*, 31 October 2001, p. 1.
67. 'Fact Sheet on Jammu & Kashmir', 20 May 2002, https://mea.gov.in/in-focus-article.htm?18987/Fact+Sheet+on+Jammu+amp+Kashmir (accessed 15 November 2020).
68. 'Twelve ultras killed in Rajouri-Poonch encounters', *Kashmir Times*, 29 April 2002, p. 1.
69. *Greater Kashmir* (Srinagar), 28 April 2002, p. 1.
70. 'Major, JCO among 11 soldiers killed in Surankote encounter', *Kashmir Times*, 28 November 2001, p. 1; 'Seven ultras, major among 10 killed in Surankote encounters', *Kashmir Times*, 14 July 2002, p. 1; 'Terrorists spray bullets at J&K bus stand, kill 12', *Hindustan Times*, 11 September 2002, p. 1; 'Three more BSF men dead, Surankote toll 16', *Kashmir Times*, 13 September 2002, p. 1.
71. Bose, *Kashmir*, pp. 143–4.
72. Shri Atal Bihari Vajpayee, 'Statement by Prime Minister Shri Atal Bihari Vajpayee in Lok Sabha on his two day visit to Jammu & Kashmir', 22 April 2003, https://mea.gov.in/Speeches-Statements.htm?dtl/4351/Statement+by+Prime+Minister+Shri+Atal+Bihari+Vajpayee+in+Lok+Sabha+on+his+two+day+visit+to+Jammu+amp+Kashmir (accessed 19 November 2020).
73. 'Musharraf: Pakistan cannot accept LoC as border', *Indian Express*, 18 January 2002, p. 1. Musharraf reiterated this four-point approach in a BBC interview in September 2002.
74. Sumantra Bose, *Contested Lands: Israel–Palestine, Kashmir, Bosnia, Cyprus, and Sri Lanka* (Cambridge, MA and London: Harvard University Press, 2007), pp. 199–200.

3. THE STONE PELTERS

1. Giorgio Agamben, *State of Exception* (Chicago and London: University of Chicago Press, 2005), pp. 1–4. Translated from the Italian by Kevin Attell.
2. 'Spirit willing, the dream lives on', *Indian Express*, 16 March 2005, p. 1.
3. Muzamil Jaleel, 'At the LoC, two armies try to bridge an old divide', *Indian Express*, 9 March 2005, p. 1.
4. 'Text of Musharraf–Singh joint statement', *Indian Express*, 18 April 2005, p. 1.
5. 'US says impressed by India–Pakistan peace moves', *Indian Express*, 17 April 2005, p. 1.
6. 'India races to fix Kashmir fence damage, stop militants', *Indian Express*, 10 April 2005, p. 1.
7. 'Race against time, nature to shut out militants', *Indian Express*, 1 August 2005, p. 1.
8. 'J&K CM inaugurates rebuilt Aman Setu', *Hindustan Times*, 21 February 2006, p. 1.
9. Chari and Cheema, *The Simla Agreement, 1972*, pp. 204–6.
10. 'Musharraf: Pakistan cannot accept LoC as border', *Indian Express*, 18 January 2002, p. 1; 'Musharraf rules out conversion of LoC into border', *Hindustan Times*, 12 September 2002, p. 1.
11. *Kashmir: Paths to Peace* (London: Chatham House, 2010).

13. Bose, *Contested Lands*, p. 197.
14. Strobe Talbott, 'Self-Determination in an Interdependent World', *Foreign Policy*, 118 (Spring 2000), pp. 152–63.
15. Sumantra Bose, 'Not even the earthquake has shaken loose old prejudices in Kashmir', *History News Network*, November 2005, https://historynewsnetwork.org/article/18591 (accessed 21 November 2020).
16. Sumantra Bose, 'Kashmir: Sources of Conflict, Dimensions of Peace', *Survival: The IISS Quarterly*, 41, 3 (1999), pp. 149–71; Sumantra Bose, 'Kashmir: Sources of Conflict, Dimensions of Peace', *Economic and Political Weekly*, 34, 13 (1999), pp. 762–8.
17. Bose, *Kashmir*, p. 207.
18. Bose, *Contested Lands*, p. 194.
19. Bose, *Kashmir*, p. 264.
20. Bose, *Kashmir*, p. 245; Bose, *Contested Lands*, p. 194.
21. Bose, 'Not even the earthquake has shaken loose old prejudices in Kashmir'.
22. Bose, *Contested Lands*, pp. 202–3.
23. Steve Coll, 'The Back Channel', *New Yorker*, 2 March 2009.
24. Coll, 'The Back Channel'.
25. Small, *The China–Pakistan Axis*, p. xiv.
26. 'An interview with the hero of 1990s', *Kashmir Patriot*, 30 March 2017, https://kashmirpatriot.com/2017/03/30/an-interview-with-the-hero-of-the-1990s/ (accessed 23 November 2020).
27. *Kashmir Times*, 28 October 2002, p. 1.
28. Press Trust of India, 'Set up independent commission to probe forced disappearances', *Business Standard News*, 26 March 2015, https://www.business-standard.com/article/pti-stories/set-up-independent-commission-to-probe-forced-disappearances-115032600845_1.html (accessed 23 November 2020).
29. Shahnawaz Khan, 'Kashmir rights groups demands probe of unidentified graves', *Voice of America*, 1 November 2009, https://www.voanews.com/archive/kashmir-rights-groups-demands-probe-unidentified-graves (accessed 23 November 2020).
30. Ishfaq Naseem, 'Centre halts probe in over 10,500 allegations of human rights violations against security forces in Kashmir', *Firstpost*, 16 August 2020, https://www.firstpost.com/india/centre-halts-probe-in-over-10500-allegations-of-human-rights-violations-against-security-forces-in-kashmir-8717041.html (accessed 23 November 2020).
31. Mark Mazzetti and Eric Schmitt, 'Pakistanis aided Kabul attack, U.S. officials say', *New York Times*, 1 August 2008, p. 1.
32. Sumantra Bose, 'Kashmir - missed chances for peace', *BBC News*, 22 August 2008, http://news.bbc.co.uk/1/hi/world/south_asia/7576393.stm (accessed 26 November 2020).
33. 'Civil curfew in Kashmir to protest Manmohan Singh's visit', *Economic Times*, 11 October 2008, https://economictimes.indiatimes.com/news/politics-and-nation/civil-curfew-in-kashmir-to-protest-manmohan-singhs-visit/articleshow/3584136.cms (accessed 26 November 2020).
34. Sumantra Bose, 'Mumbai attacks show method amid madness', *BBC News*, 28 November 2008, http://news.bbc.co.uk/2/hi/south_asia/7753876.stm (accessed 27 November 2020).
35. Shujaat Bukhari, 'CBI rules out rape, murder in Shopian case', *The Hindu*, https://www.thehindu.com/news/national/CBI-rules-out-rape-murder-in-Shopian-case/article16853371.ece (accessed 27 November 2020).
36. 'Three militants killed as army foils infiltration bid', *Outlook India*, 30 April 2010, https://web.archive.org/web/20110715024500/http:/news.outlookindia.com/item.aspx?680686 (accessed 28 November 2020).
37. Ipsita Chakravarty, 'Machil fake encounter: Case against two civilians is running parallel to the army trials', *Scroll.in*, 31 October 2017, https://scroll.in/article/856012/the-other-machil-case-running-parallel-to-the-army-trials-is-a-quiet-struggle-for-justice (accessed 29 November 2020).

38. Aijaz Hussain, 'J&K: More of the same', *India Today*, 12 June 2010, https://www.india-today.in/magazine/states/story/20100621-j-k-more-of-the-same-743200-2010-06-12 (accessed 29 November 2020).

39. Samaan Lateef, 'Family, friends, teachers recall Tufail', *Greater Kashmir*, 14 June 2010, p. 1; Lydia Polgreen, 'A youth's death in Kashmir renews a familiar pattern of crisis', *New York Times*, 11 July 2010, p. A1.

40. Sumantra Bose, 'The evolution of Kashmiri resistance', *Al Jazeera*, 2 August 2011, https://www.aljazeera.com/news/2011/8/2/the-evolution-of-kashmiri-resistance (accessed 30 November 2020).

41. Sumantra Bose, 'Kashmir's summer of discontent is now an autumn of woe', *BBC News*, 21 September 2010, https://www.bbc.co.uk/news/world-south-asia-11333788 (accessed 30 November 2020).

42. 'No decision taken on interlocutors' report on Jammu and Kashmir: Government', *Economic Times*, 22 July 2014, https://economictimes.indiatimes.com/news/politics-and-nation/no-decision-taken-on-interlocutors-report-on-jammu-and-kashmir-government/articleshow/38875849.cms?from=mdr (accessed 30 November 2020).

43. Zahid Rafiq, 'Macchil fake encounter: life term for 5 Army men', *The Hindu*, 11 November 2016, https://www.thehindu.com/news/national/other-states/Macchil-fake-encounter-life-term-for-5-Army-men/article11008202.ece?homepage=true; Ajit Kumar Dubey, 'Machhil fake encounter case: Military court suspends life sentence to five Army personnel', *India Today*, 26 July 2017, https://www.indiatoday.in/mail-today/story/machhil-fake-encounter-case-armed-forces-tribunal-kashmir-1026287-2017-07-26 (accessed 30 November 2020).

44. 'Villager confirms three Rajouri youths rented room, just 100 metres from Army camp', *Indian Express*, 12 August 2020, p. 8; 'Three killed in J&K encounter were labourers, will take action: Army', *Indian Express*, 19 September 2020, p. 1; 'Shopian: Probe looks at role of SPO posted in Srinagar, Army says it will act as per law', *Indian Express*, 4 October 2020, p. 3.

45. 'Amshipora killings: Found culpable, Major to face action', *Indian Express*, 25 December 2020, p. 1.

46. 'PM says can't be business as usual with Pakistan after 'barbaric act'', *Indian Express*, 15 January 2013, http://archive.indianexpress.com/news/pm-says-can-t-be-business-as-usual-with-pakistan-after--barbaric-act-/1059722/0 (accessed 30 November 2020).

47. Fayaz Bukhari, 'Indian PM in rare visit to Kashmir after attack on soldiers', *Reuters*, 25 June 2013, https://www.reuters.com/article/us-india-kashmir-idUSBRE95O09J20130625; Parvaiz Bukhari, 'PM on rare J&K trip after deadly attack', *Mint*, 26 June 2013, https://www.livemint.com/Politics/ZVbBaZWHatR2jH9d8K1QyN/PMon-rare-JK-trip-after-deadly-attack.html (accessed 30 November 2020).

48. Sumantra Bose, 'A historic opportunity in Jammu & Kashmir', *Mint*, 24 December 2014, https://www.livemint.com/Politics/Lc0m6QsOcOn0WCtbIwoPAL/A-historic-opportunity-in-Jammu-and-Kashmir.html (accessed 1 December 2020).

49. For example, Sumantra Bose, 'Bringing J into K', *Open*, 8 January 2015, https://openthemagazine.com/essays/open-essay/bringing-j-into-k/ (accessed 1 December 2020); Sumantra Bose, 'The power of two', *Open*, 19 February 2015, https://openthemagazine.com/essays/open-essay/the-power-of-two/ (accessed 1 December 2020).

50. Bose, 'Bringing J into K'.

51. Sumantra Bose, 'Kashmir: Can new government provide healing touch?', *BBC News*, 3 March 2015, https://www.bbc.co.uk/news/world-asia-india-31689969 (accessed 1 December 2020).

52. Sumantra Bose, 'Why the Kashmir government's fall is a tragedy', *BBC News*, 21 June 2018, https://www.bbc.co.uk/news/world-asia-india-44558098 (accessed 1 December 2020).

53. 'PM Modi: Like all Indians, I am also pained', *Indian Express*, 13 August 2016, p. 9; 'Progress through tourism: PM to Kashmir youth', *Indian Express*, 3 April 2017, p. 1.

54. 'Shah's target: Panchayat to parliament, and every state', *Indian Express*, 16 April 2017, p. 1.

55. Bose, 'Why the Kashmir government's fall is a tragedy'.

56. 'J&K | Governor's decision to dissolve Assembly "based on material available to him from multiple sources"', *The Hindu*, 21 November 2018, https://www.thehindu.com/news/national/other-states/pdp-peoples-conference-stake-claim-to-form-govt-governor-dissolves-assembly/article25556528.ece (accessed 1 December 2020).

57. '16-year-old slain J&K militant was the son of a police constable', *The Quint*, 1 January 2018, https://www.thequint.com/news/india/16-year-old-jandk-militant-fardeen-ahmad-khanday-was-son-of-a-police-constable#read-more (accessed 1 December 2020).

58. Reuters, 'Pulwama bomber Adil Ahmad Dar became terrorist after he was beaten by troops, say parents', *India Today*, 15 February 2019, https://www.indiatoday.in/india/story/pulwama-bomber-adil-ahmad-dar-became-terrorist-after-he-was-beaten-by-troops-say-parents-1457317-2019-02-15 (accessed 1 December 2020).

59. PTI, 'India Pakistan: Pakistan considering appointing NSA to resume backchannel diplomacy: Official sources', *Economic Times*, 19 May 2019, https://economictimes.indiatimes.com/news/defence/pakistan-considering-appointing-nsa-to-resume-back-channel-diplomacy-official-sources/articleshow/69402829.cms (accessed 6 December 2020).

4. THE HINDU NATIONALIST OFFENSIVE

1. Minxin Pei, 'China's Coming Upheaval', *Foreign Affairs*, May–June 2020, https://www.foreignaffairs.com/articles/united-states/2020-04-03/chinas-coming-upheaval (accessed 26 December 2020).

2. A chilling investigative account of Modi's government in Gujarat (2001–2014) can be found in Ashish Khetan, *Undercover: My Journey into the Darkness of Hindutva* (Chennai: Westland Publications, 2021).

3. On the rise of Hindu nationalism from the margins to the centre stage of India's politics, see Sumantra Bose, *Secular States, Religious Politics: India, Turkey, and the Future of Secularism* (Cambridge and New York: Cambridge University Press, 2018), Chapters 1 and 4; on the framework and content of Hindu nationalism as a political doctrine, see Chapter 6.

4. The word *rashtra* can, depending on the context of its usage, mean either 'nation' or 'state' or an amalgam: i.e., 'nation-state'.

5. Tanushree Ghosh, 'Poet of the Fall: The humane verses of Kashmir's Madhosh Balhami', *Indian Express*, 29 March 2020, https://indianexpress.com/article/express-sunday-eye/poet-of-the-fall-kashmir-madhosh-balhami-6334080/ (accessed 31 December 2020).

6. Sumantra Bose, 'Has India pushed Kashmir to a point of no return?', *BBC News*, 13 August 2019, https://www.bbc.co.uk/news/world-asia-india-49316350 (accessed 31 December 2020).

7. Sunil Ambekar, *The RSS: Roadmaps for the 21st Century* (New Delhi: Rupa, 2019).

8. 'The Sangh plan to redefine India', *Indian Express*, 29 April 2021, p. 3.

9. Rashtriya Swayamsevak Sangh, 'Vision and Mission', 22 October 2012, https://www.rss.org/Encyc/2012/10/22/rss-vision-and-mission.html (accessed 31 December 2020).

10. M.S. Golwalkar, *Bunch of Thoughts* (Bangalore: Vikram Prakashan, 1968), pp. 437–8.

11. 'How Indians identify', *Indian Express*, 30 March 2021, p. 9.

12. 'Divide J&K into four parts, create separate enclave for Pandits: VHP', *Hindustan Times*, 23 June 2002, p. 1.

13. 'Split J&K into three parts: RSS', *Indian Express*, 1 July 2002, p. 1.

14. Bose, 'Has India pushed Kashmir to a point of no return?'.

15. 'As India takes direct control of Ladakh, locals wary of outsiders', *Al Jazeera*, 5 November 2019, https://www.aljazeera.com/features/2019/11/5/as-india-takes-direct-control-of-ladakh-locals-wary-of-outsiders (accessed 1 January 2021).

16. Bose, 'Has India pushed Kashmir to a point of no return?'.

17. 'Ladakh Buddhists who hailed India's Kashmir move not so sure now', *Al Jazeera*, 14 October 2020, https://www.aljazeera.com/news/2020/10/14/kashmirs-leh-region-demands-constitutional-safeguards (accessed 1 January 2021).

18. Joanna Slater, 'In Modi's move on Kashmir, a road map for his "new India"', *Washington Post*, 15 August 2019, https://www.washingtonpost.com/world/asia_pacific/in-modis-move-on-kashmir-a-road-map-for-his-new-india/2019/08/15/1fff923a-beab-11e9-a8b0-7ed8a0d5dc5d_story.html (accessed 1 January 2021).

19. Amit Shah, 'Undoing six decades in six years', *Times of India*, 30 May 2020, p. 10.

20. Bose, 'Has India pushed Kashmir beyond a point of no return?'.

21. Shubhangi Khapre, 'Maharashtra: Want Naya Kashmir, we need to embrace all Kashmiris, says Modi in Nashik', *Indian Express*, 20 September 2019, https://indianexpress.com/article/india/maharashtra-want-naya-kashmir-we-need-to-embrace-all-kashmiris-says-modi-in-nashik-6011751/ (accessed 1 January 2021).

22. 'In PM Modi's call to embrace Kashmiris, a jab at Pak for creating mistrust', *Hindustan Times*, 1 July 2020, https://www.hindustantimes.com/india-news/kashmiris-suffered-for-40-yrs-embrace-them-rebuild-new-kashmir-pm-modi/story-M88hcPNo2C0c3kZpNhoEAP.html (accessed 1 January 2021).

23. 'Modi promises 'paradise' in Jammu & Kashmir, says wants to hug every Kashmiri', *Hindu BusinessLine*, 26 September 2019, https://www.thehindubusinessline.com/news/national/we-have-to-hug-each-kashmiri-create-new-paradise-pm-narendra-modi/article29459285.ece (accessed 1 January 2021).

24. 'Children being radicalized in J&K, isolate them gradually: Rawat', *Indian Express*, 17 January 2020, p. 1.

25. The famous 'Mughal gardens' of Srinagar, which overlook the picturesque Dal Lake in a setting of ethereal mountains, were laid out in the seventeenth century for the royal sojourners and their retinue. Jahangir died in 1627 while returning from a sojourn in Kashmir. His intestines are buried in a mausoleum located in a village called Chingus, in the present-day Rajouri district of Indian J&K's Jammu region.

26. 'Leave Kashmir ASAP: J&K govt issues advisory for Amarnath yatra pilgrims and tourists', *India News*, 2 August 2019, https://www.indiatoday.in/india/story/leave-kashmir-j-k-administration-issues-security-advisory-for-amarnath-pilgrims-1576494-2019-08-02 (accessed 12 January 2021).

27. Ashiq Hussain, '95% of tourists cleared out of Kashmir valley, NIT students leave', *Hindustan Times*, 4 August 2019, https://www.hindustantimes.com/india-news/95-of-tourists-cleared-out-of-kashmir-valley/story-qiODi5nYSuEmy6HJw47NEK.html (accessed 12 January 2021).

28. 'Amarnath pilgrims, tourists leave Kashmir after advisory; don't panic, says Guv | Top developments', *India Today*, 4 August 2019, https://www.indiatoday.in/india/story/amarnath-pilgrims-tourists-leave-kashmir-after-advisory-don-t-panic-says-guv-top-developments-1576929-2019-08-04 (accessed 12 January 2021).

29. Hussain, '95% of tourists cleared out of Kashmir valley'.

30. Krishna Bose, '*Amrai dure thele diyecchi*' [It is we who have alienated them], *Anandabazar Patrika* (Bengali), 31 August 2019, p. 4.

31. '1,999 stone-pelting incidents in 2019, 1,193 after August 5', *Hindustan Times*, 7 January 2020, p. 3.

32. 'Centre's move in J&K, blackout challenged in SC', *Indian Express*, 11 August 2019, p. 1.

33. 'J&K witnessing longest internet shutdown in history: Kashmir-based lawyer petitions NHRC, asks it to seek reply from MHA', *Greater Kashmir*, 7 January 2020, p. 1.

34. 'Want internet?: Take a ride to Banihal', *Kashmir Times*, 6 January 2020, p. 1.

35. See for example *Indian Express*, 2 January 2020, p. 16.

36. *Indian Express*, 14 May 2020, p. 6.

37. '18 months later, 4G mobile internet back in J&K', *Indian Express*, 6 February 2021, p. 1.

38. Adil Akhzer, 'In Srinagar lockdown, how a reporter got news of his sister's miscarriage', *Indian Express*, 29 August 2019, https://indianexpress.com/article/opinion/columns/kashmir-lockdown-article-370-35a-bjp-congress-amit-shah-medicine-shortage-5942564/ (accessed 16 January 2021).
39. Naveed Iqbal, 'Investor summit on cards, Valley business leaders in detention', *Indian Express*, 3 September 2019, https://indianexpress.com/article/india/investor-summit-on-cards-valley-business-leaders-in-detention-5960473/; Majid Maqbool, '"Diabetic surviving on one kidney": 76-year-old J&K lawyer's family fear for his health in prison', *The Wire*, 24 January 2020, https://thewire.in/rights/mian-abdul-qayoom-jail-jammu-and-kashmir; Mudasir Ahmad, 'Prove you "shunned separatist ideology": J&K HC upholds senior lawyer's PSA detention', *The Wire*, 29 May 2020, https://thewire.in/law/jammu-kashmir-mian-abdul-qayoom-psa (accessed 16 January 2021).
40. 'PSA detainee from J&K dies in Uttar Pradesh jail', *Indian Express*, 23 December 2019, p. 1; 'Kashmir PSA detainee dies in Uttar Pradesh jail', *Indian Express*, 24 December 2019, p. 7.
41. Gowhar Geelani, 'Concertina in our souls', *The Telegraph*, 2 August 2020, p. 9.
42. 'In PDP leader's PSA file: Referred to Geelani's book, criticized Amit Shah', *Indian Express*, 12 February 2020, p. 1.
43. 'New media policy for UT: J&K officials to rule on "fake news", take action', *Indian Express*, 10 June 2020, p. 10.
44. 'The Ministry of Truth', *Indian Express*, 12 June 2020, p. 6.
45. Bilal Kuchay, 'Kashmir journalist charged for "anti-national" social media posts', *Al Jazeera*, 20 April 2020, https://www.aljazeera.com/news/2020/4/20/kashmir-journalist-charged-for-anti-national-social-media-posts (accessed 17 January 2021).
46. The Unlawful Activities (Prevention) Act, 1967, https://www.mha.gov.in/sites/default/files/A1967-37.pdf (accessed 17 January 2021).
47. Geelani, 'Concertina in our souls'.
48. Nistula Hebbar, 'Jammu BJP raises concerns over new J&K domicile rule with national leadership, Amit Shah', *The Hindu*, 3 April 2020, https://www.thehindu.com/news/national/other-states/jammu-bjp-raises-concerns-over-new-jk-domicile-rule-with-national-leadership-amit-shah/article31245991.ece (accessed 19 January 2021).
49. Hebbar, 'Jammu BJP raises concerns over new J&K domicile rule'.
50. Press Trust of India, 'BJP betrayed trust of J&K people: Panthers Party chief on domicile law', *NDTV*, 2 April 2020, https://www.ndtv.com/india-news/domicile-law-bjp-betrayed-trust-of-jammu-and-kashmir-people-j-k-national-panters-party-chief-harsh-d-2205160 (accessed 19 January 2021).
51. Arteev Sharma, 'Domicile policy ill-conceived: Panthers Party', *The Tribune India*, 3 April 2020, https://www.tribuneindia.com/news/j-k/domicile-policy-ill-conceived-panthers-party-64726 (accessed 19 January 2021).
52. 'Political row later, Centre climbs down on J&K order, reserves all jobs for UT domiciles', *Indian Express*, 4 April 2020, p. 1.
53. 'J&K domicile: NPP torches effigy of BJP-led government to protest new rules in Jammu', *New Indian Express*, 20 May 2020, https://www.newindianexpress.com/nation/2020/may/20/jk-domicile-npp-torches-effigy-of-bjp-led-government-to-protest-new-rules-in-jammu-2145768.html (accessed 19 January 2021).
54. 'In three months, over 18 lakh issued domicile certificates in J&K', *Indian Express*, 23 September 2020, https://indianexpress.com/article/india/jammu-and-kashmir-domicile-certificates-6607010/ (accessed 21 January 2021); PTI, 'J-K govt issues 18.52 lakh domicile certificates', *Mint*, 22 September 2020, https://www.livemint.com/news/india/j-k-govt-issues-18-52-lakh-domicile-certificates-11600750207202.html (accessed 21 January 2021).
55. 'Leh body seeks protection of indigenous rights', *Indian Express*, 4 September 2020, p. 8.
56. 'Leh delegation meets Shah', *Indian Express*, 27 September 2020, p. 10.

57. 'After meeting with Shah, Ladakh leaders call off poll boycott', *Indian Express*, 28 September 2020, p. 1.

58. Safwat Zargar, 'After BJP win in Ladakh, it's all eyes on Delhi, which promised to discuss Sixth Schedule status', *Scroll.in*, 28 October 2020, https://scroll.in/article/976935/after-bjp-win-in-ladakh-its-all-eyes-on-delhi-which-promised-to-discuss-sixth-schedule-status (accessed 21 January 2021).

59. 'Governance outsourced in J&K', *Hindustan Times*, 7 January 2020, p. 2.

60. Sunil Bhat, 'BJP to woo Gujjars, Bakerwals', *India Today*, 18 August 2019, https://www.indiatoday.in/mail-today/story/bjp-woo-gujjars-bakerwals-1581881-2019-08-18 (accessed 21 January 2021).

61. Rifat Fareed, 'Kashmiris outraged as authorities fell thousands of apple trees', *Al Jazeera*, 14 Dec 2020, https://www.aljazeera.com/features/2020/12/14/indian-authorities-axe-thousands-of-apple-trees-in-kashmir (accessed 21 January 2021); 'Kashmir forest dwellers hope long-delayed law will stop evictions', *Al Jazeera*, 15 January 2021, https://www.aljazeera.com/news/2021/1/15/kashmir-forest-dwellers-hope-long-delayed-law-will-stop-evictions (accessed 21 January 2021); Aakash Hassan, 'Why are Kashmiri Muslim nomads being evicted?', *Al Jazeera*, 20 November 2020, https://www.aljazeera.com/news/2020/11/20/tribal-community-face-eviction-from-forests-in-kashmir (accessed 21 January 2021).

62. PTI, 'Domicile certificate only for jobs, does not confer right to own land, says J&K admin', *The Print*, 1 September 2020, https://theprint.in/india/domicile-certificate-only-for-jobs-does-not-confer-right-to-own-land-says-jk-admin/493666/ (accessed 21 January 2021).

63. 'Centre notifies new laws allowing any Indian citizen to buy land in Jammu and Kashmir', *Firstpost*, 27 October 2020, https://www.firstpost.com/india/centre-notifies-new-laws-allowing-any-indian-citizen-to-buy-land-in-jammu-and-kashmir-ladakh-8956781.html (accessed 21 January 2021).

64. 'Centre throws open J&K for land sale', *Indian Express*, 28 October 2020, p. 1.

65. Peerzada Ashiq, 'Now, outsiders can buy land in Jammu and Kashmir', *The Hindu*, 27 October 2020, https://www.thehindu.com/news/national/other-states/now-outsiders-can-buy-land-in-jammu-and-kashmir/article32952629.ece (accessed 21 January 2021).

66. 'Tarigami moves SC against order on land purchase in J&K', *Indian Express*, 2 December 2020, p. 4.

67. Bose, 'Has India pushed Kashmir to a point of no return?'.

68. 'District councils: No sign of assembly polls, Centre floats new local-level government in J&K', *Indian Express*, 18 October 2020, p. 1.

69. Haseeb Drabu, 'A framework of disempowerment', *Indian Express*, 24 December 2020, p. 6.

70. Ram Madhav, 'An election, a vindication', *Indian Express*, 28 December 2020, p. 7.

71. 'DDC polls: PM invokes Vajpayee, says BJP ceded power for J&K democracy', *Indian Express*, 27 December 2020, p. 1.

72. For a snapshot of the data, see *Times of India*, 24 December 2020, p. 2.

73. Safwat Zargar, '"We want justice": Families of three young Kashmiris dispute official version of a deadly shootout', *Scroll.in*, 3 January 2021, https://scroll.in/article/982979/we-want-justice-families-of-three-young-kashmiris-dispute-official-version-of-a-deadly-shootout (accessed 23 January 2021).

74. 'J&K: Drop in law-and-order incidents but uptick in militant recruitment', *Indian Express*, 25 January 2021, p. 1.

75. 'Militant bodies not handed over: DGP cites virus, crowds', *Indian Express*, 10 May 2020, p. 3; 'Hundreds defy lockdown for militant funeral', *The Telegraph*, 10 April 2020, p. 4.

76. AP, 'Empty grave for Kashmir teenager killed by Indian forces', *Al Jazeera*, 7 Jan 2021, https://www.aljazeera.com/news/2021/1/7/empty-grave-for-kashmir-teenager-killed-by-indian-forces (accessed 26 January 2021).

77. AP, 'Empty grave for Kashmir teenager killed by Indian forces'.
78. Rifat Fareed, 'Kashmiri man demanding son's body charged under anti-terror law', *Al Jazeera*, 9 February 2021, https://www.aljazeera.com/news/2021/2/9/family-of-kashmir-teen-under-anti-terror-for-demanding-his-body (accessed 11 May 2021).

5. THE 21ST-CENTURY CONFLICT

1. Marc Aurel Stein (ed. and trans.), *Kalhana's Rajatarangini: A Chronicle of the Kings of Kashmir* (Mirpur: Verinag Publishers, 1991, original 1900).
2. The Good Friday Agreement, https://www.dfa.ie/media/dfa/alldfawebsitemedia/ourrolesandpolicies/northernireland/good-friday-agreement.pdf (accessed 26 December 2020).
3. Cited in Sumantra Bose, *Contested Lands: Israel–Palestine, Kashmir, Bosnia, Cyprus, and Sri Lanka* (Cambridge, MA and London: Harvard University Press, 2007), p. 188.
4. Bose, *Contested Lands*, pp. 185–6.
5. '2020 records highest ever ceasefire violations by Pakistan along LoC in J&K in last 17 years', *India.com*, 13 November 2020, https://www.india.com/news/india/2020-records-highest-ever-ceasefire-violations-by-pakistan-in-jammu-kashmir-loc-in-last-17-years-4210069/ (accessed 26 January 2021); Asad Hashim and Rifat Fareed, 'India, Pakistan agree to stop cross-border firing in Kashmir', *Al Jazeera*, 25 February 2021, https://www.aljazeera.com/news/2021/2/25/india-pakistan-agree-to-stop-cross-border-firing-in-kashmir (accessed 25 February 2021).
6. 'India, Pakistan agree to fresh ceasefire after violent 2020', *Times of India*, 26 February 2021, p. 1.
7. Manish Tewari, 'Of India–Pakistan ties and third-party mediation', *Hindustan Times*, 5 May 2021, https://www.hindustantimes.com/opinion/of-india-pakistan-ties-and-third-party-mediation-101620236858359.html (accessed 12 May 2021).
8. 'LAC: Where it is located, and where India and China differ', *Indian Express*, 1 June 2020, p. 9.
9. M. Taylor Fravel, 'Power shifts and escalation: Explaining China's use of force in territorial disputes', *International Security*, 32, 3 (Winter, 2007–2008), p. 69.
10. John W. Garver, *Protracted Contest: Sino-Indian Rivalry in the Twentieth Century* (Seattle: University of Washington Press, 2001), pp. 100, 102.
11. 'Forty years ago, June 22, 1980: China's deal', *Indian Express*, 22 June 2020, https://indianexpress.com/article/opinion/editorials/forty-years-ago-june-22-1980-china-indira-gandhi-6470010/ (accessed 26 January 2021).
12. Garver, *Protracted Contest*, pp. 101–2.
13. Garver, *Protracted Contest*, pp. 94–5.
14. Garver, *Protracted Contest*, p. 102.
15. Agreement on the Maintenance of Peace and Tranquility [sic] along the Line of Actual Control in the India–China Border Areas, https://peacemaker.un.org/sites/peacemaker.un.org/files/CN%20IN_930907_Agreement%20on%20India-China%20Border%20Areas.pdf (accessed 26 January 2021).
16. Agreement between the Government of the Republic of India and the Government of the People's Republic of China on Confidence-Building Measures in the Military Field along the Line of Actual Control in the India–China Border Areas, https://peacemaker.un.org/sites/peacemaker.un.org/files/CN%20IN_961129_Agreement%20between%20China%20and%20India.pdf (accessed 26 January 2021).
17. 'State of play in Ladakh', *Indian Express*, 14 September 2020, p. 5.
18. Galwan published an English autobiography with the support of some of his white-skinned employers, *Servant of Sahibs: A Book to be Read Aloud* (Cambridge: W. Heffer & Sons Ltd, 1923). Francis Younghusband, a British army officer who led a brutal incursion into Tibet in 1904, wrote the book's foreword.
19. 'China's admission', *Indian Express*, 20 February 2021, p. 1.

20. 'Gallantry awards for all twenty soldiers killed in Galwan', *Indian Express*, 26 January 2021, p. 7.
21. 'We reserve the right to pre-emptively strike at Pak terror: New army chief', *Indian Express*, 1 January 2020, p. 1.
22. 'Will stand ground in Ladakh for as long as it takes: Army chief', *Indian Express*, 13 January 2021, p. 10.
23. 'Trust deficit exists: Army chief', *Indian Express*, 25 February 2021, p. 2.
24. 'State of play in Ladakh'.
25. 'How to play against China', *Indian Express*, 25 June 2020, p. 7.
26. M. Taylor Fravel, 'Regime insecurity and international cooperation: Explaining China's compromises in territorial disputes', *International Security*, 30, 2 (2005), p. 75.
27. 'The strategic road to DBO', *Indian Express*, 11 June 2020, p. 9; 'India's LAC infra upgrade unnerves China: 255-km Ladakh road seems to be the latest thorn', *Times of India*, 27 May 2020, p. 9.
28. Bruno Macaes, 'Understand China's India strategy: Nibbling territory isn't the point of it', *Times of India*, 20 June 2020, p. 14.
29. Wang Jisi, 'Westward: China's rebalancing geopolitical strategy' (International and Strategic Studies Report 73 of Peking University's Centre for International and Strategic Studies, 2012).
30. 'Pak economy: A reality check', *Indian Express*, 30 August 2019, p. 12.
31. Small, *The China–Pakistan Axis*, pp. 191–2.
32. AFP, 'China–Pakistan friendship "sweeter than honey": Nawaz Sharif', *Mint*, 5 July 2013, https://www.livemint.com/Politics/bYWGsGgm7ptn2vIu2GmymJ/ChinaPakistan-friendship-sweeter-than-honey-Nawaz-Sharif.html (accessed 2 February 2021).
33. Small, *The China–Pakistan Axis*, pp. 27–46.
34. 'China in mind, Quad statement says will counter threats to Indo-Pacific', *Indian Express*, 13 March 2021, p. 1.
35. India–Bhutan Friendship Treaty, https://mea.gov.in/Images/pdf/india-bhutan-treaty-07.pdf (accessed 2 February 2021).
36. 'Shah: Will continue to claim PoK', *Indian Express*, 7 August 2019, p. 1.
37. 'Pakistan stays on FATF grey list', *Times of India*, 26 February 2021, p. 6.
38. 'China voices Ladakh concern, India says internal affair', *Indian Express*, 7 August 2019, p. 1.
39. 'China raises J&K at Security Council, third time since August 2019', *Indian Express*, 6 August 2020, p. 5.
40. 'LAC crisis: Hardening stance, China rejects Ladakh UT, raises 1959 claim line', *Indian Express*, 30 September 2020, p. 1.
41. 'First sign of trouble in Pangong was last September, a month after change in status of J&K, Ladakh', *Indian Express*, 28 June 2020, p. 1.
42. The Boundary Agreement between China and Pakistan, 1963, https://people.unica.it/annamariabaldussi/files/2015/04/China-Pakistan-1963.pdf (accessed 2 February 2021).
43. Garver, *Protracted Contest*, pp. 187–8.
44. Small, *The China–Pakistan Axis*, p. 180.
45. Bose, 'Has India pushed Kashmir to a point of no return?'.
46. 'Trump listening, Modi says Kashmir is a bilateral issue', *Indian Express*, 27 August 2019, p. 1.
47. Zakka Jacob, 'By endorsing Trump at "Howdy, Modi", PM has walked into risky territory of American politics', *News18*, 23 September 2019, https://www.news18.com/news/opinion/by-endorsing-trump-at-howdy-modi-pm-has-walked-into-risky-territory-of-american-politics-2319277.html (accessed 2 February 2021).
48. All India, 'PM Modi speech highlights at "Howdy, Modi" event in Houston', *NDTV*, 23 September 2019, https://www.ndtv.com/india-news/howdy-modi-event-in-houston-pm-modi-speech-highlights-2105220 (accessed 2 February 2021).

49. All India, 'PM's speech at "Howdy, Modi!" event in US: Top quotes', *NDTV*, 23 September 2019, https://www.ndtv.com/india-news/howdy-modi-event-in-houston-pm-narendra-modis-speech-top-quotes-2105333 (accessed 2 February 2021).

50. Aarti Tikoo Singh, 'India ignores Donald Trump's mediation offer over Kashmir', *Mint*, 22 January 2020, https://www.livemint.com/news/india/india-ignores-donald-trump-s-mediation-offer-over-kashmir-11579695953359.html (accessed 2 February 2021).

51. 'On Kashmir and Pakistan, Donald Trump offers mediation but with a twist', *India Today*, 25 February 2020, https://www.indiatoday.in/india/story/on-kashmir-and-pakistan-donald-trump-offers-mediation-but-with-a-twist-1649930-2020-02-25 (accessed 2 February 2021).

52. 'Outrage over right-wing Euro-MPs' Kashmir visit', *BBC News*, 30 October 2019, https://www.bbc.co.uk/news/world-asia-india-50231022 (accessed 2 February 2021).

53. 'Presidential Candidate Kamala Harris on Kashmir', YouTube, 13 September 2019, https://www.youtube.com/watch?v=YmnxfgFeY_k (accessed 2 February 2021).

54. 'H. Res. 745: Urging the Republic of India to end the restrictions on communications and mass detentions in Jammu and Kashmir as swiftly as possible and preserve religious freedom for all residents', Library of Congress, 6 December 2019, https://www.congress.gov/bill/116th-congress/house-resolution/745/text (accessed 2 February 2021).

55. John Hudson, 'Top Indian official abruptly cancels meeting with congressional leaders over Kashmir criticism', *Washington Post*, 19 December 2019, https://www.washingtonpost.com/world/national-security/top-indian-official-abruptly-cancels-meeting-with-congressional-leaders-over-kashmir-criticisms/2019/12/19/29b023ea-2291-11ea-9c2b-060477c13959_story.html (accessed 2 February 2021).

56. Kamala Harris, Twitter post, 20 December 2019, https://twitter.com/VP/status/1208072080429846530 (accessed 2 February 2021).

57. 'Joe Biden's Agenda for Muslim-American Communities', JoeBiden.com, https://joebiden.com/muslimamerica/ (accessed 2 February 2021).

58. On the war and its complicated aftermath, see Sumantra Bose, *Bosnia after Dayton: Nationalist Partition and International Intervention* (New York: Oxford University Press, 2002).

59. An illuminating – and aptly titled – account of the US's involvement with the Kashmir dispute is Howard B. Schaffer, *The Limits of Influence: America's Role in Kashmir* (Washington, DC: Brookings Institution Press, 2009).

60. 'Pangong Lake: India and China to pull back from disputed border', *BBC News*, 11 February 2021, https://www.bbc.com/news/world-asia-india-56021141 (accessed 14 February 2021).

61. 'The day after, army chief flags growing footprint of Beijing, says China's moves lead to conflict', *Indian Express*, 13 February 2021, p. 1.

62. 'China refuses to leave', *Indian Express*, 18 April 2021, p. 1.

63. 'At UN, India defends pre-emptive strikes', *Times of India*, 26 February 2021, p. 6.

64. 'Alert in Valley, security convoys off roads', *Indian Express*, 15 February 2021, p. 8.

65. Geelani, 'Concertina in our souls'.

66. Sumantra Bose, *Kashmir: Roots of Conflict, Paths to Peace* (Cambridge, MA and London: Harvard University Press, 2003), p. 201.

67. *Kashmir: Paths to Peace* (London: Chatham House, 2010).

68. Balraj Puri, 'The mosaic of Jammu & Kashmir', *Frontline*, 28 April 2001, https://frontline.thehindu.com/the-nation/article30159675.ece (accessed 15 February 2021).

69. Bose, *Kashmir*, Chapter 5; Bose, *Contested Lands*, Chapter 4. For the full text of the Good Friday Agreement, see https://www.dfa.ie/media/dfa/alldfawebsitemedia/ourrolesandpolicies/northernireland/good-friday-agreement.pdf (accessed 15 February 2021).

70. Ayesha Siddiqa, *Military Inc.: Inside Pakistan's Military Economy* (Delhi: Penguin Random House India, 2017), p. 297.

71. 'Pak opposition forms alliance to oust Imran government', *Times of India*, 22 September 2020, p. 11.
72. 'Sharif blames Pak army chief', *Times of India*, 18 October 2020, p. 11; 'Pak opposition holds massive rally', *Indian Express*, 23 November 2020, p. 10; 'Pak opposition alliance holds final rally', *Indian Express*, 14 December 2020, p. 10.
73. Farzana Shaikh, 'New script in Pakistan', *Indian Express*, 30 November 2020, p. 7.
74. See Sumantra Bose, 'Why India's Hindu nationalists worship Israel's nation-state model', *The Conversation*, 14 February 2019, https://theconversation.com/why-indias-hindu-nationalists-worship-israels-nation-state-model-111450 (accessed 14 February 2021).
75. 'Joe Biden's Agenda for Muslim-American Communities'.
76. M.S. Golwalkar, *We, or Our Nationhood Defined* (Nagpur: Bharat Prakashan, 1947), pp. 55–6.
77. Bose, *Secular States, Religious Politics*, p. 339.
78. Joanna Slater, 'In Modi's move on Kashmir, a roadmap for his "New India"'.
79. 'Shah's target: Panchayat to parliament, and every state', *Indian Express*, 16 April 2017, p. 1.
80. Bose, *Secular States, Religious Politics*, p. 361.
81. 'Anti-India forces might use Covid crisis: RSS', *Indian Express*, 25 April 2021, p. 1.

Glossary

Azaadi: Literally, 'freedom'. The rallying cry of supporters of self-determination in Kashmir.

'Azad' (Free) Jammu and Kashmir: A long sliver of territory, with a population of about 4.5 million, that comprises the more populous of two distinct parts of Pakistani Kashmir (the other is Gilgit-Baltistan). 'Azad' Kashmir has supposedly autonomous institutions, but it is in reality heavily regulated by the central Pakistani government and the Pakistan Army.

Bharatiya Janata Party (BJP): The BJP (Indian People's Party) is India's Hindu nationalist political party, and holds that Indian identity and nationhood are coterminous with the Hindu faith shared by nearly four-fifths of the population. Hindu nationalist ideology – *Hindutva* (Hinduness), a very modern construct which originated in the 1920s – regards this vast and variegated Hindu society as a monolith. The Hindu nationalist movement centred on the Rashtriya Swayamsevak Sangh (RSS) seeks to politically unite this Hindu 'majority'. The movement was the far-right fringe of Indian politics until the end of the 1980s, and the BJP, formed in 1951 under a slightly different name (Bharatiya Jana Sangh, BJS), existed as a marginal party until then. The party is part of a much broader movement

– a *sangh-parivar*, or family of organisations, led by the RSS – which aims to transform India into a majoritarian Hindu nationalist republic. The BJP has been India's ruling party since 2014 and won two consecutive national elections, in 2014 and 2019, under Narendra Modi's leadership. Since August 2019, the government helmed by Modi and Amit Shah, the home (interior) minister, has been implementing a policy of draconian repression in Indian Kashmir. During Modi's premiership, democratic norms have been severely undermined in India, and since his re-election in 2019 the country has been regressing rapidly towards authoritarian rule.

Border Security Force (BSF): A paramilitary force of about 250,000 personnel responsible for securing India's land borders. It was formed just after the second India–Pakistan war in 1965 and is under the authority of the home (interior) ministry of India's central government. Although raised to guard borders, the BSF was extensively deployed throughout the 1990s in counter-insurgency operations in Indian Kashmir, particularly in the Kashmir Valley.

Central Reserve Police Force (CRPF): A paramilitary force of about 300,000 personnel under the authority of the Indian central government's home (interior) ministry. It was formed in 1949. The CRPF has been deployed in strength in Indian Kashmir for the past three decades, especially in the Kashmir Valley. Its main role is to suppress protests, which are endemic in the Valley.

Congress: The Indian National Congress was the political party, founded in 1885, which spearheaded India's mass movement for freedom from British colonial rule from the beginning of the 1920s until independence in 1947. Mohandas Karamchand (Mahatma) Gandhi (1869–1948) was its top leader. After independence, the Congress was India's dominant party until the end of the 1980s and became identified with the 'Nehru–Gandhi dynasty': Jawaharlal Nehru, prime minister from 1947 to 1964, Nehru's daughter Indira Gandhi, who was prime minister from 1966 to 1977 and 1980 to 1984, and her son Rajiv Gandhi, prime minister from 1984 to 1989. The Nehru, Indira and Rajiv governments were responsible for repressive, anti-democratic policies in Indian Kashmir which generated great discontent, especially in the Kashmir Valley, and led to large-scale insurgency from 1990. The Congress party went into long-term decline after 1989, though it did lead coalition governments in New Delhi from mid-2004 to 2014. The party's organisation and popular base have withered away across most of India, it does not have a credible leadership, and it exists today in a pale, emaciated version of its once hegemonic self.

Dogras: A Hindu community who live in significant numbers in the southern plains and foothills of Indian Kashmir's Jammu region. A dynasty of Dogra Rajputs, a martial and upper-caste sub-group of the community, founded and ruled the princely state of Jammu and Kashmir, under overarching British authority, from 1846 to 1947. The territory of this erstwhile princely state has been the subject of the India–Pakistan dispute since 1947.

Gilgit-Baltistan: Known until 2009 as Pakistan's Northern Areas, Gilgit-Baltistan is one of two distinct regions of Pakistani Kashmir (the other is 'Azad' Jammu and Kashmir). Gilgit-Baltistan is a sprawling but very mountainous and sparsely inhabited region in the high Himalayas, with a population of about 1.5 million. Gilgit-Baltistan has a long southern border with Indian Kashmir's Ladakh region, a thinly populated high-altitude desert, and a northern border of 375 miles with China's Xinjiang province.

Gujjars: A Muslim community, traditionally nomadic pastoralists, who are found in sizeable numbers in highland areas of Indian Kashmir, in both the Kashmir Valley and the Jammu region. Some Gujjars who rear sheep and goats as livestock are referred to as Bakerwals.

Hizb-ul Mujahideen (HM): The major pro-Pakistan insurgent group in Indian Kashmir. Formed in 1989, in the nascent phase of the Kashmir insurgency, HM (Organisation of Holy Warriors) displaced the independentist Jammu and Kashmir Liberation Front (JKLF) as the dominant group in the Kashmir insurgency from 1993 onwards and spearheaded the insurgency during the rest of the 1990s. From its inception, HM has been closely linked with the Indian Kashmir wing of Jama'at-i-Islami (JI), a Sunni fundamentalist movement which has branches in Pakistan, Bangladesh and both Indian and Pakistani Kashmir. As an insurgent group, HM was heavily patronised by the Pakistani military's covert operations arm, the Directorate of Inter-Services Intelligence (ISI). HM's ISI-backed attempt to assert total dominance of the Kashmir insurgency provoked a bloody backlash, as many insurgents from JKLF and other smaller groups joined the Indian counter-insurgency campaign in the second half of the 1990s to fight back against HM. During the first half of the 2000s, the Pakistani groups Lashkar-e-Taiba (LeT) and Jaish-e-Mohammad (JeM), composed of religious zealots and patronised by the ISI, took over HM's spearhead role in the Kashmir insurgency. After the decline of the insurgency from the mid-2000s, HM has had a minor, underground presence in the Kashmir Valley, a far cry from its peak in the mid-1990s when it fielded thousands of fighters in Indian Kashmir.

Hurriyat Conference: Formally the All Parties Hurriyat (Freedom, in Arabic and Turkish) Conference (APHC). An umbrella forum of about two dozen political and civil society organisations advocating for the right to 'self-determination' which was launched in 1993 in Srinagar, the Kashmir Valley's capital, at the behest of the Pakistani military's ISI agency. Most of its constituents had a pro-Pakistan orientation. The Hurriyat Conference was chronically riven by personality clashes and factional rivalries. In the 2000s, it splintered into two rival groupings, one led by Syed Ali Shah Geelani, a leading Jama'at-i-Islami figure, and the other by Mirwaiz Umar Farooq, the hereditary head preacher of Srinagar's largest mosque congregation.

Inter-Services Intelligence (ISI): The ISI is the Pakistani military's main intelligence and covert operations organisation. The ISI rose to prominence during the 1980s when, under the military regime of General Zia-ul Haq, it coordinated the US-backed mujahideen war against the Soviet Union and its allies in Afghanistan. From 1990, it became the key source of weapons and funding for the insurgency in Indian Kashmir and meddled heavily in the insurgency, particularly in building up the pro-Pakistan HM against the independentist JKLF. The ISI has remained deeply involved with Indian Kashmir ever since. From the late 1990s to the mid-2000s, the

ISI supported the activities of the Pakistani radical groups Lashkar-e-Taiba and Jaish-e-Mohammad in the Kashmir insurgency. The ISI is always headed by a Pakistan Army officer of lieutenant-general rank, and it has a major say in policy-making on both Afghanistan and Kashmir. It is also extensively involved in repression of perceived subversion and anti-army dissent within Pakistan.

Jaish-e-Mohammad (JeM): A radical Islamist group (Army of the Prophet) of Pakistan, closely linked to and supported by the Pakistan Army and the ISI, JeM became active in the insurgency in Indian Kashmir from 2000 onwards. The group's founder is Maulana Masood Azhar (b. 1968), a militant cleric who is from Bahawalpur, a city in the southern part of Pakistan's Punjab province. JeM is descended from Harkat-ul-Ansar (HuA), a similar group which became active on the margins of the Kashmir insurgency from the mid-1990s. Azhar was captured in the Kashmir Valley in 1994 and released at the end of 1999 after his associates hijacked an Indian Airlines plane flying from Kathmandu to Delhi and diverted it to Kandahar, the epicentre of Afghanistan's Pakistan-backed Taliban regime. JeM was probably responsible for a suicide attack on India's parliament building in New Delhi in December 2001, and it carried out a number of major suicide attacks in the Kashmir Valley in the early 2000s. It remains active and dangerous; in February 2019 JeM perpetrated a suicide bombing near Srinagar which killed forty Indian CRPF personnel, the single deadliest attack to date of the Kashmir insurgency since 1990.

Jama'at-i-Islami (JI): JI (Islamic Rally) is a Sunni fundamentalist movement founded in the pre-partition subcontinent in 1941 by Abul Ala Maududi, a cleric. It has wings in Pakistan, Bangladesh and in both Indian and Pakistani Kashmir. JI became an influential pressure group in Pakistan after 1947. In the 1950s it led an agitation in West Pakistan for the persecution of Ahmadis (a sect considered heretical by orthodox Sunnis), and in the 1980s it played an important role in the Islamisation of Pakistan's legal and educational systems under the military regime of General Zia-ul Haq. In 1971, the JI wing in East Pakistan emerged as the principal collaborators of the Pakistan Army's genocidal violence against the Bengali population during Bangladesh's independence struggle. JI's Indian Kashmir wing has been active for the past seven decades and traditionally focused on recruiting adherents through a network of schools, mostly in the Kashmir Valley. In 1990, it jumped on the bandwagon of armed struggle, and its affiliated insurgent group, Hizb-ul Mujahideen, became the independentist JKLF's competitor in the Kashmir insurgency. Jama'at-i-Islami has a loyal cadre and following in the Kashmir Valley but remains a minority tendency. That is because its pro-Pakistan orientation and its orthodox Sunnism are both at odds with the dominant leanings in the Valley: independentist aspirations and Sufi-influenced Islam.

Jammu and Kashmir Liberation Front (JKLF): Founded in 1965 in Pakistani Kashmir by a group of activists who aspired to establish an independent state across the territories of the former princely state (1846–1947) of Jammu and Kashmir, divided between India and Pakistan since the late 1940s. Its best-known leader was Amanullah Khan (1934–2016). JKLF was known until 1977 as the Jammu and Kashmir National Liberation Front. The organisation had almost no presence in Indian Kashmir until the end of the 1980s, when it acquired a nucleus of cadres in the Kashmir Valley – mainly in the city of Srinagar – from among young men angered by repressive Indian rule. These youths, supplied with weapons and training in Pakistani Kashmir by the established JKLF network there, launched the insurgency that began in the Kashmir Valley in 1989 and spread like wildfire from 1990. By 1993, JKLF lost its dominance of the armed struggle to Hizb-ul Mujahideen, a rival pro-Pakistan Kashmiri group linked to the fundamentalist Jama'at-i-Islami movement and supported by the Pakistan Army and the ISI. It ceased armed struggle shortly after, in the mid-1990s. JKLF exists as a political group in both Indian and Pakistani Kashmir, amid varying degrees of persecution by the authorities of both countries. It is relatively weak because of persecution, factional feuds and a deficit of effective leadership. Nonetheless, its independentist ideology has strong popular resonance in the Kashmir Valley, as well as in Pakistan's 'Azad' Kashmir region. JKLF's best-known leader in Indian Kashmir is Mohammad Yasin Malik (b. 1966), a native of Srinagar who is a survivor of the original nucleus of cadres who launched the insurgency in 1989–90. He has been incarcerated in a prison in New Delhi since early 2019.

Lashkar-e-Taiba (LeT): LeT (Army of the Pious) is an armed Islamist group of Pakistan which entered the insurgency in Indian Kashmir from the second half of the 1990s. It has close links with the Pakistan Army and particularly the ISI agency. LeT's most prominent leader is Hafiz Muhammad Saeed (b. 1950), a theologian and academic who began his political life in Pakistan's Jama'at-i-Islami before forming LeT's parent organisation in the late 1980s. LeT professes an ultra-orthodox variant of Sunnism. Initially on the margins of the Kashmir insurgency, LeT assumed centre stage from 1999 until the mid-2000s, when it launched a spate of *fidayeen* (suicide) attacks in Indian Kashmir. The peak of LeT's *fidayeen* campaign was in the early 2000s. Like Jaish-e-Mohammad (JeM), LeT is based in Pakistan – its headquarters is near the city of Lahore in Pakistan's Punjab province – and is led by Pakistani religious radicals. LeT is well funded, and through its front organisations, it runs a network of charitable activities for the poor in Pakistan, which provides a channel for recruitment. As with JeM, LeT's leading fighters in Indian Kashmir have mostly been Pakistanis (and from Pakistan's Punjab province), but supplemented by locally recruited Kashmiris. In November 2008, a 10-man LeT squad which set sail from Karachi perpetrated a mass-casualty terror attack in Mumbai, India's business and financial nerve-centre, in which 166 people were killed. The attack was plotted in probable collusion with elements of the ISI agency. LeT still has a limited underground presence in Indian Kashmir, almost entirely in the Kashmir Valley, and is, like JeM, a dangerous *provocateur* group.

Line of Actual Control (LAC): The de facto border between China and India in the western and eastern Himalayas. The entire border between China (Tibet) and India is almost 2,500 miles long. There are two sections, at the western and eastern ends, that are the subject of a Sino-Indian border dispute, unresolved since the 1950s. At the eastern end, the Indian state of Arunachal Pradesh (Sunrise Province, 56,000 square miles) is claimed by China, which refers to the territory as 'south Tibet'. At the western end,

India claims a desolate, high-altitude plateau called Aksai Chin (23,000 square miles) which is wedged between Xinjiang and Tibet and has been under Chinese control since the 1950s. India regards Aksai Chin as the north-eastern periphery of the former princely state of Jammu and Kashmir (1846–1947) and therefore as part of Ladakh, which was one of the three regions of the Indian state of Jammu and Kashmir until August 2019. The border dispute led to a fierce war in both the western and eastern sectors in October–November 1962, in which the Indians were badly defeated. The term 'actual control' is of Chinese coinage and dates to 1959. In 1960 and again in 1980, China's leaders suggested that the dispute could be resolved by reciprocally recognising 'actual control' and formalising the status quo: i.e., China's possession of Aksai Chin and India's possession of Arunachal Pradesh. The term 'Line of Actual Control' refers to both the western and eastern ends of the China–India border. In 2020, after nearly six decades of near tranquillity following the 1962 war, the LAC between Ladakh and Aksai Chin/Tibet came alive with close-range confrontations between the Chinese and Indian militaries in multiple locations. A deadly clash on the Ladakh–Aksai Chin LAC in June 2020 claimed the lives of twenty Indian soldiers and an indeterminate number of Chinese soldiers. The remilitarisation of the western LAC – which completely undermined Sino-Indian agreements in 1993 and 1996 to maintain 'peace and tranquillity' on the LAC – continued in 2021 and constitutes a new dimension of the twenty-first-century Kashmir conflict.

Line of Control (LoC): This is the major part of the de facto border between Indian Kashmir and Pakistani Kashmir. The LoC originated as a Ceasefire Line (CFL) in January 1949 at the end of the first (1947–48) India–Pakistan war over Kashmir. It was renamed the Line of Control by an intergovernmental agreement in July 1972, pending a final, negotiated settlement of the Kashmir dispute. The LoC follows the trajectory of the original CFL, barring very minor changes from the third India–Pakistan war of December 1971. The serpentine LoC traverses almost 500 miles through mostly mountainous terrain. Its southern end is just west of the town of Akhnur in Indian Kashmir's Jammu region. Its northern end is a point called NJ9842 on the border between the (Indian) Ladakh and (Pakistani) Gilgit-Baltistan regions. The LoC between the Akhnur end and NJ9842 was precisely demarcated by the Indian and Pakistani armies in 1972. There is a contested area north of NJ9842 – the Siachen glacier, located at the trijunction of Gilgit-Baltistan, Ladakh and China's Xinjiang province – where Indian and Pakistani troops have been engaged in a confrontation at altitudes of 18,000–19,000 feet above sea level since 1984. The LoC also has a southern extension or tail which runs for about 123 miles, through plains on both sides, between the south-western part of Indian Kashmir's Jammu region and Pakistan's Punjab province. The Indians regard this stretch as part of the settled International Border (IB) between India and Pakistan, while the Pakistanis refer to it as a 'working boundary'. The Line of Control in Kashmir is probably the world's most militarised frontier. In February 2021, the Indian and Pakistani armies agreed anew to observe the terms of an unravelled November 2003 ceasefire agreement on the LoC after an extraordinary spike in cross-LoC firing and shelling – 3,479 incidents in 2019, 5,133 in 2020 and 591 in the first two months of 2021.

Muslim United Front (MUF): A coalition of diverse political factions in the Kashmir Valley which came together to contest an election to constitute the legislature and government of the Indian state of Jammu and Kashmir held in March 1987. The purpose of the coalition (Muttahida Muslim Mahaz) was to provide an opposition to an unpopular electoral alliance forged by the National Conference (NC), the Valley's and Indian Kashmir's main political party, with India's ruling Congress party. The MUF's emergence as an alternative formation evoked mass enthusiasm in the Valley, particularly among the youth. Their expectations fell flat when the election was blatantly rigged in favour of the NC–Congress alliance, replicating a pattern of fraud established in elections in the Indian state of Jammu and Kashmir since the 1950s. Many among the legions of young men who had volunteered as the MUF's grassroots workers were then imprisoned for up to a year, and some tortured in detention. The 1987 election started the countdown to insurgency in Indian Kashmir, which began in 1989 and exploded from 1990. A steady trickle of young men from the Valley crossed the LoC to Pakistani Kashmir in 1988 and 1989, acquired weapons and training and returned to wage war for *azaadi* (freedom).

National Conference (NC): The All Jammu and Kashmir National Conference was historically the dominant political party of the (former) Indian state of Jammu and Kashmir. Its stronghold was the Kashmir Valley. The NC was formed in 1939 with the goal of replacing the autocratic regime of the princely state (1846–1947) with a modern, popularly mandated government. The party's top leader was Sheikh Mohammad Abdullah (1905–82). After the dissolution of the princely state in October 1947, the NC led by Abdullah came to power in the Indian state of J&K. Its rule was authoritarian, but it gained popularity by implementing major land reforms, which in the early 1950s emancipated hundreds of thousands of peasants from serfdom. In August 1953, Abdullah was toppled from power by a conspiracy engineered by the Indian government in New Delhi, and he was incarcerated almost continuously until 1975. The party's base remained loyal to Abdullah, however. Upon his release and reinstation as Indian J&K's chief minister in 1975, Abdullah revived the National Conference. After Sheikh Abdullah's death in 1982, the party's base was severely eroded under the leadership of his son and political successor, Farooq Abdullah. The party was further marginalised after the eruption of large-scale insurgency from 1990. The NC ran Indian J&K state governments from 1996 to 2002 and 2008 to 2014, but it is a pale shadow of the mass-based party it once was. The party's current leader is Farooq Abdullah's son, Omar Abdullah.

Pandits: The Pandits – also known as Kashmiri Pandits (KPs) – are the Kashmir Valley's small, indigenous Hindu minority. Their heritage, language and culture are virtually identical to those of the Valley's Muslims. Some Pandits constituted a privileged class under the princely state (1846–1947). When insurrection engulfed the Valley in early 1990, approximately 120,000 Pandits lived in the Valley, making up about 3 per cent of the Valley's population. In February–March 1990, the bulk of the Pandits (about 90,000–100,000 people) left the Valley for safety amid incidents of intimidation and sporadic killings of prominent members of the community by Kashmiri Muslim militants; most moved to the southern, Hindu-majority Indian

J&K city of Jammu or to Delhi. The rest continued to live in the violence-wracked Valley. Several massacres of Pandits by Pakistani terrorist groups which gradually became active in the Kashmir insurgency occurred in the Valley in the late 1990s and the first half of the 2000s. In addition to the post-1990 displaced Pandits and the Pandits who continue to live in the Valley today, numerous KPs whose families migrated earlier from the Valley live in cities across India.

People's Democratic Party (PDP): The Jammu & Kashmir People's Democratic Party (PDP) was formed in 1999, after a decade of relentless violence in the Indian state of J&K that began in 1990. Its purpose was to provide a progressive alternative to Indian J&K's established but weakened political party, the National Conference (NC), especially in the Kashmir Valley. The PDP's leader was Mufti Mohammad Sayeed (1936–2016), formerly a longstanding figure of India's Congress party in the Valley, and its main campaigner was his daughter Mehbooba Mufti (b. 1959). The PDP positioned itself in the middle ground between the NC and the spectrum of political groups in the Valley advocating for 'self-determination'. Like the NC, the PDP accepted the framework of Indian authority but presented itself as a reformist, pro-people party by campaigning against human rights abuses and arguing for a peace process involving all political groups as well as Pakistan to settle the Kashmir conflict. The PDP was successful in building a base of support in the Kashmir Valley, and Mufti Mohammad Sayeed served as Indian J&K's chief minister from 2002 to 2005. In 2015, the PDP formed a post-poll coalition government in Indian J&K with the Hindu nationalist BJP after state elections threw up a fractured result, with the PDP the leading party in the Kashmir Valley and the BJP in the Jammu region. The coalition government's charter promised to address the grievances of the Valley's people and pave the way to a Kashmir peace process involving all political groups as well as Pakistan. In retrospect, it is clear that the BJP, led by Narendra Modi, entered into the coalition agreement in bad faith and had no intention of acting on its commitments. The PDP–BJP government collapsed in mid-2018 after the BJP withdrew from the pact, and the PDP's credibility in the Valley has been badly damaged by the episode.

Plebiscite Front (PF): The Jammu and Kashmir Plebiscite Front (Mahaz-e-Raishumari) was formed in Srinagar in 1955 by Sheikh Mohammad Abdullah's supporters, after the Sheikh was toppled from power in the Indian state of Jammu and Kashmir in 1953 by a conspiracy engineered by the Indian central government and replaced by New Delhi's client politicians. The PF's rhetorical platform was the plebiscite (referendum) organised by the United Nations by which the Kashmir dispute between India and Pakistan was supposed to be settled in the early 1950s. The PF was continuously persecuted by the Indian authorities and their puppet governments in Indian J&K, but commanded mass support in the Kashmir Valley for twenty years. The PF self-dissolved in 1975 after Sheikh Abdullah gave up his defiance, capitulated to New Delhi's terms and was reinstated as Indian J&K's chief minister in return for his compliance. But the PF's creed of 'self-determination' remained alive in its stronghold, the Kashmir Valley.

Rashtriya Rifles (RR): The Rashtriya Rifles (National Rifles) consists of troops from the Indian Army assigned to counter-insurgency operations in the interior areas of Indian Jammu and Kashmir. The RR was formed in 1994. It has four main commands: Kilo Force operates in the northern districts of the Kashmir Valley, Victor Force in the Valley's southern districts, Delta Force in the Jammu region's Doda and Kishtwar districts, and Romeo Force in the Jammu region's Rajouri and Poonch districts. Each RR command has 10,000–12,000 soldiers, so 40,000–50,000 Indian Army personnel are dedicated to counter-insurgency duties at any one time.

Rashtriya Swayamsevak Sangh (RSS): The RSS (National Volunteer Organization) is the ideological and organisational core of India's Hindu nationalist movement. Formed in 1925, the RSS has ever since been a hierarchically structured, all-male organisation which emphasises strict discipline. The RSS was born and has been headquartered since its inception in Nagpur, a city in west-central India. Currently, the RSS has several million members, organised in nearly 60,000 local branches (*shakhas*) across India. The RSS was heavily involved in the carnage that accompanied India's partition in 1947, and its unit in the city of Jammu led massacres of Muslims in the city and its adjacent areas in late 1947. After India's independence, the RSS spawned a *sangh-parivar* (family of organisations) which make up India's Hindu nationalist movement. The Bharatiya Janata Party (BJP), which was founded in 1951 under a slightly different name, the Bharatiya Jana Sangh (Indian People's Organisation, BJS), is the RSS-led movement's political party. The RSS is dedicated to realising its original vision: of India as a *Hindu Rashtra* (Hindu nation-state). Almost all prominent BJP leaders have been indoctrinated and politically socialised in the RSS. Narendra Modi (b. 1950), India's prime minister since 2014, worked as a fulltime RSS *pracharak* (propagator of Hindu nationalist ideology) for two decades, from the early 1970s to the late 1980s. The draconian Kashmir policy being implemented by the Modi government since August 2019 through his home (interior) minister Amit Shah – another lifelong RSS member – is based on the RSS's extremely hardline view of the Kashmir conflict.

Index